MCSE Windows NT® Server 4 in the Enterprise For Dummies, 2nd Edition

Cheat Sheet

Local versus Global Groups

- Place users in global groups, which you place in local groups. You can then assign permissions to the local groups.
- You can only create global groups on domain controllers.
- You can create local groups on any Windows NT Workstation or Server.
- Local groups can have users from the local domain, as well as accounts only on the local machine.

Disk Configurations

Configuration	Description
Disk striping	Data is divided into 64K blocks and spread across the disk for speed. Doesn't provide fault tolerance. Requires at least two disks.
Disk striping with parity	Similar to disk striping, but parity information is spread across all drives that can reconstruct a failed drive for fault tolerance. Requires a minimum of three disks.
Disk mirroring	Creates a partition identical to the original on another physical disk for fault tolerance. Requires a minimum of one controller and two disks.
Disk duplexing	Same as mirroring, but includes another disk controller for even greater fault tolerance. Requires a minimum of two controllers and two disks.
Volume set	Consolidates data from multiple areas into one drive letter for maximum use. Doesn't provide fault tolerance.

Disk Configuration Performance

- Stripe sets without parity provide the best overall read/write performance.
- Stripe sets with parity provide better read/write performance than mirroring.
- Stripe sets with parity place an additional load on the CPU due to parity calculation.

Recovering from Disk Failure

- With a mirrored set, you must install a new disk, start Windows NT, and break and then re-create the mirror set.
- If you lose one disk and you use disk striping with parity, you can replace the hard disk, start Windows NT, and use Disk Administrator to regenerate the stripe set.
- If you lose more than one disk and you use disk striping with parity, you must restore from tape.
- If you have a stripe set with no parity and a volume set, one disk failure loses everything on all members of the set.

...For Dummies®: Bestselling Book Series

Cheat Sheet

Moving and Copying on NTFS Partitions

- ✔ If you copy a file within a partition, the file inherits the target folder's permissions.
- ✔ If you move a file within a partition, the file retains its original permissions.
- ✔ If you move a file across a partition, the file inherits the target folder's permissions.

The Difference between System and Boot Partitions

It sounds backwards, but the boot files are on the system partition, and the system files are on the boot partition.

Remember These Rules for Permissions

- ✔ If only one person needs access, assign permissions to only that user's account.
- ✔ Even if you belong to a group that has Full Access, if you also belong to a group with No Access, you can't access the resource.
- ✔ If resources have both file-level and share-level security, NT uses the *most restrictive* permissions.

ARC Naming Convention

multi(0)disk(0)rdisk(0)partition(1)

Parameter	Description
multi(x)	SCSI controller with BIOS enabled
scsi(x)	SCSI controller with BIOS disabled
disk(x)	SCSI disk with system files (0 when you use multi)
rdisk(x)	Physical disk with system files
partition(x)	Partition with system files

Domain Models

Model	Description
Single domain	Central location for administration with no trust relationships.
Single master domain	Central location for administration that is trusted by other domains, often resource domains.
Multiple master domain	Master domains with two-way trust relationships between them, with single domains that trust the master domains.
Complete trust domain	Each domain trusts every other domain with a two-way trust relationship.

On Exam Day . . .

Use your scratch paper to sort out the details in complex questions. This technique is especially helpful for questions on domains and global/local groups.

Manage your time wisely! Most exam takers don't have much time to go back and check answers. If you're spending too much time on a question, mark the question and come back to it later. And when you mark a question, always put an answer, even though you may need to change it. If you run out of time before you can come back to the question, you have an answer, and it may be the correct one.

...For Dummies®: Bestselling Book Series

MCSE WINDOWS NT® SERVER 4 IN THE ENTERPRISE FOR DUMMIES®

2ND EDITION

by Kenneth Majors, Dave Dermon III,
and Jeffrey Ferris

Foreword by Eckhart Boehme

IDG Books Worldwide, Inc.
An International Data Group Company

Foster City, CA ◆ Chicago, IL ◆ Indianapolis, IN ◆ New York, NY

MCSE Windows NT® Server 4 in the Enterprise For Dummies® 2nd Edition

Published by
IDG Books Worldwide, Inc.
An International Data Group Company
919 E. Hillsdale Blvd.
Suite 400
Foster City, CA 94404
www.idgbooks.com (IDG Books Worldwide Web site)
www.dummies.com (Dummies Press Web site)

Library of Congress Catalog Card No.: 99-63103

ISBN: 0-7645-0615-3

Printed in the United States of America

10 9 8 7 6 5 4 3 2 1

2B/QS/QW/ZZ/IN

Distributed in the United States by IDG Books Worldwide, Inc.

Distributed by CDG Books Canada Inc. for Canada; by Transworld Publishers Limited in the United Kingdom; by IDG Norge Books for Norway; by IDG Sweden Books for Sweden; by IDG Books Australia Publishing Corporation Pty. Ltd. for Australia and New Zealand; by TransQuest Publishers Pte Ltd. for Singapore, Malaysia, Thailand, Indonesia, and Hong Kong; by Gotop Information Inc. for Taiwan; by ICG Muse, Inc. for Japan; by Norma Comunicaciones S.A. for Colombia; by Intersoft for South Africa; by Eyrolles for France; by International Thomson Publishing for Germany, Austria and Switzerland; by Distribuidora Cuspide for Argentina; by Livraria Cultura for Brazil; by Ediciones ZETA S.C.R. Ltda. for Peru; by WS Computer Publishing Corporation, Inc., for the Philippines; by Contemporanea de Ediciones for Venezuela; by Express Computer Distributors for the Caribbean and West Indies; by Micronesia Media Distributor, Inc. for Micronesia; by Grupo Editorial Norma S.A. for Guatemala; by Chips Computadoras S.A. de C.V. for Mexico; by Editorial Norma de Panama S.A. for Panama; by American Bookshops for Finland. Authorized Sales Agent: Anthony Rudkin Associates for the Middle East and North Africa.

For general information on IDG Books Worldwide's books in the U.S., please call our Consumer Customer Service department at 800-762-2974. For reseller information, including discounts and premium sales, please call our Reseller Customer Service department at 800-434-3422.

For information on where to purchase IDG Books Worldwide's books outside the U.S., please contact our International Sales department at 317-596-5530 or fax 317-596-5692.

For consumer information on foreign language translations, please contact our Customer Service department at 1-800-434-3422, fax 317-596-5692, or e-mail rights@idgbooks.com.

For information on licensing foreign or domestic rights, please phone +1-650-655-3109.

For sales inquiries and special prices for bulk quantities, please contact our Sales department at 650-655-3200 or write to the address above.

For information on using IDG Books Worldwide's books in the classroom or for ordering examination copies, please contact our Educational Sales department at 800-434-2086 or fax 317-596-5499.

For press review copies, author interviews, or other publicity information, please contact our Public Relations department at 650-655-3000 or fax 650-655-3299.

For authorization to photocopy items for corporate, personal, or educational use, please contact Copyright Clearance Center, 222 Rosewood Drive, Danvers, MA 01923, or fax 978-750-4470.

is a registered trademark or trademark under exclusive license to IDG Books Worldwide, Inc. from International Data Group, Inc. in the United States and/or other countries.

About the Authors

Kenneth Majors, MCSE, works as a Senior Network Engineer for Levi, Ray, & Shoup, Inc., in Kansas City. Ken has more than 18 years' experience with computers and networking, including extensive experience with UNIX and Windows NT operating systems. Ken has been an MCSE since 1996. Since his initial certification on Windows NT 3.1, he has focused on the development, integration, and deployment of enterprise systems and networks based on Windows NT. He has designed and deployed Windows NT enterprises for large companies and municipalities in the Midwest. Ken has developed and taught several cram sessions for prospective MCPs, and his students have enjoyed a high success rate.

Ken is married and is training his two children to take over in the family business. He can be reached via e-mail at `kmajors@sound.net` or `kmajors@lrs.com`. You can also find him on the Web at `www.sound.net/~kmajors` or `www.lrs.com`.

Dave Dermon III, MCSE, has lived in Germantown, Tennessee for 15 years. He and his wife Valerie have two children: Dave IV, age 5, and Ella Carolyn, age 4. Dave graduated from Memphis State University, now the University of Memphis, in 1984 with a BBA. At that time, he was programming on an Apple IIe with 16K of memory! He installed and administered a small Arcnet network for Dave Dermon Insurance in 1985 and by 1989 added a XENIX system for the property management company. In 1992, Dave replaced the Arcnet system with a NetWare 3.12 network. He left the company in 1997, after he began his MCSE certification. In his current consulting business, he troubleshoots, installs, and upgrades systems for both personal and corporate clients. He has also designed several Web sites for his customers. Contact Dave via e-mail at `ddiii@dermon.com`, or visit his Web site: `www.dermon.com`.

Jeffrey Ferris is an MCSE in the Kansas City area and currently employed as an NT Systems Integrator for one of the Big Three long distance providers. Jeffrey has been working with computers since just after learning to walk, focusing on TCP/IP technologies and Windows NT for the past three years. He received his degree in Computer Information Systems at Southwest Missouri State University in Springfield, Missouri.

Syngress Media is a Boston-area firm that creates books and software for Information Technology professionals seeking skill enhancement and career advancement. Syngress Media's products are designed to comply with vendor and industry standard course studies and are geared especially to certification exam preparation.

ABOUT IDG BOOKS WORLDWIDE

Welcome to the world of IDG Books Worldwide.

IDG Books Worldwide, Inc., is a subsidiary of International Data Group, the world's largest publisher of computer-related information and the leading global provider of information services on information technology. IDG was founded more than 30 years ago by Patrick J. McGovern and now employs more than 9,000 people worldwide. IDG publishes more than 290 computer publications in over 75 countries. More than 90 million people read one or more IDG publications each month.

Launched in 1990, IDG Books Worldwide is today the #1 publisher of best-selling computer books in the United States. We are proud to have received eight awards from the Computer Press Association in recognition of editorial excellence and three from Computer Currents' First Annual Readers' Choice Awards. Our best-selling *...For Dummies*® series has more than 50 million copies in print with translations in 31 languages. IDG Books Worldwide, through a joint venture with IDG's Hi-Tech Beijing, became the first U.S. publisher to publish a computer book in the People's Republic of China. In record time, IDG Books Worldwide has become the first choice for millions of readers around the world who want to learn how to better manage their businesses.

Our mission is simple: Every one of our books is designed to bring extra value and skill-building instructions to the reader. Our books are written by experts who understand and care about our readers. The knowledge base of our editorial staff comes from years of experience in publishing, education, and journalism — experience we use to produce books to carry us into the new millennium. In short, we care about books, so we attract the best people. We devote special attention to details such as audience, interior design, use of icons, and illustrations. And because we use an efficient process of authoring, editing, and desktop publishing our books electronically, we can spend more time ensuring superior content and less time on the technicalities of making books.

You can count on our commitment to deliver high-quality books at competitive prices on topics you want to read about. At IDG Books Worldwide, we continue in the IDG tradition of delivering quality for more than 30 years. You'll find no better book on a subject than one from IDG Books Worldwide.

John Kilcullen
Chairman and CEO
IDG Books Worldwide, Inc.

Steven Berkowitz
President and Publisher
IDG Books Worldwide, Inc.

VIII WINNER

Eighth Annual Computer Press Awards ≥1992

IX WINNER

Ninth Annual Computer Press Awards ≥1993

X WINNER

Tenth Annual Computer Press Awards ≥1994

XI WINNER

Eleventh Annual Computer Press Awards ≥1995

IDG is the world's leading IT media, research and exposition company. Founded in 1964, IDG had 1997 revenues of $2.05 billion and has more than 9,000 employees worldwide. IDG offers the widest range of media options that reach IT buyers in 75 countries representing 95% of worldwide IT spending. IDG's diverse product and services portfolio spans six key areas including print publishing, online publishing, expositions and conferences, market research, education and training, and global marketing services. More than 90 million people read one or more of IDG's 290 magazines and newspapers, including IDG's leading global brands — Computerworld, PC World, Network World, Macworld and the Channel World family of publications. IDG Books Worldwide is one of the fastest-growing computer book publishers in the world, with more than 700 titles in 36 languages. The "...For Dummies®" series alone has more than 50 million copies in print. IDG offers online users the largest network of technology-specific Web sites around the world through IDG.net (http://www.idg.net), which comprises more than 225 targeted Web sites in 55 countries worldwide. International Data Corporation (IDC) is the world's largest provider of information technology data, analysis and consulting, with research centers in over 41 countries and more than 400 research analysts worldwide. IDG World Expo is a leading producer of more than 168 globally branded conferences and expositions in 35 countries including E3 (Electronic Entertainment Expo), Macworld Expo, ComNet, Windows World Expo, ICE (Internet Commerce Expo), Agenda, DEMO, and Spotlight. IDG's training subsidiary, ExecuTrain, is the world's largest computer training company, with more than 230 locations worldwide and 785 training courses. IDG Marketing Services helps industry-leading IT companies build international brand recognition by developing global integrated marketing programs via IDG's print, online and exposition products worldwide. Further information about the company can be found at www.idg.com. 1/24/99

About the Contributors

Jim Uland, MCP+Internet, MCSE+Internet, and CNA, is a Senior Systems Engineer with XLConnect Solutions, Inc., a nationwide systems integrator providing enterprise-wide information technology solutions for clients with complex computing requirements. Jim heads the Microsoft Services Practice at XLConnect's Louisville, Kentucky branch. Jim has nine years of networking experience, and his focus is on delivering sophisticated BackOffice Internet solutions using Microsoft Exchange, IIS, SQL, Proxy, and NT Servers. You can contact him via e-mail at juland@thepoint.net.

Ed Wilson, MCSE, A+, is a Senior Networking Specialist with Full Service Networking, a Microsoft Solution Provider Partner, in Cincinnati, Ohio. A former Naval Officer, he has a BA in Journalism from the University of Mississippi, and an AS in Industrial Electronics from Maysville Community College. He is actively involved in teaching Windows-based classes in an Adult Education program, and is currently working on developing A+ certification classes with Maysville Community College. He has been working with computers for 15 years, and has worked with NetWare and Windows NT networks for the last five years. He lives in Hamilton, Ohio with his wife Teresa, and can be reached on the Internet at Ewilson@One.Net.

Robert Aschermann, MCP, MCSE, MCT, has been an IS professional for nearly ten years, and has been involved with networking the entire time. During his career, he has worked in technical support, systems design, consulting, and training. Robert has been an MCSE for almost three years and has passed 15 Microsoft certification exams. At the time of this writing, he is working on his MCSE+I certification. Robert works as a trainer and consultant for one of Microsoft's oldest and largest Authorized Technical Education Centers. He leads such courses as Networking Essentials, TCP/IP, SNA Server, Windows NT Administration, Windows NT Core Technologies, and Windows NT in the Enterprise. He is also a Certified Sylvan-Prometric Test Administrator. Prior to joining Empower Trainers & Consultants, he worked for IBM, providing technical support and services for IBM's RISC/ 6000 hardware platform and AIX operating system. He concentrated on networking and communications. At one point, he led the support team responsible for TCP/IP, SNA, and NetView/6000 support.

Bradley John Schaufenbuel is a consultant on the Internet Architecture team, which is a part of the Technology Infrastructure Services group at Arthur Andersen Technology Solutions in Chicago, Illinois. Brad has designed and implemented the infrastructure for numerous Internet and intranet projects, including the Arthur Andersen KnowledgeSpace℠ Web site, which recently won *InternetWeek* magazine's "Business On The Internet — Best Business Information Site" award. Brad has been working with the Windows NT operating system and several Microsoft BackOffice server products for more than two years. He is pursuing a Master of Business Administration degree in MIS at DePaul University in Chicago. He received his Bachelor of Arts degree in MIS from the University of Northern Iowa in Cedar Falls.

Jason Nash, MCSE and MCT, lives in Raleigh, North Carolina, with his wife Angie (another CNE and MCSE!) and works for Advanced Paradigms, Inc. (www.paradigms.com), one of the top Microsoft Solution Providers in the country. In addition to MCSE and MCT, his certifications include Novell CNE and CNP (Certified Network Professional). He is currently completing his MCSD and working on a Bachelor of Science degree in computer science. He welcomes comments from readers; his e-mail address is jnash@intrex.net, and his home page is at www.intrex.net/nash.

Derrick Woo, MCSE, is a consultant for numerous Southern California firms and educational institutions, including UCLA. He works primarily with Windows NT and Backoffice solutions and is part of the support team for the world's largest fully switched Ethernet network. In his spare time, he enjoys online chatting and weight training.

Jeremy N. Myers, MCSE, holds a master's degree in Computer Information Systems from Florida Institute of Technology and currently works as an MIS and NT Administrator for a Fortune 500 company in Melbourne, Florida. Because focusing on any one area of study would be too mundane, Jeremy started his career in computer science by obtaining a Bachelor of Arts degree in anthropology from the University of California, Riverside. While obtaining the degree, he worked as a Macintosh system administrator for an advertising firm and as a private computer consultant primarily for clients in the legal field. In his pursuit of an advanced, more technical (and practical) degree, Jeremy took his beautiful wife and daughter to a less mountainous part of the country.

Michael Cross, MCSE, MCP Specialist: Internet, is not your typical computer geek . . . although his certifications and experience seem to show otherwise. He has spent the past 17 years glued to a computer. He is a computer programmer, network support specialist, and an instructor at local private colleges. In addition (as if that weren't enough), Michael runs his own business (consulting, programming, Web page design, hardware, networking, and freelance writing). He lives in London, Ontario, Canada with his lovely fiancée, Jennifer, and two spaz cats.

Garrett Jennings, MCT, MCSE, CNI, CNE, CCSE, CCSI, is president of Jennings Computer Systems, Inc. Prior to forming his own company, Garrett worked as a technical instructor at TeKnowlogy Education Centers in Chicago, where he did training for Novell and Microsoft classes, developed training documentation, and automated class setup implementation. In 1996, he was voted the Instructor of the Year for TeKnowlogy Inc., Chicago. Garrett holds a BS in general engineering from the University of Illinois, Champaign, Illinois. He can be reached via e-mail at jen@mcs.com, and his Web site is www.mcs.com/~jen/jcsi.htm.

Authors' Acknowledgments

We would like to thank the people at IDG Books who worked to bring this book to market — especially Diane Steele, Jill Pisoni, Mary Corder, and Mary Bednarek. Thanks to John Pont, our project editor, for guiding us through the development of this book. For their insights, their careful attention to detail, and their helpful suggestions for improving the manuscript, we thank Paula Lowell, our copy editor, and Nickolas Landry, Michel Aumont, and Tullio Galati, our technical reviewers. We also want to thank Constance Carlisle for her efforts in copyediting several chapters. Thanks to everyone in IDG's Media Development department for their efforts in assembling the CD-ROM that accompanies this book, and to the talented production people who transformed our manuscript into this finished product.

Publisher's Acknowledgments

We're proud of this book; please register your comments through our IDG Books Worldwide Online Registration Form located at http://my2cents.dummies.com.

Some of the people who helped bring this book to market include the following:

Acquisitions, Editorial, and Media Development

Project Editors: John W. Pont, Pat O'Brien

Senior Acquisitions Editor: Joyce Pepple

Copy Editors: Paula Lowell, Constance Carlisle

Technical Editor: Nickolas Landry, MCSD

CD-ROM Exam Reviewers: Joe Wagner, MCSE, Systems Engineer, ST Labs, Inc.; Steven A. Frare, MCP, Network Engineer, ST Labs, Inc.

Technical Reviewers: Michel Aumont, MCSE; Tullio Galati, MCSE

Media Development Technical Editor: Marita Ellixson

Associate Permissions Editor: Carmen Krikorian

Media Development Coordinator: Megan Roney

Editorial Manager: Rev Mengle

Media Development Manager: Heather Heath Dismore

Editorial Assistants: Donna Love, Jamila Pree

Production

Project Coordinator: Tom Missler

Layout and Graphics: Linda M. Boyer, Angela F. Hunckler, Brent Savage, Janet Seib, Michael A. Sullivan

Proofreaders: Nancy Price, Marianne Santy, Janet M. Withers

Indexer: Liz Cunningham

Special Help

Beth Parlon; Barry Pruett; Suzanne Thomas; Prime Synergy; Development of the QuickLearn Game by André LaMothe of Xtreme Games, LLC; CD-ROM Exam authored by Stewart A. Simpson, MCSE, and Eric Charbonneau, MCSE, MCP + Internet

General and Administrative

IDG Books Worldwide, Inc.: John Kilcullen, CEO; Steven Berkowitz, President and Publisher

IDG Books Technology Publishing: Richard Swadley, Senior Vice President and Group Publisher

Dummies Technology Press and Dummies Editorial: Diane Graves Steele, Vice President and Associate Publisher; Mary Bednarek, Director of Acquisitions and Product Development; Kristin A. Cocks, Editorial Director, Branded Consumer; Mary C. Corder, Editorial Director, Branded Technology

Dummies Trade Press: Kathleen A. Welton, Vice President and Publisher; Kevin Thornton, Acquisitions Manager

IDG Books Production for Dummies Press: Michael R. Britton, Vice President of Production and Creative Services; Cindy L. Phipps, Manager of Project Coordination, Production Proofreading, and Indexing; Shelley Lea, Supervisor of Graphics and Design; Debbie J. Gates, Production Systems Specialist; Robert Springer, Supervisor of Proofreading; Debbie Stailey, Production Control Manager; Tony Augsburger, Supervisor of Reprints and Bluelines

Dummies Packaging and Book Design: Patty Page, Manager, Promotions Marketing

◆

The publisher would like to give special thanks to Patrick J. McGovern, without whom this book would not have been possible.

◆

Contents at a Glance

Cartoons at a Glance

By Rich Tennant

page 453

page 443

page 387

page 31

page 167

page 9

page 251

page 73

page 303

Fax: 978-546-7747 • E-mail: the5wave@tiac.net

Table of Contents

· ·

Foreword

Certification makes computer professionals stand out. Technical managers recognize the Microsoft Certified Professional (MCP) designation as a mark of quality — one which ensures that an employee or consultant has proven experience with and meets the high technical proficiency standards of Microsoft products. The ...*For Dummies* series from IDG Books Worldwide, Inc., really stands out in the marketplace and can help you achieve your goal of certification.

The ...*For Dummies* series of MCP Approved Study Guides is based on the exam's objectives — and designed to help you meet them. By partnering with Microsoft, IDG Books has developed the MCSE series to ensure that every subject on the exam is covered. Every Microsoft Approved Study Guide is reviewed and approved by an independent third party.

And certification will help you stand out from the crowd as one of the best in your industry. Microsoft training and certification let you maximize the potential of Microsoft Windows desktop operating systems; server technologies, such as the Internet Information Server, Microsoft Windows NT, and Microsoft BackOffice; and Microsoft development tools. In short, Microsoft training and certification provide you with the knowledge and skills necessary to become an expert on Microsoft products and technologies — and to provide the key competitive advantage that every business is seeking.

Research shows that MCP training and certification also provides these other benefits to businesses:

- A standard method for determining training needs and measuring results — an excellent return on training and certification investments
- Increased customer satisfaction and decreased support costs through improved service, increased productivity, and greater technical self-sufficiency
- A reliable benchmark for hiring, promoting, and career planning
- Recognition and rewards for productive employees by validating their expertise
- Retraining options for existing employees so that they can work effectively with new technologies
- Assurance of quality when outsourcing computer services

As an MCP, you'll also receive many other benefits, including direct access to technical information from Microsoft; the official MCP logo and other materials to identify your status to colleagues and clients; invitations to Microsoft conferences, technical training sessions and special events; and exclusive publications with news about the MCP program.

The challenges — both for individuals and for the industry — are out there. Microsoft training and certification will help prepare you to face them. Let this book be your guide.

— Eckhart Boehme,
Marketing Manager, Certification and
Skills Assessment, Microsoft Corporation

Introduction

. . . .

*Y*our mission, should you choose to accept it, is to increase your marketability, ensure secure employment for years to come, and substantially increase your salary potential. If you've purchased this book, you already know that becoming a Microsoft Certified Systems Engineer (MCSE) is the first step in completing your mission. We created this book to help you prepare for the 70-068 exam, Implementing and Supporting Windows NT Server 4.0 in the Enterprise.

When we first started down the path to our MCSE credentials, we didn't know what to expect. We had worked with Windows NT 4.0 since it was released in beta, but enterprise computing seemed to have so many different aspects. How could we possibly prepare for an exam that covered such a wide range of topics? Which topics wouldn't be on the exam? Just how detailed would the questions be? Most of the available study materials covered every possible aspect of Windows NT, but from a technical application level. Oh, how we longed for a book that focused on the information we needed for the Enterprise exam. Unfortunately, our hopes were in vain. We knew the product inside and out, but we still had no idea what to expect on the exam.

You may be a little hesitant to purchase an *MCSE . . . For Dummies* book at first. We can assure you that unless you have time to wade through forests full of extraneous information, you shouldn't hesitate. The *MCSE . . . For Dummies* series targets people who have experience with Windows NT — people who have decided to take the extra step and get the certification. We omit all the confusing, extraneous information, and focus on the information you need for passing your exam. We give you tips on what you need to know — as well as what you don't need to know — and we provide you with sample questions similar to those you may see on your exam.

So are you ready? Do you accept your mission? Do you want to pass your exam, without giving up countless nights ignoring your friends and loved ones while you wade through book after book of technical information you'll never even see on the exam? Then read on, and get ready to pass that exam!

Using This Book

We wrote this book to give you everything you need while you prepare for the Enterprise exam. Of course, having some experience with Windows NT in a functioning network environment is helpful.

If at all possible, follow along on your own Windows NT 4.0 Server as you read each chapter. Pay special attention to the sidebars, the tips, the warnings, and the figures throughout each chapter. Give yourself time for the exercises and the prep questions we provide in each chapter.

This book is a complete path to prepare for the exam. Just start with Chapter 1 and work your way to the end. At every step, we show you how to decide what you need to study and what you can skip.

This book follows the order of the Microsoft published exam objectives when that's the best way to study. If changing the order makes a topic easier to learn, we change the order.

Don't worry about memorizing the exact names and order of Microsoft's objectives for the exam. You aren't asked to recite the objectives like the rules of arithmetic in grade school.

Part I: You're Wondering Why I Called This Meeting

The two chapters in Part I provide an introduction to the Enterprise exam. You find out what types of questions you can expect, how many questions the exam has, and what the Enterprise exam covers. We also cover the fundamentals of NT Server 4.0. If you need to brush up before you begin your study process, Part I is the place to do it.

Part II: Planning

One of the key focus areas on your Enterprise exam involves planning and implementing an effective Enterprise security model. That's what we cover in Part II of this book. We look at the different networking models available, we explore the different roles NT Server can fulfill, we examine trusts, and we discuss the major domain security models available for an NT environment.

Part III: Installation and Configuration

Before you can implement an effective NT enterprise solution, you
need to know some basics. You must be able to set up NT, and your
hardware must be capable of running your operating system efficiently.
Then you have partitioning schemes and file systems for your hard
drives, licensing issues, and network protocol considerations.

After you design your hardware and network environments and install
NT, you must be able to manage your enterprise environment. You
need to worry about domain management, Security Accounts Manager
(SAM) database replication between domain controllers, your browser
services, printing. . . . Where's an NT administrator to begin? Well, we
suggest you turn to Part III. In this part of the book, we cover all the
aforementioned topics, and we even include a chapter on the intricacies of TCP/IP, and another on Windows Internet Name Service (WINS)
and Domain Name Server (DNS).

Part IV: Managing User Resources

Implementing a network doesn't do you any good if your users can't
access it. In Part IV, we look at managing user accounts in your NT
domains. We also discuss group management for local and global
groups — and we can guarantee that you'll see plenty of this information on your Enterprise exam. Getting a little more advanced, we
explore the possibilities you have for establishing account policies,
user rights policies, and audit policies.

Also in Part IV, we look at resource management on a user-by-user
basis. You can set security and permissions for each user on both local
resources and network resources, and in this part, we show you how.
We also explore the wonderful world of user profiles, system policies,
hardware profiles, and client administration.

Part V: Managing Network Resources

In all likelihood, you've already been introduced to basic network
resource management and TCP/IP. So what, you wonder, can Part V do
for you? Well, for starters, we introduce you to internetwork routing,
including the services that NT includes for routing IP, IPX, and DHCP
packets.

Another big focus point on your Enterprise exam is using NT in a mixed-platform environment. We discuss the NetWare connectivity provided with NT, from the NWLink protocol to the Client and Gateway services. We also look at the benefits that the Migration Tool for Netware offers for projects that involve implementing NT on a NetWare-based network.

We also examine Macintosh connectivity issues. We cover not only Macintosh connectivity and configuration issues, but also requirements you may see in the installation and configuration portion of the Enterprise exam.

Part VI: Managing External Resources

Our focus for Part VI is on Internet Services and Remote Access Services (RAS). We take you through installing and configuring Internet Information Server (IIS) and its various components for your intranet or Internet server. We cover the basics of RAS, including installation and configuration, connectivity options, and security configuration. We also explore the client side issues of RAS, such as client installation and configuration, creating dial-up connections, security, and scripts.

Part VII: Monitoring and Optimization

Another important subject area for your Enterprise exam involves monitoring and improving the performance of the different components in your enterprise network. You must know how to work with Performance Monitor to analyze issues ranging from hardware utilization to network services. You also need to understand the ins and outs of using Network Monitor to provide greater insight to network-related performance issues. In Part VII, we walk you through the finer points of these applications.

Part VIII: Troubleshooting

What network environment would be complete without its bucketful of troubleshooting issues? In Part VIII, we examine troubleshooting of numerous common problems you may see in questions on your exam. We cover some basic techniques for resource troubleshooting and repair strategies, as well as advanced problem resolution. We also look at the importance of fault tolerance in keeping your system up and running. And we cover hardware configuration, from installing new hardware to failure in the boot process, and working with your Boot.ini file.

Part IX: The Part of Tens

In Part IX, we provide top-ten lists with information that can help you pass the exam. We list the top ten resources that are certain to help you pass the exam and become an MCSE. We also offer ten nuggets of advice gathered from veteran exam takers to make your Enterprise exam experience more enjoyable, and of course, to help you pass the exam.

Part X: Appendixes

Appendix A is a complete practice exam — all the exam questions you need to practice without the pressure! Appendix B explains what you can find on the CD-ROM that accompanies this book. The CD-ROM includes some powerful study aids and other resources. You can find another practice exam at the ...*For Dummies* Web site (www.dummies.com). And to help you understand how the Enterprise exam fits into the big picture, this Web site also offers a guide to the various Microsoft certifications.

Studying Chapters

MCSE Windows NT Server 4 in the Enterprise For Dummies is a self-paced method of preparing for the exam. But you don't have to guess what to study. Every chapter that covers exam objectives guides you with

- Preview questions
- Detailed coverage
- Review questions

This step-by-step structure identifies what you need to study, gives you all the facts, and rechecks what you know. Here's how it works.

First page

Each chapter starts with a preview of what's to come, including

- Exam objectives
- Study subjects

Not sure you know all about the objectives and the subjects in the chapter? Keep going.

Quick Assessment questions

At the beginning of each chapter, you find a quick self-assessment test that helps you gauge your current knowledge of the topics the chapter covers. Take this test to determine which areas you need to focus more attention on, and to determine which areas you already understand:

- ✔ In a hurry? Just study sections for the questions you miss.
- ✔ Get every one? Jump to the end of the chapter and try the practice exam questions.

Study subjects

When you study a chapter, carefully read through it just like any book. Each subject is introduced — very briefly — and then you see what you need to know for the exam.

MCSE Windows NT Server 4 in the Enterprise For Dummies doesn't just recite the dry facts. As you study, special features show you how to apply everything in the chapter to the exam.

Labs

We include labs throughout the book to give you a feel for what's involved in using NT Server. These labs are useful for simulating often-tested topics, such as installation and configuration of services. Performing the labs can help clear up areas that may be difficult to explain through straight documentation.

We simplify each lab step so you understand the ideas of the process at the same level as they are tested, as in the following example.

Lab 9-2	Adding Static Mappings for non-WINS Clients

1. **Open up WINS Manager.**

2. **Choose Mappings⇨Static Mappings.**

   If you have added any NetBIOS names to IP address static mappings, they are listed in the dialog box that's displayed.

3. **Click Add Mappings.**

   A dialog box appears for you to enter the computer name, IP address, and the type of mapping.

4. **Enter the name of the computer for the mapping.**

5. **Enter the IP address.**

6. **For the mapping type, select Unique.**

7. **Click Add.**

8. **Click Close.**

   You see three entries for the mapping you just made in the Static Mappings dialog box. The three entries are for the NetBIOS service types of Redirector, Messenger, and Server.

Icons

Throughout the book, we use the following icons to highlight key points that can help you pass the Enterprise exam:

The Time Shaver icons point out tips that can help you manage and save time while studying or taking the exam.

The Warning icons flag problems and limitations of the technology that may appear on the exam.

Instant Answer icons highlight tips to help you recognize correct and incorrect exam answers by context.

Remember icons point out important advantages of the technology that may appear on the exam.

Tables

Sometimes, you need just the facts. In such cases, tables are a simple way to present everything at a glance, as the following example demonstrates.

Table 9-1	Static Mappings and Their Characteristics
Type	*Description*
Unique	Type of address that permits only one address per name. The unique name is the name of the computer.
Group	A normal group that doesn't have IP addresses stored for the computers in the group. A normal group is used for broadcasts and browsing the domain.
Internet Group	A group that can contain IP addresses for as many as 25 primary and backup domain controllers. This type is used for domain controllers to communicate with each other.
Multihomed	Similar to a Unique mapping, but this address can contain as many as 25 addresses that are used for *multihomed systems* (computers with more than one network interface card and IP address).

Prep Tests

The prep questions at the end of each chapter gauge your understanding of the entire chapter's content. We structure these prep test questions in the same manner as those you may see on your exam, so be sure to try your hand at these sample questions. If you have difficulties with any questions on the prep test, review the corresponding section within the chapter.

Like the exam, Prep Test questions have circles to mark when only one answer is right. When questions can have more than one answer, the answers have squares to mark.

What's Next?

MCSE Windows NT Server 4 in the Enterprise For Dummies is your guide to the exam. No need for sweaty palms.

Dig in!

Part I

You're Wondering Why I Called This Meeting

The 5th Wave   By Rich Tennant

"Oddly enough, it came with a PCI bus slot."

In this part . . .

This part provides an introduction to the Enterprise exam. In Chapter 1, you find out what types of questions you can expect, how many questions the exam has, and what you can expect when you take the Enterprise exam.

In Chapter 2, we present your exam prep roadmap. This chapter reviews NT Server basics. If you need a refresher course or are new to NT Server, you should start with Chapter 2. If you're comfortable with foundation-level material, skip Chapter 2.

Chapter 1

The NT Server 4.0 in the Enterprise Exam

. . . .

In This Chapter

▶ Taking a look at the Enterprise exam

▶ Understanding what's being tested

▶ Reviewing the ins and outs of taking the Enterprise exam

. . . .

*T*he Enterprise exam is often considered the most difficult of the core MCSE requirements. This isn't necessarily because of the difficulty of the questions, so much as the wide scope of material the questions can cover. In this chapter, we look over some of the basics of the Enterprise exam.

What Can You Expect from the Enterprise Exam?

We hope the Enterprise exam isn't going to be your introduction to the Microsoft certification experience. Before you take the Enterprise exam, you should at least take the Implementing and Supporting Windows NT Server 4.0 exam, and if possible, the Implementing and Supporting Windows NT Workstation 4.0 exam. Most of the material on the NT Server exam translates easily to information that the Enterprise exam covers. All the Microsoft exams are structured in the same way, so if you've taken one, you know the format to expect for the others.

 Check out the *...For Dummies* Web site at www.dummies.com for more information on Microsoft MCSE and other certifications. You will also find information on how the Enterprise exam fits into the certification picture.

If you've never taken a Microsoft exam, we suggest running the tutorial before you begin. Before you start your exam, you see an option to take a brief tutorial. After you click the Tutorial button, you walk through the various types of questions you can expect, the important areas of the testing interface, and special features such as marking questions. You also learn how to properly navigate through the test. The tutorial can be quite beneficial in saving time if you're unfamiliar with the testing interface.

How are the questions structured?

As we mention in a previous section in this chapter, the Enterprise exam is structured just like any of the other Microsoft certification exams. You must answer numerous multiple-choice questions. Some are knowledge based, and some are scenario based. Some questions have more than one correct answer; others have a single correct answer. The Prep Tests throughout this book can give you a good idea of the types of questions you can expect on your exam.

The questions that allow you to choose multiple answers have check boxes instead of circular check areas — but remember, just because you see a check box doesn't mean the question has more than one correct answer.

How long will the exam take?

If you're comfortable with the material, you'll find that an hour and a half is more than enough time to complete the exam. Take your time when you read the questions on this exam.

Read each question carefully, and read every available answer just to make sure you aren't missing anything. You may see several questions that look exactly the same, but subtle differences in one or two words may mean the difference between the right answer and a wrong one.

What does the Enterprise exam cover?

The Enterprise exam has six main sections. The structure of this book closely matches those primary focus areas. The focus areas, from Microsoft's Exam Preparation grid, cover the following objectives:

✓ **Planning:**

- Plan the implementation of a directory services architecture. Considerations include selecting the appropriate domain model, supporting a single logon account, and allowing users to access resources in different domains.

- Plan the disk drive configuration for various requirements. Requirements include choosing a fault-tolerance method.

- Choose a protocol for various situations. Protocols include TCP/IP, TCP/IP with DHCP and WINS, NWLink IPX/SPX Compatible Transport Protocol, Data Link Control (DLC), and AppleTalk.

✔ **Installation and configuration:**

- Install Windows NT Server to perform various server roles. Server roles include primary domain controller, backup domain controller, and member server.

- Configure protocols and protocol bindings. Protocols include TCP/IP, TCP/IP with DHCP and WINS, NWLink IPX/SPX Compatible Transport Protocol, DLC, and AppleTalk.

- Configure Windows NT Server core services. Services include Directory Replicator and Computer Browser.

- Configure hard disks to meet various requirements. Requirements include providing redundancy and improving performance.

- Configure printers. Tasks include adding and configuring a printer, implementing a printer pool, and setting print priorities.

- Configure a Windows NT Server computer for various types of client computers. Client computer types include Windows NT Workstation, Windows 95, and Macintosh.

✔ **Managing resources:**

- Manage user and group accounts. Considerations include managing Windows NT user accounts, managing Windows NT user rights, managing Windows NT groups, administering account policies, and auditing changes to the user account database.

- Create and manage policies and profiles for various situations. Policies and profiles include local user profiles, roaming user profiles, and system policies.

- Administer remote servers from various types of client computers. Client computer types include Windows 95 and Windows NT Workstation.

- Manage disk resources. Tasks include creating and sharing resources, implementing permissions and security, and establishing file auditing.

✔ **Connectivity:**

- Configure Windows NT Server for interoperability with NetWare servers by using various tools. Tools include Gateway Service for NetWare and Migration Tool for NetWare.

- Install and configure multiprotocol routing to serve various functions. Functions include Internet router, BOOTP/DHCP relay agent, and IPX router.

- Install and configure Internet Information Server.

- Install and configure Internet services. Services include World Wide Web, DNS, and intranet.

- Install and configure Remote Access Services (RAS). Configuration options include configuring RAS communications, configuring RAS protocols, and configuring RAS security.

✔ **Monitoring and optimization:**

- Establish a baseline for measuring system performance. Tasks include creating a database of measurement data.

- Monitor performance of various functions by using Performance Monitor. Functions include Processor, Memory, Disk, and Network.

- Monitor network traffic by using Network Monitor. Tasks include collecting data, presenting data, and filtering data.

- Identify performance bottlenecks.

- Optimize performance for various results. Results include controlling network traffic and controlling server load.

✔ **Troubleshooting:**

- Choose the appropriate course of action to take to resolve installation failures.

- Choose the appropriate course of action to take to resolve boot failures.

- Choose the appropriate course of action to take to resolve configuration errors. Tasks include backing up and restoring the registry and editing the registry.

- Choose the appropriate course of action to take to resolve printer problems.

- Choose the appropriate course of action to take to resolve RAS problems.

- Choose the appropriate course of action to take to resolve connectivity problems.

- Choose the appropriate course of action to take to resolve resource access and permissions problems.

- Choose the appropriate course of action to take to resolve fault-tolerance failures. Fault-tolerance methods include tape backup, mirroring, and stripe set with parity.

- Perform advanced problem resolution. Tasks include diagnosing and interpreting a blue screen, configuring a memory dump, and using the Event Log service.

Exam Day Advice

Here are some general tips to make your exam experience more successful:

✔ Try to arrive at least 15 minutes before your scheduled exam. By doing so, you give yourself a few minutes to relax and some time to quickly review any study materials.

✔ Don't leave a question unanswered. An unanswered question counts against your score just as much as an incorrectly answered question. You should take a guess rather than leave a question unanswered — with a guess, you have at least a chance of a correct answer.

✔ Read the questions carefully. Read every available answer before making your selection, and pay close attention to wording.

You get a piece of scratch paper to use during your exam. Keep in mind that the clock doesn't start ticking until you click the start button. So if you have an area that gives you problems, look it over before you start the exam. Then, when you sit down, but before clicking the start button, take some time to write out everything you can remember about your troublesome topic area, or any mnemonic devices you may have memorized. Later in the exam, if you run into a question dealing with that subject, you can refer to your scratch paper, and that security can do a lot to calm your nerves.

When you show up for your exam, don't forget, you must have a valid photo ID available, such as a driver's license, passport, or state identification card.

Getting Your Score

The exam software stops automatically when your time is up. The software grades your exam, displays your results on the screen, and prints your results. The exam coordinator at the testing center notarizes the printed results, and you can take them with you. This printout serves as your official report. Congratulations!

Registering for the Exam

So, are you ready to schedule your test? Some people schedule a week or two ahead of time; others wait until a few days before. The exam fee is $100, well worth every penny when you pass!

You can register for the exam by contacting either of the following two companies:

- ✔ Sylvan Prometric at 1-800-755-EXAM, or you can register online at www.sylvanprometric.com.
- ✔ Virtual University Enterprises at 1-888-837-8618, or online at www.vue.com.

Chapter 2

Exam Prep Roadmap: Windows NT Server in the Enterprise Basics

---

In This Chapter

▶ Reviewing Windows NT executive and kernel

▶ Understanding the Windows NT security model

▶ Working in a heterogeneous network

▶ Understanding the minimum requirements for using NT Server

---

*I*f you haven't spent some quality time with NT Server 4.0, or if you're just a little rusty, we can help you get up to speed in a hurry. In this chapter, we discuss the basics of NT Server 4.0 and we give you a handle on which of its features you need to grasp for the Enterprise exam. Unlike subsequent chapters in this book, this chapter doesn't address specific exam objectives. Instead, we focus on the NT Server fundamentals that you must understand before you take the Enterprise exam.

If you are already familiar with Windows NT Server 4.0, you may be able to skip this chapter.

In this chapter, we cover the basics of Windows NT and the minimum requirements for loading and running the operating system. You need to know the minimums for the exam. Make sure you know the requirements for both X86 and RISC-based servers.

Sorting Out NT Server and Windows

Windows NT 3.*x* was designed, not as an upgrade to an existing product, but as an entirely new operating system. The designers kept the familiar Windows 3.*x* interface and designed a modular architecture for the core of the operating system. The design model also includes support for 32-bit processing. This design targets the high-end workstation and server markets, and it brings Windows from the desktop to the enterprise.

Since its initial release in 1993, the Microsoft Windows NT Server operating system has established itself as a multipurpose network operating system. Combining an application server, a file and print server, a communications server, and an Internet/intranet server, Windows NT Server is designed to be easy to manage, use, and scale.

With Windows NT 4.0, the user interface changed to match Windows 95. NT provides tools to connect users around the corner or around the world and offers better tools for sharing data with these users.

Although their user interfaces look similar, Windows NT and Windows 95 can't share much on the same computer. The two operating systems use completely different formats for their respective Registries, and no upgrade path exists from Windows 95 to Windows NT. If you require a dual-boot system, you must perform a new installation of Windows NT.

If you want to share an application on a dual-boot system, you must install it twice — once for each operating system. You can place both installations in the same directory, and you don't need two separate copies of the application. You perform the separate installations to register the application into each operating system's Registry.

You can configure Windows 95 as a diskless workstation and boot from a Windows NT Server. Windows 95 computers can act as clients to all Windows NT Servers. The NT Installation CD has server management tools for both Windows NT Workstation and Windows 95.

Reviewing Windows NT Server's Features

In addition to the capabilities of previous versions, Windows NT Server 4.0 offers the following features:

Windows 95 interface	DNS server
Internet Explorer 3.0	Multiprotocol routing
Internet Information Server	DirectX support
Exchange Client	Remote booting of Windows 95 desktops
Telephony API	Remote administration
Enhanced TCP/IP protocol	Connectivity with Novell NetWare 4.*x* servers running NDS

Examining the Windows NT kernel

The microkernel is the heart of the operating system. It schedules activities for the processor. If the system has multiple processors, the microkernel synchronizes the activities of the processors. With Windows NT 4.0, Microsoft added more function to NT's microkernel. Figure 2-1 shows the Windows NT architecture model.

The scheduled activities are known as threads. Threads are the most basic entity in the system that the microkernel can schedule. They define the context of a process, which represents an address space, a set of objects visible to the process, and a set of threads that runs in the context of a process. Basically, every process has at least one thread. The processor performs threads. A multithreaded application has the capability to increase performance by utilizing multiprocessors.

The main thing to remember about the Windows NT microkernel is that it's the only way that software can interface with hardware. The microkernel communicating with the HAL (Hardware Abstraction Layer) manages all hardware.

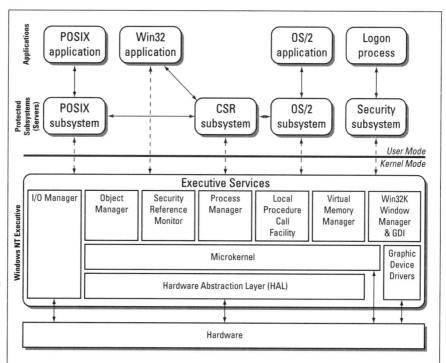

Figure 2-1:
The
Windows NT
architecture.

Security

Windows NT was designed to meet the National Computer Security Center (NCSC) C2 rating. Among the many processes and requirements for becoming certified, the most important ones to remember are

- **Mandatory logon:** Accountability
- **Discretionary access control:** An enforceable security policy
- **Auditing:** Accountability, again

Security is provided by the security subsystem. Figure 2-2 shows the process flow on security.

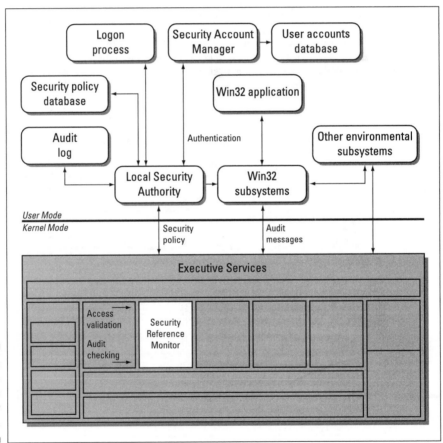

Figure 2-2:
The Windows NT security subsystem.

You need to understand Windows NT's logon process and the security subsystem:

1. When you boot the system, it uses information contained in the Registry to load drivers and services. The system is completely operational, but a user must log on before interactive use can take place. Windows NT requires that every user log on to the system.

2. When a user attempts to log on, the WinLogon process passes the user's ID and password to the security subsystem.

3. The LSA (Local Security Authority) queries its User Account Database and either validates or denies the user's request. The key to Windows NT security is the From box in the Windows Logon dialog box. It tells the WinLogon process which SAM to query.

4. WinLogon dispatches a process for the user that contains a token. This user's process can now attempt to access resources, and the token is used to validate each request for discretionary access control. Information in the token is compared with information in the resource to verify that this user has permission to use the resource.

To successfully log on to Windows NT, a user must have a valid user name and password. The password may be blank. Each user is assigned a Security Identifier (SID). A user's SID is generated when you create the account. If you delete and then re-create a user, a different SID is generated.

Fault tolerance

Windows NT supports fault tolerance in many ways — for example:

✔ Windows NT supports file system RAID 0, 1, and 5. We discuss fault tolerance in Chapter 24.

✔ NTFS (NT File System) supports a hot-fix feature, which automatically moves data written to a bad sector to a good sector, and removes the bad sector from service.

✔ NTFS also provides a log file that you can use to restore files in the event of a disk failure.

✔ Symmetric multiprocessing provides redundancy in case of a processor failure.

Preemptive multitasking

In preemptive multitasking, the operating system can take control of the processor without the task's cooperation. (A task can also give it up voluntarily, as in cooperative multitasking.) The term *preemption* refers to the process in which the operating system takes control from a task.

Windows NT uses preemptive multitasking for all processes except 16-bit Windows 3.1 programs. As a result, a Windows NT application can't take over the processor in the same way as a Windows 3.1 application can.

A preemptive operating system takes control of the processor from a task in two ways:

- **When a task's time quantum (or time slice) runs out.** Any task is given control for only a set amount of time before the operating system interrupts it and schedules another task to run.

- **When a task that has higher priority becomes ready to run.** Regardless of whether it has time left in its quantum, the currently running task loses control of the processor when a task with higher priority is ready to run.

Symmetric multiprocessing

The Windows NT microkernel takes maximum advantage of multiprocessor configurations by implementing symmetric multiprocessing (SMP). SMP allows the threads of any process, including the operating system, to run on any available processor. Furthermore, the threads of a single process can run on different processors at the same time.

The Windows NT microkernel allows processors to share memory and assigns ready threads to the next available processor or processors. In this way, NT ensures that no processor is ever idle or is executing a lower priority thread when a higher priority thread is ready to run. Allowing the operating system to run on multiple processors has significant advantages, especially when it's running processor-intensive applications. Server processes can respond to more than one client at a time.

SMP systems provide better load balancing and fault tolerance than single processor servers. Because the operating system threads can run on any processor, the chance of hitting a CPU bottleneck is greatly reduced. In the SMP model, processor failure only reduces the computing capacity of the system.

Windows NT Server's capability to run on machines with as many as 32 processors is one of the operating system's most important features and is fundamental to the design of the kernel. The technology necessary to achieve genuine, load-balancing, symmetric multiprocessing is intrinsic to all components of Windows NT Server.

Windows NT Server ships with support for four processors. Systems with more processors require a vendor-supplied HAL.

Platform independence

Platform independence, or portability, means that Windows isn't designed for just one type of processor. You can install Windows NT Server 4.0 on the following types of processors:

- ✔ Intel 80486, Pentium, Pentium Pro, Pentium II
- ✔ DEC Alpha AXP RISC
- ✔ MIPS R4000 RISC
- ✔ PowerPC

As of Service Pack 3, support is no longer provided for the MIPS and PowerPC platforms.

Exploring the Windows NT File System (NTFS)

You have two file system choices for Windows NT:

- ✔ FAT (File Allocation Table)
- ✔ NTFS (NT File System)

Although FAT has a lower overhead than NTFS, it isn't really suitable for a server because it lacks security and recoverability. Also, NTFS supports larger partitions than a FAT file system can. You can convert a partition from FAT to NTFS without losing data.

On a RISC-based machine, you need a 2MB FAT partition for boot purposes. You can format all other partitions as NTFS. Only computers running Windows NT can access an NTFS partition directly. Network users can access files on an NTFS partition without difficulty, provided they have the access permission to do so.

Reliability

NTFS can recover in the event of a failure because it completes the logging of transactions before it carries out the transactions. This technique is known as a *lazy write*.

NTFS also constantly monitors its disk areas. If it finds damage, it takes the bad area out of service and moves the data to a good sector on the disk. This process is called a *hot fix*. The hot-fix process is invisible to all processes, applications, and users.

Security

Maintaining file security has two main aspects:

- ✔ Controlling access to the file
- ✔ Protecting the integrity of the file

NTFS allows for control of user access at both the folder and the file levels. A person may have Full Access to a folder but No Access to all the files within the folder, or vice versa. Table 2-1 lists the standard permissions for folders. Table 2-2 lists file permissions. The individual file attributes are

- ✔ Read (R)
- ✔ Write (W)
- ✔ Execute (X)
- ✔ Delete (D)
- ✔ Change Permissions (P)
- ✔ Take Ownership (O)

Table 2-1	Standard Folder Permissions
Folder Permission	*Description*
No Access	The user can't access the folder even if that user belongs to a group that has Full Access.
List	The user can list the files and subfolders in this folder and can change to subfolders of this folder. The user can't gain access to files created in this folder by other users.
Read	The user can read the files and run the applications contained in the folder.
Add	The user can add files to the folder but can't read or change the files that the folder currently contains.
Add & Read	The user can add and read files but can't change them.
Change	The user can add, change, and read files.
Full Control	The user can add, change, and read files; change permissions for the folder and its contents; and take ownership of the folder and its contents.

Table 2-2	Standard File Permissions
File Permission	*Description*
No Access	The user can't gain access to the file even if that user belongs to a group that has Full Access.
Read	The user can read the contents of the file and can run any applications.
Change	The user can read, change, and delete the file.
Full Control	The user can read, change, delete, set permissions for, and take ownership of the file.

To set permissions, click the Permissions button on the Security tab in the File (or Folder) Properties dialog box. Figure 2-3 shows the resulting File Permissions dialog box.

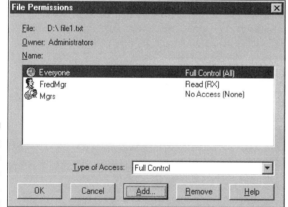

Figure 2-3:
The File
Permissions
dialog box.

You need to know the various permissions and what a user can do with each type. Your Enterprise exam will have many questions pertaining to permissions. The big key is that No Access means *no access* — it overrides all other permissions.

Reviewing networking services

Enabling communications across a network is essential for using Windows NT Server. Having a server is almost pointless if clients can't connect to it. For this reason, an NT Server has several methods for communicating. In Part III, we cover these topics in more detail but we touch on the main features here.

You set up all network functions from the Control Panel's Network applet. Figure 2-4 shows the Network Services tab.

Protocol support

Windows NT Server comes with many protocols that you can enable for connectivity to various other computer systems:

- ✔ Network Basic Input/Output System (NetBIOS)

- ✔ NetBIOS Extended User Interface (NetBEUI)

- ✔ Transmission Control Protocol/Internet Protocol (TCP/IP)

- ✔ NWLink Internetwork Packet Exchange/Sequenced Packet Exchange (IPX/SPX)

- ✔ Data Link Control (DLC)

- ✔ AppleTalk

In addition to these protocols, different network vendors can provide protocols for Windows NT. You can load additional protocols via the Control Panel's Network applet.

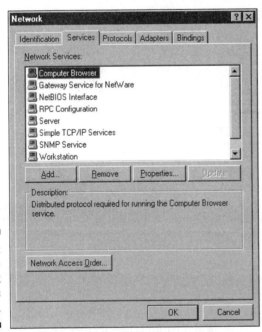

Figure 2-4:
The
Network
Services
tab.

For the Enterprise exam, you need to know what each default protocol is and in what type of situation you would use each one. We cover these protocols in depth later in the book, but here's a quick take on the protocols and what you should remember as a foundation for your study process:

- ✔ NetBIOS is loaded automatically. NT uses it for browsing and interprocess communication. It is not routable.

- ✔ NetBEUI is a simple network protocol requiring no configuration. It's small and fast but is not routable.

- ✔ TCP/IP is the standard for the Internet and is loaded by default. It's routable and has good cross-platform support.

- ✔ NWLink (IPX/SPX) is routable and is used for connectivity to NetWare.

- ✔ DLC is used to communicate to network-attached printers and IBM SNA computers.

- ✔ AppleTalk is used for connecting to Macintosh networks and providing services to them. Macintosh support is only available on NTFS partitions.

Multiple clients

Windows NT Server supports several clients:

- ✔ MS-DOS
- ✔ Windows 3.1*x*
- ✔ Windows 95
- ✔ Windows NT
- ✔ Macintosh
- ✔ NetWare

These clients are supported by the Services for Microsoft, Services for Macintosh, and Services for NetWare. You can use other support services by loading the appropriate service drivers from the network vendors.

You can configure Windows NT to allow from one to an unlimited number of connected users to shared resources. You configure this capability on the Sharing tab in a folder's Properties dialog box. Figure 2-5 shows the Sharing tab. You control how many users can connect to a shared resource by selecting the appropriate option in the User Limit box.

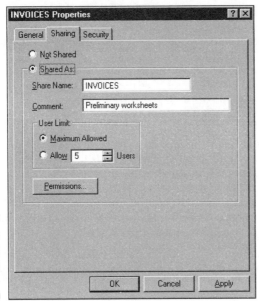

Figure 2-5:
Sharing
properties
for a folder.

Integrating Windows NT with Other Servers

Windows NT Server can communicate and interoperate with many other operating systems. Several tools and utilities are included with Windows NT Server to assist you in integrating into an existing environment. Integration with some operating systems may require additional third-party supplied tools.

Novell NetWare

Windows NT Server easily integrates with NetWare 2.*x*, 3.*x*, and 4.*x* infrastructures to increase resource utilization and become the platform for client/server solutions. To ease this integration, Microsoft developed a set of utilities that enables you to add Windows NT Server seamlessly to NetWare-based networks.

Windows NT Server supports numerous utilities that enable it to fully integrate with most NetWare networks. Several of these utilities ship with NT Server:

- Client Services for NetWare
- Gateway Services for NetWare
- NWLink, an IPX/SPX-compatible protocol
- The Migration Tool for NetWare

You can also purchase two add-on utilities separately that greatly enhance Windows NT Server and NetWare interoperability:

- File and Print Services for NetWare
- Directory Service Manager for NetWare

Banyan Vines

Windows NT doesn't integrate directly with Vines. Agents are available from Banyan to integrate Windows NT Servers with Vines servers.

UNIX

Windows NT Server easily integrates with existing UNIX infrastructures to increase resource utilization and enable a smooth migration to Windows NT Server from a legacy UNIX environment. Windows NT Server includes several utilities that ship with the base product and also supports many third-party utilities that allow it to fully integrate with all of today's UNIX networks.

Windows NT and UNIX interoperability ranges from low-level protocols to high-level end-user applications. Windows NT Server is built on an industry-standard TCP/IP stack that transparently interoperates with TCP/IP running on UNIX. Other protocols commonly found on UNIX systems — for example, DNS, DHCP, HTTP, Gopher, Telnet, FTP, and LPR/LPD — are all built-in. File service interoperability is available in various forms, with NFS clients, servers, and gateways available from numerous vendors. And native Windows NT file services (SMBs) are available for UNIX clients and UNIX servers.

Macintosh

With built-in services for Macintosh, Windows NT Server provides a power-ful integration platform for mixed Windows and Macintosh-based networks. Windows NT Server makes it easy for Macintosh and Windows users to collaborate and share information on a network. Services for Macintosh lets Macintosh users access the file server and print server through the familiar interface of the Chooser. Macintosh clients don't know that a Windows NT Server is on the network.

Reviewing Windows NT Hardware Requirements

Being a robust and powerful operating system, Windows NT needs a computer with adequate resources to provide optimum performance and accessibility to clients. In this section, we list the bare minimum and a recommended minimum configuration. Of course, the more resources that Windows NT Server has, the better performance it can achieve.

✔ **Microprocessor:** An Intel 80486/25 is the minimum processor specified. An 80486/66 or higher processor is recommended. A Pentium or Digital Alpha RISC is recommended for domain controllers, application servers, and other high-use servers.

A Windows NT Server can support four processors out of the box. Servers with more processors come with a vendor-supplied HAL.

✔ **Memory:** A minimum of 12MB of RAM is required for x86-based servers, and 16MB to 32MB is recommended. A minimum of 16MB is required for RISC-based servers, with 32MB preferred.

✔ **Disk space:** For x86-based systems, you need a hard drive with at least 124MB of free disk space on the partition that will contain the Windows NT system files. RISC-based systems require 159MB of free disk space for Windows NT. Recommendations are 200MB or more for additional features and options.

✔ **Peripherals:** You need the following peripheral devices for your server:

  • A VGA display is adequate unless you plan to work at the server a lot.

  • A high-density 3.5-inch or 5.25-inch disk drive. You may need to use floppies for the setup disks to get started. Windows NT Server comes with 3.5-inch setup disks.

  • A 4X or better CD-ROM drive is required for RISC-based computers and recommended for x86 servers. If you don't use a CD-ROM on x86 servers, you can perform a network installation.

  • A network adapter is required to configure any of the networking components. Windows NT Server can support multiple network adapters.

  • A mouse or other type of pointing device is recommended.

Part II
Planning

"Sure, at first it sounded great — an intuitive network adapter that helps people write memos by finishing their thoughts for them."

In this part . . .

One of the main focus areas on your Enterprise exam will be on planning and implementing an effective Enterprise security model. That's what we cover in this part of the book. We look at the different networking models available, we explore the different roles NT Server can fulfill, we examine trusts, and we discuss the primary domain security models available for an NT environment.

Chapter 3
Networking Models

Exam Objectives

▶ Selecting the appropriate domain model

▶ Introducing trust relationships

▶ Understanding the different roles of servers

▶ Building an effective structure

*T*he topics we discuss in this chapter provide the foundation for setting up Windows NT on an enterprise network. The information we cover throughout the rest of the book builds on this foundation.

This relatively short chapter addresses several important topics that you can expect to see on the Enterprise exam:

- ✔ You must understand the fundamentals of network models for the Enterprise exam.

- ✔ Be sure to study the different domain models, because the exam includes questions about these models.

- ✔ Pay close attention to the roles of NT Servers in the domain.

- ✔ Be sure to study the authentication methods in case they show up in a troubleshooting question on the exam.

Quick Assessment

1 A network with worldwide locations and separate administrators needs to use the _____ domain model.

2 Which are more secure — workgroups or domains?

3 A two-way trust is actually two _____ trusts set up between two _____.

4 A domain is a logical grouping of _____ and _____ organized for _____ purposes. The trust provides a _____ link between two domains.

5 If Domain A trusts Domain B, does B trust A?

6 How many primary domain controllers are needed in a domain for fault tolerance?

7 The four uses for a Windows NT Server in a domain are _____, _____, _____, and _____.

8 The four keys to building an efficient domain structure are an appropriate number of _____, appropriate server _____, efficient _____, and efficient _____ authentication.

Answers

1 *Multiple master.* See "Reviewing the Networking Models."

2 *Domains.* See "Reviewing the Networking Models."

3 *One-way; domains.* See "Reviewing the Networking Models."

4 *Users; computers; administrative; communication.* See "Welcome to the Starship Enterprise Environment."

5 *No.* See "Reviewing the Networking Models."

6 *One.* Review "Exploring NT Server Roles."

7 *PDC; BDC; member server; workstation.* See "Exploring NT Server Roles."

8 *Servers; location; synchronization; passthrough.* Review "Building an Effective Structure."

Welcome to the Starship Enterprise Environment

One of Windows NT Server's strong points is its scalability. Scalability may sound like another new buzzword in networking, but it's very important. The term *scalability* refers to a server's capability to accommodate growth in an organization. If a system doesn't scale well, it may not be able to keep up as your network grows.

Windows NT Server's scalability comes from its system of servers and domains. *Domains* are logical groups of servers and workstations that share and use the same security and resource information. Without domains, users would need separate accounts on each server they needed to access, which could quickly become a nightmare for the poor administrator!

To simplify your job as an administrator, you must carefully plan these domains and servers. Administering a well-planned domain is easy, and sometimes a pleasure, while a poorly planned strategy presents lots of problems. Before we get any deeper into domains, however, we need to explain the difference between workgroups and domains, as well as the different domain models. We examine trusts in more detail in Chapter 4.

Reviewing the Networking Models

In a Windows NT network, you can use either domains or workgroups. The correct choice depends on the size and the requirements of your network. Larger networks, and those needing tighter security, definitely need to use one of the domain models.

The workgroup model

Workgroups are useful in small office environments where centralized security is not a concern. Workgroups are made up of individual computers that normally act as clients and servers to all the other network participants. The great thing about workgroups is that you don't need any sort of administrator to handle the network. Each user manages his or her own resources. Although this simplicity may seem attractive, it can become scary very quickly when a network grows to more than about 10 computers.

In a workgroup, each computer keeps track of its own user and group account information and doesn't share this information with other computers. Each Windows NT computer that participates in a workgroup maintains its own security policy and security account databases. This decentralization of management allows for very little security. Each user has full control over resources on his or her machine.

Each Windows NT computer in a workgroup setting maintains its own Security and User databases. The information in these databases is not shared with the other members of the domain. A user would need an account on every machine in order to use those machines.

The domain models

Domains are designed to support large networks. Unlike the chaos and lack of order in a workgroup, domains have an established chain of command.

Security in a domain is shared and used by all members of a domain. In this way, a user needs only one account in the domain to be able to access all the resources shared from computers in that domain. An administrator needs to manage only one set of user accounts or directory permissions. Everyone's life is easier!

In a Windows NT domain, you have a few different types of participants:

- ✔ Exactly one primary domain controller (PDC)
- ✔ An optional number of backup domain controllers (BDCs)
- ✔ Member servers
- ✔ Workstations

A workgroup can contain computers running nothing but Windows 95, Windows NT Workstation, and NT Server as a member server, but a domain requires at least one computer to run Windows NT Server and act as the PDC.

Four types of domain models exist:

- ✔ The single domain model
- ✔ The single master domain model
- ✔ The multiple master domain model
- ✔ The complete trust domain model

We discuss these domain types in the following sections and in Chapter 4. On the exam, you must know when to use each domain structure.

The single domain model

In most cases, you can use the single domain model. In this model, the network has only one domain. You create all users and global groups in this domain. The single domain has a PDC with one or more BDCs. Each BDC supports user accounts to validate user logons and provide fault tolerance. All the clients get their resources from the different servers, not each other.

The single master domain model

If you need to split the network into domains for organizational purposes, but the network has a small enough number of users and groups, the master domain model may be the best choice. This model gives you both centralized administration and the organizational benefits of multiple domains. Figure 3-1 shows a network that uses the single master domain model. The network has a PDC, a BDC, and even plain servers for each domain. All the accounts reside in the master, and all the resources reside in separate resource domains.

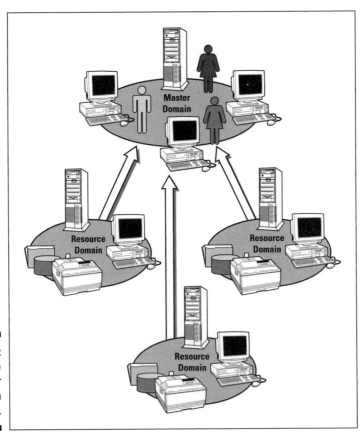

Figure 3-1:
The single master domain model.

Because multiple domains are involved, you must set up trusts between them. If one domain "trusts" another domain, the users of the trusted domain have access to the trusting domain. By placing all user accounts in the trusted domain, the administrator alleviates the problems associated with managing user accounts. In diagrams, an arrow is used to show a trust, with the arrow pointing to the trusted domain.

Trusts are not transitive. A trust relationship provides a communication link between two — and only two — domains. Trusts are one way only. (A two-way trust is actually two one-way trusts!) If A trusts B, and B trusts C, and C trusts A, A doesn't trust C.

With this model, one domain — the *master domain* — acts as the central administrative unit for user and group accounts. All other domains on the network trust this domain, which means they recognize the users and global groups defined there. The master domain is the trusted domain. The others are trusting domains. Because of this trust, users in the master domain have access to resources in the trusting domains.

All users log on to their accounts in the master domain. Resources, such as printers and file servers, are located in the other domains. Each *resource domain* establishes a one-way trust with the master (account) domain, enabling users with accounts in the master domain to use resources in all the other domains. The network administrator can manage the entire multiple-domain network and its users and resources by managing only a single domain.

The single master domain model is particularly well suited for meeting the following needs:

- ✔ **Centralized account management.** User accounts can be centrally managed; you can add, delete, and change user accounts from a single point.

- ✔ **Decentralized resource management or local system administration capability.** Each department domain can have its own administrator who manages the resources in the department. The administrator can group resources logically, corresponding to local domains.

The multiple master domain model

In the multiple master domain model, the network has two or more single master domains. Like the single master domain model, the master domains serve as account domains, with every user and computer account created and maintained on one of these master domains. A company's MIS groups can centrally manage these master domains. As in the single master domain model, the other domains on the network are called resource domains. They don't store or manage user accounts, but they do provide resources such as shared file servers and printers to the network.

Figure 3-2 shows a multiple master domain, and all the trusts associated with one. Each master has two one-way trusts with the other masters. Because each resource domain trusts each master, a user needs only one account to access any network resource.

In this model, every master domain is connected to every other master domain by a two-way trust relationship. Each resource domain trusts every master domain with a one-way trust relationship. The resource domains can trust other resource domains, but they are not required to do so. Because every user account exists in one of the master domains, and because each resource domain trusts every master domain, every user account can be used on any of the master domains.

The multiple master domain model incorporates all the features of a single master domain and also accommodates

✔ Organizations of more than 40,000 users. The multiple master domain model is scalable to networks with any number of users.

✔ Mobile users. Users can log on from anywhere in the network, anywhere in the world.

✔ Centralized or decentralized administration.

✔ Organizational needs. You can configure domains to mirror specific departments or internal company organizations. You can also distribute BDCs between sites to facilitate LAN-WAN interactions.

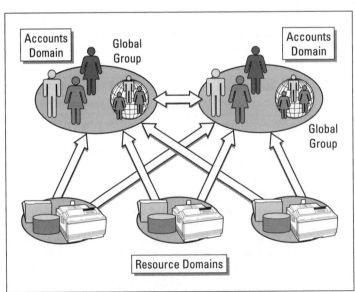

Figure 3-2:
The multiple
master
domain
model.

For the multiple master domain model to work, all the masters must trust each other via two one-way trusts.

The complete trust model

In a complete trust environment, every domain trusts every other domain. This model can quickly grow into a nightmare due to the number of trusts involved. You should only use the complete trust model if you don't have a centralized MIS group, or when you must distribute the management of users and resources among different departments. The key here is that no centralized management exists.

Figure 3-3 shows a complete trust environment. Notice how each arrow is double headed, indicating two one-way trusts.

You will definitely see questions on the exam asking whether to use a workgroup model or a domain model. The key thing to remember is whether you need centralized account management and security. Keep these points in mind when preparing for the exam:

- ✔ **Workgroup model:** Decentralized account and security management. Useful for small networks with no more than 10 users.

- ✔ **Domain model:** Centralized account and security management. Effective for medium to large networks.

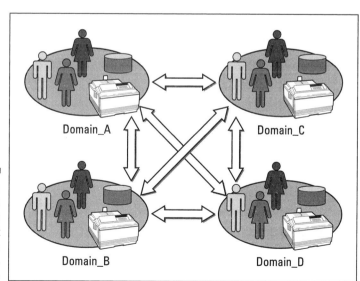

Figure 3-3:
The complete trust domain model.

Domain_A   Domain_C

Domain_B   Domain_D

Exploring NT Server Roles

In a domain, a few different types of servers exist. Some help to maintain order and security, and others exist simply to share resources. At a minimum, both types of domain controllers must run Windows NT Server. The different types of servers in a domain are

- Primary domain controllers (PDCs)
- Backup domain controllers (BDCs)
- Member servers

Primary domain controllers

A primary domain controller (PDC) is in charge of the domain. It maintains the master list of all user account information, known as the Security Accounts Manager (SAM) database, or the directory database.

The master copy of the directory database is stored on one server, replicated to backup servers, and then synchronized on a regular basis to maintain centralized security. When a user logs on to a domain, Windows NT Server software checks the user name and password against the directory database. Whenever an administrator makes a change to a domain account, the change is recorded in the directory database on the PDC. The PDC is the only domain server that receives these changes directly. Figure 3-4 shows how the PDC can replicate to BDCs.

PDCs may also handle logging on if no BDCs exist to handle that task. You must configure Windows NT Server to be a domain controller at the time of installation. You may then designate the server as a primary or backup domain controller.

Remember that you can have only one primary domain controller in a domain! Should the PDC fail, you need to manually promote a BDC in its place. If you promote a BDC while the PDC is still active, the PDC is demoted automatically to a BDC.

Backup domain controllers

Backup domain controllers (BDCs) keep a copy of the SAM database and use it to log on users and authenticate them to resources. In a previous section of this chapter, we state that BDCs are optional; however, Microsoft always counts on at least one per domain.

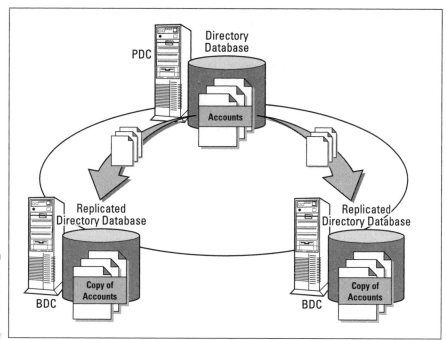

Figure 3-4:
A PDC
replicating
to BDCs.

You can have no BDCs, or 100 — it's up to you. The number you use depends on how much fault tolerance you have as well as the number of users in your domain. Each BDC can handle about 2,000 users under normal circumstances.

Microsoft recommends that you have one BDC for every 15 computers on your network. Keep this recommendation in mind on the exam.

Should the PDC fail, you can promote a BDC to its place. You do this through Server Manager. BDCs handle all logon requests if they are available, and thus keep the load off the PDC.

Member servers

Member servers are simply servers that belong to the domain but don't keep copies of the SAM database. These servers can see and use the domain security information so that they can give domain users access to their resources. You can't promote a member server to a domain controller. Member servers may be application servers, print servers, or RAS servers.

The only way to upgrade a member server to a domain controller is to reinstall Windows NT Server.

Building an Effective Structure

Windows NT domains require careful planning. A well-planned domain is much easier to administer than a poorly planned domain. In the following sections, we provide guidelines for planning the optimum network design.

Number of controllers

A network must have the proper number of domain controllers. Each domain requires one PDC. You must determine how many BDCs you need. A BDC can usually handle 2,000 accounts. However, remember that other uses of a BDC, such as being a resource server, affect this number.

Appropriate server location

Knowing where to place servers can make the difference between creating an efficient network that serves its users, or one that's just a collection of servers and workstations. Within a domain, the PDC should be in or near the heaviest network administrative and support activity. You should place the BDCs closer to user locations to decrease WAN traffic, especially during periods of heavy logon and logoff, and validation time. Across WANs, remember line speed, bandwidth, reliability, access, protocols, and user authentication requirements.

Efficient synchronization

Synchronization occurs when a PDC copies the directory database to the BDCs within a domain. Consider these aspects of synchronization:

- ✔ The overall process
- ✔ How much time it takes
- ✔ The effect of different links on performance
- ✔ The ways to optimize the process

To ensure proper synchronization, never set the Replication Governor Registry entry below 25 percent.

Efficient passthrough authentication

User logons must be validated as efficiently as possible. Because logons may all occur during a short time span, you must plan to ensure that they don't interfere with normal business communication. Passthrough authentication is the heart of trusts. It allows for One User, One Account networking!

Passthrough authentication occurs when a user account must be authenticated, but the local computer can't authenticate the account. In this case, the user name and password are forwarded to a Windows NT Server computer that can authenticate the user, and the user's information is returned to the requesting computer.

Passthrough authentication occurs in the following instances:

- At interactive logon when a user at a Windows NT Workstation computer or a Windows NT Server computer that is not a domain controller is logging on to a domain or trusted domain
- At remote logon when the domain specified is a trusted domain

Prep Test

1 To demote a PDC to a BDC you must _____ a BDC.

A ○ demote
B ○ promote
C ○ trust
D ○ log on to

2 With four domains, and 4,000 users, _____ domain controllers are recommended.

A ○ 1
B ○ 2
C ○ 4
D ○ 8

3 The _____ network model should be chosen for an organization with three offices, each with its own resources, account management, and administration.

A ○ workgroup
B ○ single master
C ○ multiple master
D ○ complete trust

4 Jane works in an office with eight other people. They all work on their own documents. They occasionally need to share these documents as well as printers and CD-ROMs. You should choose the _____ model for this organization.

A ○ workgroup
B ○ single domain
C ○ single master domain
D ○ multiple master domain

5 How do you make a member server a BDC?

A ○ Promote the member server.
B ○ Demote the PDC.
C ○ Reinstall Windows NT.
D ○ Change its properties in Network Properties.

6 Which domain model should you use for a company with 5,000 employees, spread out over six floors of an office tower, with each floor being a separate department?

A ○ Workgroup

B ○ Single domain

C ○ Single master domain

D ○ Multiple master domain

7 Angie works in an office with 35 other people. They are all working on one large product that is in development and must be kept fairly secure. They have two people on staff to handle the IS functions. Which domain model would you choose for Angie?

A ○ Workgroup

B ○ Single domain

C ○ Single master domain

D ○ Multiple master domain

8 In a small company with less than 10 computers, where everyone may use a different computer daily, which network model should you use?

A ○ Workgroup

B ○ Single domain

C ○ Single master domain

D ○ Multiple master domain

9 You have been hired as a consultant for a very large company looking at moving to Windows NT. The company has 25,000 people who will need user accounts. The company has the luxury of a single IS department that maintains this organization. Supervisors at the branch offices want to be able to maintain the security on resources at their sites. Which domain model would you suggest for this situation?

A ○ Workgroup

B ○ Single domain

C ○ Single master domain

D ○ Multiple master domain

10 Which domain controller(s) handle(s) logon requests?

A ❏ PDC

B ❏ BDC

C ❏ Member servers

D ❏ File and print servers

Answers

1 *B. promote.* The only way to demote a PDC is by promoting a BDC. When you promote a BDC, the PDC is automatically demoted (if it is available). *See "Exploring NT Server Roles."*

2 *D. 8.* You need four PDCs and four BDCs. You can use additional BDCs, but they aren't required. *Review "Exploring NT Server Roles."*

3 *D. complete trust.* Each site is a separate master domain because they all have account management. Each master should trust the other masters, allowing users to access all resources. *See the section "Reviewing the Networking Models."*

4 *A. workgroup.* A domain model is unnecessary because you don't need any central accounts or security, and resource sharing is light. *See "Reviewing the Networking Models."*

5 *C. Reinstall Windows NT. Review "Exploring NT Server Roles."*

6 *C. Single master domain.* This model creates logical domains for the re-sources on each floor, and one master for all the user accounts. *See "Review-ing the Networking Models" for more information.*

7 *B. Single domain.* This model is perfect for this situation due to centralized account and security requirements. *See "Reviewing the Networking Models."*

8 *B. Single domain.* The users move from machine to machine, and maintain-ing a centralized SAM is easier than maintaining multiple user accounts for each user. *See "Reviewing the Networking Models."*

9 *D. Multiple master domain.* Any time you talk about centralized account management and multiple sites, the master domain model is the answer. Due to the large number of user accounts needed, you need the multiple master domain model. *See the section "Reviewing the Networking Models."*

10 *A, B. BDC, PDC.* BDCs handle logon requests if they are found on the network. If no BDCs are installed, PDCs handle the requests. *See "Exploring NT Server Roles."*

Chapter 4

Trust Relationships

● ●

Exam Objectives

▶ Reviewing trust relationships

▶ Selecting domain models

▶ Logging on in the domain environment

▶ Understanding groups in the domain environment

● ●

*T*rusts allow for "One User, One Account," which means that each user has only one user account in the network. No matter where a user logs on, that user's account and permissions remain the same. This feature of trusts greatly reduces the load for administrators, because fewer accounts mean fewer permission problems. In this chapter, we introduce the key elements of trust relationships and we discuss how they are applied in various domain settings.

You need to understand the strengths and weaknesses of the four domain models, which we discuss in this chapter:

✔ The single domain

✔ The single master domain

✔ The multiple master domain

✔ The complete trust

After you choose a domain model, you place users into groups and assign access rights. Permissions are then assigned at logon based on a combination of user and group rights. As we explain in this chapter, the NetLogon service handles user logons and passthrough authentication when a user logs on in a remote domain.

Quick Assessment

Reviewing trust relationships

1 You set up trust relationships using the _____ tool in Windows NT.

2 (True/False). Trusts are transitive.

Selecting domain models

3 In a large corporation with a central MIS department, you should use the _____ domain model.

Logging on in the domain environment

4 Passthrough authentication allows you to log on to a computer using a _____ or _____ domain account.

5 Using "One User, One Account," a user needs _____ logon profile(s) on the network.

6 You should put user accounts in _____ groups.

Under-standing groups in the domain environment

7 You should assign resource permissions to _____ groups.

Answers

1 *User Manager for Domains.* See the section "Reviewing Trust Relationships: Trust Us!" for more information.

2 *False.* See "Reviewing Trust Relationships: Trust Us!"

3 *Multiple master.* See "Selecting Domain Models."

4 *Local; trusted.* See the section "Logging on in the Domain Environment: NetLogon" for more information.

5 *One.* See "Logging on in the Domain Environment: NetLogon."

6 *Global.* See "Understanding Groups in the Domain Environment."

7 *Local.* Review "Understanding Groups in the Domain Environment."

Reviewing Trust Relationships: Trust Us!

Domains are pretty simple. But because of such circumstances as physical location or number of users, you may need to have more than one domain. If you have lots of separate domains, you may defeat the purpose of creating domains. With multiple domains, you lose the ability to have one user account with which you can access all the resources you need.

Fortunately, NT Server has an answer to this problem. Trust relationships allow you to connect domains so that users from one domain may access resources in another domain. When one domain trusts another domain, the trusting domain can see all the users in the trusted domain.

Be sure to know the correct terminology for trust relationships:

- **Trusting domain:** The domain that can see the user accounts in the other domain. This domain is trusting the other domain and the users in the other domain. Also known as a resource domain.

- **Trusted domain:** The domain that allows itself to be trusted. It's also known as an account domain, because user accounts reside here.

Figure 4-1 shows a diagram of two domains in a trust relationship. The arrow points to the trusted domain.

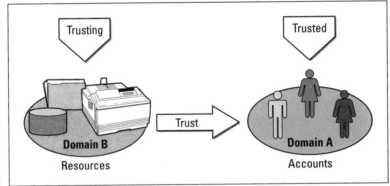

Figure 4-1:
A trust
relationship.

You will see diagrams similar to the one in Figure 4-1 on the exam. Remember that the arrow always points to the trusted domain. A simple way to remember the relationship is by thinking "Always point to those you trust."

In Figure 4-1, Domain B trusts Domain A. This relationship means that an administrator in Domain B can see all accounts in Domain A. In addition to seeing the accounts, the administrator can assign rights and permissions to those accounts. This relationship allows users in Domain A to access resources in Domain B.

Establishing a one-way trust

The term *one-way trust* describes a relationship in which one domain trusts another domain, but the second domain doesn't trust the first domain. Figure 4-1 shows an example of a one-way trust between domains.

To create a trust, you use the User Manager for Domains tool and you must be logged on as an Administrator. You find Trust Relationships listed in the Policies menu. Setting up a trust — even a one-way trust — is a two-step process. You must have access to an Administrator account in both domains to set it up, or work with someone in the other domain to handle that end. Turning off the computer doesn't affect the trust.

In Lab 4-1, we walk you through the steps for setting up a one-way trust between domains. The two domains we use in this lab are PRODUCTION1 and SALES1. SALES1 trusts PRODUCTION1. You can use any domain names you want.

Lab 4-1   Setting Up a One-Way Trust

1. **For the first part of the lab, log on to the trusted domain as an Administrator.**

2. **Start User Manager for Domains by choosing Start⇨Programs⇨ Administrative Tools⇨User Manager for Domains.**

3. **Choose Policies⇨Trust Relationships.**

4. **In the Add Trusting Domain dialog box, enter the name of your trusting domain.**

   For the example, enter **SALES1**.

5. **In the Initial Password and Confirm Password fields, enter a password for this trust relationship, and then click OK.**

   You need this password to set up the other side of the trust. Choose a password that you can easily remember.

   In the Trust Relationships dialog box, you see the specified domain listed in the Trusting Domains list, as shown in Figure 4-2.

6. **Click Close and then exit User Manager for Domains.**

   The next part of the lab takes you through the steps for setting up the other side of the trust. You should be logged on to the computer in the trusting domain as an Administrator.

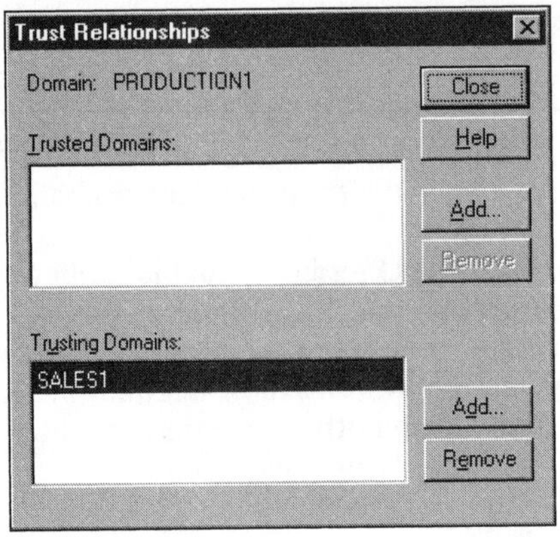

Figure 4-2: The Trust Relationships dialog box shows the new trusting domain.

7. **Choose Start➪Programs➪Administrative Tools➪User Manager for Domains.**
8. **In the User Manager window, choose Policies➪Trust Relationships.**
9. **In the Add Trusted Domain dialog box, enter the name of the trusted domain and the password for the trust relationship, and then click OK.**

   The example uses PRODUCTION1 as the trusted domain.

   After a short time, you should receive a message saying that the trust relationship has been established.

10. **Click OK.**

    Figure 4-3 shows the Trust Relationships window with the PRODUCTION1 domain listed in the Trusted Domains list.

11. **Click Close and exit User Manager for Domains.**

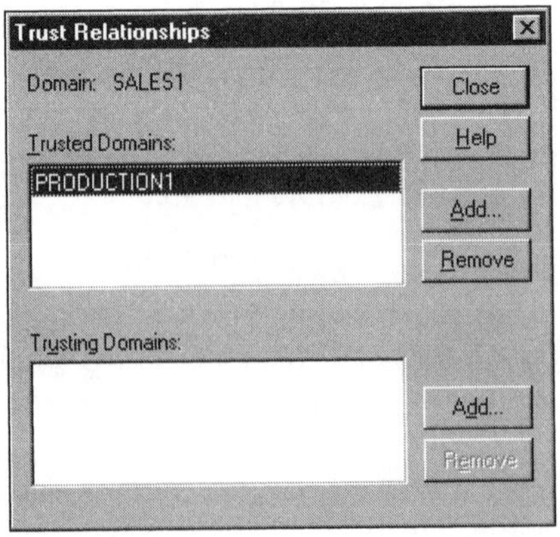

Figure 4-3: The Trust Relationships dialog box shows the new trusted domain.

You should usually set up the trusted domain first, and then do the trusting domain. If you reverse the order, the trust gets established, but you get a trust relationship message and the trust may take up to 15 minutes to become active.

Setting up a two-way trust

In some cases, you need more than a one-way trust. Two-way trusts allow two domains to see each other's user accounts and resources. Two-way trusts are really just separate one-way trusts going both directions.

To set up a two-way trust, simply follow the steps in Lab 4-1, and then repeat the process with the domains switched. In this way, you set up two separate one-way trusts.

Are trusts transitive?

Figure 4-4 shows three domains: Research, Production, and Marketing. Look at Figure 4-4 and decide whether the Marketing domain is trusted by the Research domain.

The Research domain trusts the Production domain. The Production domain trusts the Marketing domain. Does Research trust Marketing? The answer is no. Trusts are not transitive.

If you want Research to trust Marketing, you need to set up a separate trust as shown in Figure 4-5.

This important tip is worth repeating: Trusts are not transitive!

Removing trusts

To remove a trust, you simply go into User Manager for Domains and choose Policies⇨Trust Relationships. Highlight the trust you want to break and click Remove. Also, remember to remove the trust from the opposite domain or you may receive errors in your Event Viewer.

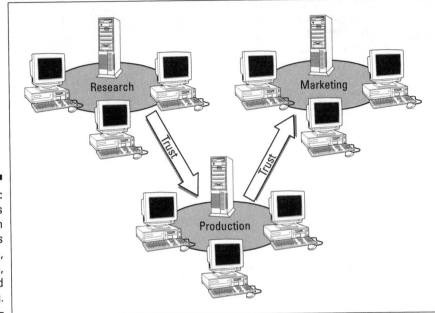

Figure 4-4:
Trusts
between
domains
Research,
Production,
and
Marketing.

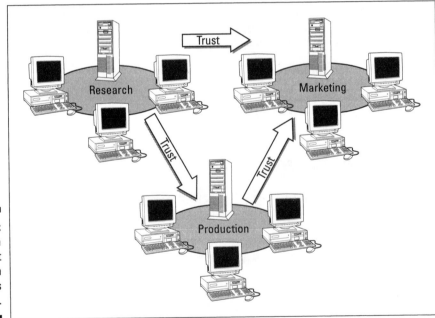

Figure 4-5:
Adding a
trust so that
Research
trusts
Marketing.

Selecting Domain Models

In addition to understanding how you create trust relationships, you must know how to make them work together nicely and get along. As we discuss in Chapter 3, you can choose from four main domain models:

- ✔ The single domain model
- ✔ The master domain model
- ✔ The multiple master domain model
- ✔ The complete trust domain model

Figure 4-6 depicts the four domain models. The model you choose depends on the number of users, servers, sites, and resources that you have, as well as their location and how they are managed. Choosing the best domain model for your network is a major step in making your life easier. Redoing the domain model on an existing network is a nightmare!

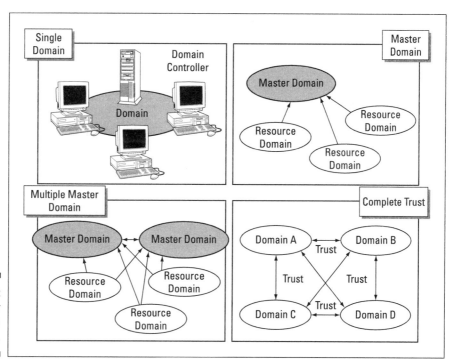

Figure 4-6:
The four domain models.

Table 4-1 lists the advantages and disadvantages of the four domain models. Review this table to help you determine when to use each model.

Table 4-1	Advantages and Disadvantages of the Four Domain Models	
Model	*Advantages*	*Disadvantages*
Single Domain	Centralized management of user accounts and resources	No groupings of users into departments
	No management of trust relationships necessary	No grouping of resources
Single Master	User accounts are centrally located	Local groups must be defined in each domain
	Resources grouped logically	Trusting domains rely on master domain for global groups
	Define global groups only once	
Multiple Master	Many users — scalability	Define groups multiple times
	Central MIS department	More trusts to manage
	Logical resource grouping	Not all accounts in one domain
Complete Trust	Scalable to any number of users	Very large number of trust relationships to manage
	Each department has full control over its user accounts and resources	Each department must trust that the other departments will not put inappropriate users into global groups
	Both resources and user accounts are grouped into departmental units	No centralized MIS department

The single domain model

The single domain model is very simple. It consists of one domain and no trust relationships. The one domain contains all computer accounts, user accounts, groups, rights, permissions, and resources.

You typically use the single domain model in small networks where the administrative staff is on-site in the same building or facility. If you have more than one location, you usually split up your domains. However, you may spread a single domain model over multiple sites if you have sufficient bandwidth between them.

The single domain model has some limits, but they can be very hard to reach. For example, the single domain model can accommodate as many as 40,000 users. If you have computer accounts and group accounts, that number can drop to around 25,000. With that many computers in a single domain, network browsing can become very slow.

Although domains can contain as many as 40,000 accounts, Microsoft only recommends up to 10,000. Keep this figure in mind on the exam. Also remember that accounts and users are different. Each user and Windows NT computer has an account. Therefore, when an NT computer is logged on, it is using two accounts.

The master domain model

Its potential size and its ease of administration make the single master domain model a very popular model. This model consists of one domain that contains user accounts — that is, the account domain — and other domains that trust it and contain resources — in other words, resource domains. Figure 4-7 shows trust relationships in a single master domain model.

The single master domain model is very good for medium-sized networks, especially with a centralized account management system. The resource domains can be administered locally so that each division can control its own servers and other resources.

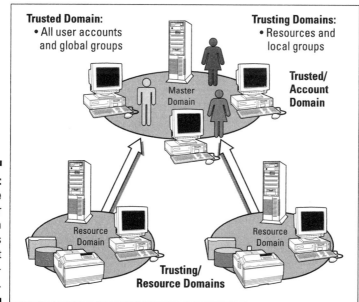

Figure 4-7: The single master domain model's trust relationships.

Keep in mind that because all accounts are stored in a single domain, the single master domain model can contain the same number of user accounts as a single domain model.

Trust-related questions on the Enterprise exam usually focus on the master domain model. Know how this model functions and remember the difference between resource domains and account domains.

The multiple master domain model

If the single domain model and the master domain model are too small for your needs, the multiple master domain model is your answer. The multiple master domain model has more than one account domain and any number of resource domains. Figure 4-8 shows trust relationships in a multiple master domain model.

Notice that each resource domain trusts each account domain, and each account domain trusts the other account domains. These trust relationships enable an administrator in any account domain to manage the entire network.

This model is very customizable to your needs. You can scale the multiple master domain to any network size by simply adding more account domains. Large organizations use this model because of this scalability. You can divide the multiple account domains by region, department, or any other way that you need.

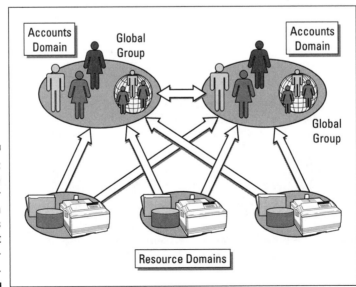

Figure 4-8:
The multiple master domain model's trust relationships.

To determine the number of trusts in a multiple master domain model, use the following formula:

$$M \times (M - 1) + (R \times M)$$

where *M* is the number of master domains, and *R* is the number of resource domains.

Using Figure 4-8 as an example, you can calculate the number of trusts as follows:

$$2 \times (2 - 1) + (3 \times 2) = 8$$

The complete trust domain model

The complete trust model is a decentralized model made up of multiple domains that trust all other domains. Each domain has a two-way trust with every other domain in the organization. Figure 4-9 shows an example of a complete trust domain model.

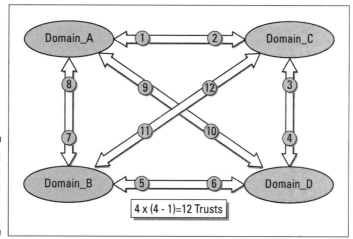

Figure 4-9:
The
complete
trust domain
model.

Figure 4-9 shows a complete trust model with four domains and 12 trust relationships. You can administer four separate domains with no problems, but with six or ten domains, the number of trusts quickly becomes an issue. You calculate the number of trusts needed in a complete trust domain model by using the following formula:

$$n \times (n - 1)$$

where *n* is the number of domains involved. A complete trust model with six domains requires 30 trusts. Ten domains require 90 trusts! You can see that the required number of trusts quickly becomes a major problem.

The only time that this model is recommended is within organizations that don't have any sort of centralized administration or control of resources. A lot of trust is placed in the administrators of each site to maintain the integrity of the network.

A full trust should only be used for the smallest of networks — those that will never be larger than three or four domains. This model is by far the worst way to set up a network from an administrative standpoint.

Logging On in the Domain Environment: NetLogon

The process for logging on to a domain account differs from that of a local computer account. In this section, we cover the logon process steps and give some detailed examples of which processes handle which operations.

The NetLogon service is in charge of handling user logons. It installs automatically when you install NT, and is set to start on boot. NetLogon is responsible for managing the following tasks:

- ✔ The logon process
- ✔ Passthrough authentication
- ✔ Synchronization of the backup domain controllers with the primary domain controller

The logon process

In this section, we cover the process that Windows NT goes through when you log on. The logon process uses the NetLogon service, the SAM (Security Accounts Manager) database, and SIDs (security identifiers) to complete the process.

Windows NT gives each object in the SAM a SID during creation. Every user, group, and computer account gets a SID. A SID is a unique number that no other object has. You may specify users or groups by their names, but Windows NT uses the SID. NT stores these SID numbers in the SAM database. The SAM is stored in the <systemroot>\system32\Config directory.

Here is the process for logging on to a Windows NT computer using a local account (not a domain account):

1. When the Windows NT computer boots, you get the familiar Ctrl+Alt+Delete screen. Press these keys and you see the logon screen. If this computer is part of a domain, you also see a drop-down box showing the domain list. To log on to a local account, change that drop-down box to show the name of the Windows NT computer you are on, not a domain name.

2. After you enter your user name and password, click OK. Windows NT passes your logon information, user name, password, and computer name to the NetLogon service. The NetLogon service then checks your information against the SAM database to see whether you're authorized to log on. If your account is validated, the NetLogon service retrieves your SID and any SIDs for groups of which you are a member. These SIDs are combined to form what is known as an *access token*.

3. After you have an access token, you are logged on to the computer.

The access token is used to authenticate you to other resources on the network. When you request access to a shared resource, the SIDs in your access token are compared against those in the ACL (Access Control List) of the shared resource. If your SID is listed and has the rights for the access you request, you are properly authenticated.

If you log on to an account that is not contained on the local workstation, you use passthrough authentication.

Passthrough authentication

Passthrough authentication allows a user to log on to a Windows NT computer from a domain account, or an account on a trusted domain. Passthrough authentication gives the Microsoft domain model the capability to have a single logon for all resource access — that is, "One User, One Account." This capability enables users to log on even if they don't have an account on the local machine, or in the local domain.

The passthrough authentication process happens whenever the local NetLogon service can't authenticate the account you are using to log on. Instead, the local NetLogon service forwards your logon request to the domain controller for your domain. The domain controller authenticates you and passes the SID information back to your computer's NetLogon service. The access token is then created for you. In the following sections, we describe some examples of passthrough authentication.

Using a local domain account

In this example, User 1 is logging on to a Windows NT computer in the North American domain. The user's account is in the North American domain:

1. User 1 enters the correct user name, password, and domain name in the logon box.

2. The local NetLogon service determines that this account isn't local and forwards the logon request and information to a domain controller in the North American domain.

3. The NetLogon service on the domain controller validates the account information and then passes back the user's SID and any SIDs for groups to which the user belongs.

4. The local NetLogon service creates the access token for the user and then finishes the logon process. Figure 4-10 shows this process.

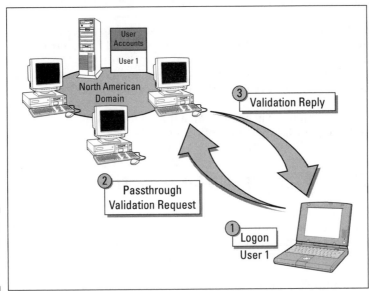

Figure 4-10:
Passthrough
authenti-
cation.

Using an account from a trusted domain

The process for logging on with an account from a trusted domain is slightly longer than the process we describe in the preceding section. When User 1 enters the logon information, it is forwarded to a local domain controller as in the preceding example. In this case, however, the domain controller forwards the information to a domain controller in the trusted domain for authentication. Figure 4-11 shows this scenario.

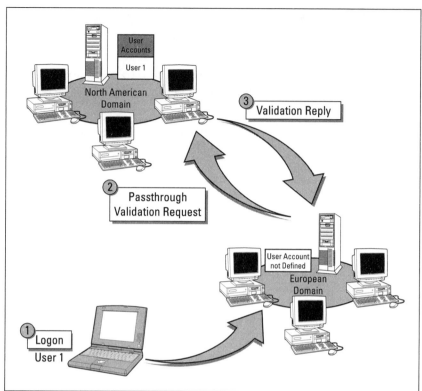

Figure 4-11:
Logging on
using a
trusted
domain
account.

1. User 1 in the European domain is logging on using an account in the North American domain.

2. The European domain controller forwards the request to a domain controller in the North American domain.

3. The controller in the North American domain sends back the appropriate SID information to the European controller.

4. The European controller sends the SID information to the local workstation, where an access token is created, and User 1 is allowed to log on.

Understanding Groups in the Domain Environment

Two types of groups exist in an NT domain environment: global and local. Only global groups can cross a trust to use resources in a different domain. You assign permissions to local groups for resources within a particular domain.

Managing access to resources across trusts: AGLP

The abbreviation AGLP sums up the keys to group strategy. Use AGLP to remember the following method for managing access to resources across trusts:

- ✔ Place User **A**ccounts in **G**lobal groups in the trusted domain.
- ✔ Place these Global groups inside **L**ocal groups across the trust in the trusting domain.
- ✔ Assign **P**ermissions for using various domain resources to the Local groups.

Figure 4-12 shows the AGLP strategy of placing users in global groups, which are in local groups, which have permissions assigned to them.

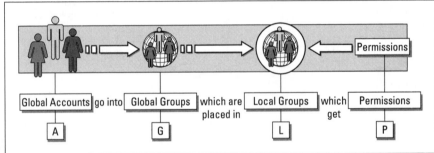

Figure 4-12:
The keys to group strategy: AGLP.

Coordinating these components correctly makes it possible for an administrator to manage even the largest enterprise network from a single computer. In the following sections, we look at each component of AGLP.

A — Accounts

In Windows NT Server, the network management process begins with global accounts. Global accounts (user accounts) can cross trusts, while local accounts can function only in the domain in which they were created.

Because global accounts can cross trusts, they can move from domain to domain to access resources in any domain on the network. Using local accounts leads to a multiple-account environment and all the problems involved in having to keep track of multiple accounts, duplicate logons, separate permissions, and several passwords.

So, in a multidomain environment, global accounts are essential to efficient account management. But after you create global accounts in one domain, the question remains, how do global accounts actually get across trusts from their home domain to a remote resource domain?

G — Global groups

Global accounts can move from domain to domain on their own. However, it is much more efficient to include them in groups (which can also move from domain to domain), because groups are easier to manage than separate individuals.

Therefore, to get accounts from one domain to the next, the administrator creates global accounts and puts them in a global group. This way, accounts can go from one domain to the next in a neat, organized manner. Remember, however, that global groups contain only user accounts from a single domain. You can't place user accounts from a trusted domain in a global group of a trusting domain.

But one problem with global groups is that they shouldn't be granted permissions to use resources. After the members of a global group get to a remote domain, how can they get permissions to use resources in that remote domain?

The exam can be very tricky when it comes to groups. Remember where permissions are assigned and accounts are located. If an exam question about groups doesn't include a diagram, draw it yourself.

L — Local groups

Local groups can be granted permissions to use resources in the domain in which they were created. When you assign a local group permission to use a resource, the permission to use that resource automatically extends to everyone in the local group.

Not only can you assign individual accounts to local groups, but you can also assign global groups to local groups. This is the first half of the real key to managing large networks. The second half of the key involves permissions.

To answer our previous question about how global groups receive permissions to use resources in a remote domain, the administrator assigns the global group to a local group that has access to the resource in the remote domain. After the global group becomes a member of the local group, all the members of the global group automatically have access to the resource. Because all members of the local group have access to the resource, all members of the global group automatically have access to the resource as well.

However, you still need to figure out what kind of access members of the global group have in the resource, and how to determine that access. If the resource is a database, for example, can they only read the information or can they change it or even delete it?

P — Permissions

You can assign permissions to local groups; the permissions automatically include all members of the local group. You can grant permissions to global groups, but this practice is not recommended by Microsoft. Therefore, the best way to grant permissions to users in global groups is to add the global groups to local groups.

After you add global groups to local groups, any permissions that the local group has are automatically given to any global group assigned to it, and those permissions extend to members of the global group.

If you make a global group part of the local group that has access to a resource, all the members of the global group automatically have the same access to the resource as the members of the local group. This is the second half of the key to managing large networks.

In a well-planned, efficient, enterprise network that uses the strategy of putting global groups into local groups and granting permissions to local groups, an administrator has to grant permissions to only one component — the local group. In this way, the administrator automatically grants those permissions to

✔ Members of the local group

✔ Members of the global group assigned to the local group

Considering the potential numbers of accounts in local and global groups, an administrator only has to grant permissions once — to a local group — in order to grant permissions to tens of thousands of users from every domain in the network.

Therefore, by combining four Windows NT components (global **A**ccounts, **G**lobal groups, **L**ocal groups, **P**ermissions — AGLP), an administrator can simplify account and resource management in even the largest network.

Remember AGLP! The exam emphasizes the proper use of groups, permissions, and trust direction. Know where to place users (global) and resources (local). Questions pertaining to groups are on the exam.

Domain controllers implement this strategy by default. For example:

✔ When a user account is created, it is automatically made a member of the global group Domain Users.

✔ Domain Users is a member of the local group Users in each trusting domain. Therefore, the new user is a member of each local group Users.

✔ When a computer running Windows NT Server or Workstation joins a domain, the global group Domain Users is automatically made a member of the new computer's Local Users group.

Built-in groups

Windows NT has several built-in groups, both local and global, which you should utilize for AGLP. If these built-in groups are not sufficient, you can easily add more groups. Although you don't need to know all these groups for the exam, you should know some of the basic group categories. The built-in local groups are

✔ **Administrators:** Members have full capabilities on the computer.

✔ **Operator Groups:** Members have limited administrative control. Server Operators and Print Operators are examples of these groups.

✔ **Other:** Members are given specific capabilities to perform tasks.

NT Server also has three built-in global groups:

✔ **Domain Admins:** Belongs to the local Administrators group.

✔ **Domain Users:** Belongs to the local Users group.

✔ **Domain Guests:** Belongs to the local Guests groups (usually disabled for security purposes).

Prep Test

1 If a local user can't see a resource in a remote domain, which group should the user most likely need to be added to?

A ○ Domain Admins

B ○ Local Users

C ○ Domain Users

D ○ Guest

2 Which of the four domain models requires the most administrative effort in a large setting?

A ○ Single

B ○ Master

C ○ Multiple master

D ○ Complete trust

3 (True/False). If Domain D trusts Domain E, and E trusts F, then Domain D trusts F.

A ○ True

B ○ False

4 What are the major responsibilities of the NetLogon service? (Choose all that apply.)

A ❑ Logon validation

B ❑ Synchronization

C ❑ Maintaining trusts

D ❑ Passthrough authentication

5 John is trying to set up a two-way trust. He goes into User Manager for Domains and only sees a way to make a one-way trust. No option exists for two-way trusts. What does he do?

A ○ Exit User Manager and use Server Manager to set up the two-way trust.

B ○ Set up a one-way trust. The system will automatically create a two-way trust.

C ○ Set up two one-way trusts.

D ○ It can't be done between these domains.

6 (True/False). Only one SID is required for each user on a network.

A ○ True

B ○ False

7 What are the extra steps needed when you log on using an account from a trusted domain instead of an account from the local domain? (Choose all that apply.)

A ❑ The local domain controller authenticates the logon.
B ❑ The local domain controller forwards the logon.
C ❑ The trusted domain controller authenticates the logon.
D ❑ The trusted domain controller returns the appropriate SID information.

8 (True/False). Passthrough authentication makes it possible for users to log on to the network from computers or domains in which they have no account.

A ○ True
B ○ False

Answers

1 *C. Domain Users.* This group will be placed in the remote Local group with the proper permissions. *See "Understanding Groups in the Domain Environment."*

2 *D. Complete trust.* The complete trust model requires the most administrative work due to the large number of trusts to be maintained, and because no centralized account domain exists. *See "Selecting Domain Models."*

3 *B. False.* Trusts are not transitive. *See the section "Reviewing Trust Relationships: Trust Us!" for more information.*

4 *A, B, and D. Logon validation, synchronization, and passthrough authentication. See "Logging on in the Domain Environment: NetLogon."*

5 *C. Set up two one-way trusts.* A two-way trust is nothing more than two one-way trusts. He needs to set up a one-way trust going from each domain to the other domain. *See "Reviewing Trust Relationships: Trust Us!"*

6 *B. False.* Each domain requires a unique SID because all user authentication is based on the account's SID. *Review "Logging on in the Domain Environment: NetLogon."*

7 *B, C, D.* When you log on to an account from a trusted domain, your local domain controllers must forward the request to controllers in the trusted domain. The trusted domain's controllers then send back the appropriate SID information. *Review "Logging on in the Domain Environment: NetLogon."*

8 *A. True.* Users can log on to the network from computers or domains in which they have no account. *See "Logging on in the Domain Environment: NetLogon."*

Part III
Installation and Configuration

The 5th Wave   By Rich Tennant

DANG! I TOLD 'EM A 486 MILKING MACHINE, WAS ONE UPGRADE TOO MANY.

In this part . . .

Before you can implement an effective NT enterprise solution, you need to know some of the basics. You must be able to set up NT, and your hardware must be capable of running your operating system efficiently. Then you have partitioning schemes and file systems for your hard drives, licensing issues, and network protocol considerations.

After you design your hardware and network environments and install NT, you must manage your Enterprise environment. You need to worry about domain management, Security Accounts Manager (SAM) database replication between domain controllers, your browser services, printing. . . . The list goes on and on. In this part of the book, we cover all the aforementioned topics, and we even include a chapter on the intricacies of TCP/IP, and another on Windows Internet Name Service (WINS) and Domain Name Service (DNS).

Chapter 5

Installation, Hesitation, and Perspiration

. . . .

Exam Objectives

▶ Installing Windows NT Server

▶ Installing Windows NT Server to perform various server roles

▶ Configuring protocols

▶ Choosing between the two types of partitions — system or boot

. . . .

*I*nstallation is one of the more straightforward topics that you will be asked about on the Enterprise exam. You can successfully answer any exam questions on installation if you do two things:

> ✔ Read this chapter and memorize the lists of options and the distinctions between the options.
>
> ✔ Practice installing NT Server at least a dozen times.

In this chapter, we highlight the information you need for planning the installation, and we discuss the installation options you must understand. To ensure that you understand all the installation-related issues that may come up on your Enterprise exam, we also cover the following topics:

> ✔ Determining the right file system — FAT or NTFS
>
> ✔ Understanding the minimum hardware requirements
>
> ✔ Choosing between per-server and per-seat licensing modes
>
> ✔ Running the WINNT.EXE setup program
>
> ✔ Recognizing the differences between CD-ROM and network installations
>
> ✔ Understanding the four or five phases of setup
>
> ✔ Anticipating problems that require troubleshooting

Quick Assessment

Installing
Windows NT
Server

1 The minimum disk space required for installing NT Server on an Intel system is _____ MB.

2 If you don't know your system's hardware configuration, you can run the _____ utility.

3 Always check the current version of the _____ before installing NT Server with your hardware.

4 If you need to install Windows NT from across a network or by using an unsupported CD-ROM, you can use _____.

5 Removing Windows NT from a(n) _____ drive requires deleting the partition and reinstalling all data.

Installing
Windows NT
Server to
perform
various
server roles

6 Each domain has only one _____, which maintains the security information for the entire domain.

7 You may need the _____ protocol if you are connecting to a Novell NetWare server.

Configuring
protocols

8 When installing _____, you are asked whether you want to use Dynamic Host Configuration Protocol (DHCP).

Choosing
between the
two types of
partitions

9 To support really large drives, you should choose the _____ file system as opposed to the _____ file system.

Answers

1 *125.* Review "Meeting NT's hardware requirements" — in particular, Table 5-1.

2 *NT Hardware Qualifier (NTHQ) tool.* Review "Meeting NT's hardware requirements."

3 *Hardware Compatibility List (HCL).* Review "Meeting NT's hardware requirements."

4 *WINNT.EXE.* Review "Installing NT Server."

5 *NTFS.* Review "Uninstalling Windows NT."

6 *Primary domain controller.* Review "Domain planning."

7 *NWLink IPX/SPX.* Review "Choosing your protocols."

8 *TCP/IP.* Review "Choosing your protocols."

9 *NTFS; FAT.* Review "Choosing a file system: Vanna, I'd like a vowel."

Planning for NT Server

The Windows NT 4.0 Server in the Enterprise exam questions reinforce the notion that the key to a successful Windows NT installation is planning.

While studying, keep in mind the age-old tailor's adage, "Measure twice; cut once." In the real world, if you plan well, you only need to install Windows NT once. The following sections discuss aspects of installation that you should think about before you actually install NT Server — for example, hardware requirements, types of servers, and domain models. We focus on the issues you must consider to plan a successful installation.

For the Enterprise exam, you need to remember a few key points from this chapter:

- **The requirements for installing Windows NT Server.** These requirements are important in determining whether you can use Windows NT on a computer. Exams have been known to include questions about hardware requirements.

- **The different licensing modes.** Be familiar with how the licensing is calculated. You may encounter a question that uses both types of licensing at once.

- **The choice of file system type.** Pay attention to the requirements specified in the exam questions concerning disk size, security requirements, and attributes.

- **Procedures for troubleshooting installation problems.** Microsoft is well known for putting troubleshooting questions in its exams. Keep studying!

Meeting NT's hardware requirements

Before you begin your Windows NT installation, you must ensure that your computer meets the minimum system requirements. You can be certain that the exam will include questions about at least one of the following topics:

- The minimum hardware requirements for installing NT Server
- The Hardware Compatibility List (HCL)
- The NT Hardware Qualifier (NTHQ) utility

Although Windows NT supports either Intel-compatible processors or RISC processors, expect only one or two RISC questions at most. Your time is best spent understanding the requirements of Intel-based systems. Table 5-1 shows the requirements for Intel systems as set by Microsoft. Table 5-2 shows the Digital Alpha requirements.

Table 5-1	Minimum Windows NT System Requirements for Intel Computers	
---	---	
Hardware Component	*Server Requirements*
Processor	80486 33 MHz
RAM	16MB
Hard disk space	125MB
Display	VGA
Floppy disk	3.5-inch floppy
CD-ROM drive	Supported CD-ROM
Network adapter	Optional
Mouse	Supported mouse

The version of Windows NT Server on the CD-ROM includes support for up to two processors. You can get support for as many as 32 processors for Windows NT Server from the manufacturer of your computer system.

Table 5-2	Minimum Windows NT System Requirements for RISC Computers	
---	---	
Hardware Component	*Server Requirements*
Processor	Compatible RISC processor
RAM	16MB
Hard disk space	160MB
Display	VGA
Floppy disk	3.5-inch floppy
CD-ROM drive	Supported CD-ROM
Network adapter	Optional
Mouse	Supported mouse

Although the Windows NT CD-ROM includes software for Intel, Digital Alpha, MIPS, and PowerPC, you should know that support for MIPS and PowerPC has been discontinued. You won't be asked about these two platforms.

The requirements in Table 5-1 are the minimum requirements, but in the real world, not too many servers run on the minimum. For purposes of the exam, however, you need to commit the minimum requirements to memory.

In addition to knowing the minimum requirements, you need to know whether Windows NT supports your particular hardware. The one and only sure way to check this information is to use the Hardware Compatibility List (HCL). This list constantly changes, so make sure you always work from the current version. You can obtain the latest copy of this list from www.microsoft.com/hwtest.

You may also be asked how to determine what hardware is in your computer. The answer is to run the NT Hardware Qualifier (NTHQ), which you can find in the SUPPORT\HQTOOL directory on your Windows NT CD-ROM. To use this tool, you must make a bootable floppy disk by using the MAKEDISK.BAT command.

After you're sure that you have the proper hardware for installation, you can decide on the software configuration.

Partitioning the hard disk

The first installation decision you need to make is how to set up your hard drive partitions. You must divide hard disks into partitions before you can use them. Carefully review Tables 5-1 and 5-2 to ensure that the partition you plan to use doesn't exceed the minimum available disk space.

You need to be aware of two types of partitions:

- ✔ **System partition.** The system partition is on the active primary partition of the first hard disk in the computer. Windows NT loads its boot files from this partition. These boot files include NTLDR, NTDETECT.COM, BOOT.INI, and sometimes BOOTSECT.DOS (for dual-boot systems), and NTBOOTDD.SYS. These files may vary depending on the hardware configuration of the computer system.

  On the exam, make sure that you know what NTBOOTDD.SYS does for Windows NT Server. You must have this file installed so that Windows NT can recognize your SCSI drive.

- ✔ **Boot partition.** The boot partition can be either a primary partition or an extended partition. The boot partition contains the Windows NT system files. These files are stored in the WINNT directory by default.

The names of these two partitions confuse many people. You would think that Windows NT would boot from the boot partition, not the system partition, but this is not the case. Keep this point in mind when installing Windows NT and taking any Windows NT exams!

Often, the system partition and the boot partition are on the same drive. If you install the Windows NT system files onto the same partition that your computer boots from, they will coexist fine.

Choosing a file system: Vanna, I'd like a vowel

After you choose an installation partition, you must decide on the file system to use. Windows NT supports two different file systems:

- ✔ **FAT.** The file allocation table (FAT) file system is the one you are probably already familiar with. MS-DOS, OS/2, Windows 3.*x*, Windows 95, and Windows NT support the FAT file system. If you need to dual boot between Windows NT and MS-DOS or Windows (and have Windows NT on the same drive as the other operating system), you need to use the FAT file system.

- ✔ **NTFS.** The Windows NT file system (NTFS) is the native file system for Windows NT. It is not supported by any other major operating system. NTFS supports much larger drives than FAT, and also supports extended attributes and permissions.

Windows NT does not support the new FAT32 file system. It's also important to know that Windows NT 4.0 Server does not support the high performance file system (HPFS). It was supported in Windows NT 3.51, but not in 4.0. Be careful not to be tricked on an exam question.

Table 5-3 compares the FAT and NTFS file systems.

Table 5-3	Comparing FAT and NTFS	
Characteristic	*FAT*	*NTFS*
Compatibility	MS-DOS, Windows 3.*x*, 95, and NT	Windows NT
Security	None	Full file- and directory-level permissions tied to Windows NT logon security
Maximum file size	4 gigabytes	64 gigabytes
Maximum partition size	4 gigabytes	16 exabytes
File compression	None	File- and directory-level compression
Filenames	8.3 filenames (Can store 255 character filenames with certain operating systems)	255 characters

If you are unsure of which file system you want to use, the best choice is FAT. Windows NT supports a utility called CONVERT.EXE that lets you convert a FAT partition to NTFS. Windows NT does not have a conversion utility to convert from NTFS to FAT. Your only option is to back up the data from the drive, reformat the drive to FAT (and possibly reinstall Windows NT if it is on the drive to be converted), and then restore all the data to the reformatted drive.

Also be aware that Windows NT no longer supports the high performance file system (HPFS). Previous versions of Windows NT supported this file system, but this support was removed in Version 4.0. If you have a computer that you want to install NT on with HPFS, you must back up all the data, install Windows NT, and restore the data.

Choosing a licensing mode

Before you can use Windows NT, you must have a license for it. Windows NT Server supports two different types of licenses:

- ✓ **Per server.** In the per-server licensing mode, you must purchase one client access license (CAL) for each connection to the server. For example, if you have 250 users who need to access a server, but only 125 will ever be on at one time, you only need to purchase 125 client access licenses.

- ✓ **Per seat.** Per-seat licensing is more straightforward. With per-seat licensing, you must purchase a license for any user who connects to the server. So if you have 250 users, you must buy 250 per-seat licenses because 250 different connections will be made.

Make a good decision on which type of licensing you use, because after you choose the per-seat type, you can't change back!

If a server reaches its maximum number of licensed connections when using per-server licensing, it refuses any new connections and you receive an error in the event log. You must either close some connections or add more licenses to the server using License Manager.

You may be asking yourself why anyone would choose the per-seat licensing option. It all depends on how your network is set up. If you have multiple servers, the per-seat option may be advantageous.

For example, if you have a network with 250 users and three servers that each user must connect to, you only have to buy 250 per-seat licenses. You need only one per-seat client license for each user, but each user can connect to all three servers. On the other hand, if you decide to use per-server licenses, you must purchase 250 licenses for each server, for a total of 750.

Naming your workstation

During the installation of Windows NT, you need to enter the computer name you want to use. This name is often referred to as the NetBIOS name. The name should have some meaning as to its purpose or follow a set naming standard. You can change this name later if necessary.

Be sure that the computer name you give your server is unique.

Domain planning

Before you install Windows NT Server, you need a domain plan. Depending on how you install Windows NT Server, you may not be able to change the domain of which it is a member without completely reinstalling the system. Remember the following points:

- ✔ You can't move domain controllers between domains.
- ✔ You can move stand-alone and member servers between domains.
- ✔ You can change domain names and server names.

You can install Windows NT Server as one of four different types of servers. Planning is very important here because you may not be able to change the server type after you install Windows NT Server. (You can find more information on domain management in Chapter 6.) The four server types are

- ✔ **Primary domain controller (PDC).** The PDC maintains the security database for the entire domain. Only one PDC exists in any domain. Be aware that the PDC may need extra processor power and memory due to the overhead of maintaining the security database.

- ✔ **Backup domain controller (BDC).** The BDC is responsible for handling user logon requests. The BDCs maintain copies of the security database. They may also require extra processing power and memory to handle the user logon requests.

- ✔ **Member server.** The member server is part of a domain, but doesn't handle any of the security overhead. You can grant permissions allowing members of the domain to access resources on a member server. Most member servers handle your file/print and application duties instead of processing logons from the users.

- ✔ **Stand-alone server.** The stand-alone server is part of a workgroup, not a domain. Consequently, you can't grant permissions to resources on the server to members of a domain. All accounts you plan to use on this server must be created locally on the server.

A member server can leave a domain and become a stand-alone server. A stand-alone server can also join a domain to become a member server. This capability is useful if you need to move a server to another domain.

Choosing your protocols

Even though Windows NT supports many different protocols, you only need to study a few of them to prepare for the exam:

- ✔ **TCP/IP.** Transmission Control Protocol/Internet Protocol (TCP/IP) is quickly becoming the most popular protocol in the world due to the Internet. Almost all network operating systems today support TCP/IP, including Windows NT, Windows 95, UNIX, MS-DOS, Macintosh, and OS/2. It is very popular on routed networks such as the ever-popular Internet.

  When installing TCP/IP, you are asked whether you want to use Dynamic Host Configuration Protocol (DHCP). DHCP allows administrators to automatically configure computers that support TCP/IP. Without DHCP, you must configure each device manually, which allows room for mistakes. A DHCP server must be installed and must be running before anybody selects "Yes" on an installation.

- ✔ **NWLink IPX/SPX.** NWLink is the IPX/SPX-compatible protocol that comes with Windows NT. You may need this protocol if you are connecting to a Novell NetWare server. A significant advantage to NWLink is its ease of configuration. It is also very fast on small, routed networks.

  The only major configuration setting you may need to make with IPX/SPX is the frame type to use. If you are not sure which frame type to use, you can select the Auto Detect option, although it is advisable to manually set the frame type your network uses. Auto Detect may choose an incorrect frame type should one server be misconfigured on your network.

- ✔ **NetBEUI.** NetBEUI is a small, very fast protocol. The major disadvantage is that you can't use it on a routed network. Due to the overhead required, it is advisable not to use this protocol except on very small networks.

- ✔ **DLC.** Data Link Control is a more primitive protocol than TCP/IP, NWLink, or NetBEUI, and cannot support the Server and Workstation services on its own. The primary use for DLC is to allow connectivity to Hewlett-Packard printers and support for IBM's SNA communications. The DLC protocol does not need to be installed on the network clients, only on the server. Unlike most protocols, DLC is not mainly used for communication between computers. As with most other protocols

> under Windows NT, you have the choice of configuring the protocol during installation of your server or after the installation is complete. You can always install the DLC protocol from the Network icon in the Control Panel.
>
> ✔ **AppleTalk.** Before you install the AppleTalk protocol on your NT Server, you need to install Services for Macintosh. Services for Macintosh allows Macintosh computers to access file and printer resources on an NT Server. You have the option of installing Services for Macintosh during the installation of your Windows NT Server, but you can always add this service through the Network icon in the Control Panel.

As a rule, the configuration of your network determines which protocols to use. Again, to prepare for the exam, make sure you understand the differences between these protocols, and know the situations for which each is best suited.

Installing NT Server

After you make the major decisions regarding your Windows NT configuration, you can begin the installation. In this section, we walk you through the process.

Choosing an install method: Easy as one, two, three . . .

You can install Windows NT in a few different ways. The method you use depends on whether you plan to install from a CD-ROM or across a network, and from which operating system. You can start the setup process by using WINNT.EXE, WINNT32.EXE, or the disks that ship with Windows NT.

Installing on Intel x86 computers

The first step of installation depends on the hardware platform that you use. With an Intel x86 compatible computer, you normally use the Windows NT CD-ROM and the three disks included with Windows NT. Your computer must boot from the setup disk and load drivers from the other two disks. You don't necessarily have to use the three Windows NT setup disks if you decide to use the /B switch for installation (check out Table 5-4, later in this chapter, for more information about this switch). Also located on the CD-ROM, you find numerous utilities and add-ons for Windows NT Server.

If Windows NT does not support your CD-ROM drive, you can use WINNT.EXE to start the installation. If your CD-ROM supports the "El Torrito" bootable CD-ROMs, you can boot directly from the CD.

Installing on RISC computers

If you have a RISC computer such as a Digital Alpha or PowerPC, you do not use the three floppy disks. Instead, you just use the CD-ROM. Depending on the type of RISC system you have, starting the installation may be very simple. Some Digital Alpha computers have a simple menu option when you boot them that says "Install Windows NT from CD-ROM." You choose that option and off it goes.

The important thing to remember is that after you begin setup, the rest of the procedure is exactly the same across all supported platforms.

Using WINNT.EXE

If you need to install Windows NT from across a network or by using an unsupported CD-ROM, you can use WINNT.EXE. You can execute WINNT.EXE from MS-DOS or Windows 95, but not from Windows NT.

WINNT.EXE supports many different parameters. WINNT.EXE has the following syntax:

```
WINNT [/S[:]sourcepath] [/T[:]tempdrive] [/I[:]inffile]
      [/O[X]] [/X | [/F] [/C]] [/B] [/U[:scriptfile]]
      [/R[X]:directory] [/E:command]
```

Don't let the number of parameters scare you! Table 5-4 lists the meaning of each parameter.

Table 5-4	WINNT.EXE Parameters
Parameter	**Specifies**
/S[:]sourcepath	The source location of Windows NT files. Must be a full path of the form x:\[path] or \\server\share[\path]. The default is the current directory.
/T[:]tempdrive	A drive to contain temporary setup files. If not specified, setup attempts to locate a drive for you.
/I[:]inffile	The filename (no path) of the setup information file. The default is Dosnet.inf.
/OX	You want to create boot floppies for CD-ROM installation.
/X	You do not want to create the setup boot floppies.
/F	You do not want setup to verify files as they are copied to the setup boot floppies.
/C	You want to skip free-space check on the setup boot floppies you provide.

Parameter	Specifies
/B	Floppyless operation (requires /S).
/U[:*scriptfile*]	Unattended operation and an optional script file (requires /S).
/R:*directory*	Optional directory to be installed.
/RX:*directory*	Optional directory to be copied.
/E:*command*	A command to be executed at the end of GUI setup process.

For the exam, you should pay particular attention to three Windows NT setup switches: /B for diskless installation, /OX to create the three Windows NT setup disks, and /U for unattended setup. These switches are more than likely to appear on the exam.

If you want to install Windows NT from across a network, you must first set up an installation point. You can do this in two ways:

✔ Use the XCOPY command to copy the \I386, \MIPS, or \ALPHA directories from the CD-ROM to a shared directory on a server. Be sure to use the /S parameter for XCOPY so that all subdirectories are also copied.

✔ You can share out the \I386, \MIPS, or \ALPHA directories directly from the Windows NT CD-ROM. Although this method is slower than sharing the data off a hard disk, it is simpler to set up.

After sharing the directories, you can just connect to them from the computer on which you want to install Windows NT. Use the /S parameter for WINNT.EXE or WINNT32.EXE to point to the shared files.

Using WINNT32.EXE

WINNT32.EXE is the Windows NT executable equivalent of WINNT.EXE. WINNT32.EXE serves the same purpose as WINNT.EXE, but does not run under MS-DOS or Windows 95 — it is for Windows NT only. It supports all the same parameters as WINNT.EXE except for /F and /C.

Going through the many phases of setup

The Windows NT setup process goes through several phases. Each phase handles a different set of tasks or configuration settings. The number of phases depends on whether you use the three floppies, WINNT.EXE, or WINNT32.EXE. In the following sections, we review each phase of installation.

Make sure that your computer meets the minimum requirements and has supported hardware. If you are unsure about your hardware, check the Windows NT Hardware Compatibility List.

If your CD-ROM is not compatible with Windows NT, you need to use WINNT.EXE to start your installation. We discuss the parameters for this command in the section "Using WINNT.EXE." For the following labs, use the three boot disks that come with Windows NT.

If you lose your disks that come with Windows NT, you can remake them with the WINNT.EXE /OX command or the WINNT32.EXE /OX command.

Pre-copying files

The pre-copying phase only happens if you use WINNT.EXE or WINNT32.EXE. During the pre-copy phase, the Windows NT setup process performs the following tasks:

- ✓ **Creates three setup floppy disks.** These disks are not the same disks that you receive with Windows NT. They are changed to point to the copy of Windows NT that was pre-copied to your local hard drive. If you use the /B or /U switches, setup doesn't create these disks.

- ✓ **Creates a folder named WIN_NT.~1S.** This temporary folder is deleted after Windows NT installs. After this folder is created, setup copies the Windows NT source files from the location you specified into the temporary folder.

- ✓ **Prompts you to reboot.** If you had setup create the three floppy disks, you need to insert the first disk before rebooting.

Phase 0

The first real setup phase begins after you reboot your computer. If you use WINNT.EXE /B, setup automatically launches and you don't need to worry about swapping floppy disks. During Phase 0, the setup process copies from the CD-ROM a limited version of Windows NT, which allows the setup process to use the multithreading capability of Windows NT. Setup performs the following tasks during Phase 0:

- ✓ Giving you the option of manually specifying mass storage devices or having setup try to automatically detect them. Even if you have it try to detect them, you have the option of specifying any others not detected.

- ✓ Displaying the license agreement for Windows NT. You must agree to continue.

- ✓ Asking whether you want to do an upgrade or install a new copy of Windows NT into another directory, if setup detects that you already have a copy of Windows NT installed.

- ✓ Prompting you to enter the destination directory for installing NT, if you choose to do a new installation.

- ✓ Displaying a list of the hardware on your system. You can either agree to this list or make any necessary changes.

You may notice that the video adapter detected is VGA. This is normal, so don't change it. You get an option later in the setup to specify exactly which video adapter you have. The VGA selection is the fallback setting that Windows NT uses later.

✔ Asking you which partition you want Windows NT to be installed on.

✔ Prompting you to choose which type of file system to use on that partition. If the partition is already formatted as FAT, you have the option to convert it to NTFS or leave it as is.

✔ Checking your hard disk for any corruption. You have the option of doing an exhaustive secondary check if you want. The secondary check is a good idea in that it does a more thorough scan, which you want on an important server.

Phase 1

Phase 1 begins the graphical part of the installation. This phase gathers more information about your computer and how you want Windows NT installed. You enter the following configuration settings during this phase:

✔ Your name and the name of your organization.

✔ Your 10-digit CD key. This key is located on the back of your CD-ROM case.

✔ The type of licensing you want. Choose either per server or per seat. If you choose per server, you must enter the number of licenses that you currently own.

✔ The NetBIOS computer name that you decided on.

✔ The type of server you want this system to be: primary domain controller, backup domain controller, member server, or stand-alone server. If you choose to join a domain, you may need to enter an administrator account name and password if a computer account has not been created for you.

✔ The password for the administrator account that will be created on this system. You also need to confirm this password.

✔ Whether you want to make an emergency repair disk.

✔ The optional components that you want to install.

Phase 2

Phase 2 covers the network installation section of the setup process. You need to enter the following information during this phase:

✔ The type of networking to install. You can choose LAN or dialed in (Remote Access). If you choose not to install networking, Phase 2 ends.

✔ Whether you want to install Internet Information Server.

> ✔ The type of network card to install. You may also be prompted for the configuration settings for the card, such as IRQ, I/O, and transceiver type.
>
> ✔ Which network protocols you want to install and their configurations.
>
> ✔ Any additional network services you want to install.
>
> ✔ The workgroup or domain to join.

Phase 3

Phase 3 is the final phase of setup. You are prompted for the following information:

> ✔ Time zone, date, and time
>
> ✔ Exchange Inbox configuration (if you selected to install Exchange)
>
> ✔ Video driver configuration

After you click Finish at the end of Phase 2, the Time Zone dialog box appears, and you're ready to begin Phase 3. Lab 5-4 details the steps for completing Phase 3.

Welcome to Windows NT Server!

Troubleshooting the Windows NT Installation Process

You may hit a snag when installing Windows NT. In this section, we list the most common problems and solutions to your installation blues. Check out Table 5-5 for help.

Table 5-5	Common Installation Problems and Solutions
Problem	*Possible Solution*
Media errors	This problem is usually caused by a bad CD-ROM. Try the CD in another CD-ROM drive. If the CD works, do an over-the-network install. For a replacement CD, contact Microsoft.
Non-supported adapter	Replace the adapter with a supported card. Use the WINNT.EXE command from MS-DOS. Do an over-the-network installation.

Problem	Possible Solution
	Check with your adapter manufacturer. Some manufacturers offer drivers that you can put on the Windows NT setup disks.
Not enough disk space	A very common problem. The simple answer to this problem is to delete some unneeded applications.
Dependency service doesn't start	This problem usually involves an incorrect network card setting. Because the driver can't talk to the network card, the other network services can't talk to the driver. Check the Event Log and see which service was the first one to fail and work from there. Make sure that your corresponding service is correctly configured.
Can't find the domain controller	This error sometimes has nothing to do with the error you receive. First, verify that you do have a working network connection and the domain controller is available.
	Second, double-check your logon name and the password you're using. You also get this error if you enter the wrong administrator account or password (we told you it sometimes didn't have to do with the error you received). Make sure that your networking is working and that you have sufficient privileges to connect to the domain controller.

Uninstalling Windows NT

You may never need to uninstall NT, but you should cover this procedure so that you'll be prepared if it appears on the exam. Remember, Windows doesn't have an uninstall function. In the following sections, we describe the steps for uninstalling Windows NT, depending on the file system you're using.

Removing Windows NT from a FAT file system

The FAT file system is the easiest one to remove Windows NT from. You most often have this situation when you have a dual-boot system and want to make it boot Windows 95 only. To remove Windows NT, use the following steps:

1. Boot the computer with an MS-DOS or Windows 95 disk that contains the SYS.COM command.

2. From the boot disk, type SYS C: to make the C: drive boot under the MS-DOS or Windows 95 operating system.

3. Remove the boot disk from drive A:, and then reboot the computer off the hard disk.

4. You can now remove the Windows NT files from the computer. You can safely remove the following files:

   - C:\PAGEFILE.SYS

   - C:\BOOT.INI

   - C:\NT*.*

   - C:\BOOTSECT.DOS

   - All files and directories under the WINNT directory

   - All files and directories under the \Program Files\Windows NT directory

Removing Windows NT from an NTFS drive

The bad news is that removing Windows NT from an NTFS drive requires deleting the partition and reinstalling all data. To remove the NTFS partition, use the following steps:

1. Start the computer from the Windows NT setup disk.

2. When you get to the partition options, select the partition with Windows NT installed, and press D to delete it.

3. Press F3 to exit setup.

Prep Test

1 You have a computer that uses a proprietary type of CD-ROM. The computer currently has MS-DOS on it, but you want to install Windows NT. How can you do this using your current CD-ROM?

A ○ Use WINMSD.EXE.

B ○ Use WINNT.EXE.

C ○ Use NTBOOTDD.SYS.

D ○ Use REGEDIT.EXE.

2 (True/False). During setup, you receive a critical error and the setup process exits. You notice a new directory on your hard drive called WIN_NT.~1S. You can delete this directory.

3 You are planning to install five different Windows NT Servers in your network. To make the process easier, you want to install them across the network without using any boot disks. Which switch do you use?

A ○ WINNT.EXE /B

B ○ WINNT.EXE /OX

C ○ WINNT.EXE /U

D ○ WINNT.EXE /T

4 What are the requirement differences between installing Windows NT Server on an Intel computer and on a RISC computer?

A ○ More memory

B ○ Faster processor

C ○ More hard disk space

D ○ SCSI CD-ROM

5 Which service helps you with the configuration of many TCP/IP computers by configuring them automatically?

A ○ LMHOSTS

B ○ Workstation

C ○ Server

D ○ DHCP

6 What is the best licensing mode for a network with 300 users who all need to connect to three different Windows NT Servers?

A ○ Per user

B ○ Per seat

C ○ Per workstation

D ○ Site license

7 You are installing a new server that will store personal documents. You want the best security possible for this information. Which file system should you install?

A ○ HPFS

B ○ FAT-32

C ○ FAT-16

D ○ NTFS

8 You are installing Windows NT Server on a computer with four CPUs. When Windows NT Server boots, it shows that only two CPUs were detected. What do you need to do to fix this problem?

A ○ Get an OEM Version of Windows NT Server.

B ○ Install Service Pack 3.

C ○ Run SMP utility.

D ○ Run Windows NT Diagnostics.

Answers

1 *B. WINNT.EXE.* You can either run WINNT.EXE and let it copy the files to your hard drive and create the three setup disks, or use the /B option to skip creation of the three disks. *Review "Installing NT Server" — in particular, see the subsection titled "Using WINNT.EXE."*

2 *True.* The directory you found is a temporary directory created by Windows NT setup. Because setup failed and you need to start over anyway, you can safely delete this directory. *Check out "Installing NT Server."*

3 *A. WINNT.EXE /B.* You must first create the shared installation point from which to get Windows NT Server. To do this, you can either XCOPY the appropriate directories (depending on your hardware platform) to the server and share them, or simply share out the CD-ROM itself. After you share out the source files, you need to go to each computer and connect a drive to the shared files. Then, you can run WINNT.EXE /B /S:*Path_To_Your_Files*. This command starts the setup process by copying the Windows NT files to your local hard disk. *See "Installing NT Server."*

4 *C. More hard disk space.* You need 160MB for a RISC computer compared to 125MB for an Intel computer. *Review "Meeting NT's hardware requirements."*

5 *D. DHCP.* DHCP is a simple service that allows administrators to configure TCP/IP settings on computers automatically. *See "Choosing your protocols."*

6 *B. Per seat.* In a per-user setting, you only need to purchase 300 licenses. In contrast, if you use per-server licensing, you need to buy 900 licenses. *Review "Choosing a licensing mode."*

7 *D. NTFS.* The FAT file system does not provide any security for the files and directories that it stores. NTFS provides fully integrated security. *Review "Choosing a file system: Vanna, I'd like a vowel."*

8 *A. Get an OEM Version of Windows NT Server.* To support more than two CPUs, you need to contact the manufacturer of your computer. By default, Windows NT Server supports only two CPUs. *Check out "Meeting NT's hardware requirements" for more information.*

Chapter 6

Domain Management

. . . .

Exam Objectives

▶ Working with Server Manager

▶ Reviewing PDC/BDC account synchronization

▶ Exploring the Computer Browser service

. . . .

*I*n this chapter, we explore the areas of domain management that you can expect to see on your Enterprise exam. We focus on three areas of domain management: Server Manager, account synchronization, and the Computer Browser service.

Server Manager is a powerful tool for administering computer accounts and servers within a domain. Account synchronization involves the automated and manual processes for replicating changes to the Security Accounts Manager (SAM) database. The Computer Browser service — one of the basic services installed with Microsoft Networking — allows you to view network resources active on your network.

For the topics we cover in this chapter, the exam covers theory much more than application. In particular, the exam stresses the following topics:

✔ Forcing replication of the SAM to update account settings on the backup domain controllers (BDCs), and determining when you may need to perform this action.

✔ Understanding the available functions within Server Manager from a remote management standpoint.

✔ Using the Registry to change synchronization settings.

✔ Promoting and demoting servers in a domain.

Quick Assessment

Working
with Server
Manager

1 (True/False). Server Manager displays *only* a list of member and domain controller Windows NT Servers in your domain.

2 You can use _____ to promote a BDC to a PDC.

Reviewing
PDC/BDC
account
synchroni-
zation

3 To change the frequency at which the master accounts database replicates, you use _____.

4 You use the _____ utility to force synchronization of the primary domain controller's (PDC) and backup domain controller's (BDC) SAM.

5 By default, the PDC replicates changes to the SAM to a BDC every _____.

Exploring
the
Computer
Browser
service

6 Which platforms may be browsers?

7 By default, a machine that's not actively performing a browser role sends an announcement packet to a master browser every _____.

8 You access the browse list via the _____ desktop icon.

Answers

1   *False.* Review "Working with Server Manager."

2   *Server Manager.* Review "Working with Server Manager."

3   *Regedit or Regedt32.* Review "PDC/BDC SAM Synchronization."

4   *Server Manager.* Review "PDC/BDC SAM Synchronization."

5   *5 minutes.* Review "PDC/BDC SAM Synchronization."

6   *NT Server acting as a domain controller, NT Server acting as a member server, NT Workstation, Windows 95, Windows for Workgroups, Windows 3.1.* Review "Exploring the Computer Browser Service."

7   *12 minutes.* Review "Exploring the Computer Browser Service."

8   *Network Neighborhood.* Review "Exploring the Computer Browser Service."

Working with Server Manager

One of the many tools available within the Administrative Tools group on NT Server is Server Manager, and the exam expects you to know just which functions the Server Manager can perform. Server Manager provides a domain management interface through which you can perform the following functions:

- Managing server and workstation computer accounts in a domain
- Managing domain controllers
- Forcing domain account replication

In addition to these functions, you can manage services, shared directories, and properties such as replication on local or remote computers. Only the Domain Admins, Server Operators, and Account Operators groups have rights to access Server Manager.

Managing computers

When you open Server Manager, the first thing you see is a display of all the systems with computer accounts in your current domain. If you are unsure of your current domain, check the title bar in the Server Manager window.

The Server Manager window has three columns that list the computer's NetBIOS name, the role the computer plays in the domain, and an optional description. To edit the description for a system, double-click the computer name in Server Manager, and enter the description in the Description box.

Figure 6-1 shows the Server Manager window for a domain called DOMAIN1. Three machines are currently in the domain: PDC, the primary domain controller; BDC1, a backup domain controller; and WORKSTATION1, a workstation in the domain. You can tell at a glance the online status of systems visible in the domain. In Figure 6-1, the PDC is online and active, and the gray icons indicate that the BDC and the workstation are currently offline.

To manage a specific system, double-click its name in the Server Manager window. If the computer is active and your permissions in the domain allow you to manage the system you have selected, the resulting Properties dialog box allows you to perform several management tasks on the selected system:

- View or disconnect user sessions
- Display, create, or delete shared resources
- List or close currently opened resources

| ✔ Manage replication
| ✔ Manage administrative alerts

Although you may need to know the available management functions for your exam, you won't be expected to know specific details on how to use or configure any of these functions, with the possible exception of directory replication.

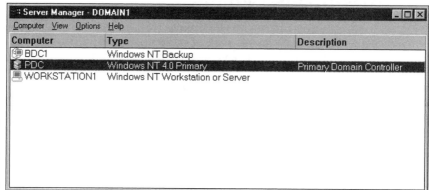

Figure 6-1:
Server
Manager.

Replicating directories

The Replication button on the Properties dialog box enables you to configure and monitor directory replication. Replication occurs when a directory structure is duplicated from an export computer to an import computer. Changes made to the export computer's replicated directory structure are duplicated in the directory structure of the import computer. A single export computer can replicate to numerous import computers. Any files changed on the import computer are overwritten the next time replication occurs.

Directory replication is commonly used to replicate logon scripts from a PDC to the BDCs in the domain. It is important to remember, however, that replication can occur either within a single domain, across different domains, or completely independent of any domain. By default, logon scripts are located in the NETLOGON share of a domain controller. The local directory structure of the NETLOGON network share is, by default, WINNT\SYSTEM32\REPL\IMPORT\SCRIPTS on any Windows NT domain controller.

Also by default, your export server replicates the structure contained in the WINNT\SYSTEM32\REPL\EXPORT directory. Your import server receives these replicated files and folders under the WINNT\SYSTEM32\REPL\IMPORT directory.

Your exam may ask which types of systems can fill particular roles in the replication process. Only NT Servers can be used as export computers, but either NT Servers or Workstations can be used as import computers. For the replicator service to function properly, the service must be configured to log on under a user account that is a member of the Replicator local group.

Managing domains

As we mention in the introduction to this section, Server Manager can assist in domain management, in addition to managing individual computers. Domain management is a very important aspect of Server Manager, and you can expect to see questions on the Enterprise exam dealing with promoting and demoting domain servers and on manual replication of the SAM. You can see more information on manual replication in the section "PDC/BDC SAM Synchronization," later in this chapter.

You should already know that you can't promote a stand-alone server to a domain controller, or demote a domain controller to a member server, without reinstalling NT Server. You can, however, force a role-reversal between a PDC and a BDC, and you can make this change via Server Manager. If your PDC fails, or you want to take your PDC offline for maintenance, you need to promote one of your BDCs to a PDC.

If you see any question on your exam that refers to promoting a member server to a domain controller, or demoting a domain controller to a member server, remember that the only way you can accomplish these changes is by reinstalling Windows NT Server. Look for an answer that involves reinstalling from scratch, and you'll know that you have the right answer. Be careful, though; the solution may be hidden in an answer such as, "By running Winnt32.exe from the command line."

Reinstalling Windows NT Server also applies to moving a BDC or a PDC to the control of a different, existing domain. You can rename an existing domain if you change the domain name on all domain controllers, member servers, and member workstations. However, if you want to make a BDC or a PDC a member server of a different, *existing* domain in your Enterprise, your only choice is to reinstall Windows NT Server.

You can promote a BDC to a PDC in two ways. The method you use depends on whether the PDC is still online when you perform the promotion. The preferred situation is to perform the promotion while the PDC is online and operating normally. In this case, you simply select the BDC you want to promote in Server Manager, and choose Computer⇨Promote to Primary Domain Controller, as shown in Figure 6-2. The BDC is promoted, and the PDC is automatically demoted to a BDC.

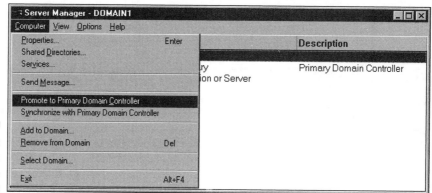

Figure 6-2:
Promoting a
BDC.

The other possible situation involves promoting a BDC when your PDC is offline. Your initial steps are the same: Select the BDC you want to promote in Server Manager, and then choose Computer⇨Promote to Primary Domain Controller. In this scenario, you must perform an additional step when your PDC comes back online. Through Server Manager, you need to select your original PDC and choose Computer⇨Demote Primary Domain Controller. This option only becomes available when a BDC has been promoted with a PDC offline, and the original PDC has been brought back online.

PDC/BDC SAM Synchronization

Any time you change your User Accounts database, the changes must be replicated to all domain controllers to maintain proper domain security. By default, your domain automatically synchronizes the SAM every five minutes. You can also force replication through Server Manager by manually replicating SAM changes to your entire domain, or selectively to a specific BDC within your domain.

Two types of synchronization exist: full and partial. Full synchronization occurs when a PDC sends the entire SAM to a BDC, and always happens when a new BDC is brought online. Partial synchronization occurs every time the PDC sends incremental SAM updates to a BDC.

Automatic synchronization

Once every five minutes, the PDC database notifies the BDCs whether changes have been made to the SAM. If a change has occurred, the BDC replies by sending a packet to the PDC requesting replication of those changes. The PDC then responds by sending SAM updates to the BDC requesting replication.

To change the default replication frequency, you must use the Regedit utility on the Registry of the PDC. You need to change the Pulse and PulseConcurrency values under the following Registry key:

```
HKEY_LOCAL_MACHINE\SYSTEM\CurrentControlSet\Services\Netlogon\Parameters
```

In situations where you must edit the Registry, we usually refer to the *Regedit* utility. You may, however, also use the *Regedt32* utility. Either of these two utilities allows you to set or change Registry keys. We prefer Regedit, because Regedit is easier to use when searching the Registry for a specific key or value.

The Pulse setting — a REG_DWORD value — defines the pulse frequency (in seconds) during which time changes are collected for a PDC. When the time expires, a pulse is sent to each BDC that needs to make changes. A pulse isn't sent to a BDC with a current database, with the exception of a default pulse sent every two hours regardless of the state of a BDC's database. Valid ranges for this parameter are from 60 to 3,600 seconds.

The PulseConcurrency setting — also a REG_DWORD value — defines the maximum number of simultaneous pulses that may be sent to the BDCs, signaling them to begin replication. Increasing the PulseConcurrency setting increases the load on the PDC. Decreasing this value increases the time required for replicating SAM changes to a large number of BDCs. The default for this value is 20, and the value can range anywhere from 1 to 500.

Under the same registry structure for the BDC, you can specify a ReplicationGovernor REG_DWORD value that determines how often a BDC responds to a PDC's synchronization announcement, and how much of the changed data is transferred upon each connection. This value is a percentage, with a range of 0 to 100, with 100 being the default setting. This value is especially helpful for limiting the amount of bandwidth used over a WAN link for account replication. Use caution when modifying this value. If you set the ReplicationGovernor too low, replication will never complete. If you set a zero value, replication will never even begin.

If you see a question on your exam asking how to control SAM synchronization to BDCs over a slow WAN link, you can ignore any answers concerning the Pulse and PulseConcurrency settings on the PDC. Instead, look for answers involving the ReplicationGovernor setting on the BDC. Your key phrase here is *slow WAN link*. You can have multiple BDCs in a domain, and three of them may be connected with your BDC via a high-speed LAN link. However, suppose you have one system connected via 56K in a building down the street. You may need to make sure your bandwidth isn't chewed up every five minutes as the one BDC attempts to replicate the SAM database; however, you have no reason to prevent the local BDCs from performing a complete database replication.

Manual synchronization

If you make numerous changes to the SAM, and you want to immediately force synchronization across your domain, you can use Server Manager to initiate a manual synchronization. To synchronize the entire domain, select your PDC in Server Manager, and choose Computer⇨Synchronize Entire Domain, as shown in Figure 6-3. To synchronize a specific BDC to the PDC, select the BDC you want to synchronize, and choose Computer⇨Synchronize with Primary Domain Controller.

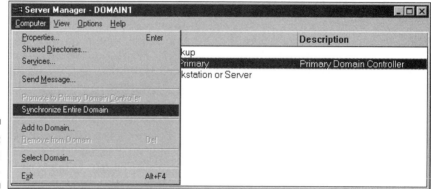

Figure 6-3:
Synchronizing
a domain.

Exploring the Computer Browser Service

If you've ever opened Network Neighborhood to find the name of a forgotten resource, you've probably had a brush with the Computer Browser service. Windows NT uses the Computer Browser service to identify and display a list of available network resources on your domain.

The Enterprise exam may include a question about the benefits of the Computer Browser service. The Computer Browser service selects certain systems from those available on the network and assigns them the responsibility of maintaining lists of available network resources. This prevents other systems from having to maintain their own local resource lists.

Can you think of any benefits of assigning specific computers the browser role, rather than allowing each system to maintain a local resource list? With fewer systems maintaining a browser list, less network traffic is created by list maintenance activities. In addition, the systems can use fewer CPU cycles doing a simple list lookup than would be required to create a list every time a system needed to browse the network.

You install the Computer Browser service in the same way you install most network resources: from the Services tab of the Network option in your Control Panel (see Figure 6-4). The Computer Browser service is actually one of the default network services, and should be installed unless it was deselected during the initial network component setup process or manually removed after installation.

Choosing browser computers

Computers running NT Workstation or NT Server can perform any of the possible browser service roles listed in Table 6-1. Every 12 minutes, any computer not currently assigned an active browser role (the first three entries in Table 6-1) sends an announcement packet to the nearest system participating in the browsing process. The master browse list is replicated between participating systems every 15 minutes.

Table 6-1	Browser Service Roles
Role	**Description**
Domain master browser	Only one domain master browser exists per NT domain. By default, this role is always filled by the PDC. The domain master browser maintains a master list of available resources, and distributes this list to a *master browser* on each subnet in the domain.
Master browser	One master browser exists for each subnet in a domain. If a BDC exists on the subnet, it defaults to the role of master browser. The master browser sends its local browse list to the domain master browser, and receives the domain master browse list in return. This master list of available resources is then distributed down the line to backup browsers on the same subnet as the master browser.
Backup browsers	Backup browsers receive their copy of the master browse list from master browsers on the same segment. By default, BDCs are used to fill the role of backup browsers, unless the PDC is unavailable, in which case, one BDC is chosen to assume the role of master browser. Backup browsers then distribute the browse list to browse clients on request.
Potential browser	Any computer that is capable of becoming a backup or master browser is considered a potential browser. In times of need, a master browser can request that a capable system pick up the responsibility of maintaining a browse list.

Role	Description
Non-browser	A non-browser is a computer that has been set up in such a way as to prevent the system from becoming a browser server.

Each browser-capable system on a network is ranked on certain criteria during a browser election to determine its place in the browser food chain. You may need to know the correct order on your exam, and you should definitely know which systems are able to take on the role of a browser during the election process. The operating systems that can become network browsers include, in order of selection ranking:

- ✔ Windows NT Server acting as a domain controller

- ✔ Windows NT Server acting as a member server

- ✔ Windows NT Workstation

- ✔ Windows 95

- ✔ Windows for Workgroups 3.11

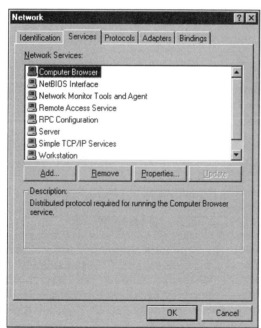

Figure 6-4:
The
Computer
Browser
service.

In addition to the operating system in use, two more criteria may be used in an election. First, the browser election may further subdivide a particular OS category by version. This means, for example, that NT Server 4.0 takes precedence over NT Server 3.51. The second is a system's current ranking in the browser hierarchy — master, backup, or potential browser. Furthermore, NT Server 3.51 takes precedence over NT Workstation 4.0, because the computer role takes precedence over OS version number.

In the event of two systems running the same OS type and version, the computer that has been on the network longer wins. If the systems have been on the network for the same amount of time, the alphanumeric computer names are compared, and the first system in alphabetic order wins the election.

The exam may ask how you go about allowing only certain systems to participate in the browser process. The answer is in the Registry. Although you shouldn't need to know the specific key for the test, here it is, for your reference:

```
\HKEY_LOCAL_MACHINE\SYSTEM\CurrentControlSet\Services\Browser\
         Parameters\MaintainServerList
```

The three possible values for this key are all string settings:

- ✔ **Yes.** Attempt to become a browser service. This is the default setting for NT domain controllers.

- ✔ **No.** Never participate as a browser service. You may want to set this value on systems that are frequently taken off the network, such as notebook computers.

- ✔ **Auto.** The system may become a browser server, depending on the number of active browsers. This system is known as a *potential browser*. This is the default setting for non-domain controller NT systems, both workstations and servers.

Browsing within an enterprise

Browsing within a LAN is fairly automatic. But suppose your domain spans an enterprise infrastructure. In a strictly TCP/IP-based subnetted network environment, browser broadcasts don't automatically pass through your routers. So the question — one you may see on the exam — is: How do you allow the browser service to successfully maintain lists that include services on the other subnets of your WAN?

You have three possible solutions to the problems with WAN browsing:

- ✔ You can implement WINS on your network.
- ✔ You can use LMHOSTS files — don't forget your #PRE and #DOM tags!
- ✔ You can configure your routers to forward browser activity through UDP port 137.

For more information on configuring WINS and LMHOSTS files, check out Chapter 8.

Recognizing browser failures

Ever wonder just what your system is really doing during all that time it takes to shut down? Well, if it's on a network, one part of the shutdown process sends an announcement to the master browser, letting it know that the computer is no longer available for network services. When the master browser receives this packet, the sending computer is removed from the master browse list.

If a computer is powered off without performing a proper shutdown, however, it doesn't have a chance to send the announcement packet. As a result, the master browser may think the system is still available, and fail to remove it from the browse list. The computer remains on the browse list until it misses three successive announcement periods, meaning that it could incorrectly appear in the lists for up to 36 minutes, in addition to any time it may take to replicate the changes in the list to the backup browsers.

When a backup browser fails to check back in with a master browser through three browse list replication periods (45 minutes), it is removed from the browse list. On the other hand, if a master browser is not detected during a single announcement period, the backup browser that detected the missing master immediately broadcasts a packet to force the election process for a new master browser.

Prep Test

1 You want to limit the amount of bandwidth used on your WAN for SAM database synchronization. Which of the following Registry values should you modify?

A ○ The Pulse setting on each BDC

B ○ The PulseConcurrency setting on each BDC

C ○ The ReplicationGovernor setting on each BDC

D ○ The ReplicationGovernor setting on the PDC

E ○ The DatabaseReplication setting on the PDC

2 You recently added numerous BDCs to your network, dramatically increasing network traffic related to SAM synchronization and slowing down your network. Which changes should you make to your PDC's Registry to correct this issue? (Choose all that apply.)

A ❑ Decrease the Pulse setting

B ❑ Decrease the PulseConcurrency setting

C ❑ Increase the Pulse setting

D ❑ Increase the PulseConcurrency setting

3 Rank the following systems in the order by which they will win browser elections:

A ○ Windows 95

B ○ Windows NT Server 3.51 configured as a member server

C ○ Windows NT Server 4.0 configured as a member server

D ○ Windows NT Server 3.51 configured as a backup domain controller

E ○ Windows NT Workstation 4.0

4 You have just added 50 new user accounts to the PDC for your domain. Some users from one of your remote sites complain that they still can't log on, and 10 minutes have passed since your last change to the PDC. Users at other sites are having no problems. What is the first thing you should try to do to fix this problem?

A ○ Promote the BDC at the remote site to a PDC.

B ○ Power down the remote BDC so users are forced to authenticate at the PDC.

C ○ Open Server Manager, highlight the BDC at the remote site, and choose Computer➪Synchronize with Primary Domain Controller.

D ○ Open Server Manager, highlight the PDC, and choose Computer➪Synchronize Entire Domain.

E ○ Stop and restart the Replicator service.

5 You have just replaced your PDC with a faster server, and demoted your original PDC to a BDC in the process. You no longer want this BDC to perform user authentication, so you plan to demote it to a member server. What is the easiest way to accomplish this?

A ○ From Server Manager, highlight the BDC and choose Computer⇨Demote to Member Server.

B ○ From the Network Control Panel, select the Identification tab. Under the Domain option box, select the Server Will Not Participate in Domain Security check box.

C ○ Reinstall Windows NT Server.

D ○ Modify the Registry parameter ServerRole under the NETLOGON parameters key.

6 You want your computer to be visible to others who are browsing the network, but you do not want your computer to become a browser on the network. What should you do to accomplish this?

A ○ Disable the browser service.

B ○ Set the MaintainServerList parameter in the Registry to No.

C ○ Set the MaintainServerList parameter in the Registry to 0.

D ○ Delete your computer account from the Server Manager list for your domain.

7 Your network is running TCP/IP as the only network protocol. When accessing the browse list, you can see only computers located on the same physical subnet as your workstation. Which of the following steps can you take to enable your browser service to work across subnets? (Choose all that apply.)

A ❑ Configure forwarding for UDP port 137 on your routers.

B ❑ Enable WINS on your network.

C ❑ Enable DNS on your network.

D ❑ Enable DHCP on your network.

8 By default, which role of the five available browser service roles will a BDC play?

A ○ Domain master browser

B ○ Master browser

C ○ Backup browser

D ○ Potential browser

E ○ Non-browser

9 To access Server Manager, to which group or groups must a user belong? (Choose all that apply.)

A ❑ Account Operators

B ❑ Domain Admins

C ❑ Backup Operators

D ❑ Server Operators

E ❑ Users

Answers

1 *C. The ReplicationGovernor setting on each BDC.* The Pulse and PulseConcurrency settings are both for controlling replication behavior from the PDC. The ReplicationGovernor setting on each BDC is the value that you need to modify for controlling SAM replication over a WAN. *Review "Automatic synchronization" — in particular, see the Instant Answer in that section.*

2 *B and C.* The Pulse setting on the PDC represents the number of seconds between synchronization requests initiated by the PDC. The PulseConcurrency setting on the PDC determines how many BDCs are allowed to synchronize their databases at the same time. Making these changes reduces traffic by increasing the time between synchronizations and decreasing the number of systems attempting to simultaneously synchronize. *Review "Automatic synchronization."*

3 *D, C, B, E, A.* The computer's role in your domain and the OS platform are the first criteria. Next, to break ties between similar roles (such as two domain controllers or two member servers), the OS version is used. *Review "Choosing browser computers."*

4 *C. Open Server Manager, highlight the BDC at the remote site, and choose Computer⇨Synchronize with Primary Domain Controller.* You should force synchronization only on the BDC at the remote site that is having problems. It is possible that the BDC has not fully replicated the SAM because of the ReplicationGovernor setting in the Registry. By forcing synchronization, the BDC will update the entire domain database regardless of settings in the Registry. You don't need to synchronize the entire domain because no other locations appear to be having problems. *Review "Automatic synchronization."*

5 *C. Reinstall Windows NT Server.* You can't promote a member server to a domain controller, or demote a domain controller to a member server, without reinstalling NT. *Review "Automatic synchronization."*

6 *B. Set the MaintainServerList parameter in the Registry to No.* This Registry parameter has three possible values: Yes, No, or Auto. Setting the value to No allows your computer to browse and be browsed on the network, but prevents your system from winning a browse election. *Review "Choosing browser computers."*

7 *A and B.* Browser activity in a strictly TCP/IP network occurs through UDP port 137, so enabling forwarding on the routers allows browser traffic to cross subnets. Enabling WINS or using the LMHOSTS file also allows the browser to see systems in other subnets. *Review "Browsing within an enterprise," and see Chapter 8 for more information.*

8 *C. Backup browser.* The BDCs all act as backup browsers unless otherwise configured in the Registry. In the event of a domain master browser failure, one of the BDCs immediately assumes the responsibility. *Review "Choosing browser computers" — in particular, Table 6-1.*

9 *A, B, and D.* Only Domain Admins, Server Operators, and Account Operators have access to Server Manager. *Review "Working with Server Manager."*

Chapter 7

Printers: Don't Be Fooled by Spools and Pools

* *

Exam Objectives

▶ Adding and configuring a printer

▶ Implementing a printer pool

▶ Printer connectivity

▶ Setting print priorities

* *

*Y*ou'll find enough questions on printing to make it worth your while to know this information. Enterprise printing can be a fairly robust topic — we were surprised at the complexity of some of the questions on our exams.

While you review for your exam, remember the following points:

✔ The five main areas of printing you want to spend the most time with before your Enterprise exam are spooler settings, print clients, creating printer pools, security, and scheduling.

✔ The Enterprise exam doesn't ask questions about basic printer installation. You are more likely to see such questions on your Server and Workstation exams. You may, however, see questions dealing with advanced post-installation configuration and optimization.

✔ The questions dealing with printing will most likely be scenario-based questions. If you've taken any of the Microsoft exams, you know what we mean. If not, check out Question 8 in the Prep Test at the end of this chapter for an example.

✔ Although you don't need to know how to configure Services for Macintosh, File and Print Services for NetWare, or the TCP/IP Printing Service, you need to know that, by installing these services, you enable printing from Macintosh, NetWare, and UNIX clients, respectively.

Quick Assessment

Adding and configuring a printer

1 You manage printers through NT's _____.

2 Having multiple physical print devices associated with a single printer is known as a _____.

3 For users to delete print jobs other than their own, they must have _____ access for the specified NT printer.

Implementing a printer pool

4 When printing to a TCP/IP print device, you must use the UNIX command _____.

Printer connectivity

5 Which of the following client platforms can print to an NT print server?

A. NT Workstation 3.51

B. Windows 95

C. UNIX

D. Macintosh

E. Novell NetWare

6 When configuring a user's or group's printer priority, _____ is the lowest priority, and _____ is the highest.

7 You have NetWare clients on your Enterprise network, and you want them to be able to access file and print resources on your server. To allow access without having to install and configure software on every NetWare client workstation, you need _____.

Setting print priorities

8 You can use a _____ page to switch between PostScript and PCL printing, as well as to help users find their documents among others at a printer.

Answers

1 *Printers folder.* Review "The NT print utility: Working with the Printers folder."

2 *Printing pool.* Review "Diving into printer pools."

3 *Full Control or Manage Documents.* Review "Assigning permissions."

4 *LPR.* Review "NT print clients."

5 *All of them!* Review "NT print clients."

6 *One; 99.* Review "Setting printing priorities: Tough love."

7 *File and Print Services for NetWare (FPNW).* Review "NetWare clients."

8 *Separator.* Review "Managing NT Printers."

Preparing for Enterprise Printing

In terms of cost, purchasing a print device for every desktop in an enterprise environment is never feasible. By the same token, having every user in a large-scale environment printing to the same print device is highly inefficient. The Enterprise exam tests your skills in designing and implementing a printing environment that uses a minimum number of printing devices, while offering maximum productivity and convenience for your users.

Microsoft has specific definitions for its technologies that you need to be familiar with for the exams. Don't fall into the trap of thinking your technical vocabulary will match the definitions used on the tests. Review the definitions in Table 7-1, and pay close attention to the relationships between a printer, a print device, and a printing pool.

Table 7-1	Printing Definitions
Term	*Definition*
Printer	The software interface between a print device and the operating system.
Print device	The physical printer — the hardware — that produces your final document.
Printing pool	A collection of physical print devices associated with a single printer.
Print server	Network servers on which shared printers are defined. Client computers submit their print jobs to print servers for processing and management.
Print driver	Software that allows the operating system to communicate with a specific type of print device.
Print processor	Software that renders a print job depending on its content to prepare it for printing.
Local printer	A printer using a physical port of and being controlled by the attached computer. Only local users of the attached computer are able to print to the printer.
Network printer	A printer that both local and network users can use.

The NT printing process

As you probably know, the NT printing process begins when a client attempts a connection with a printer, and ends when a print device receives processed data and produces a printed document. We review the entire printing process here. While you prepare for the exam, remember to focus on Step 1, the initial client connection. We list all the other steps for your reference, but you don't need to memorize them for the exam:

1. Whenever you add a new network printer to a client machine, and any time a client machine attempts to send a print job to a print server, if the client is running NT or Windows 95, the client first checks the version of the print driver on the server. If the server has a more recent driver, the client downloads the driver from the NT Server into memory. If the version is the same or earlier, the client uses its local print driver. This version checking and automatic downloading can only occur with NT clients and Windows 95 clients attaching to an NT Server.

2. The print job is sent to the client's local spooler via a remote procedure call (RPC), and the local spooler then forwards the job to the server spooler. This step doesn't occur if the client and the server are the same computer.

3. The server-side spooler passes the document to the router, which then determines the data type and passes the information to the appropriate print processor on the local print provider.

4. The print processor analyzes the type of data and determines whether further processing is required before returning the document to the local print provider.

5. If a separator page is to be used, the page is created and attached to the beginning of the print job.

6. The print job is passed to the print monitor, which determines when the job should print and which port it should print through.

7. The print device receives processed data and produces a printed document.

NT print clients

NT Server supports print services for a wide variety of client platforms — all of which are fair game for the exam. You'll see questions on which clients are able to print to an NT print server without requiring client-side driver installations, which platforms can print to NT, and what additional software is required to give different platforms the capability to print to an NT print server.

The following client platforms can print to NT Server:

✔ Windows NT clients

✔ Windows 95 clients

✔ Windows 3.*x* and Windows for Workgroups (WFW) clients

✔ DOS clients

✔ TCP/IP (UNIX) clients

✔ NetWare clients

✔ Macintosh clients

Windows NT and Windows 95 clients

NT print servers can provide print drivers to NT and 95 clients automatically. When an NT 4.0 client sends a print job to an NT print server, the client is able to automatically download and use driver software from the server. To allow similar operation of NT 3.x clients and Windows 95 clients, you can install the device drivers for the different operating systems on the print server by using the Alternate Drivers box on the Sharing tab of the Printer Properties dialog box. By installing alternate drivers on the print server, you avoid the need for installing driver software on each client system.

Windows 3.x, WFW, and DOS clients

Using a Microsoft Networking Client Redirector allows print jobs to be sent from DOS or Windows applications to an NT Print Share. Each DOS application requires its own internal print drivers, while Windows applications all use a single print driver that you must install on each client machine.

TCP/IP clients

TCP/IP-based printing clients, particularly UNIX clients, can print to NT print servers that are running the Microsoft TCP/IP Printing Service (also known as the Line Printer Daemon, or LPD). Clients submit print jobs using the LPR (Line Printer Request) command, and a client can view the TCP/IP printer queue using the LPQ (Line Printer Queue) command.

NetWare clients

Two methods exist by which a NetWare client can use NT print servers, and both are fair game on the Enterprise exam. In the first scenario, you need File and Print Services for NetWare (FPNW) installed on your NT Server. FPNW is a Windows NT network service that allows a computer running NT Server to act as a NetWare 3.12-compatible file and print server. Using FPNW, NetWare clients can transparently access print services on a Windows NT Server without requiring additional client-side software.

The other option for NetWare clients is to install a client-side Microsoft Networking Client Redirector for NetWare Clients. Although you can still print from any of these NetWare clients, this method has a downside: You must add and configure software on every NetWare client workstation.

Macintosh clients

Did you know that Macintosh clients can print to NT without additional client software? Faced with an exam question on Macintosh printing, look for an answer that has "Services for Macintosh" in it. This advice may at least eliminate some of the incorrect answers for you. To allow Macintosh clients to submit print jobs to your NT Server, simply install and configure the Services for Macintosh on your NT Server.

You'll see questions on the exam about printing from non-NT clients. If you see a question that includes a phrase similar to, "without requiring configuration on the client workstation," you can eliminate answers containing the word *redirector*. Instead, look for answers containing the word *services*. A redirector is client-side software that you use to allow a non-Microsoft client access to Microsoft network services. A service, in this case, is a server-side solution that can mimic the print server component of a client's native environment.

The NT print utility: Working with the Printers folder

Windows NT uses the Printers folder as the central print management utility. The Printers folder provides your interface for adding, sharing, deleting, and managing resources in the NT printing environment. You can access the Printers folder in four ways:

- ✔ Choose Start⇨Settings⇨Printers.
- ✔ Choose Start⇨Settings⇨Control Panel⇨Printers.
- ✔ Choose My Computer⇨Printers.
- ✔ Navigate through NT Explorer.

Your best tool is experience. If you haven't worked with NT's Printers folder, take some time to explore. You don't need to know every detail of every screen, but be familiar with some of the main tabs.

Adding and Configuring Printers: Plug 'n' Pray

You're more likely to see questions about the basic creation of a printer on the Workstation and Server exams. In contrast, the Enterprise exam will quite likely test your knowledge of post-installation configuration and optimization. The NT Add Printer Wizard can assist you in either endeavor, and you should know its ins and outs.

To access the NT Add Printer Wizard, open the Printers folder and double-click the Add Printer icon. The Wizard presents you with numerous configuration options identical to those available with the post-installation configuration options that we cover throughout the rest of this chapter.

You'll probably see a question on the exam dealing with the Hewlett-Packard Network Interface Print Device. Most people aren't likely to have experience with this technology, but we can give you a quick rundown on what you may need to know:

✔ Using an HP network interface print device requires the installation of the DLC network protocol. After you install the DLC network protocol, you see the HP network interface device as an option under the Ports dialog for your printers.

✔ If you are unable to connect to an HP network interface print device, another user may be attached using Continuous Connection mode. Users should not be using the Continuous Connection mode on a shared printer.

Sending Print Jobs to Network Printers

You may be a master at creating printers, but how do you submit the print jobs and configure the advanced options? In particular, you want to focus on option settings for spooling and pooling, which we discuss in the next two sections of this chapter.

To spool, or not to spool

On the Settings tab in your Printer Properties dialog box, you find the two primary settings for your print spooler:

✔ **Spool Print Documents So Program Finishes Printing Faster:** The exam may ask questions about either of the suboptions available within this selection. Spooling saves pending print jobs in a directory on your server before forwarding them to the print device. If you select this option, you are presented with two additional choices:

• **Start Printing After Last Page Is Spooled:** If any of these options are to show up as answers on your exam, this option is the most likely candidate. This option ensures that a print job occupies the print device for the least amount of time; efficient resource utilization such as this is an important goal of enterprise design.

The spooler doesn't forward the job to the print device until the entire job has been submitted by the client, avoiding delays while the print server waits for the individual pages of a document to be processed.

- **Start Printing Immediately:** Selecting this option causes a print job to start as soon as the first page has been spooled. If you have a fast print device and it can print pages faster than a client can provide them, this option causes a bottleneck as the device waits for spooled pages.

✔ **Print Directly to the Printer:** For the exam, you only need to know that selecting this option bypasses the spooler. This option is never used in an enterprise environment because it limits your ability to manage documents, and it slows the speed of document completion in a multi-user environment. This option is useful only for troubleshooting, allowing you to bypass the spooler and print directly to the print device.

We didn't see any questions about the Hold Mismatched Documents, Print Spooled Documents First, and Keep Documents After They Have Printed options on our exams. Just know they exist.

Diving into printer pools

You'll most likely see at least one scenario-based question on the Enterprise exam referencing printing pools. Make sure that you are clear on the following point: The term *printer pooling* means associating multiple print devices with a single printer as defined in the NT Printers folder. Be careful not to confuse this term with associating multiple NT printers to a single print device.

You enable printer pooling from the Ports tab in the Printer Properties dialog box by clicking the Enable Printer Pooling box and selecting multiple ports in the Port box (see Figure 7-1).

To use printer pooling, the printers that you plan to include in the printer pool must be able to use a common print driver, and they must all be connected to the same print server. From a network design standpoint, it's helpful to have all the printers in a printer pool located in close physical proximity. You don't want to have your users wandering around the building trying to find where their documents were printed.

On the other side of the spectrum, associating multiple printers with a single print device facilitates scheduling and priority assignments. This feature has no special name, but you certainly don't want to overlook it when you are preparing for your exam. For more information, see the section "Setting printing priorities: Tough love," later in this chapter.

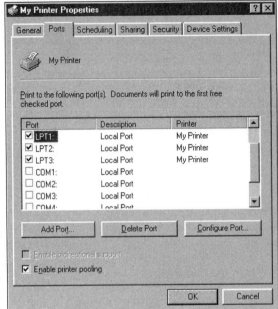

Managing NT Printers

After you become a whiz at setting up new printers, you should look at some of the management functions you're likely to see on the exam. These functions include pausing printing, setting default printers, setting document defaults, purging print documents, setting up network sharing of your printer, and setting a printer's properties. You can open the printer management functions by double-clicking either a Printer icon in the Printers folder, or the Printer icon in the System Tray when you have active print jobs.

Did you know that you can use a separator page to do more than just identify and separate different users' documents? You can also use a separator page to switch a printer between PostScript and PCL mode.

You should briefly review each of the available functions before exam day:

✔ **Printer:** The following menu selections are available under the Printer menu. Again, we stress the importance of actually exploring the software before taking the exam. Use the following list as a guide to finding some of the subjects you may not be familiar with. Open a printer, poke around a bit, and see if you can break anything.

- **Pause Printing:** When a printer is paused, users can still submit print requests, but the jobs aren't forwarded to the print device until the printer is restarted.

- **Set As Default Printer:** If this option is checked, Windows applications use this printer by default.

- **Document Defaults:** The window opened by this item contains different options depending on the print device and the print driver associated with the NT printer. Common options include settings for paper size, printer resolution, and page orientation.

- **Sharing:** Under sharing, you can select whether a printer is shared. If it's shared, you can set the printer's share name on the network. Oh, and don't forget, if you want a shared printer, but you don't want everyone to be able to see it, adding a dollar sign ($) after the share name makes it invisible to a network browser. The Sharing option also enables you to select and install additional drivers for other Windows client platforms for automatic download.

- **Purge Print Documents:** Selecting this option deletes all documents currently in the printer's queue.

- **Properties:** Properties include general settings, port configuration, scheduling options, printer priorities, sharing, security, and device settings.

- **Close:** We'd explain this option, but we're willing to bet you wouldn't be taking the exam if you didn't know what it does.

✔ **Document:** The options in the Document menu are specific to a print job in the main window for the printer you're working with. You can pause, resume, restart, or cancel a particular print job from this menu. Pausing puts the print job on hold until you choose Resume. Resume picks up a print job from the point at which it was interrupted. Restart starts printing a document from the beginning. The Properties option allows you to view or change document-specific settings for documents already in the print queue. Cancel, as we're sure you've guessed, cancels a print job and deletes it from the spooler.

Setting printing priorities: Tough love

On the Enterprise exam, you need to find solutions to scenarios involving different functional user groups who need to be able to use the same print device in a method that allows access based on the types of jobs submitted. Print priority and availability come into play in these scenarios. As you can see in Figure 7-2, you set both priority and availability on the Scheduling tab in the Printer Properties dialog box.

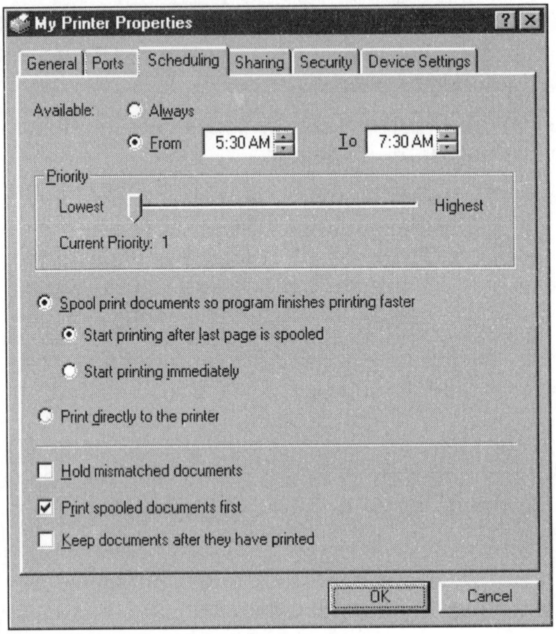

Figure 7-2:
The Printer
Properties
Scheduling
tab.

To prepare for the scheduling questions you may see on the exam, focus on the following highlights:

- Your priorities can range from 1 to 99, with 1 being the lowest priority, and 99 being the highest priority.

- You set priorities in the Printer Properties dialog box, and then set user rights to define who accesses the printer. Priorities aren't assigned to users; they are assigned to printers.

- A single printer can't have multiple priority assignments. For each new priority you want to assign to a print device, you must create a new printer definition and then set security and access privileges through that printer's security dialog from the Security tab of the Printer Properties dialog box.

- Availability doesn't prevent a user from submitting a print job to a printer at any given time. Rather, availability settings cause submitted print jobs to be held in the spooler until the time falls within the availability constraints. The spooler then forwards the held jobs to the print device.

- You can define multiple printers with similar availability settings, but different priorities. When the print jobs go active within the availability constraints, the system looks at the priorities of the multiple printers, and completes all the jobs in the print queue of the higher-ranked printer before starting any of the jobs in the queue of the lower-ranked printer.

Availability as you'll see it on the exam is most frequently used in situations involving large documents that are not time sensitive. The key words here are *not time sensitive*. If you see these key words on the exam, you can eliminate answers that don't involve scheduling or availability.

Print Priority and Availability will likely be combined in questions on the exam. Here's an example: Suppose you have two user groups — Accountants and Managers. The Accountants print two types of documents: documents with 200 pages or more, which can tie up the printer for hours at a time, or one- to two-page memos. Their large documents are printed only for archival purposes, and have minimal time sensitivity. The memos need to be printed shortly after being submitted to the print queue.

The Managers only print one- to two-page memos, which they want to print immediately. In addition, the Managers have requested that their print jobs be given priority over other users. Your print server has only one physical print device. How do you optimize your printing environment?

Solution: You need to define three NT printers, all of which point to the same physical print device. Create a Management Memo printer with a printing priority of 99. Point the members of the Managers group to this printer. Next, create two printers for the Accountants group: Accounting Memos and Accounting Archives. Give both printers a print priority of 1, and schedule the Archive printer to be available only after 5:00 p.m. Instruct your accounting users to send their large documents to the Archive printer and their memos to the Memo printer.

In this solution, you apply scheduling by directing the large print jobs to a printer that is available only after 5:00 p.m., and you apply priority assignments that allow the management print jobs to print before the accounting print jobs.

Assigning permissions

You can assign group permissions to printers in the same way that you can assign permissions to files and folders, but with one major difference. You can assign only four permissions to an NT printer. Table 7-2 lists the available permissions. Figure 7-3 shows the default group permissions granted to a newly created printer on a domain print server.

Table 7-2	Printer Permissions
Permission	*Description*
Print	Allows users to print documents and manage queued documents they have sent to the printer.
Manage Documents	Allows users to manage documents in the queue, regardless of who sent them. Document management includes pausing, restarting, resuming, and deleting existing documents.
No Access	Denies users all access to the printer or the print queue.
Full Control	Allows users to create, manage, and delete printers or documents.

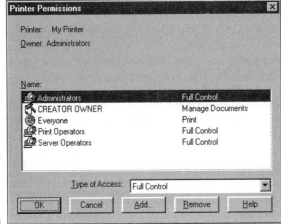

Figure 7-3:
Group
permissions.

Prep Test

1 You are creating a printing pool with two different print devices so that users from the Accounting group can print jobs on either device. Which of the following statements best describes a printing pool? (Choose all that apply.)

A ❑ All print devices must use the same type of printer port.

B ❑ All print devices must be using TCP/IP Printing.

C ❑ All print devices must be able to use a common driver.

D ❑ You can direct certain print jobs to a specific print device in the printing tool without the need to define a second printer.

E ❑ All print devices in the printing pool must be connected to the same print server.

2 You run a small domain with two user groups: Managers and Peons. Your boss asks you to make sure any documents submitted by the Managers group are printed before documents submitted by the Peons group. Which of the following steps must you take to accomplish this task? (Choose all that apply.)

A ❑ Create a separate printer for users in the Managers group, and configure the printer to start printing immediately.

B ❑ Create a separate printer for users in the Managers group, and set the print priority to 1.

C ❑ Create a separate printer for users in the Managers group, and set the print priority to 99.

D ❑ Create a separate printer for users in the Peons group, and set the print priority to 1.

E ❑ Create a separate printer for users in the Peons group, and set the print priority to 99.

3 What is the functional difference between the Print permission and the Manage Documents permission for a printer?

A ○ Manage Documents permission allows users to submit jobs to printers, as well as manage documents submitted by any other user. Print permission allows users to submit jobs to a printer, but only allows them to manage their own documents.

B ○ Manage Documents permission allows a user to submit jobs to a printer, as well as manage documents submitted by any other user. Print permission only allows a user to submit a job to a printer.

C ○ Manage Documents permission allows a user to manage documents in a print queue, but doesn't allow users to submit their own jobs to a printer. Print permission allows users to submit their own print jobs.

D ○ Manage Documents permission allows users to manage print jobs they have submitted to the printer. Print permission allows a user to submit jobs to a printer.

4 One of your users has submitted a print job, and the print device fails. The job has not yet cleared from the print queue. Your user has already shut down his system, and doesn't want to re-create the document. After correcting the problems with the print device, you open the Printer Management window from the Printers folder. What can you do as an administrator to reprint the entire document?

A ○ Choose Document⇨Resume.

B ○ Choose Document⇨Restart.

C ○ Choose Printer⇨Restart.

D ○ Choose Printer⇨Resume.

5 DLC is installed on your computer, and you are trying to print to an HP-series network interface print device that also uses Data Link Control (DLC). You have reset the printer, but you still can't print successfully to the network interface print device. What may be causing the problem?

A ○ The DLC protocol isn't installed on the network interface print device.

B ○ Someone else is connected to the printer using DLC in Continuous Connection mode.

C ○ Someone else is connected to the printer using the Microsoft TCP/IP Printing Service, preventing DLC from accessing the network interface print device.

D ○ You are using the RAW data type.

6 Which option do you set in Printer Properties to make sure that large documents occupy a print device for the least amount of time?

A ○ Start Printing Immediately

B ○ Print Directly to Printer

C ○ Print Spooled Documents First

D ○ Start Printing After the Last Page Is Spooled

7 You want to enable printing to an NT print server from your existing NetWare client workstations. You want to minimize the administrative effort required, and your solution shouldn't require installation of additional software on the NetWare clients. Your NetWare clients are running only the IPX/SPX protocol. You are running only the NWLink protocol on your NT Server. What else must you do to allow the NetWare clients to print to the NT print server?

A ○ Install the Microsoft TCP/IP Printing Service.

B ○ Install the NetWare Client Redirector software on your server.

C ○ Install the File and Print Services for NetWare on your server.

D ○ Install the File and Print Services for NetWare on each client.

8 You are the administrator for your company's NT domain. Users of the local group Payroll are currently using a printer, and you want to restrict access to the printer so that only the users in the Payroll group have access to the printer.

Required results: Only users of the Payroll group are able to submit jobs to the printer.

Optional desired results: Users should be allowed to manage only their own print jobs.

Individuals should be able to view all jobs sent to the printer.

Solution: You remove the Everyone special group from the printer's Security tab. You add the Payroll group to the printer's Security tab, and grant the group Print permissions.

This solution

A ○ Accomplishes the required result, and both optional desired results.

B ○ Accomplishes the required result, but only one optional desired result.

C ○ Accomplishes only the required result.

D ○ Doesn't produce the required result.

9 You have just created a new printer share on your NT print server. Your print server is named NTPRTSRV, and you name the newly created share COLORLSR$. When you connect to the server NTPRTSRV through Network Neighborhood, you can see other printer shares, but you can't see COLORLSR$. What do you need to do to make the print share visible to Network Neighborhood browsers?

A ○ The name is too long. You should rename the printer CLRLSR$.

B ○ You must reboot the print server to make newly created printers visible.

C ○ Remove the $ from the share name, making it COLORLSR.

D ○ Do nothing. It can take up to 30 minutes for a new print share to show up under Network Neighborhood.

10 By default, what permissions do members of the Administrators group have on a newly created NT printer?

A ○ No Access

B ○ Print

C ○ Manage Documents

D ○ Full Control

Answers

1 *C and E.* To successfully implement a printing pool, all printers must be able to use a common driver, and must be connected to the same print server. However, you can use different types of printer ports, such as one Local port (LPT1) and one Network port. When implementing a printing pool, all print devices act as a single physical unit; it isn't possible to direct a print job to a specific device without creating an additional NT printer. *Review "Diving into printer pools."*

2 *C and D.* You set printer priority on the Scheduling tab in the Printer Properties dialog box. The highest priority is 99, and the lowest is 1. *Review "Setting printing priorities: Tough love."*

3 *A.* Manage Documents allows a user to manage any jobs that are submitted to the printer, but doesn't allow a user to manage the properties of the printer itself. *Review "Assigning permissions."*

4 *B.* Document⇨Resume attempts to pick up printing from where the device left off. Restart prints a document from the beginning, but you must restart the document before it's deleted from the spooler. *Review "Managing NT Printers."*

5 *B.* If another computer has connected to the HP network interface print device using Continuous Connection mode, you can't access the device. *Review "Adding and Configuring Printers: Plug 'n' Pray."*

6 *D.* This option prevents delays while the print server waits for the client to render individual pages in a print job. *Review "To spool, or not to spool."*

7 *C.* If you don't want to install software on every client system, you should install the File and Print Services for NetWare on your NT Server. Installing Microsoft Redirector software on the clients works, but doesn't satisfy the requirement of not installing software on client systems. TCP/IP print service won't work unless you are printing from TCP/IP clients to a TCP/IP server. *Review "NT print clients."*

8 *A.* Print permission allows users to see any jobs in the print queue, but doesn't give users management capabilities over those documents. You remove the Everyone special group from the printer to restrict access not specifically granted, rather than changing the permission to No Access, because No Access prevents *all users*, including the Payroll group, from being able to access the printer. *Review "Assigning permissions."*

9 *C.* Just as with shared folders, a $ at the end of the share name creates a hidden share. You can still attach to the printer, but you must enter the full UNC name — in this case, \\NTPRTSRV\COLORLSR$. *Review "Managing NT Printers."*

10 *D.* Administrators, by default, have Full Control permissions on a newly created printer. This permission means they can manage documents, manage the printer itself, and submit print jobs to the printer. *Review "Assigning permissions."*

Chapter 8

Do You See What I TCP/IP?

Exam Objectives

▶ Internetworking with TCP/IP

▶ Using TCP/IP tools and utilities

▶ Reviewing Dynamic Host Configuration Protocol

*T*CP/IP, the Transport Control Protocol/Internet Protocol, is one of the most common network protocols in use today. Implementing TCP/IP on your Windows NT network allows for easy interconnectivity with various systems, including UNIX, Macintosh, and any other platform capable of running the TCP/IP protocol suite. You can use TCP/IP on networks ranging from just a handful clients, to the world's largest data network, the Internet. The Internet without TCP/IP would be like New York City without street signs or traffic lights. Okay, make up your own analogy, but you get the picture.

Microsoft's implementation of TCP/IP for Windows includes numerous useful utilities. One of these utilities is DHCP — a service that makes managing and configuring TCP/IP on client workstations a much more manageable task. In this chapter, we tell you what you need to know about TCP/IP and DHCP for the Enterprise exam.

Quick Assessment

Internetworking with TCP/IP

1 Is UDP connectionless or connection-oriented?

2 To use NT to communicate with an IP device on a remote subnet, you must configure an IP address, a(n) _____, and a(n) _____.

3 The difference between TFTP and FTP is that TFTP is _____, and FTP is _____ -oriented.

Using TCP/IP tools and utilities

4 To display current TCP/IP configuration information, you use the _____ command-line utility.

5 ARP translates an IP address into a physical _____ address.

6 To test whether an IP address is active and reachable, you can run the _____ command-line utility.

Reviewing Dynamic Host Configuration Protocol

7 In DHCP, a(n) _____ refers to the range of addresses that a DHCP server has available to assign to clients.

8 If you want to dynamically configure TCP/IP on your client workstations, you should install the _____ service.

9 (True/False). DHCP can assign IP addresses, as well as DNS server addresses and WINS server addresses.

Answers

1 *Connectionless*. Check out "Understanding the core protocols."

2 *Subnet mask; default gateway*. Take a look at "Understanding IP addressing."

3 *Connectionless; connection*. Review "Hooking up with the TCP/IP connectivity utilities."

4 *IPCONFIG*. See "Examining the TCP/IP diagnostic tools."

5 *MAC*. See "Understanding the core protocols."

6 *PING*. Review "Examining the TCP/IP diagnostic tools."

7 *Scope*. Review "Installing and configuring DHCP servers."

8 *DHCP*. Review "Using Dynamic Host Configuration Protocol (DHCP)."

9 *True*. Review "Reaping the rewards of DHCP."

The TCP/IP Protocol Suite

Unless you live in a cave, at the bottom of an ocean, or on one of the outer moons of Saturn, you know that TCP/IP is the collection of network protocols used on the Internet. TCP/IP may not be the smallest, fastest, or easiest to configure protocol available, but it's by far the most common, and one of the more robust. Literally billions of computers throughout the world communicate through the magic of TCP/IP.

Microsoft, as it has done with many technologies, has added a few of its own features to the TCP/IP protocol suite, making TCP/IP one of the best protocol choices for mid- to large-sized networks. Installing TCP/IP on Windows NT includes numerous core protocols, connectivity utilities, and diagnostic utilities. We explore these components in the following sections.

Understanding the core protocols

TCP/IP is not, as many people think, a single network protocol. TCP, the Transport Control Protocol, and IP, the Internet Protocol, are the two primary components of the TCP/IP suite. Some of the other core protocols that you may see referenced on your exam are the Address Resolution Protocol (ARP), the Internet Control Message Protocol (ICMP), and the User Datagram Protocol (UDP). In the following sections of this chapter, we explore each of these suite component categories in greater detail.

Throughout this chapter, I refer to the Open Systems Interconnect (OSI) network model. You don't need to worry about memorizing the seven OSI layers for the Enterprise exam, but you need more information before you take the Networking Essentials exam. Check out the Networking Essentials study guide for a more in-depth exploration of the OSI model.

TCP: Making the connection

TCP, the Transport Control Protocol, is a reliable, connection-oriented, transport layer protocol. A connection is set between the two communicating devices to send and receive data. If this data is out of order, TCP reorders the information. If the expected information isn't received, it is requested again.

Think of TCP communication as a telephone conversation. A connection is made between the source and destination devices, sometimes referred to as a "virtual circuit." Files, or programs, can be transferred during the session. After the information transfer completes, both sides can agree on termination of the connection.

On your exam, you need to know the difference between TCP and UDP. The most important thing to remember is that while both are transport layer protocols, TCP is connection oriented, with guaranteed delivery. UDP is connectionless, and contains no built-in reliability.

IP: Move along, little packet

IP, the Internet Protocol, functions at the network layer of the OSI model, and is used to route packets across an internetwork. This protocol is the core of the TCP/IP suite. IP packets are delivered on a connectionless delivery system, meaning that packets are not guaranteed to arrive in the correct order, if they arrive at all.

Packets are routed based on the IP address. This unique numeric address consists of two sections: a network address and a host address. The source and destination IP addresses are glued as headers to the beginning of packets of information, in much the same way as a letter has a destination and a return address — except, fortunately, IP packets move quite a bit faster. This header information tells a network where a packet is headed, and from where it originated.

UDP or not UDP; where's the connection?

UDP, the User Datagram Protocol, is a connectionless, transport layer protocol that provides no built-in reliability. UDP offers no guarantee that data will arrive in order, if it arrives at all.

UDP is fast because it doesn't have to wait to receive acknowledgments from the destination computer. The UDP protocol is commonly used for broadcasting, which has only recently begun holding a more active stake in Internet technologies.

Resolving with ARP

ARP, the Address Resolution Protocol, as you need to know on your exam, is a network layer protocol that allows one computer to communicate with another computer by mapping the IP address — a logical, software-configured address — to the physical Media Access Control (MAC) address burned into the network interface card (NIC) in your computer. If your computer needs to send information to another computer on a TCP/IP-based network, your computer checks to see whether it has sent information to that computer before. Your computer first looks in its cache to see whether the destination computer's network card address is listed. If the address isn't listed in the cache, ARP broadcasts the IP address to the network and asks everyone to take a look at it. If a system recognizes the address, it sends a reply directly to the system that made the ARP request. ARP now knows the destination network card's physical address, and stores the address in local cache for approximately two minutes.

ICMP, what do you see?

ICMP, the Internet Control Message Protocol, is a network layer protocol essential for diagnostics and error reporting for the TCP/IP protocol suite. While you shouldn't expect to see ICMP on your Enterprise exam, it is an important part of the suite, so we give you a quick rundown. The utilities PING (Packet InterNet Groper), which is used to see whether an IP address is active and reachable, and TRACERT, which TRACEs the RouTe an IP packet takes from source to destination, both use this protocol. ICMP provides error messages when IP transmissions run into problems such as time-outs or unreachable destinations.

You may see a question or two referring to connection-oriented versus connectionless TCP/IP protocol components. If you see a question asking about a connectionless protocol, look for answers dealing with UDP, IP, ICMP, or TFTP.

Hooking up with the TCP/IP connectivity utilities

As far as TCP/IP connectivity utilities go, dozens, if not hundreds, of options are available. Fortunately, NT includes only eight of these utilities — FINGER, FTP, LPR, RCP, REXEC, RSH, TELNET, and TFTP — and these are the only eight utilities you need to focus on for the exam. Table 8-1 provides descriptions of these utilities.

Table 8-1	TCP/IP Connectivity Utilities
Utility	*Description*
FINGER	FINGER retrieves user and account information from a remote computer.
FTP	The File Transfer Protocol provides a connection-oriented file transfer between systems running TCP/IP.
LPR	Line Printer Request sends a print request to a printer running the Line Printer Daemon (LPD) service. (See also LPQ in Table 8-2.)
RCP	The Remote Copy Program copies files from a client computer to a UNIX-based system running the Remote Shell Daemon (rshd).
REXEC	Use Remote EXECution to execute commands on a remote UNIX-based computer.
RSH	Use the Remote Shell utility to control a command interpreter on a remote UNIX-based host.

Utility	Description
TELNET	The Telnet utility provides terminal emulation from a client computer to a host computer.
TFTP	The Trivial File Transfer Protocol is the connectionless, UDP implementation of the File Transfer Protocol, and is used to transfer files between two TCP/IP systems.

Examining the TCP/IP diagnostic tools

Much like connectivity utilities, dozens of TCP/IP diagnostics tools are available. The nine included with Windows NT — ARP, HOSTNAME, IPCONFIG, LPQ, NBTSTAT, NETSTAT, PING, ROUTE, and TRACERT — all are fair game on the Enterprise exam. You can use these utilities to diagnose, trace, and troubleshoot TCP/IP problems. Table 8-2 provides more information on these nine utilities.

Table 8-2	TCP/IP Diagnostic Tools
Tool	**Description**
ARP	Allows one computer to communicate with another computer by mapping the IP address — a logical, software-configured address — to the physical MAC address burned into the NIC in your computer. For more information about ARP (the Address Resolution Protocol), see "Understanding the core protocols," earlier in this chapter.
HOSTNAME	Displays your system's host name.
IPCONFIG	Displays your system's current IP configuration, and releases or refreshes an IP address assigned by a DHCP server.
LPQ	Displays the contents of a print queue on a system running the Line Printer Daemon (LPD) service.
NBTSTAT	Displays the statistics of the current NBT (NetBIOS over TCP/IP) session.
NETSTAT	Displays current TCP/IP statistics.
PING	Tests whether an IP address is active and reachable. (PING is an acronym for Packet InterNet Groper, running over ICMP.)
ROUTE	Displays or modifies the local routing table.
TRACERT	Displays the path taken by a TCP/IP communications packet from one system to another. This tool runs over ICMP.

The IPCONFIG utility has several available switches. You should be aware of these switches for your exam:

/?   Display the help message that describes the available switches.

/all   Display full configuration information.

/release   Release the DHCP-assigned IP address for the specified adapter.

/renew   Renew the DHCP-assigned IP address for the specified adapter.

Understanding IP addressing

You don't need to know much about IP addressing on the Enterprise exam. If anything, you may need to know some of the basic theory behind TCP/IP addressing.

Each host on your network must have a unique IP address. Any system you want to use to interface with the Internet must have an IP address unique to the Internet. A registry organization known as the InterNIC assigns that unique IP address. When combined with a subnet mask, an IP address provides two important pieces of information: the network number to which a host belongs, and the unique host ID on that network.

Here's a simple example of using a subnet mask to determine the network number and host ID. Suppose your IP address is 192.168.104.39, and your subnet mask is 255.255.255.0. The network number in this case is 192.168.104.0, and the host ID is 39. The first three octets of the subnet mask are 255, meaning you use the first three octets of the IP address to determine the network number, and the non-masked octet, the last number, as the host ID.

Installing and viewing TCP/IP configuration information

If you didn't choose TCP/IP during the installation of Windows NT, you can add it through the Network Control Panel's Protocols tab. To view and configure Windows NT TCP/IP protocol configuration information, select TCP/IP from the Protocols tab, and then click the Properties button to open the dialog box shown in Figure 8-1. The initial tab, IP Address, displays your most basic, required TCP/IP information, including the IP address, the subnet mask, and the default gateway. You can enter Domain Name Server (DNS) and Windows Internet Name Service (WINS) configuration on the corresponding tabs. We cover WINS and DNS in more detail in Chapter 9.

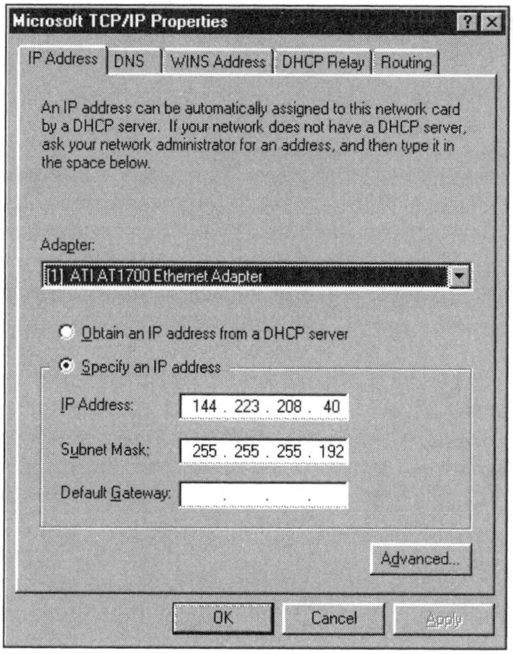

Figure 8-1:
The TCP/IP
Properties
dialog box.

Suppose you're running DHCP. It's quite possible that none of your IP configuration information is listed on this interface — you may only have the Obtain an IP Address from a DHCP Server option turned on. In this case, viewing your IP configuration requires some work from the command line. From the command line, you can issue the IPCONFIG command to see basic IP information. For more detailed information, including DNS and WINS server information, you can enter IPCONFIG /ALL.

Using Dynamic Host Configuration Protocol (DHCP)

Without properly configured IP information, your computer can't communicate with other systems on a network. At a minimum, to communicate with systems on your local subnet, you must configure the IP address and subnet mask. To communicate with systems on remote subnets, you must also define a default gateway. Additionally, if you use WINS or DNS for your network, you need to enter the addresses of the corresponding servers on the TCP/IP Properties configuration tabs. Entering all this information on hundreds of systems throughout an enterprise leaves a great deal of room for error — and that's where DHCP comes in.

Reaping the rewards of DHCP

The Dynamic Host Configuration Protocol takes some of the headache out of tracking and configuring IP hosts. With DHCP, an administrator can create a range of IP addresses called a *scope,* with addresses that can be leased to the DHCP clients. Leasing allows addresses to be assigned on a temporary basis. Clients renew an IP lease after one-half the lease period defined in the DHCP configuration utility. In addition to assigning the IP addresses, DHCP can set the subnet mask, default gateway, WINS servers, DNS servers — anything that would otherwise need to be set manually for TCP/IP.

You can also benefit from using DHCP if you have fewer IP addresses than workstations, but don't require connectivity for all your workstations at the same time. You can use DHCP to assign addresses to clients on an "as-needed" basis. For example, suppose your office is open 24 hours a day, and you have three different shifts of agents, each with his or her own work-station. Only one-third of the workstations are ever in use at a time.

If you use DHCP, you don't need to have a static address assigned to each workstation; your DHCP server can assign IP addresses as the workstation boots. You can set your lease time to around four hours, and set a scope of IP addresses containing perhaps only half as many IP addresses as you have workstations. In this way, you can have fewer IP addresses than workstations.

Using DHCP to configure TCP/IP on the client computers offers several benefits:

- ✔ Administrators can enter and send additional TCP/IP information to the client computer, such as WINS and DNS server IP addresses.

- ✔ Administrators don't have to visit each client to configure TCP/IP.

- ✔ The DHCP server won't assign the same address twice.

- ✔ Global information (DNS, WINS servers) is entered only once, minimizing the possibility of errors. And if these server IP addresses change, the address only needs to be corrected in one place.

- ✔ DHCP can automatically reconfigure a client that moves to another subnet, making it ideal for mobile or notebook users who attach to your network from various subnets.

- ✔ The Administrator can control which IP addresses are assigned to specific systems in cases where you want to make sure a particular client always receives a particular IP address.

Configuring DHCP clients

On the exam, you may be presented with a question similar to the following example: Your network is a mixed environment, consisting of Windows NT Workstation, NT Server, Windows 95, Windows for Workgroups, and MS DOS 3.0 Network clients. Which of the systems must be manually configured, and which ones are capable of receiving their information from a DHCP server?

Answer: All these systems are capable of receiving IP information from a DHCP server.

Locally configured information, such as DNS and WINS server information, overrides DHCP-assigned settings, so configuring a client to use DHCP requires two steps. First, make sure the Obtain an IP Address from a DHCP Server option box is selected. (As shown in Figure 8-1, you find this option on the IP Address tab in the TCP/IP Properties dialog box.) Next, check other tabs in the TCP/IP Properties dialog box, and clear away DNS addresses, WINS addresses, or other variables that you are assigning via DHCP.

A final note on clients: When changing from a static IP to a DHCP-assigned address, you don't need to reboot the client computer. However, if you change from DHCP back to a static IP address, you must reboot before your changes are applied.

Installing and configuring DHCP servers

Microsoft Windows NT 4.0 Server includes a DHCP Server service. In fact, Microsoft has included a DHCP Server service since the release of NT 3.5. You install the DHCP Server service in the same way as any other network service — through the Services tab in the Control Panel's Network applet. After you install the service, you find the administrative interface under the Programs⇨Administrative Tools program group.

In the DHCP management utility, you define a *scope* of valid IP addresses that the server will be able to assign. You must define one scope per valid subnet that you want the server to manage. If you have statically assigned IP addresses on any non-DHCP systems (such as network print devices or UNIX servers) within the range of IP addresses in your scope, you must exclude these addresses from your scope to prevent the DHCP server from assigning an IP address already in use on your network. If you have a DHCP client that must always have the same IP address, such as a DNS server, you can create a *client reservation,* forcing DHCP to assign a specific IP address based on the MAC address of the client you want to make static.

Prep Test

1 For what purpose would you implement the Dynamic Host Configuration Protocol on your network?

A ○ Resolving fully qualified domain names to IP addresses

B ○ Assigning and maintaining IP address information on a TCP/IP network

C ○ Dynamically assigning original NetBIOS names to clients on your network

D ○ Providing dynamic connectivity to UNIX file and print services

2 Tim, one of your end users running NT Workstation 4.0, is unable to resolve the IP address for your corporate intranet Web server. You recently began using DHCP on your network to assign IP information, and DHCP configures the clients with your corporate DNS server for IP resolution. No one else on your network is reporting any problems getting to the intranet. You check your DHCP scope, and everything appears correct. You can PING the Web server by IP, but not by name. What should you try next?

A ○ Remove NWLink from the list of network protocols, because it can interfere with IP resolution.

B ○ Check to see whether Tim has locally configured a DNS server address, and if so, remove the address.

C ○ Tim can't access the intranet without a static IP. Exclude his address from the DHCP scope, and manually configure his TCP/IP information.

D ○ Check to see whether Tim has locally configured his DNS service, and manually add the server address if he hasn't.

3 Which of the following components of the TCP/IP protocol suite are considered connectionless? (Choose all that apply.)

A ❑ TCP

B ❑ IP

C ❑ TELNET

D ❑ ICMP

E ❑ UDP

4 You are setting up a client PC on your TCP/IP network. You assign the address 130.30.5.15, and you assign the value 255.255.0.0 for the subnet mask. What is the network number for this subnet?

A ○ 15

B ○ 130.30.0.0

C ○ 5.15

D ○ 130.30.5.0

5 You are setting up a client PC on your TCP/IP network. You assign the address 130.30.5.15, and you assign the value 255.255.0.0 for the subnet mask. What is the host ID for this client?

A ○ 15

B ○ 130.30.0.0

C ○ 5.15

D ○ 130.30.5.0

6 Which of the following settings must be configured in order to communicate with a TCP/IP host on a remote subnet? (Choose all that apply.)

A ❑ Subnet mask

B ❑ Default gateway

C ❑ IP address

D ❑ ARP cache location

7 Your network is a mixed environment, consisting of Windows NT Workstation, NT Server, Windows 95, Windows for Workgroups, UNIX, and MS-DOS 3.0 Network clients. Which of these systems *cannot* take advantage of DHCP?

A ○ Windows NT

B ○ Windows 95

C ○ Windows for Workgroups

D ○ UNIX

E ○ MS-DOS 3.0

8 Which of the following TCP/IP utilities can you use to display the path taken by a TCP/IP communications packet from one system to another?

A ○ PING

B ○ TELNET

C ○ ROUTE

D ○ TRACERT

9 You are setting up a DHCP server in your enterprise. You're using a TCP/IP network interface print device on one of the segments where you will be implementing DHCP. What must you do to prevent the DHCP server from assigning the IP address for the print device to a client on your network?

A ○ Make up an arbitrary IP address for the print device.

B ○ Exclude the print device IP address from your scope in the DHCP management utility.

C ○ Make a client reservation in the DHCP management utility that will always assign the same IP address to the print device.

D ○ Do nothing. DHCP automatically checks an IP address before assigning it, so you won't have any duplicate IPs assigned.

Answers

1 B. Assigning and maintaining IP address information on a TCP/IP network. DHCP facilitates automatic assignment of IP addresses and configuration of numerous address-specific IP services. *See "Using Dynamic Host Configuration Protocol (DHCP)" for more benefits to implementing a DHCP server.*

2 B. Check to see whether Tim has locally configured a DNS server address, and if so, remove the address. Locally defined IP settings, such as DNS or WINS server addresses, override settings defined on a DHCP server. *See "Configuring DHCP clients" for more information.*

3 B, D, and E. IP, ICMP, and UDP are all connectionless components of the TCP/IP protocol suite. Another prominent connectionless utility is TFTP. FTP, on the other hand, is connection-based. *Review "Understanding the core protocols" and the subsections that discuss these protocols.*

4 B. 130.30.0.0. Because the first two octets are masked by the subnet mask, the first two octets specify the network number. *Review "Understanding IP addressing."*

5 C. 5.15. After blocking off the network number, the last two octets remain, designating the host ID as 5.15. *Review "IP addressing."*

6 A, B, and C. All three are required to communicate to a system on a remote subnet. To communicate only with systems on the same subnet, you don't need to define a default gateway. No ARP cache location setting exists. *See "Using Dynamic Host Configuration Protocol (DHCP)" for more information.*

7 D. UNIX. UNIX can't take advantage of the DHCP service. If you have UNIX machines on the same subnets as clients that you plan to manage with DHCP, you need to exclude their addresses when you create the DHCP scopes. *The section "Installing and configuring DHCP servers" discusses this topic.*

8 D. TRACERT. TRACERT displays the address of each IP device that a packet passes through on the way to its destination. *See "Examining the TCP/IP diagnostic tools" — in particular, Table 8-2 for a list of the TCP/IP utilities.*

9 B. Exclude the print device IP address from your scope in the DHCP management utility. Excluding the address of the print device keeps NT from assigning a duplicate to one of the DHCP clients. DHCP doesn't check for the existence of an IP address before assigning an address to a client, so you must make sure you don't duplicate any IP addresses in your scope definitions. You can only make a client reservation for systems that can act as a DHCP client, a function that network interface print devices can't perform. *Review "Configuring DHCP clients."*

Chapter 9

Windows Internet Name Service (WINS)

• •

Exam Objectives

▶ Understanding the WINS technology

▶ Installing and configuring a WINS server

▶ Configuring static mappings in the WINS database

▶ Configuring WINS replication

• •

*Y*our Enterprise exam may cover some aspects of WINS, but many other features of WINS won't be covered on the exam. In this chapter, we show you what you should know about WINS for the exam, and what you can safely overlook. We offer an overview of WINS, and we discuss the installation and configuration of a WINS server — two potential topics for exam questions. We also discuss other aspects of WINS that you may encounter on the Enterprise exam, such as replication and static mappings.

Make sure you have a good understanding of the following concepts, because they are likely exam question candidates:

✔ Installing a WINS server, and what is required for the installation.

✔ Knowing how and where to add a static mapping for a non-WINS client.

✔ Understanding the use of the WINS proxy, and that it is required for non-WINS clients.

✔ Understanding database replication, such as with push and pull partners. Understand when you should configure a WINS server as a push or pull partner.

We include several hints in this chapter for you to keep in mind when you see these scenario-based questions on the exam.

Quick Assessment

Under-
standing
the WINS
technology

1 A WINS server resolves _____ to IP addresses.

2 WINS is a dynamic replacement for _____.

3 A WINS server can be queried if a _____ server can't resolve a name.

Installing
and
configuring
a WINS
server

4 (True/False). If a client attempts to register a name and the name already exists, a *name query request* is sent to the existing computer.

5 (True/False). A WINS server must be on some type of domain controller, such as a primary or backup.

Configuring
static
mappings in
the WINS
database

6 Which type of static address mapping permits only one address per name?

7 A non-WINS client must have a static mapping or use a(n) _____ to use WINS.

Configuring
WINS
replication

8 The replication partner that "forces" its updates to another partner is the _____ partner.

9 The replication partner on the opposite end of a WAN link should be the _____ partner.

10 (True/False). Entries in the WINS database are either Active, Renewed, or Released.

Answers

1 *NetBIOS names.* Review "Understanding the WINS Technology."

2 *LMHOSTS.* Review "Understanding the WINS Technology."

3 *DNS.* See "WINS/DNS Integration."

4 *True.* Review "Using WINS."

5 *False.* Refer to "Implementing WINS."

6 *Unique.* Check out "Configuring the WINS Server."

7 *WINS proxy.* Refer to "Configuring the Non-WINS Client."

8 *Push.* Review "Database Replication."

9 *Pull.* Review "Database Replication."

10 *False.* See "Maintaining the WINS Database."

Understanding the WINS Technology

To help you understand where WINS fits in the whole Microsoft networking scheme, we need to discuss the evolution of WINS, and the purpose WINS serves. Understanding the role of the WINS server is important for the exam.

As you may know, the NetBIOS interface is important for Microsoft Windows-based operating systems. NetBIOS names are required for communicating with other machines on the network. NetBIOS networks have traditionally been broadcast-based networks, which works fine for smaller networks. However, broadcasts aren't recommended for larger networks, especially WANs, because routers by default don't pass broadcast messages. Also, the more computers on the network broadcasting, the more these broadcasts use precious bandwidth.

The LMHOSTS file was a solution to the problem of NetBIOS broadcasts on the network. This static text file maps NetBIOS computer names to IP addresses. This solution limits broadcasts on the network, and is also much easier to maintain than the other static text file, the HOSTS file.

If you are using an LMHOSTS file for each computer on the network, whenever a computer's name or IP address changes, you must update the LMHOSTS file to reflect the new configuration. The LMHOSTS file, unlike the HOSTS file, has the capability to be centrally managed, which decreases the amount of time and effort needed to maintain the file. All you need to do is modify the central LMHOSTS file and have the clients include or import this file, as we discuss later in the chapter.

To overcome the need for maintaining static configuration files, the Windows Internet Name Service (WINS) was developed as a means for dynamically resolving NetBIOS names to IP addresses on the network. You can think of WINS as a dynamic, centralized LMHOSTS file.

For the exam, know that WINS offers the following benefits:

- A dynamic database that minimizes maintenance effort for the administrator
- Centralized NetBIOS name management
- Elimination of the need for static LMHOSTS files, unless they are used for fault tolerance in addition to the WINS server
- Decreased broadcast traffic
- The capability to be used with clients on remote subnets

In the following sections, we emphasize the aspects of WINS that you're most likely to see on the exam. If you don't see much coverage on a specific aspect of WINS, you can safely ignore it. It probably won't be on your exam.

WINS/DNS Integration

A WINS server can be used to resolve names for the DNS server. If a DNS client issues a request in which the server must resolve a DNS host name, the client can then query the WINS server if the DNS server is unable to resolve this name (if the client has been configured to use the WINS server). The name can be resolved and returned to the client.

Unlike the WINS database, a DNS database isn't dynamic. The static nature of a DNS database is what makes the integration between WINS and DNS so important.

Using WINS

To understand the WINS name registration and resolution process for the exam, you need to know how clients interact with the WINS server. Clients must register, renew, and sometimes release their registered names with the WINS server. In the following sections, we discuss some important details that happen during each step in the WINS registration, renewal, and release process.

Registering names

When a NetBIOS computer initializes on the network, it must register its name. Computers on the network first began using broadcasts, but now with WINS, the *name registration query* messages are sent directly to the WINS server and registered in the WINS database. You designate the WINS server to be used by the client in the Control Panel's Network applet under the TCP/IP properties.

The name registration query includes the source IP address and the NetBIOS name to be registered, as well as the destination computer's IP address. The WINS server checks the database to determine whether an entry already exists for this computer name. If no entry exists for this name, the server sends a *positive name registration response* with a time at which the client needs to renew its registration. If an entry already exists in the database, the server challenges the holder of the current registration to respond. If the current holder responds successfully, the server sends a negative registration response to the computer that's attempting to register the existing name. The server knows the address of the source computer because it was sent in the registration query message.

Renewing names

The registered name for a computer must be re-registered after a period of time known as the time-to-live (TTL). The WINS server enforces this requirement by timestamping the entries in the database as they are added and deleted. Renewing the registered names purges the entries that have expired. Entries that aren't renewed are marked as released in the WINS database.

You have control over the length of time before a computer name must be renewed. By default, this period of time is 96 hours, or four days. Adjusting the period for renewal has the following effects:

✔ If you increase the amount of time, the WINS database may become outdated and incorrect.

✔ If you decrease the amount of time, more traffic appears on the network as computers attempt to renew their names more often.

When the client must renew its name, it sends the *name refresh request* to the server, asking to refresh its registration. This request includes the IP address and the name of the source computer that wants to be renewed. The WINS server responds to the name refresh request with a *name refresh response,* which specifies a new time-to-live.

Releasing names

A computer releases a name through an orderly system shutdown. When your computer shuts down, it informs the WINS server that the names that have been registered for this computer can be removed from the database. The computer that's shutting down sends a *name release request* to the server, specifying the IP address and name that can be released.

When the WINS server receives the name release request, it searches the WINS database for the entry. The server then removes the entry from the database, and sends a *name release response* that contains the name that was requested to be released. This response doesn't mean much, because a positive or negative response doesn't affect the client computer's shutdown.

Please note that broadcasting plays no part in this process. The WINS client and server know each other's addresses from the registration requests and responses that began the process, and also from the IP address for the WINS server that you specify on the client computer.

Understanding name queries and responses

As we discuss earlier in this chapter, in the section "Registering names," a WINS client attempts to register its name with the WINS server upon initialization. The WINS server checks the database for any existing entries with that name. If a name already exists, a *name query request* is sent to the existing computer. If this computer responds with a *name query response,* the server rejects the name request by the second computer. The new name is accepted if the existing computer doesn't respond to the name query request.

Implementing WINS

We've found that planning is a significant topic in any exam, and you must consider numerous planning issues in a WINS implementation. In this section, we discuss the planning issues that may appear on your Enterprise exam.

A WINS implementation involves numerous planning issues — for example:

- ✔ How many WINS servers do you need for the number of clients on the network?
- ✔ How many WINS servers do you need for fault tolerance, backup, or recovery?
- ✔ Can the network bandwidth support WINS traffic?
- ✔ What about name registration and renewal for non-WINS clients?

In the section "Understanding the WINS Technology," we mention that the WINS servers and clients generate traffic for name registration and renewal. However, this traffic is considerably less than in broadcast-based implementations.

Although you can estimate the amount of network traffic WINS uses, you aren't required to do so for the exam. However, you may need to know the Microsoft recommendations for the number of servers required based on the number of clients on the network.

For every 10,000 clients on the network, you should have one primary WINS server and one secondary WINS server. Of course, these figures are rough estimates. If you do happen to see a question on the exam regarding this topic, just scale the recommended ratio of one server (and one backup) to 10,000 clients accordingly. For example, if you're asked how many WINS servers should be used for a network of 50,000 clients, answer five servers (and five backups). However, it's highly unlikely that you will see a question like this one on your exam.

With multiple WINS servers, database replication is important. If one WINS server becomes unavailable, the secondary WINS server can have a current database to maintain the client registrations and renewals. Later in this chapter, in the "Database Replication" section, we discuss the various methods used for maintaining the WINS server database on multiple servers.

Depending on your network topology, you must determine whether you can support WINS traffic on your network. The exam won't cover physical network implementation and WINS in terms of traffic, and we don't cover those topics either. We do cover the configuration of the WINS server to support non-WINS clients in the section "Configuring the WINS Server," later in this chapter.

Reviewing WINS server requirements

The hardware and software requirements for Microsoft products always appear on the exam. For the WINS server, one server can handle all the name registration and renewal for an entire network, even with remote subnets. The WINS packets can cross routers, unlike broadcast-based name registration methods.

Although one WINS server can support a whole network, you should add another server for fault tolerance. A secondary WINS server can replicate with the primary server and continue the registration and renewal process when the primary server goes down.

Adding a secondary server is easy — just add the IP of the secondary WINS server in the space directly below the primary WINS server on the WINS Address tab in the Control Panel's Network applet. The secondary WINS server is contacted only if the first server doesn't respond.

A few requirements for a WINS server make great exam questions. Make sure you memorize these WINS server elements:

✔ The WINS server must be running on Windows NT Server 3.5 or higher, and it doesn't have to be a domain controller.

✔ The WINS server must have static TCP/IP information such as the IP address, default gateway, and subnet mask.

Installing a WINS server

Configuring your Windows NT Server as a WINS server requires installing WINS. You add this service on the Services tab in the Control Panel's Network applet. You use the same method for installing other services — for example, the DHCP service and the DHCP Relay Agent. Lab 9-1 shows you how to configure your Windows NT Server as a WINS server.

Lab 9-1	Installing WINS

1. **Open the Network applet from the Control Panel.**

2. **Select the Services tab.**

   You see a list of installed services on your computer.

3. **Click Add.**

   You see a list of network services that are available for installation.

4. **Select the Windows Internet Name Service.**

   You may be asked to provide the Windows NT Server 4.0 CD for files to be copied. You must restart the computer for the changes to take effect. After you restart the computer, you can find an icon for the WINS Manager in the Administrative Tools program group.

Configuring the WINS Server

To configure the WINS Server, you use the WINS Manager utility that's created during installation. Before you can configure your WINS server, you must add a WINS server to WINS Manager. In addition to the local WINS server, you can add remote servers that will be managed by your local WINS Manager.

After you add the WINS server, you can configure it with the WINS Manager graphical interface. To configure a WINS server, you must be a member of the Administrators group on that server. This requirement prevents unauthorized users from wreaking havoc on the network. You have numerous configuration options in the WINS Server Configuration dialog box, shown in Figure 9-1. To access the WINS Server Configuration dialog box, choose Server⇨Configuration.

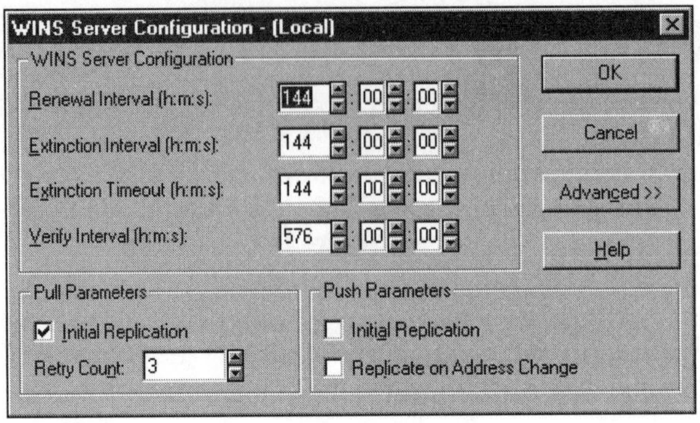

Figure 9-1:
The WINS
server
configuration.

It's difficult to predict which of these configuration options may make it to your exam, so we briefly discuss them all, and focus on the most important items to know for the exam. If you have access to WINS Manager, we recommend that you follow along, taking note of how you specify these options.

Here's a listing of the configuration options for the WINS server (we list the default values where possible, because the exam often includes questions about these values):

- **Renewal Interval.** The duration before the WINS clients must renew their leases. Default is 96 hours.

- **Extinction Interval.** The interval between entries marked as released before they become extinct. The default is the same as the setting for the renewal interval.

- **Extinction Timeout.** The length of time before extinct entries are scavenged from the database. The default is the same as the setting for the renewal interval.

- **Verify Interval.** The amount of time before the server verifies whether entries from other WINS servers are still active. Default is 576 hours (24 days).

- **Pull Parameters.** Check box that determines whether this server pulls information from the replicating WINS servers. This option also includes the number of times the server retries connecting to a remote WINS server. Default is checked, with a retry count of 3.

- **Push Parameters.** Check box that determines whether the server notifies the partners that the local database has changed.

- **Replicate on Address Change.** Check box that specifies whether the server notifies other partners when a name registration changes.

Don't expect any really in-depth questions regarding these options, with the exception of push and pull partners, which have their own section later in this chapter.

In addition to these options, you can set some advanced options. But based on our experience, as well as the experiences of many other people we've talked to, these advanced options won't be on the exam. WINS server configuration has way too many details to be covered effectively.

Adding static mapping for clients

As we discuss in the section "Understanding the WINS Technology," earlier in this chapter, WINS is for Microsoft Windows-based machines that use NetBIOS names to establish and maintain sessions between computers. If your network includes non-Windows-based computers, or machines that you don't plan to configure as WINS clients, you must do some additional configuring to accommodate these clients.

Adding static mappings for clients in the WINS database is a fairly easy task. You must manually add the mapping of the NetBIOS name to the IP address on the server. Remember, you can achieve the same effect by using LMHOSTS, but this method is more efficient for a couple of reasons:

✔ The WINS server is queried before the LMHOSTS file is parsed.

✔ LMHOSTS files must be maintained for these non-WINS clients.

Another reason for creating a static mapping for clients is to reserve the name for an important machine, such as a server that must maintain the same name. For example, if a machine were to register a name that was being used by a server that's down for repair, when the server reinitializes, it couldn't use its existing name because that name has been taken. A static mapping avoids this situation.

You add, modify, and delete static mappings by using options in the WINS Manager's Mappings menu. Table 9-1 describes the various static mapping types and the purpose of each type. To prepare for the exam, be sure you know the types of mappings that you can create.

Table 9-1	Static Mappings and Their Characteristics
Type	*Description*
Unique	Type of address that permits only one address per name. The unique name is the name of the computer.
Group	A normal group that doesn't have IP addresses stored for the computers in the group. A normal group is used for broadcasts and browsing the domain.
Internet Group	A group that can contain IP addresses for as many as 25 primary and backup domain controllers. This type is used for domain controllers to communicate with each other.

(continued)

Table 9-1 *(continued)*	
Type	**Description**
Multihomed	Similar to a Unique mapping, but this address can contain as many as 25 addresses that are used for *multihomed systems* (computers with more than one network interface card and IP address).

Lab 9-2 demonstrates how you add these static mappings to the WINS database.

Lab 9-2   Adding Static Mappings for Non-WINS Clients

1. **Open up WINS Manager.**

2. **Choose Mappings⇨Static Mappings.**

   If you have added any NetBIOS names to IP address static mappings, they are listed in the dialog box that's displayed.

3. **Click Add Mappings.**

   A dialog box appears for you to enter the computer name, IP address, and the type of mapping.

4. **Enter the name of the computer for the mapping.**

5. **Enter the IP address.**

6. **For the mapping type, select Unique.**

7. **Click Add.**

8. **Click Close.**

You see three entries for the mapping you just made in the Static Mappings dialog box. The three entries are for the NetBIOS service types of Redirector, Messenger, and Server.

Reviewing WINS client requirements

Microsoft certification exams often include questions concerning minimum hardware or software requirements for using the product, and the WINS client requirements are no exception. Here are the operating systems required of a WINS client:

✔ Windows NT 3.5 or higher, Server or Workstation

✔ Windows 95, or Windows for Workgroups 3.11 with TCP/IP services installed

- ✔ Microsoft MS-DOS network client 3.0 or higher
- ✔ LAN Manager Server 2.2c or higher

You must specify the use of a WINS server, either manually at the client, or through the use of DHCP.

Almost every Microsoft exam we've taken has included questions concerning integrating other operating systems such as UNIX and Novell NetWare. Integrating non-WINS clients into the network is another example of this type of question. These non-WINS clients must use one of two methods:

- ✔ You can create a static mapping for the non-WINS client in the WINS server database. The static mapping consists of a NetBIOS name and IP address mapping. You create the static mapping with the WINS Manager utility.

- ✔ You can install a WINS proxy on the subnet with non-WINS clients to listen for NetBIOS broadcasts and to relay those messages to the WINS server. Remember, b-node broadcasts can't pass through routers, so the non-WINS clients must be on the same subnet as the WINS proxy, and you may also need a WINS proxy for each subnet of non-WINS clients.

You can find more information about static mappings and the WINS proxy in the next section of this chapter.

Configuring a WINS Client

You can configure the client to use WINS in two ways: through the use of DHCP, or by manually configuring the client. This section describes the requirements for each method as it applies to the exam.

For a DHCP-enabled client, you need to specify two DHCP options at the server in DHCP Manager:

- ✔ 044 WINS/NetBIOS Name Service Servers
- ✔ 046 WINS/NetBT Node Type

In addition to these settings, you have to configure your client to use DHCP. You configure your client to use DHCP by using the Control Panel's Network applet.

For manual configuration of the client, you must enter the IP address of the primary WINS server, and optionally, the IP address of the secondary WINS server in the TCP/IP properties. You enter these settings on the WINS Address tab in the TCP/IP Properties dialog box.

Another client configuration issue you should understand involves the roles of the primary and secondary WINS servers. Although you can configure your clients to use both of these servers, the clients use only the primary server. The clients use the secondary server only if the primary server becomes unreachable. Even though the client is registering and renewing with the secondary server, the client continually checks the primary server until it comes back online.

Configuring the Non-WINS Client

You should understand that non-WINS clients don't really need to be configured to take advantage of the WINS server for name registration and resolution. However, these clients need a WINS proxy. A WINS proxy listens for and intercepts the name-query broadcast messages that it hears on the local subnet. The WINS proxy is the intermediary between the non-WINS client and the WINS server. Non-WINS clients make great candidates for static mappings in the DHCP Manager utility.

Database Replication

Replication between WINS servers maintains current mappings for clients so that any computer in the enterprise network can resolve any other computer's NetBIOS name. Two different methods exist for replicating changes to other WINS servers: push or pull partners.

It's a tug of war: Push or pull partners

Exam questions on push and pull often involve scenarios in which you must determine the best combination of push or pull partners. These challenging questions require a thorough understanding of the two methods.

Push partners send their updated information to the replicating pull partner. They inform the partners that the database has changed, and they send the new entries to the pull partners. A push partner can be configured to notify the partners that the database has changed in two ways:

✔ By a predetermined amount of WINS updates specified by the administrator in the WINS Manager.

✔ By immediately replicating the updated entries, which is also specified by the WINS administrator in the WINS Manager.

Think of a push partner as "forcing" its updates to the partners, and a pull partner as being more civilized, waiting for an interval of time before asking its partner for an update.

Pull partners request entries that have higher version numbers than entries existing in the WINS database. As with push partners, pull partners can perform these requests at predetermined amounts of updates, or by immediately replicating the updated entries.

Configuring replication

You must make several considerations when determining whether to make a server a push or a pull partner. Here are the two most important considerations for determining whether to make it a push or pull partner:

- ✔ Whether the partner crosses a WAN link
- ✔ The importance of maintaining a current database

A WINS server on the other end of a WAN link is a great candidate for a pull partner. By configuring the servers in this way, you can control when the pull partner requests the updates from the push partners on the other side of the WAN link. For example, you can have the pull partner request updates every 12 hours. If this server were configured as a push partner, you would have no control over when this server would push its updated entries across the WAN link. In Figure 9-2, Server 2 is configured as a pull partner to request updated entries every 12 hours because it's on the opposite side of the WAN link.

If you're on a much faster link, such as a LAN, you should configure both servers to act as push and pull servers for each other. By doing so, you ensure that the entries in the database are as current as possible. In Figure 9-3, Server 1 and Server 2 are both configured as push and pull partners of each other to take advantage of the faster LAN link.

Remember this rule when you are faced with the placement of WINS servers for replication: The longer the distance, (which most often equals the slowest link), the less frequent the updates. For example, if you have links between two schools in one city, the replication frequency can be more frequent, such as every 15 minutes or less. If these schools must replicate with another server across the country, the replication frequency should be less frequent — for example, every hour.

If you remember the placement of the servers in relation to the WAN link, these types of questions should be no problem for you.

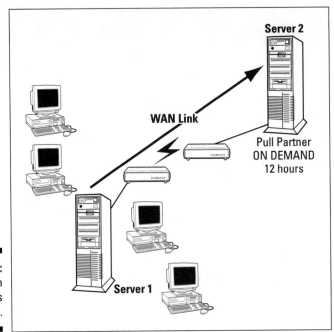

Figure 9-2:
Replication
across
WAN links.

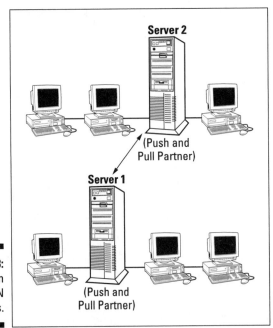

Figure 9-3:
Replication
across LAN
links.

You must remember one very important fact about primary and secondary WINS servers as far replication is concerned: They must be push and pull partners to each other. This setup ensures that the client can continue with the secondary WINS server if the primary server becomes unavailable. The client also continually checks to see whether the primary server is available.

Maintaining the WINS Database

The Enterprise exam doesn't cover maintaining the WINS database in as much detail as name registration and renewal or replication, but we must discuss this topic. You must perform numerous actions on the WINS database, similar to those you perform with the DHCP database. These actions include backing up, restoring, and compacting the database. As you can imagine, lots of activity takes place within the WINS database, such as adding and updating leases, resolving names, and housekeeping.

Table 9-2 shows the components that make up the WINS database. Remember these components just in case you are asked what makes up the WINS database.

Table 9-2	Components of the WINS Database
Component	*Description*
Wins.mdb	The WINS server database
Winstmp.mdb	A temporary file created by the WINS database for maintenance
J50.log and J50#####.log	A log with database transactions to recover data if necessary
J50.chk	The checkpoint file

Backing up the database

Within WINS Manager, you have tools for backing up the WINS database. You need to specify a directory in which you want to back up the database, and then the database is automatically backed up at the intervals you specify — every three hours is the default. For a complete backup, also back up the Registry entries for the WINS server.

We can just see a question on the exam that resembles this example: "What must be done prior to backing up the database of a WINS server?" Of course, the answer is obvious after reading the preceding paragraph.

When you are preparing for an exam, make sure that you're studying the latest material to avoid test disaster. For example, the default automatic backup interval of the WINS database has changed from Windows NT 3.51 to Windows NT 4.0. We discovered the installation default for the automatic backup for Windows NT 4.0 is every three hours, but the default for Windows NT 3.5 is every 24 hours.

Restoring the database

If you see a question on the exam covering restoring the WINS database, you should know that you can do this task in two ways:

- ✔ You can use WINS Manager.
- ✔ You can manually move the database files.

When you are restoring using WINS Manager, simply point to the directory in which the good database files are located.

Manually moving the database files involves deleting the J50.log, J50#####.log, and Winstmp.mdb files from the WINS directory, and then copying only the Wins.mdb file to the WINS directory. After you restart WINS, the log and temp files are created automatically.

Compacting the database

Although Windows NT 4.0 automatically compacts the WINS database, you may need to manually compact the database anyway. Like the DHCP database or a hard drive, the WINS database can become fragmented. When entries are removed, they leave gaps that aren't often filled with new entries. Compacting the database not only decreases the size of the database, but also speeds up transactions. Microsoft recommends compacting the database when it grows larger than 30MB.

Using the Jetpack utility

You can use the Jetpack utility to compact the WINS database. Any question regarding compaction will most likely be on the command-line syntax of this utility. The Jetpack.exe utility has the following syntax:

```
jetpack database_name temp database_name
```

The temp database is used for the compaction process and is deleted after the process completes.

In addition to knowing the Jetpack syntax, remember that you must stop the WINS server before the compaction process, either by using the Services applet in the Control Panel or by entering the following command:

```
net stop wins
```

Good news! The syntax for the Jetpack utility is the same as for the DHCP database. Everything we tell you in this section works for the DHCP database, except that you stop WINS here, and not the DHCP service.

Removing obsolete database entries

Each entry in the WINS database is in one of three states:

- ✔ Active
- ✔ Released
- ✔ Extinct

The process of removing obsolete database entries is called *scavenging*. Looking at the list of three states, you can see that you want to scavenge the extinct entries from the database. The only thing you should probably remember about the scavenging process is that it occurs automatically, based on the settings you enter for the Renewal and Extinction Intervals in the WINS Server Configuration dialog box (refer to Figure 9-2, earlier in this chapter). Obsolete entries are removed more quickly if you configure entries to become extinct more rapidly.

Prep Test

1 What is the default interval before a computer name must be renewed?

A ◯ 2 days

B ◯ 3 days

C ◯ 4 days

D ◯ 6 days

2 What must be configured to allow WINS packets to cross routers to remote WINS clients?

A ◯ IP forwarding must be enabled.

B ◯ A WINS proxy must be on the same subnet.

C ◯ An entry in the routing table must be specified.

D ◯ Nothing.

3 You have eight subnets with 500 computers on each subnet. This network is DHCP-enabled with non-WINS clients on some of the subnets. How many WINS servers do you recommend, and why?

A ◯ Only one WINS server, because that's all you need for a network of this size

B ◯ One primary and one secondary WINS server, because that's all you need for a network of this size

C ◯ Two primary and two secondary WINS servers, because you have reached the limit of just one server

D ◯ One primary server, with a secondary server for each remote subnet that contains non-WINS clients

4 If you're manually restoring the WINS database, what step do you take after deleting the files in the WINS directory?

A ◯ Stop WINS.

B ◯ Copy the backup Wins.mdb file to the WINS directory.

C ◯ Start WINS.

D ◯ Copy the backup Wins.mdb, J50.log, J50#####.log, and Winstmp.mdb files to the WINS directory.

5 At your corporate headquarters in Atlanta, you have four WINS servers that are configured to replicate with a WINS server in Boston and another in Seattle. How do you configure replication for these servers?

A ○ Configure Atlanta's WINS servers on the LAN as push and pull partners of each other, and configure Boston and Seattle as pull partners.

B ○ Configure Atlanta's WINS servers on the LAN as push and pull partners of each other, and configure Boston and Seattle as push partners.

C ○ Configure Atlanta's WINS servers on the LAN as push partners of each other, and configure Boston and Seattle as push partners.

D ○ Configure Atlanta's WINS servers on the LAN as pull partners of each other, and configure Boston and Seattle as push partners.

6 Which is not a factor when considering whether a WINS server should be a push or pull partner?

A ○ Whether the database must be updated often for accuracy

B ○ Whether you have remote subnets with non-WINS clients

C ○ Whether a WAN link is involved

D ○ Whether the server is primary or secondary

7 For a DHCP-enabled client that's configured to use the WINS server, which DHCP options do you have to configure at the server?

A ○ 046 WINS/NetBIOS Name Service Servers, and 048 WINS/NetBT Node Type

B ○ 044 WINS/NetBIOS Name Service Servers, and 046 WINS/NetBT Node Type

C ○ 046 WINS/NetBT Node Type, and 045 WINS/NetBIOS Name Service Servers

D ○ 045 WINS/NetBT Node Type, and 046 WINS/NetBIOS Name Service Servers

8 What information is required when adding a static entry in the WINS database for a non-WINS client?

A ○ IP address, mapping type, and name

B ○ Name, unique mapping type

C ○ IP address, node type, and group name

D ○ IP address, mapping type, node type, and name

Answers

1 *C. 4 days.* You can adjust this default value, but doing so affects the database by either creating too much renewal traffic, or leaving outdated entries in the database. *See "Renewing names" for more information.*

2 *D. Nothing.* Although you must have a WINS proxy on the same subnet as non-WINS clients, you don't have to configure the WINS server in any way for the packets to reach the remote clients. *Review "Configuring the Non-WINS Client."*

3 *B. For a network of this size, you need only one primary and one secondary WINS server.* It's always recommended to use a secondary WINS server for fault tolerance, even when you haven't exceeded the limits of one WINS server. *Review "Implementing WINS."*

4 *B. Copy the backup Wins.mdb file to the WINS directory.* This is the only file that you need to copy to the WINS directory after the other files have been deleted or moved. WINS automatically creates the other files. *See "Maintaining the WINS Database" for more information, and review Table 9-2.*

5 *A. Configure Atlanta's WINS servers on the LAN as push and pull partners of each other, with Boston and Seattle configured as pull partners.* Remember, remote WINS servers make excellent candidates for pull partners because you can configure them to pull information at certain intervals. *Review "Configuring the WINS Server."*

6 *B. Whether you have remote subnets with non-WINS clients.* This makes no difference in terms of push or pull partners, unless the remote subnets are across WAN links. *Review "Configuring the WINS Server."*

7 *B. 044 WINS/NetBIOS Name Service Servers, and 046 WINS/NetBT Node Type.* If the client is configured via DHCP, you must manually specify the IP address of the WINS server(s) at each client. *See "Configuring a WINS Client."*

8 *A. IP address, mapping type, and name all are required for the static mapping.* Remember, this is one of the exam objectives. *For more information, see "Adding static mapping for clients," as well as Table 9-1.*

Part IV
Managing User Resources

The 5th Wave   By Rich Tennant

"You the guy having trouble staying connected to the network?"

In this part . . .

None of NT's complicated installation and configuration work would be necessary if you didn't have to deal with those pesky users. The Enterprise exam places great emphasis on user and group management, and that's our focus in Part IV. In this part, we discuss the proper method for creating global and local groups, we explain which groups you should place users in, and we discuss the groups to which you assign permissions. We also focus on establishing account policies, user rights policies, and audit policies to restrict and track user actions. Also in Part IV, we discuss resource management by means of user profiles, system policies, hardware profiles, and client administration.

Chapter 10

Users: A Necessary Evil

Exam Objectives

▶ Creating user accounts

▶ Deleting, disabling, and renaming user accounts

▶ Managing user properties

▶ Using templates

*T*he heart of Windows NT Server is the idea of a single logon for access to the entire enterprise. To accomplish this simple goal, you create a database of user accounts and Windows NT distributes it to all account domain controllers in the enterprise.

The Enterprise exam has many questions dealing with user accounts, policies, rights, and profiles. You must understand how to perform all tasks pertaining to users. In this chapter, we explain what you need to know about managing user accounts.

Quick Assessment

Creating user accounts

1 A user name can contain as many as _____ characters.

Deleting, disabling, and renaming user accounts

2 Creating a group of users with the same basic attributes is best accomplished with a(n) _____.

3 Renaming a user account retains the _____ assigned to the account.

4 When a user will be gone for an extended period of time, you should _____ that person's account.

Managing user properties

5 _____ is the primary tool for managing user accounts.

6 _____ sets the minimum password length.

7 _____ and _____ are the default user accounts created by Windows NT Server.

8 You can control access to the network by setting parameters in the _____ and _____ properties of User Manager for Domains.

9 You can set a temporary account to automatically expire by clicking the _____ button in User Manager for Domains.

Using templates

10 (True/False). You can recover a deleted user account.

Answers

1 *20.* See "Creating a New User" for more information.

2 *Template.* The section "Using Templates" gives you the details.

3 *SID.* To find out more, read the section "Renaming User Accounts."

4 *Disable.* See "Disabling and Deleting User Accounts."

5 *User Manager for Domains.* For more information, review "Managing User Accounts in NT Server."

6 *Account Policy.* See "Managing User Properties."

7 *Administrator; Guest.* The section "Creating a New User" covers this information.

8 *Hours; Logon To.* See the section "Managing User Properties" for all the properties.

9 *Account.* See "Managing User Properties" for all the details.

10 *False.* To find out why, review the section "Disabling and Deleting User Accounts."

Managing User Accounts in NT Server

In most network operating systems, you manage users on a per-user basis. This approach to user management is a cumbersome and administratively taxing process. Windows NT Server uses the User Manager for Domains for user management. The User Manager for Domains provides the tools you use for administering users and groups. Its capabilities greatly simplify the task of managing users in an enterprise environment consisting of multiple domains. Figure 10-1 shows the User Manager window.

To simplify management, Windows NT employs a group administration philosophy. You can easily place users into groups and assign rights and permissions to the group. When you assign a user to a group, that user inherits all the rights and access permissions of the group. We discuss group management in more detail in Chapter 11.

Creating a New User

When you install Windows NT Server, only two user accounts are created: Administrator and Guest. These accounts aren't suitable for the everyday user, so you must create new ones. As we show you in Lab 10-1, the process for creating new user accounts is pretty easy.

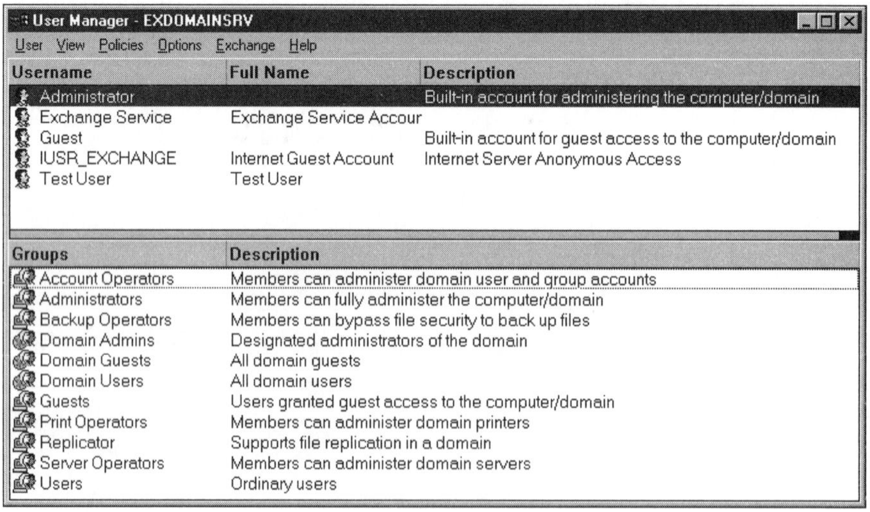

Figure 10-1:
User
Manager
for
Domains.

```
User Manager - EXDOMAINSRV                                          _ □ ✕
User  View  Policies  Options  Exchange  Help

Username              Full Name              Description
👤 Administrator                              Built-in account for administering the computer/domain
👤 Exchange Service    Exchange Service Accour
👤 Guest                                      Built-in account for guest access to the computer/domain
👤 IUSR_EXCHANGE      Internet Guest Account  Internet Server Anonymous Access
👤 Test User           Test User

Groups               Description
👥 Account Operators   Members can administer domain user and group accounts
👥 Administrators      Members can fully administer the computer/domain
👥 Backup Operators    Members can bypass file security to back up files
👥 Domain Admins       Designated administrators of the domain
👥 Domain Guests       All domain guests
👥 Domain Users        All domain users
👥 Guests              Users granted guest access to the computer/domain
👥 Print Operators     Members can administer domain printers
👥 Replicator          Supports file replication in a domain
👥 Server Operators    Members can administer domain servers
👥 Users               Ordinary users
```

Lab 10-1 Creating a New User Account

1. Open User Manager for Domains.

2. Choose User⇨New User.

As shown in Figure 10-2, User Manager displays the New User dialog box.

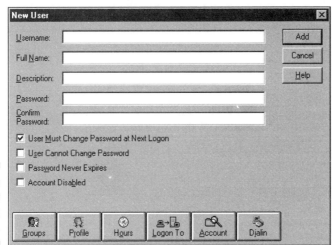

Figure 10-2:
The New
User dialog
box.

3. Complete the five fields in the top half of the New User dialog box.

A user name can be up to 20 characters long and must be unique to the domain or computer being administered. It can contain any uppercase or lowercase characters except the following symbols:

" / \ [ ] : ; | = , + * ? < >

A user name can't consist solely of periods (.) and spaces.

4. Select the relevant check boxes in the bottom half of the dialog box to specify the following controls:

- The user must change the password at the next logon.

- The user cannot change the password.

- The password never expires.

- The account is disabled.

5. Click Add.

Don't worry about the other buttons just yet; we cover them a little later. That's all you need to do to create a new user.

Later in this chapter, we show you a quick method for creating lots of users (see the section "Using Templates").

Disabling and Deleting User Accounts

To prevent a user from logging on, you disable or delete the user account. Disabling and deleting a user account may sound like the same task, but they're actually quite different:

- ✔ A disabled user account still exists, but the user isn't permitted to log on. A deleted user account is completely removed.

- ✔ A disabled account still appears in the user account list of the User Manager for Domains window. A deleted account is removed from the user account list and can't be restored.

- ✔ You can re-enable a disabled account at any time.

To prevent accidental deletions, first disable a user account, and then periodically delete the disabled accounts.

If you delete a user account that has read access to a certain shared directory and then create another user account with the same user name, the new account does *not* have access to the directory. You must reapply permissions to the shared directory. When you create a user account, a unique Security Identifier (SID) is created for that user. Internal processes in Windows NT Server refer to a user account's SID rather than its user name.

If a user is going to be absent for an extended period of time, disable that user's account. You can disable user accounts with the User Manager for Domains. Just double-click the user name and then click the Account Disabled check box in the User Properties dialog box.

To delete a user account with User Manager for Domains, just select the user name that you want to delete, choose User➪Delete, and then click Yes in the resulting Warning dialog box. The user account is deleted.

Renaming User Accounts

When a new user takes the place of an existing one, rename the existing account rather than create a new one. All group memberships and access permissions remain because the user's SID hasn't changed, only the user name. Lab 10-2 guides you through the process.

Lab 10-2	Renaming a User Account

1. **Open User Manager for Domains and select a user.**

2. **Choose User⇨Rename.**

3. **In the resulting dialog box, enter the new user name.**

4. **Click OK.**

The exam may include a question about a new user taking over from another user for whom you've set numerous individual access privileges. This type of question asks you how to give the new user the same access privileges as the old one. The answer is to rename the old user account for the new user and then change the password.

Managing User Properties

Each user has several properties. The individual settings are contained in the first page of the User Properties dialog box. Of these properties, only the Description is copied from account to account. The main user properties are

- ✔ **Username:** The name used by the user for logging on to the network.

- ✔ **Full Name:** The user's full name. You can use this name as a sort key in User Manager for Domains.

- ✔ **Description:** Text to further describe the user. If you use a template to create user accounts, the description is copied from account to account.

- ✔ **Password:** The password can be up to 14 characters long. Your Account Policies control the specific rules for creating a valid password. Passwords are case sensitive. You access Account Policies via the Policies menu in User Manager for Domains. (The NT Server exam covers Account Policies.)

- ✔ **Confirm Password:** Verifies the entry of the password.

The six option buttons at the bottom of the dialog box govern many of the user's capabilities:

- ✔ **Groups:** Clicking this button opens the Group Memberships dialog box, which enables you to add or remove a user who is to be a member of one or more groups.

- ✔ **Profiles:** This button allows you to define a user's profile, logon script, and home directory. You set these properties in the User Environment Profile dialog box.

✔ **Hours:** Clicking this button opens the Logon Hours dialog box, which enables you to set the times in which a user can log on to the network. By default, a user has 24-hour access to the network. If a user is already logged on when a restricted time period is reached, the user may remain logged on but can't log back on until the allowed time. A user can be forcibly logged off at the specified time. The Account Policies set this control.

✔ **Logon To:** You can restrict a user to one or more specific computers in the domain. By default, a user is allowed to use all workstations.

✔ **Account:** Clicking this button opens the Account Information dialog box, which you use for specifying the length of time an account remains active. This setting is useful for accounts used by temporary employees and contractors. The default is Never. You can also assign an account as Local or Global.

✔ **Dialin:** This button opens the Dialin Information dialog box, which lets you establish a user's right to dial in to the network as well as establish callback security, if desired.

Managing User Properties for Multiple User Accounts

With User Manager for Domains, you can control the user properties of multiple users by selecting all users who share common attributes and then choosing User⇨Properties (or simply pressing Enter). This command opens the User Properties dialog box shown in Figure 10-3. Just make the appropriate changes and click OK.

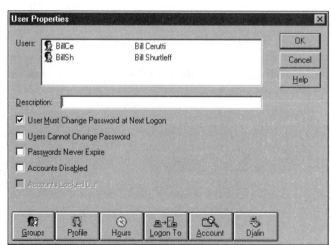

Figure 10-3: The User Properties dialog box.

This dialog box offers a convenient method for changing properties for groups of existing users instead of changing each user's properties individually.

Using Templates

If you have an existing user account that is substantially the same as a new account you want to create, you can copy the existing account and modify the copy as necessary. *Template accounts* are regular user accounts that are disabled. You can build a template for each type of user on the network, and then copy the appropriate template whenever you need to add a new user. In this way, template accounts speed the process of creating many new user accounts.

When you copy a user account, the copy contains all the information from the original except the user name, full name, and password.

To copy a user account, follow these steps:

1. **Open User Manager for Domains.**

2. **Select the user account you want to copy.**

3. **Choose User⇨Copy.**

4. **Enter the information for the new user, make any necessary modifications to the Groups, Hours, Logon To, Profile, and Dialin settings, and then click Add.**

Prep Test

1 As the Administrator of a Windows NT domain, you need to allow a group of people to dial in to the network. What's the most efficient method for accomplishing this task?

    A ○ Edit the properties of each user to allow dial-in access by using User Manager for Domains.

    B ○ Use the Remote Access Administrator and select the Grant All check box.

    C ○ Select all users requiring dial-in access in User Manager for Domains and press Enter. In the Dialin dialog box, allow them dial-in access.

    D ○ Use Server Manager to configure the Remote Access service.

2 You are the administrator of a Windows NT domain. You have a large number of contractors coming in to work on a project. This project will last for 60 days. After that time, you won't need these user accounts. What's the most effective method for creating these user accounts?

    A ○ Have a member of your team create each user account and make sure they are all in the same groups. Then monitor the status of the project and delete all the contractor accounts when they are finished.

    B ○ Assign a single user account for all the contractors to use and set the concurrent login flag to a 1 in the Registry. When the project is finished, delete the account.

    C ○ Create a single user account and use Server Manager to set up a contractor share. Allow access to this share by only that account. Delete the user account and take ownership of the share when the project is finished.

    D ○ Create a template user account and set the properties in the Account tab for the accounts to expire in 60 days. Then copy the template account for each of the contractors.

3 Joe is leaving the company and Sandy is replacing him. What's the best way to give Sandy access to all the resources previously used by Joe?

    A ○ Create an account for Sandy, using Joe as a template. Then delete Joe's account.

    B ○ Rename Joe's account in User Manager and tell Sandy to change the password when she logs on for the first time.

    C ○ Create an account for Joe using Sandy's account as a template. Then tell Joe to change his password the next time he logs on.

    D ○ Create an account for Sandy using Joe as a template. Then disable Joe's account.

4 Which is a valid user name for a Windows NT user?

A ○ Sandra B Majors

B ○ Sandra;B;Majors

C ○ Sandra,B,Majors

D ○ Sandra*B*Majors

5 At 5:00 p.m., KeithM logs out. He returns at 6:00 p.m. and can't log on again. Identify a possible cause.

A ○ Account Policies in User Manager

B ○ A setting in the Account dialog box in User Manager

C ○ A user profile

D ○ A setting in the Hours dialog box in User Manager

6 You are the administrator of a Windows NT domain. You have a consultant who works at your location frequently. She requires an account with the same access each time she comes out. You should

A ○ Create a user account each time she comes out, and then delete it when she leaves.

B ○ Leave a generic consultant account on the system for these instances.

C ○ Create a user account each time she comes out, and then disable it when she leaves.

D ○ Grant the necessary user rights to the guest account and allow her to use it.

7 A member of your team mistakenly deletes a user's account. How can you recover the account?

A ○ Re-create the user's account using the same user name. Put the user into all the same groups he was a member of before the accident. Allow the user to take ownership of his home directory and grant him access to all the files and folders he had access to before.

B ○ Stop the replication process on the PDC. Promote a BDC and synchronize the domain to use the SAM from the BDC to recover the user's account.

C ○ Re-create the user's account with the same user name. Assign the user name the same SID as the deleted account, using the Registry Editor.

D ○ In User Manager for Domains, choose User⇨Undelete.

8 Which default users are built when you install Windows, and what is their status?

A ○ User and Administrator; both accounts are active.

B ○ Administrator and Guest; Guest is disabled.

C ○ User and Administrator; User is disabled.

D ○ Guest and Administrator; both accounts are active.

9 How many user names are required to access all resources in the enterprise?

A ○ One

B ○ One in each domain

C ○ One on each server

D ○ One for each resource

10 After a reorganization, the names of the departments have all changed. All user accounts are built with templates. What's the most efficient way to change the Descriptions field to reflect the new department names?

A ○ Edit the Description field for each template to reflect the new department. Then re-create all the user accounts for that department using the new template.

B ○ Edit the Description field for each template to reflect the new department. Highlight all users from the same department, press Enter, and then edit the Description field in the User Properties dialog box.

C ○ Edit each department user's Description field to reflect the new department name. Edit the template user accounts for each department to reflect the new name.

D ○ Update a single account in each department with the new Description field. Then copy that account for each member in the department. Edit the Description field for each template to reflect the new department name.

Answers

1 C. *Select all users requiring dial-in access in User Manager for Domains and press Enter. In the Dialin dialog box, allow them dial-in access.* User Manager for Domains enables you to manage the properties of multiple user accounts simultaneously. *See "Managing User Properties for Multiple User Accounts."*

2 D. *Create a template user account and set the properties in the Account tab for the accounts to expire in 60 days. Then copy the template account for each of the contractors.* Using a template and setting the accounts to expire in 60 days is the most efficient use of the administrator's time. This method also allows for the automatic expiration of the temporary accounts. *Review the section "Using Templates."*

3 B. *Rename Joe's account in User Manager and tell Sandy to change the password when she logs on for the first time.* Renaming Joe's account gives Sandy exactly the same accesses as Joe had. *See "Renaming User Accounts."*

4 A. *Sandra B Majors.* A user name can be up to 20 characters long but cannot contain the following symbols:

" / \ [ ] : ; | = , + * ? < >

See "Creating a New User."

5 D. *A setting in the Hours dialog box in User Manager.* The Hours properties control when a user can log on to the network. *See "Managing User Properties" for more information.*

6 C. *Create a user account each time she comes out, and then disable it when she leaves.* This method protects your domain and allows the consultant the same user name and access each time she is on your site. *See "Managing User Properties."*

7 A. *Re-create the user's account using the same user name. Put the user into all the same groups he was a member of before the accident. Allow the user to take ownership of his home directory and grant him access to all the files and folders he had access to before.* You can't recover an account after you delete it. *See "Disabling and Deleting User Accounts."*

8 B. *Administrator and Guest; Guest is disabled.* These are the two default accounts built for a domain controller. The Guest account is disabled by default. *See "Managing User Properties."*

9 A. *One.* You need only one user account to access all resources in the enterprise. *See "Managing User Properties."*

10 B. Edit the Description field for each template to reflect the new department. *Highlight all users from the same department, press Enter, and then edit the Description field in the User Properties dialog box.* You can edit properties for multiple accounts at the same time with User Manager for Domains. *For more information, see "Managing User Properties for Multiple User Accounts."*

Chapter 11

Groups: Deciding Who Gets In and Who Doesn't

Exam Objectives

▶ Creating and using local groups

▶ Creating and using global groups

▶ Deleting groups

▶ Managing groups across domains

▶ Reviewing security policy management

Group accounts are collections of user accounts. By giving a user account membership in a group, you give that user all the rights and permissions granted to the group. Group membership provides an easy way to grant common capabilities to sets of users. By managing user accounts in groups, you can more easily manage and track users' access to resources.

In a large, multiple-domain enterprise with several offices and resource domains, using groups greatly simplifies the account domain administrator's job. By using groups in combination with user templates, which we discuss in Chapter 10, you can quickly and efficiently set up a new user and grant access rights and permissions. Even in smaller single domains, building global and local groups to manage users remains a valid technique. The domain may grow or you may incorporate a different model, but you have a framework that allows migration with a minimum of reconfiguration.

Group management is a key topic on the Enterprise exam. You must fully understand the concepts of groups. You need to know the built-in groups and the rights and permissions that each group inherits. The Enterprise exam includes many questions pertaining to local and global groups and how they interact within a domain.

Quick Assessment

Creating
and using
local groups

1 The _____ and _____ local groups on a domain controller can create a user account.

2 Who belongs to the group Everyone?

3 How many users do you assign to the Replicator group?

4 Local groups can contain _____ and _____.

Creating
and using
global groups

5 By default, all members of the domain are members of the _____ global group.

6 You create global groups by using _____.

7 Global groups can contain _____.

Managing
groups
across
domains

8 When you assign a user to a group, user rights are _____.

9 By default, members of the _____ and the _____ can add workstations to the domain.

Reviewing
security
policy
manage-
ment

10 The _____, _____, and _____ built-in groups can perform backups.

Answers

1 *Administrator; Account Operators.* Review "Using built-in local groups."

2 *Everyone.* Refer to "Everyone."

3 *None.* See "Replicator."

4 *User accounts; global groups.* See "Creating local groups."

5 *Domain users.* See "Default global groups."

6 *User Manager for Domains.* Review "Creating global groups."

7 *User accounts.* Check out "Creating global groups."

8 *Inherited.* See "Global Groups."

9 *Account Operators; Administrator.* See "Using built-in local groups."

10 *Administrator; Backup Operators; Server Operators.* Review "Using built-in local groups."

Local Groups

A local group contains user accounts and global groups from one or more domains grouped together under one local group account name. Local groups make it possible to quickly assign rights and permissions for the resources on one domain (that is, the local domain) to users and groups from that domain and other domains that trust it. You can add users and global groups from outside the local domain to the local group only if they belong to a trusted domain. (If you want to review trust relationships, refer to Chapter 4.)

Local groups also exist on member servers and computers running Windows NT Workstation, and they can contain user accounts and global groups. A local group can't contain other local groups.

To remember the roles of the different types of groups, keep the following points in mind:

- ✔ Global groups contain domain users only.
- ✔ Local groups contain global groups and any users.
- ✔ Nothing contains a local group.
- ✔ For management, you want to put users into global groups and global groups into local groups. Grant rights and permissions to the local group.

Creating local groups

In addition to understanding the importance of local groups, you need to know how to create one. Lab 11-1 steps you through this process. You want to pay attention to the dialog boxes and explore any options that they present. Overall, the process is straightforward and relatively simple.

Lab 11-1   Creating Local Groups

1. **Start User Manager for Domains by choosing Start⇨Programs⇨ Administrative Tools⇨User Manager for Domains.**

2. **Choose User⇨New Local Group.**

   As shown in Figure 11-1, User Manager for Domains displays the New Local Group dialog box.

Figure 11-1:
The New
Local
Group
dialog box.

3. Enter the name and description of the new local group.

You can also select any initial members of the local group by clicking Add and then completing the Add Users and Groups dialog box. Notice that the global groups show up in the Add Users and Groups dialog box.

If you need to create a number of similar groups, you can create one, assign rights to this group, copy the group, and then assign members. To copy a group, use the Copy function in User Manager for Domains. Lab 11-2 shows you how.

Lab 11-2   Copying a Group

1. Start User Manager for Domains.

2. Select the group you want to copy.

3. Choose User⇨Copy.

User Manager for Domains displays the New Local Group dialog box.

4. Enter the new name and change the description.

5. Click Add, add or remove users as necessary, and then click OK.

6. Click OK to create the new group and return to User Manager.

Using built-in local groups

The built-in local groups differ depending on the role of the server. You need to be aware of the differences and what all the local groups are allowed to do.

For servers acting as domain controllers, the local groups are

- Administrators
- Account Operators
- Backup Operators
- Print Operators
- Server Operators
- Replicator
- Users
- Guests

For servers acting as member servers, the local groups are

- Administrators
- Backup Operators
- Power Users
- Replicator
- Users
- Guests

Note the difference in the local groups based on server roles. The Power Users group exists only in a member server. The only Operators group that exists on a member server is the Backup Operators group.

On the exam, you will be asked situational questions about which groups can perform which jobs. You need to know all the built-in groups and their capabilities. Table 11-1 describes the built-in local groups.

Table 11-1	Built-in Local Groups
Group Name	*Description*
Administrators	Members can administer fully the server/domain.
Account Operators	Members can administer domain user and group accounts.
Backup Operators	Members can bypass file security to back up and restore files.
Print Operators	Members can administer domain printers.
Server Operators	Members can administer domain servers.

Group Name	Description
Replicators	Supports file replication in a domain.
Users	Ordinary users.
Everyone	Anyone with a user account.
Guests	Users granted access to the computer/domain.

Administrators

The Administrators group is the most powerful local group. It has complete control over the domain and the domain controllers and servers, and is the only local group automatically granted every capability and every right in the system. When you install Windows NT, the Domain Admins global group is automatically a member of this local group.

Account Operators

Account Operators can create user accounts and groups for their home domain using User Manager for Domains. They can modify or delete most user accounts and groups. They can also add workstations to the domain. They can't change or modify the Domain Admins, Administrators, Backup Operators, Print Operators, Server Operators, or Account Operators groups.

Backup Operators

Members of the Backup Operators group can back up and restore files and folders on servers and domain controllers. They can't change security settings.

Print Operators

The Print Operators group members can manage every aspect of printing. They can share and stop sharing printers.

Power Users

Power Users is a local group that exists only on member servers and workstations. Power Users can modify only user accounts and groups they create. They can also add and remove users from the Power Users group, as well as share and stop sharing folders and printers.

Replicator

The Replicator group is unlike the other local groups. No one is automatically a member of the Replicator group. Don't assign any users to this group. Establish a special account and assign it to this group. Use this group to manage the replication of files and folders on the domain controllers.

Server Operators

The Server Operators local group is on domain controllers and can do most of the administrative jobs on a server except manipulate security options. Server Operators can perform the following tasks:

- ✔ Locking and overriding the lock on a server
- ✔ Formatting the server's hard drive
- ✔ Creating common groups
- ✔ Sharing and stopping the sharing of folders and printers
- ✔ Backing up and restoring files and folders
- ✔ Changing the system time

The key to remembering the difference between the Account Operators group and the Server Operators group is in their names:

- ✔ Account Operators can manage things dealing with user accounts. They can do most things with user accounts except modify security.
- ✔ Server Operators can do almost anything pertaining to a server. They have nothing to do with user accounts. They can create a group. They can't manipulate security.
- ✔ Administrators are the only ones who can do it all, including manage security.

Users

The Users group is the default group for all users. This group gives its members rights to perform end-user tasks such as logging on to a workstation; accessing the network; running an application; printing, creating, and managing their own local groups; keeping a personal profile; and locking and unlocking their workstation. Users don't have the right to log on locally to a server.

Guests

The Guests local group is for one-time or occasional network users. Guests have no rights on any of the servers, but they can log on at a workstation. A guest user can shut down the system, however, because all members of the group Everyone have that right.

Everyone

This group isn't a group in the strictest sense. Anyone with a user account in a domain is a member of that domain's Everyone local group by default. Granting access to a file or folder to Everyone means just that — everyone can access the file or folder. The same applies to user rights. Be careful with this group.

Global Groups

A global group contains numerous user accounts from one domain that are grouped together under one group account name. A global group can contain only user accounts from the domain where the global group is created.

After you create a global group, you can grant it permissions and rights in its own domain, on member servers, or in trusting domains. Your best bet is to grant rights and permissions to local groups and use the global group as the means for adding users to local groups.

You can add global groups to local groups in the same domain, in domains that trust that domain, or to member servers or computers running Windows NT Workstation in the same or a trusting domain. Global groups contain only domain user accounts. You can't create a global group on a computer running Windows NT Workstation or on a computer running Windows NT Server as a member server.

The Enterprise exam focuses on trust relationships, which we discuss in Chapter 4. Global groups are best used in the account domain. If a resource domain trusts an account domain, you can use the global groups in the account domain in the local groups of the resource domain.

Creating global groups

You build global groups at the account domain. A global group can contain only user accounts from that domain. Global groups are very convenient for managing large or diverse groups of users. The process for creating global groups is similar to creating local groups. In Lab 11-3, we show you how to create a new global group. Notice the differences and think of ways to use a combination of local and global groups to solve problems regarding access to resources in a domain.

Lab 11-3 Creating a Global Group

1. **Start User Manager for Domains by choosing Start⇨Programs⇨ Administrative Tools⇨User Manager for Domains.**

2. **Choose User⇨New Global Group.**

   As shown in Figure 11-2, User Manager for Domains displays the New Global Group dialog box.

3. **Enter the name and description of the new global group.**

   You can also select any initial members of the global group.

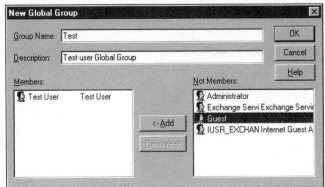

Figure 11-2:
The New
Global
Group
dialog box.

Default global groups

On a domain's primary and backup domain controllers, you have three
built-in global groups:

✔ Domain Admins

✔ Domain Users

✔ Domain Guests

You can't delete any of these groups.

For a quick comparison of the built-in global groups, check Table 11-2. The
name of each global group gives you a clue as to the group's purpose.

Table 11-2	Built-in Global Groups
Group Name	**Description**
Domain Admins	Designated Administrators of the domain
Domain Users	All domain users
Domain Guests	All domain guests

Domain Admins

The Domain Admins global group is initially a member of the Administrators local group for the domain and of the Administrators local group for
every computer in the domain running Windows NT Workstation or
Windows NT Server. The built-in Administrator user account is a member
of the Domain Admins global group. The Administrator user account is
also a member of the Administrators local group, and you can't remove it.
Because of these memberships, a user logged on as an Administrator can

administer the domain, the primary and backup domain controllers, and all other computers running Windows NT Workstation and Windows NT Server in the domain.

To provide administrative-level capabilities to a new account, add the account to the Domain Admins global group. Members of this group can administer the domain, the servers and workstations of the domain, and a trusting domain to which you've added the Domain Admins global group from this domain to the Administrators local group in the trusted domain.

Domain Users

The Domain Users global group initially contains the domain's built-in Administrator account. By default, all new accounts created thereafter in the domain are added to the Domain Users group, unless you specifically remove them.

The Domain Users global group is, by default, a member of the Users local group for the domain and of the Users local group for every computer in the domain running Windows NT Workstation or member servers running Windows NT Server. Domain Users is the default primary group for each user. Because of these memberships, users of the domain have normal user access to and capabilities for the domain and the computers in the domain running Windows NT Workstation and Windows NT Server as member servers.

Domain Guests

The Domain Guests global group initially contains the domain's built-in Guest user account. If you add user accounts that you intend to give more limited rights and permissions than typical domain user accounts, you may want to add those accounts to the Domain Guests group and remove them from the Domain Users group. The Domain Guests global group is a member of the domain's Guests local group.

Special Groups

Four special groups exist in Windows NT Server that are only used to show how a user is using the system at a particular time. These groups have no actual members, but membership is implied by access to a resource:

- ✔ **Interactive:** Any user who is logged on locally.
- ✔ **Network:** Any user who has gained access through the network.
- ✔ **System:** The operating system.
- ✔ **Creator/Owner:** Anyone creating a file, folder, or print job.

Assigning a User to a Group

Groups aren't much good until you put users in them. In most cases, you assign users to a global group, then assign the global group to a local group. Just remember that you *can* assign a user directly to a local group. In Lab 11-4, we show you the process for assigning users to a group. Notice in the lab that global groups show up on the list of users when assigning to a local group.

Lab 11-4   Assigning Users to a Group

1. **Start User Manager for Domains by choosing Start⇨Programs⇨ Administrative Tools⇨User Manager for Domains.**

2. **Double-click the desired group name in the bottom half of the window to open the Local Group Properties dialog box.**

   Figure 11-3 shows the Local Group Properties dialog box.

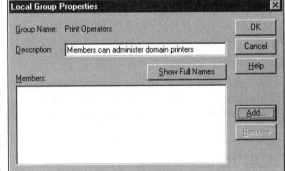

Figure 11-3:
The Local
Group
Properties
dialog box.

3. **Click Add to open the Add Users and Groups dialog box.**

   Figure 11-4 shows the Add Users and Groups dialog box.

4. **Select the desired group members, click Add, and then click OK.**

   Notice that the users are added to the group.

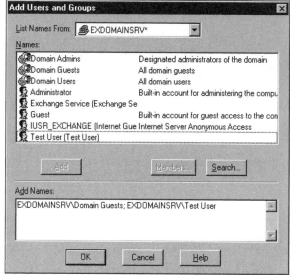

Figure 11-4:
The Add
Users and
Groups
dialog box.

Deleting Local and Global Groups

You can delete only the groups that you create with User Manager for Domains. You can't delete any of the built-in groups.

After you delete a group, you can't recover it because the SID for the group is removed when you delete the group. If you decide you want to re-create a group that you've deleted, you must re-create it from scratch, including all the permissions associated with it. In Lab 11-5, we show you how to delete a group.

Lab 11-5   Deleting a Group

1. **Start User Manager for Domains.**

2. **Select the group to delete.**

3. **Press the Delete key or choose User⇨Delete.**

   You see the warning message shown in Figure 11-5.

4. **Click OK to delete the group and then click Yes.**

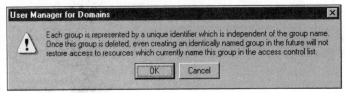

Figure 11-5:
The group
deletion
warning.

Managing Groups Across Domains

The real advantages of using groups appear in a multidomain environment. When working with groups across trust relationships, follow these guidelines:

✔ **Gather users into global groups.** Remember that a global group can contain only users from the same domain. You may have the same global group name in more than one domain.

✔ **If you have more than one account domain, use the same name for the global group that has the same type of users in each domain.**

✔ **Remember that you must create the local group where the resource is located.** If the resource is on a domain controller, create the local group in that domain's account database. If the resource is on a member server or a Windows NT Workstation, create the local group on the local system's account database.

✔ **Be sure to set permissions for the resource to the local group before assigning the global group as a member so that security has been set for the resource.**

You use the User Manager for Domains to manage groups from a trusted domain to all trusting domains and to all member servers of its domain and all member servers of trusting domains. You select the domain or member server by choosing User⇨Select Domain.

When multiple domains are involved, the group name is referred to as DOMAIN/GROUP.

Administering Security Policies

You must make various policy decisions for users in Windows NT Server — everything from the times users can log on, to the length of their passwords. The policies may control desktop settings, screen savers, and configuration settings. Because these policies apply to all users or groups of users, you need to plan a policy that will work for the selected group.

The Enterprise exam has questions covering all types of policies. Most of these questions include exhibits. You must understand the desired action of all the switches and fields of the different policy tools. You set account policies, the audit policy, and user rights from the User Manager. Use the Policy Editor for creating and editing system policies. You set file and folder auditing and sharing in the properties of the file or folder.

Managing the account policy

Account policies deal with passwords. To access the Account Policy dialog box shown in Figure 11-6, in User Manager for Domains, choose Policies⇨ Account Policies. You use this dialog box for setting the following password-related policies:

- **Maximum Password Age** sets the maximum amount of time a user's password can remain the same without forcing the user to change it.

- **Minimum Password Age** defines the minimum time a password must be used before a user can change it. With this setting, you prevent users from circumventing the Maximum Password Age setting. By setting the Minimum Password Age, you ensure that users don't change their passwords when required and then immediately change back to their old passwords.

- **Minimum Password Length** sets the minimum number of characters a password must contain. Set the minimum length to six to eight characters because short passwords are easy to guess.

- **Password Uniqueness** specifies a minimum number of passwords a user must choose before reusing an old favorite. A value here requires a value in the Minimum Password Age block.

The next group of options in the Account Policy dialog box deals with account lockout. These useful features can foil hackers trying to guess user passwords by repeatedly attempting to log on:

- **Lockout After** sets the number of failed attempts users can have before their accounts are locked.

- **Reset Count After** sets the number of minutes the system waits after a bad set of logon attempts before resetting the count. If a user reaches the maximum number of failed attempts without successfully logging on, the account remains locked out until released by an administrator.

- **Lockout Duration** sets the amount of time a user's account remains locked out before being released by the system. This setting saves many calls to the administrator.

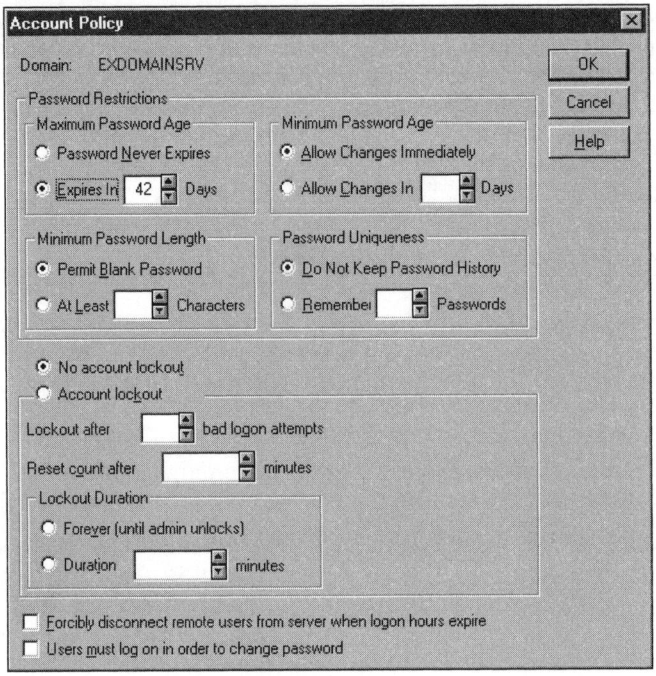

Figure 11-6:
The
Account
Policy
dialog box.

The first of the two boxes at the bottom of the Account Policy dialog box relates to the hours a user is allowed to log on. This check box forces users to log off when their allowed time frame is up. This option doesn't affect users not running Windows NT.

The second check box requires users to log on to the system before they can change their passwords. A user with an expired password can't change the password without help from the administrator.

Managing the user rights policy

Users must be able to log on and get to the resources they need. What a user can do — and can't do — depends on the rights and permissions you grant to that user. Rights and permissions are not exactly the same things:

- ✓ **Rights** generally apply to the system as a whole, and you set rights with User Manager for Domains. An administrator can give or take away such rights as the capability to back up files or log on to a server. Rights can be assigned to individual users but are more commonly assigned to a group. Then users are assigned to that group.

- ✓ **Permission** is the access a user or group has to specific files or folders.

You grant user rights by using the dialog box shown in Figure 11-7. User rights fit in one of two categories: regular and advanced. Regular rights are the most common that pertain to what a user is allowed to do. The built-in groups in Windows NT Server have whole sets of user rights assigned to them. You don't usually need to edit these rights. Table 11-3 lists regular user rights.

Figure 11-7:
The User
Rights
Policy
dialog box.

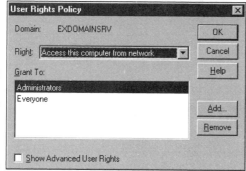

Table 11-3	Regular User Rights	
Regular Right	**Definition**	**Default Assignment**
Access this computer from the network	Allows user to log on to this computer through the network	Administrators, Everyone
Add workstations to domain	Allows a user to create computer accounts in the domain	None
Back up files and directories	Grants a user the right to back up all files on this computer	Administrators, Backup Operators, Server Operators
Change the system time	Allows a user to set the computer's time clock	Administrators, Server Operators
Load and unload device drivers	Permits a user to install and remove device drivers on this computer	Administrators
Log on locally	Allows a user to log on to the Server	Administrators, Backup Operators, Server Operators, Account Operators, Print Operators

(continued)

Table 11-3 *(continued)*

Regular Right	Definition	Default Assignment
Manage auditing and security log	Permits a user to manage the auditing policy	Administrators
Restore files and directories	Permits a user to restore files and folders. Supersedes any permission restrictions	Administrators, Backup Operators, Server Operators
Shut down the system	Allows a user to shut down a server	Administrators, Backup Operators, Server Operators, Account Operators, Print Operators
Take ownership of files or other objects	Allows a user to take ownership of objects owned by other users	Administrators

You may see a question about a user who can access files and folders via the network and can log on from a workstation, but can't log on at the server. You need to set the user right Log on Locally for this user.

The advanced rights are used more by programmers and applications than by users. You need to know the following advanced rights:

- **Bypass Traverse Checking:** This right allows users to pass through a folder they don't have permission to access. The users can't change or read anything — they can only pass through.

- **Log On as a Service:** This right permits a user account to log on as a service. This right is used by the account that's used to run the Replicator.

Managing the audit policy

You set the basic audit policy for the server in the Audit Policy dialog box. You can refine the policy to audit specific files, folders, and printers, but you can't extend it beyond what you set in the Audit Policy dialog box. Lab 11-6 shows you how to set up auditing.

Lab 11-6   Setting up Auditing

1. **Open User Manager for Domains.**

2. **Choose Policies⇨Audit.**

   User Manager for Domains displays the Audit Policy dialog box.

3. **Click Audit These Events.**

4. **Select the event you want to audit on success or failure and click OK.**

You set up file and folder auditing in the Properties dialog box for the individual file or folder. Lab 11-7 guides you through the process of setting up auditing for a file or a folder.

Lab 11-7   Setting Up Auditing on a File or Folder

1. **Right-click the file or folder you want to audit, and then choose Properties from the resulting pop-up menu.**

2. **On the Security tab in the Properties dialog box that's displayed, click Auditing.**

   If you have selected a folder, use the Replace Auditing on Subdirectories and Replace Auditing on Existing Files check boxes to specify the extent of your auditing.

3. **Select the user whose files or folders you want to audit, and then click Add to open the Add Users and Groups dialog box.**

4. **Select the users or groups whose use of the files or folders you want to audit. Click Add until all the names are in the Add Names box. Click OK.**

5. **Select the events you want to audit and click OK to save the information.**

You can audit printers in much the same way as you audit files and folders. You can perform the procedure in Lab 11-8 to find out who is using all the printer paper.

Lab 11-8   Auditing a Printer

1. **Open the Printer Properties dialog box by right-clicking a printer and choosing Properties from the pop-up menu that's displayed.**

2. **On the Security tab in the Printer Properties dialog box, click Auditing.**

3. **Click Add to open the Add Users and Groups dialog box.**

4. **Select the users or groups you want to audit. Click Add until all the names are in the Add Names box. Click OK.**

5. **Select the events you want to audit and click OK to save the information.**

Prep Test

1 Your company plans to hire numerous temporary employees to work on a project. You'll need to create and rename several user accounts every day. Response for these changes must be fast. The project leader is willing to take responsibility for managing these changes. In which built-in group should you place the project leader to perform only these tasks?

A ○ Server Operators

B ○ Administrators

C ○ Account Operators

D ○ Replicators

2 A department in your company has a local group assigned with the name of the department as the group name. After a reorganization, the department name changes. The department head wants the name of the local group changed to reflect the current name of the department. How do you accomplish this task?

A ○ Create a new global group, and pull the old local group into it as a member.

B ○ Copy the old local group, assign a new name to it, and delete the old local group.

C ○ Rename the local group.

D ○ Create a new local group and pull the old local group into it as a member.

3 TabithaM has no problems logging on to the network and attaching to her resources. While in the computer room, she tries to log on to one of the servers, and she is denied access. What could be the cause?

A ○ She is a member of the Print Operators global group.

B ○ She is a member of the Domain Users global group.

C ○ She is a member of the Backup Operators global group.

D ○ She is a member of the Server Operators global group.

4 The following group memberships apply:

JoeS is a member of the Administrators group.

BettyM is a member of the Server Operators group.

KeithM is a member of the Backup Operators group.

DavidC is a member of the Account Operators group.

BobA is a member of the Print Operators group.

DavidC has to leave for a business trip and wants to leave his duties to his assistant. Who can place his assistant into the Account Operators group?

A ○ JoeS
B ○ BettyM
C ○ DavidC
D ○ BobA
E ○ KeithM

5 For security, the server has been locked. Which group can override the lock on the server?

A ○ Print Operators
B ○ Backup Operators
C ○ Server Operators
D ○ Account Operators

6 Who can make changes to the Domain Users global group?

A ○ Backup Operators
B ○ Server Operators
C ○ Account Operators
D ○ Replicators

7 By default, who is a member of the Replicator group?

A ○ All valid users
B ○ Only users with local accounts
C ○ Only the Administrator
D ○ No one

8 Someone has been using the printer excessively. To find out who it is, you can

A ○ Turn on auditing on the printer.
B ○ Turn on Security passwords for printing resources.
C ○ Set No Access permissions on the printer.
D ○ Limit access to the printer to only managers with a system policy.

9 SandyB tries to change her password. She receives a message indicating that her new password is not long enough. Password length is set by

A ○ User Manager
B ○ Password Manager
C ○ Account Policy
D ○ Policy Editor

10 Global groups generally contain

A ○ Resources
B ○ Users
C ○ Domains
D ○ Local groups

Answers

1 *C. Account Operators.* The Account Operators group allows the project leader to manage the user accounts and not much else. *Review the section "Account Operators" for more information.*

2 *B. Copy the old local group, assign a new name to it, and delete the old local group.* You can't rename groups but you can copy them and assign new names. *See "Creating local groups."*

3 *B. She is a member of the Domain Users global group.* The other groups all have the right to log on locally to a server. *For more information, review "Managing the user rights policy" — in particular, Table 11-3.*

4 *A. JoeS.* Only a member of the Administrators group can assign a user to the Account Operators group. *See "Using built-in local groups."*

5 *C. Server Operators.* Server Operators and Administrators can override the lock on a server. *See "Server Operators."*

6 *C. Account Operators.* Account Operators and Administrators are the only two groups that can create a user account. *Review "Managing the user rights policy" — in particular, Table 11-3.*

7 *D. No one.* No one is assigned to the Replicator group by default. This is a special group. *Reread the "Replicator" section.*

8 *A. Turn on auditing on the printer.* You can audit several events on printers, files, and folders. *For more details on what you can audit, see "Administering Security Policies."*

9 *C. Account Policy.* Account policy is where all password parameters are set. *Review "Administering Security Policies" for more details.*

10 *B. Users.* Global groups contain user accounts. *See "Global Groups."*

Chapter 12

Permission to Manage Resources, Sir!

- -

Exam Objectives

▶ Setting permissions for local resources

▶ Setting permissions for network resources

▶ Combining local and network resources

▶ Auditing file and folder access

- -

*W*ith the capability to allow multiple users access to the same physical system, and the capability to connect users to resources shared over a network, you face the necessity for managing those shared resources. The Enterprise exam has numerous questions dealing with resource management, and in this chapter we explore the information you need to know.

As we discuss in this chapter, NT's security layer enables you to manage security permissions for local resources and network resources, and it allows combinations of different security privileges for those resources. You can also set up auditing to see how privileges you allow for resources on your network are being utilized.

Quick Assessment

Setting permissions for local resources

1 The _____ resource permission *always* overrides any other granted access.

2 What are the default NTFS security permissions on a newly created local file or directory?

3 A user belongs to two groups with different NTFS security privileges on a local resource. One group has the Change permission. The other group has the Read permission. When logged on locally, which permissions does the user have?

4 (True/False). You can set the same security permissions on an NTFS partition as you can on a FAT partition.

5 (True/False). You can set NTFS permissions at the file level and the directory level.

Setting permissions for network resources

6 What are the default share security permissions on a newly created network share?

7 (True/False). After you change a user's group membership, the user has immediate access to all resources with access defined for that group.

Combining local and network resources

8 When comparing NTFS permissions to Network share permissions, which permission takes priority: the least restrictive or the most restrictive?

Auditing file and folder access

9 You view NT's security audit logs through the _____ utility.

10 Before setting audit events for files and folders, you must turn on File and Object Auditing through the _____ utility.

Answers

1 *No Access.* Review "Understanding NTFS security."

2 *The Everyone group has Full Control.* See "Implementing local security."

3 *The least restrictive permission — in this case, Change.* For details on how you determine the effective permissions, see "Understanding NTFS security."

4 *False.* See "Managing Local Resources."

5 *True.* Review "Managing Local Resources" for details on file and directory permission settings.

6 *The Everyone group has Full Control.* Review "Setting permissions on network shares."

7 *False.* Check out "Goin' with the resource access flow."

8 *The most restrictive.* Review "Working together: Local and network security."

9 *Event Viewer.* See "Auditing File Resources."

10 *User Manager for Domains.* You can find details in the section "Auditing File Resources."

Understanding NT Security and Permissions

Resource sharing, as you know, is perhaps the greatest benefit of networking. With the capability to share resources, however, comes an obvious requirement for security. After all, you don't want to give your Marketing department the capability to change the product requirement documents on your development team's local drives.

Fortunately, NT includes a complete security system, including a secure file system, local and network resource permissions, and file and resource auditing. In fact, with NT security, resource sharing is not limited to the network. You can actually define security settings for resources on a user-by-user basis on a local machine!

Remember the following points as you prepare for this part of the Enterprise exam:

- ✔ Focus on the various rights that NT Server grants with a specific permission.

- ✔ Remember that No Access always overrides other permissions.

- ✔ Within a resource category, NT Server always grants the least restrictive permission (unless you specify No Access, of course).

- ✔ If you cross resource categories, however, NT grants the most restrictive permission. The two resource categories are local NTFS File and Object resources and Network Share resources.

- ✔ Resource permission priority is perhaps the most important topic we cover in this chapter. Most of the resource management questions on your exam involve permission priority.

- ✔ If you change resource permissions, a user must log off and log back on before the changes take effect. This requirement results from the resource access flow that Windows NT follows. You may see a handful of troubleshooting questions that refer to resource access flow.

Managing Local Resources

Any resource physically located and managed on a machine on which you're working is considered a *local resource*. Local security settings apply only to users logged on at the machine on which the resource and settings are defined. Managing local security for file resources requires the use of the NTFS, rather than the FAT file system.

If you see a question on your exam asking about local resource security settings for a FAT drive, look for an answer that says the solution won't work. You can only set local resource security settings for NTFS drives.

Suppose your office is open 24 hours a day. The office has three shifts per day, and each workstation may have as many as three different users assigned. You don't share network file space; all resources are managed locally. You don't want users to be able to change each other's documents. To facilitate this security, you must be using the NTFS file system, and you must implement security settings on the local files and directories.

Understanding NTFS security

NTFS security is important! You'll see some questions on the exam that ask about various aspects of NTFS security.

NTFS allows you to set permissions on folders and individual files — a feature that FAT can never provide. FAT only allows you to add permissions to a share; any subdirectories and files within that share contain the same permissions.

With NTFS, each file in the share can have different permissions. This feature is convenient when you want to give someone access to a particular file or folder, but you don't want to create a whole new share for it. For example, if you have a share on an NTFS volume called Documents, you can set up the share permissions to give everyone Full Control. If you put a file called Page1.doc in the Documents directory and set the NTFS permissions for that file to allow everyone No Access, then everyone can access all the files except Page1.doc.

Throughout this chapter, as well as on your exam, the terms *folder* and *directory* are used interchangeably, as are the terms *subfolder* and *subdirectory*.

Remember: Any time a user belongs to multiple groups with different access permissions, the least restrictive of those permissions applies to the user. The exception to this rule is if one of the groups has been assigned the No Access permission. We can't say it enough: No Access *always* overrides every other granted permission.

Also remember that the FAT permissions are still available to NTFS. If a file or folder has Full Control and the Read-Only flag is set on the Properties page, then the file or folder is read-only.

You will see questions on your exam that ask you what rights someone has to an NTFS file or folder. Read these types of questions carefully. With NTFS permissions, even if you have permission to access a file or folder with your user account, if you are a member of a group that has been granted No Access to the file or folder, then you have no access.

Implementing local security

By default, every newly created folder or file grants Full Control to the Everyone group. This default permission means all users can do anything they want to any file or folder for which security has not been explicitly defined. To set permissions on a file or folder, you must first remove the Everyone group from the permissions list, and define permissions from that point. An important exception to this rule becomes apparent when a file or folder is added to an existing directory structure with permissions already defined. Newly created files and folders inherit the security permissions of parent folders.

You can expect to see a question on your Enterprise exam dealing with assigning No Access versus not assigning permissions to the Everyone group. Notice, when defining security, you want to *remove* the Everyone group from the permissions list. You don't want to set the Everyone group to No Access. Setting No Access for the Everyone group overrides any other permissions you may assign for all users or groups.

To access the security properties for files and folders, right-click the file or folder, choose Properties from the pop-up menu, and select the Security tab. Table 12-1 lists the available permissions for an NTFS folder. NTFS file permissions are similar, but only include the settings No Access, Read, Change, Full Control, and Special File Access.

Table 12-1	NTFS Folder Permissions
Permission	*Description*
No Access	Indicates that the specified user or group has no rights to the folder. No Access always overrides all other explicitly assigned group or user permissions.
List	Allows the specified user or group to view the directory name and change to a subfolder within the directory.
Read	Allows the same functions as the List permission, with the added capability to view data files or run applications within the folder.
Add	Allows specified users or groups to add files and subdirectories to the folder.
Add & Read	Combines the rights available through the Add and Read permissions.
Change	Combines the rights available through Add, List, and Read, with the added permission to modify data files or delete files and subdirectories.

Permission	Description
Full Control	Allows all permissions granted through Add, List, Read, and Change, with the added permission to set security permissions or take ownership for files and subdirectories.
Special Directory Access	Allows customized security permissions for folders and subdirectories. Available permissions include Full Control, Read, Write, Execute, Delete, Change Permission, and Take Ownership.
Special File Access	Allows customized security settings for files, including Unspecified (inherits Special Directory Access settings), Full Control, Read, Write, Execute, Delete, Change Permissions, and Take Ownership.

Reviewing directory permissions options

After you define security on a directory, all subsequently created files under that directory structure inherit the same security permissions.

Directory-level permissions include two options that are not available with security at the file level:

- ✓ **Replace Permissions on Subdirectories:** This option sets the permissions specified in the Name box for all folders below the current directory level.
- ✓ **Replace Permissions on Existing Files:** This option sets the permissions specified in the Name box for all files in the current directory.

If you select both of these options, all files and folders — including files in subfolders of your current directory — inherit the security permissions specified in the Name box. If neither option is selected, permissions apply only to the directory and any subsequently created files. The default options are to replace permissions on files, but not on subdirectories.

Managing Network Resources

As we mention earlier in this chapter, resource sharing is perhaps the greatest benefit of having a network. With the capability for users to store data on shared resources, you must have capabilities for controlling access to those resources on a user-by-user basis. Sharing disk resources allows for centralized management of your enterprise file space. By centralizing management, you minimize the storage space requirements on local workstations, making it easier for users to share data, and allowing you to back up all user data at the same time — much easier than backing up every workstation in your enterprise.

Creating and sharing resources

You will definitely see a couple of questions on your exam relating to sharing network resources. You can set network sharing on folders through My Computer, Windows NT Explorer, or Server Manager. To set up network resources, you must be a member of either the Administrators or the Server Operators group.

The process couldn't be easier: Simply right-click a folder, choose Sharing from the pop-up menu, and click the Shared As option button in the resulting dialog box. You can either accept the defaults, or set additional options.

By default, your share name is the same as your folder name. For example, if you're sharing a folder named Documents, the default share name is Documents.

Here's a fact you need to know for the exam: As with all shared resources, adding a dollar sign ($) to the end of a share name makes the resource invisible to network browsers.

By default, no user limit is defined on a shared resource. By defining this option, you prevent more than the specified number of users from connecting to a network resource at one time.

The Comments text box, which is blank by default, allows you to set a comment string for a share. This comment string has no effect on the function of the network share.

Setting permissions on network shares

To set network permissions, click the Permissions button on the Sharing properties tab. Table 12-2 describes your available network permissions, which you should know for your exam.

Table 12-2	Network File Permissions
Permission	*Description*
No Access	The specified user or group has no rights to the shared resource. No Access always overrides all other explicitly assigned group or user permissions.
Read	The user can view files and directories within a network share. With this permission, the user can open documents on a read-only basis, execute programs, and navigate subdirectories.
Change	In addition to the rights associated with the Read permission, a user can add files and subdirectories, change existing data or directories, and delete files and directories.
Full Control	This permission allows all permissions granted through Read and Change, with the added permission to set security permissions or take ownership for files and subdirectories on NTFS partitions.

You don't have as many available network resource permissions as local resource permissions. By default, the Everyone group has Full Control permissions on a newly created network share. Unlike local resource permissions, you can grant network share permissions to directories on any file system, and you can't grant network permissions at the file level.

As with local resource permissions, if a user belongs to multiple groups with different access permissions, the least restrictive of those permissions applies to the user. The exception to this rule is if one of the groups has been assigned the No Access permission. Just in case we haven't run this point completely into the ground: No Access *always* overrides every other granted permission.

Accessing network resources

After you configure a network resource, domain users with appropriate permissions can access it from remote workstations. For example, using the network share, you may have a directory shared with the share name Documents. Assume that this share is located on a server with the computer name PDC. You can access this resource in several ways.

One of the easiest ways to view a shared resource is through the network Neighborhood. In Figure 12-1, you can see the computer name PDC under Network Neighborhood. After you select PDC, a window opens up displaying the available share names for that computer. As you can see in Figure 12-1, the Documents network share is displayed, along with the NETLOGON share, which shows up on every domain controller, and a Printers share, which shows up on every system running a server service on your network.

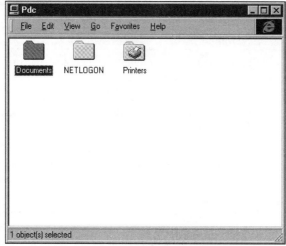

Figure 12-1:
Network
shares
on PDC.

If you know a computer name and share name for a resource, you can type the Universal Naming Convention (UNC) name directly into the Start⇨Run dialog box. In the preceding example, the UNC name is \\PDC\Documents. By entering this name in the Run dialog box, you open an Explorer window that allows additional browsing of the files and subdirectories. In addition, simply typing \\PDC in the Run dialog box opens a window displaying the available shares on the computer PDC. In this example, a Documents folder would be displayed, and opening it would bring you to the same place as the previous method.

If you frequently access a network resource, you may want to associate the share with a drive letter on your system, as shown in Figure 12-2. For this purpose, you create what's known as a *persistent network connection*. Every time you log on to your system, the network connection attempts to re-establish itself. We show you how to create a persistent network connection in Lab 12-1.

Lab 12-1   Creating a Persistent Network Connection (Mapping a Drive)

1. **Log on to the workstation from which you want to create the persistent network connection.**

   For purposes of this lab, assume that you have a network with a single domain named DOMAIN1, a single domain controller with the computer name PDC, and a single workstation with the computer name WKST1. Your domain user name is JFERRIS. JFERRIS is a member of the Users group. You have already created a share on your PDC named DOCUMENTS. So for this example, log on to WKST1 as JFERRIS in the DOMAIN1 domain.

Figure 12-2:
Mapping a
network
drive.

2. **Choose Start➪Programs➪Windows NT Explorer.**

3. **Choose Tools➪Map Network Drive.**

   You see the dialog box shown previously in Figure 12-2.

4. **From the Drive drop-down list, select an available drive letter.**

   For this example, select S:.

5. **Make sure the Reconnect at Login box is checked.**

6. **In the Shared Directories box, expand Microsoft Windows NT Network.**

7. **Locate the share to which you want to create the drive mapping.**

   In the example, you expand PDC, and select the Documents folder.

8. **Click OK.**

   In the example, drive S: for user JFERRIS on workstation WKST1 is mapped to the \\PDC\DOCUMENTS share every time the user logs on. The drive letter appears in Windows NT Explorer, My Computer, at the DOS command prompt, and anywhere else that lists available local drives.

Goin' with the resource access flow

Although you don't need to know the details of resource access flow for the exam, you need to understand one specific concept. As you can see from the process we outline in this section, an access token is created at logon. NT security checks for privileges against that token. If you add a user to a new group, the token doesn't contain the group Security Identifier (SID), and will not be re-created until the user logs off and logs back on to the network.

The access flow is as follows:

1. When a user logs on, a security access token is generated. This token contains the SIDs for the user account, and any groups of which the account is a member.

2. When a resource is accessed, NT's security layer checks that token against the Access Control List for that resource to see whether an account is able to access the resource.

3. If the account is present on the Access Control List, NT's security layer checks the Access Control Entries to determine which privileges the account has been granted.

So what does that all mean? Assume you have a shared resource on your network named LAWSUITS, and only members of your LEGAL group are able to access that resource. Jeffrey just transferred to your Legal department, and you add his user account to the LEGAL group. Jeffrey calls to say he still can't access the LAWSUITS share. Even though you added his account to the LEGAL group, until Jeffrey logs off and logs back on to the network, his system still checks the Access Control List against the originally created token, which doesn't yet reflect his addition to the LEGAL group.

Working together: Local and network security

Local and network security in NT are good friends. You can configure them in a similar method, and you can assign them similar permissions. They can also work together. If you define both NTFS permissions and share permissions for a directory, the most restrictive access determines what a network user can do. If a user accesses a shared resource from the machine on which it is defined using the physical path and directory name instead of the UNC name, only the NTFS permissions apply.

Auditing File Resources

After you set up security for your local and network resources, how can you tell when your users take advantage of their various permissions? This is where file and object access auditing comes in. Before you can define audit requirements for your various resources, you must enable file and object access auditing for your domain. As we show you in Lab 12-2, you enable file and object access auditing by using the User Manager for Domains.

Lab 12-2   Enabling File and Object Access Auditing

1. **To start the User Manager for Domains, choose Start➪Administration Tools➪User Manager for Domains.**

2. **Choose Policies➪Audit.**

   The User Manager for Domains displays the Audit Policy dialog box shown in Figure 12-3.

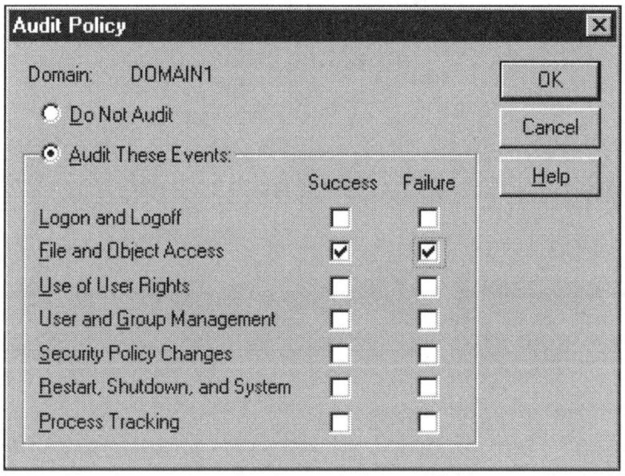

Figure 12-3:
Enabling file and object access auditing.

3. **Select both check boxes for File and Object Access and then click OK.**

   With file and object access auditing enabled, you can set audit flags on various local and network resources. You set these flags on the Security tab in the Properties dialog box for a specified file or folder.

4. **To access the Security properties for a specific file or folder, right-click the file or folder, select Properties from the resulting pop-up menu, and then click the Security tab in the Properties dialog box.**

5. **Click Auditing.**

   For folders, you see the dialog box shown in Figure 12-4.

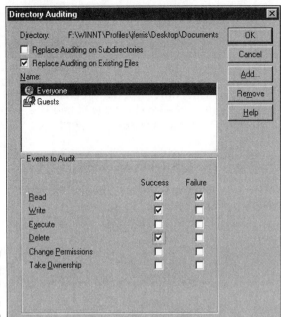

Figure 12-4:
Folder
auditing.

6. **Add the users or groups for which you want to enable auditing, and select the events you want to audit from the available check boxes.**

   To view the auditing records, you must use the Event Viewer.

7. **Choose Start➪Programs➪Administrative Tools➪Event Viewer.**

   Audit events are listed under the Security Log.

Prep Test

1 You have created a share for the Documents directory on a computer named FILESERV1. You haven't modified any of the default permissions for the newly created share. Which type of access exists for this share?

A ○ The Administrators group has Full Control. You must grant access to specific users and groups to allow others to access the newly created share.

B ○ The Everyone group has Full Control. You must remove access for the Everyone group if you want to set group- or user-based security.

C ○ The Everyone group has No Access. You must explicitly grant access on newly created network shares.

D ○ The account you were using when you created the share is the only account with access. You must add all users or groups manually.

2 Shawn is a member of the Accounting group, the Finance group, and the Users group. You have a share on your FILESERV1 server named FINANCE for which the Accounting group is allowed Read Access, the Finance group has Full Control, and the Users group is allowed No Access. Shawn can't access the FINANCE share. What must you do to allow Shawn to access this resource?

A ○ Add Shawn's user account to the Access Control List for Finance.

B ○ Remove Shawn's account from the Users group.

C ○ Give the Accounting group Full Access.

D ○ Remove Shawn's account from the Accounting group.

3 Tim wants to create a new network share from your WIDGETS directory. Of which group must Tim be a member to allow him to create a network share? (Choose all that apply.)

A ❑ Administrators

B ❑ Server Operators

C ❑ Account Operators

D ❑ Users

4 Which utility must you use to view audit logs generated by file and object access auditing?

A ○ User Manager for Domains

B ○ Notepad

C ○ Server Manager

D ○ Event Viewer

5 You have a network share named DOCUMENTS for which you have enabled file and object access auditing through the Securities tab on the Properties dialog box. You have enabled Success and Failure logging for the Read and Write events for the Everyone special group. When you attempt to generate an audit event, it doesn't show up in the security log. What else must you do to enable auditing?

A ○ You must enable auditing through the Audit menu of the Server Manager.

B ○ You must start the Auditing service from the Services Manager.

C ○ You must enable file and object access auditing from the Audit menu in the User Manager for Domains.

D ○ You must enable file and object access auditing from the Event Viewer's Audit menu.

6 You have a folder on an NTFS drive named ACCOUNTING. The folder is also shared on the network as ACCOUNTING. James is a member of the Accounting group and the Users group. Which type of access does he have from across the network if access privileges to the folder are as follows?

Local NTFS Folder Security	*Network Share Security*
Accounting Group: Change	Accounting Group: Read
Auditing Group: Read	Auditing Group: Read
Administrators: Full Control	Administrators Group: Full Control

A ○ No Access

B ○ Change

C ○ Read

D ○ Full Control

7 Patricia, a member of the Photographers and Users groups, is attempting to access the STOCKPHOTO network share. Which access does Patricia have from across the network if access privileges to the folder are as follows?

Local NTFS Folder Security	*Network Share Security*
Photographers Group: Full Control	Photographers Group: Full Control
Users Group: Read	Users Group: Read
Reporters Group: No Access	Reporters Group: No Access

A ○ No Access

B ○ Change

C ○ Read

D ○ Full Control

8 Matt is attempting to access files in the network share APPS. He is a member of the Users and the Agents groups. Which access does Matt have from across the network if access privileges to the folder are as follows?

Local NTFS Folder Security	*Network Share Security*
Users Group: Add & Read	Users Group: Read
Agents Group: Change	Agents Group: Full Control
Administrators: Full Control	Administrators Group: Full Control

A ○ No Access
B ○ Change
C ○ Read
D ○ Add & Read
E ○ Full Control

9 How can you prevent users from seeing a network share while browsing the network through the Network Neighborhood?

A ○ Select the Create Share as Hidden option box on the Sharing properties tab.
B ○ Add a dollar sign ($) to the end of the share name.
C ○ Add a percent sign (%) to the end of the share name.
D ○ Select the Make Hidden option box on the Share name under the Server Manager.

10 Which permission always overrides any other explicitly granted group or user permissions?

A ○ Full Control
B ○ No Access
C ○ Special File or Folder Access
D ○ List

Answers

1 *B. The Everyone group has Full Control. You must remove access for the Everyone group if you want to set group- or user-based security.* The default setting for a newly created share is to grant Full Control to the Everyone group. *Review "Setting permissions on network shares."*

2 *B. Remove Shawn's account from the Users group.* The No Access privilege always overrides other privileges. You must remove Shawn from the Users group, or remove the No Access privilege for the Users group on the FINANCE share. *Review "Understanding NTFS security."*

3 *A and B.* Only Administrators or Server Operators can add new shares. *Review "Creating and sharing resources."*

4 *D. Event Viewer.* In the Event Viewer, viewing the Security log displays audit events. *Review "Auditing File Resources."*

5 *C. You must enable file and object access auditing from the Audit menu in the User Manager for Domains.* Before audit events can be recorded in the Event Viewer, you must enable them by choosing Policies⇨Audit in the User Manager for Domains. *Review "Auditing File Resources."*

6 *C. Read.* James has Read access because Read is the most restrictive of the NTFS or Network Share settings. *Review "Working together: Local and network security."*

7 *D. Full Control.* Patricia has Full Control. When combining resource permissions for multiple group membership, the least restrictive permission applies, unless No Access is specified. No Access always overrides other settings. In this case, the NTFS resource permissions are the same as the Network share permissions. *Review "Working together: Local and network security."*

8 *B. Change.* Matt has Change access. Because he is a member of both Agents and Users, the least restrictive NTFS permission is Change, and the least restrictive Network permission is Full Control. Change and Full Control are both for the Agents group. The most restrictive of the permission settings between the Local and the Network resource is the NTFS Change permission for the Agents group. Therefore, Matt has the Change permission for the APPS share. *Review "Working together: Local and network security."*

9 *B. Add a dollar sign ($) to the end of the share name.* Adding a dollar sign to the end of any shared resource prevents the resource from showing up on the Network Neighborhood browse list. *Review "Creating and sharing resources."*

10 *B. No Access.* In case you can't tell by how many times we repeat this point throughout the chapter, No Access *always* overrides any other granted permission. *Review "Understanding NTFS security."*

Chapter 13

User Profiles, System Policies, and Hardware Profiles, Oh My!

- -

Exam Objectives

▶ Managing the user environment

▶ Understanding user profiles and hardware profiles

▶ Reviewing user, group, and computer policies

- -

*M*anaging the user's environment is a key part of your job as an administrator and a key part of the Enterprise exam. You need to be familiar with all the different tools and methods that you can employ to perform this task. You also need to know how to implement these tools and you need to understand the differences among them.

System policies and user profiles assist in the centralization of management in a Windows NT domain. System policies help an administrator implement common Registry settings across the enterprise. User profiles store the user portion of the Registry. You can implement these profiles as either local or roaming profiles. Roaming profiles enable users to have the user portion of their configuration follow them wherever they log on to the network.

 For the exam, make sure you understand the processes for creating local user profiles, setting up roaming user profiles, and establishing mandatory profiles. You also want to know what a system policy contains and how to create a hardware profile.

Quick Assessment

Managing the user environment

1 The _____ contains the specifics of a user's working environment.

2 _____ control(s) user environments.

Understanding user profiles and hardware profiles

3 You can force a user to maintain specific desktop settings by using a _____.

4 Roaming profiles are stored on a network _____.

5 To designate a specific user profile, you use the _____.

6 Policies can be applied to _____, _____, and _____.

Reviewing user, group, and computer policies

7 You use the _____ to create policies.

8 Computer policies alter the Registry subkey _____.

9 You can display a logon banner by using a _____.

10 Group system policies use _____ group memberships.

Answers

1 *User profile.* See "Understanding User Profiles."

2 *System policies.* See "Setting System Policies."

3 *Mandatory profile.* See "Understanding User Profiles."

4 *Server.* See "Understanding User Profiles."

5 *User Manager for Domains.* See "Understanding User Profiles."

6 *Users; groups; computers.* See "Understanding User Profiles" and "Configuring Hardware Profiles."

7 *Policy Editor.* See "Setting System Policies."

8 *HKEY_LOCAL_MACHINE.* See "Setting System Policies."

9 *Computer system policy.* See "Setting System Policies."

10 *Global.* See "Specifying user and group system policies."

Managing the User Environment

A *user environment* defines the following information:

- ✔ The submenus available from the Start menu
- ✔ Taskbar settings
- ✔ Screen colors
- ✔ Mouse settings
- ✔ Printer and network connections
- ✔ Icons on the desktop

Windows NT Server has a number of tools for managing a user's environment. User profiles and logon scripts offer two of the most important methods for managing these settings.

User profiles are only effective on workstations running Windows NT Workstation. In a mixed-network environment (for example, one running MS-DOS, Windows for Workgroups, or other operating systems), a logon script works best.

Understanding User Profiles

You define the specific properties of a user's working environment in the User Environment Profile dialog box, shown in Figure 13-1. You access this dialog box in User Manager for Domains. Double-clicking the desired user name brings up the properties page for that user. By clicking the Profiles button at the bottom of this page, you open the User Environment Profile dialog box. To set up a User Profile, you must be a member of the Administrators or Account Operators groups.

You define the following properties in the User Environment Profile dialog box:

- ✔ **User Profile Path:** The network path to the user's profile folder. The user profile contains the desktop and program settings for a user. You specify the path in the following form: *server\profiles folder*.
- ✔ **Logon Script Name:** The name of a batch file that runs when a user logs on to the network.
- ✔ **Home Directory:** The user's default directory for opening and saving files. It can be located on a server or a workstation.

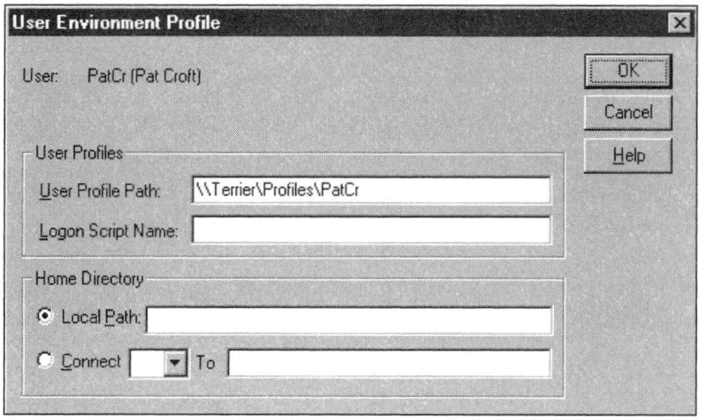

Figure 13-1:
The User
Environment
Profile
dialog box.

Reviewing the benefits of defining profiles

As an administrator, you need to ensure that NT Server and the client workstations offer a consistent look and feel for users throughout the enterprise network. At the same time, users may want to customize their desktops. User profiles give you the flexibility to balance an administrator's need for consistency with the users' desire for personalized work environments.

Profiles offer several advantages to the user:

- ✔ When users log on to their computers, the settings and the desktop are the same as when the users last logged off.

- ✔ Several people can use the same computer, and each user can have a customized desktop.

- ✔ You can save a user profile as a roaming profile on a server so that the user has the same environment at any Windows NT computer on the network.

Profiles also offer the administrator several advantages:

- ✔ You can create special profiles that don't include extraneous items and provide a consistent environment for users.

- ✔ You can create a profile and assign it to a specific group of users.

- ✔ You can assign mandatory profiles so that users can't change their desktop settings.

- ✔ You can control access to resources.

- ✔ You can make resources accessible to a group of users sharing the same profile.

Creating local user profiles

When a user logs on to a workstation for the first time, Windows NT creates a profile by recording any changes made to the profile during that session and stores them in that person's local user profile. Those settings are specific to that workstation. The profiles are normally stored in C:\WINNT\PROFILES.

You can save many settings in a user profile. Table 13-1 lists the settings that you can save.

Table 13-1	User Profile Settings
Source	*Saved Setting*
Windows NT Explorer	All user-controlled settings — for example, view settings and folder arrangement settings
Control Panel	All user-controlled settings — for example, screen colors and mouse pointers
Accessories	All user-controlled settings in the listed applets
Taskbar	All personal programs and groups and their settings, and all taskbar settings
Printers	Network Printer connections
Windows NT applications	All user-configurable settings in multiuser programs
Online Help bookmarks	Bookmarks that a user places in the Help system

Setting up roaming user profiles

The administrator can set up a roaming profile for users so that their settings travel with them. When you provide a profile path in a user account, the user sets up the desktop and, when the user logs off, a copy of this local profile is saved both locally and in the user profile path location. The profile on the server is entered in the Universal Naming Convention (UNC), which is *servername**sharename*. Lab 13-1 shows you how to implement a roaming profile. As with all actions dealing with user accounts, you must be logged on as an Administrator or an Account Operator.

Lab 13-1	Creating a Roaming Profile

1. **Open User Manager for Domains, and then double-click the user's account to open the User Properties dialog box.**

2. **Click the Profile button to open the User Environment dialog box.**

3. **Enter the profile path in the User Profile Path text box.**

   This step creates an empty folder, where the self-configured user's profile will be stored.

4. **Under Home Directory, assign a path to a home directory on a server.**

If a domain controller is unavailable at logon, the user can't receive the mandatory profile. When this happens, Windows NT uses the user's last locally cached profile or the default profile assigned to the workstation. Windows NT uses the locally cached profile if the user has successfully logged on to the domain in the past. If the user has never logged on before, Windows NT uses the default profile.

Establishing mandatory user profiles

You can force users to maintain settings by establishing mandatory profiles. To produce a mandatory profile:

1. **Establish a roaming profile for a user.**

2. **Copy that profile to a shared directory.**

3. **Assign the appropriate users to the profile.**

4. **Change the name of the Ntuser.dat file to Ntuser.man, and enter the profile path into the User Profile Path dialog box in the User Environment Profile dialog box for each user.**

Setting System Policies

System policies control user environments and actions. You create system policies with the System Policy Editor, which you launch by choosing Start⇨Programs⇨Administrative Tools(common)⇨System Policy Editor. Figure 13-2 shows the System Policy Editor.

The System Policy Editor gives you the following capabilities:

✔ Specifying which programs are available in the user's Control Panel

✔ Specifying network settings

✔ Controlling network access

✔ Customizing user desktops

✔ Setting the Start menu program options

You can set a default system policy for all users, computers, groups, or individual users. By setting up policies, you modify Registry settings in the HKEY_LOCAL_MACHINE and HKEY_CURRENT_USER hives.

To define a system policy as the default policy, you must save the policy in \winnt\system32\Repl\Import\Scripts with the filename of Ntconfig.pol. This path is shared by default as NETLOGON. After starting replication, the default system policy is copied to all BDCs in the domain.

Figure 13-2:
The System
Policy
Editor.

If you define a system policy, you must choose between two modes: Registry and Policy File mode. To choose the desired mode:

1. **Open the File menu in the System Policy Editor.**

2. **Choose either Open Policy or Open Registry.**

   Open Policy lets you edit an existing policy. Open Registry leads you to the Registry hives HKEY_LOCAL_MACHINE and HKEY_LOCAL_USER.

   The Open Registry option enables you to edit the Registry of a remote computer.

3. **Make your changes and then save them.**

Specifying user and group system policies

You can set policies on a user-by-user basis. When a user logs on, NT Server checks Ntconfig.pol to determine whether a policy exists for that user. If no user policy exists, NT Server uses the default user policy for the logon process. Figure 13-3 shows the Default User Properties dialog box. To access this dialog box, start System Policy Editor and then choose File⇨Open.

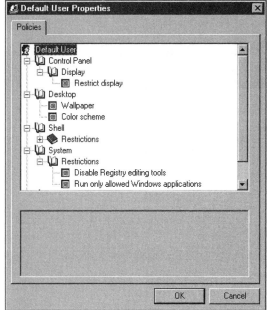

Figure 13-3:
Default
User
Properties
dialog box.

Here are some common restrictions that you can place on users through policies:

- ✔ Locking down the display properties. You can prevent users from changing all or some of the display properties.

- ✔ Setting a default color scheme or wallpaper.

- ✔ Standardizing the desktop. By deciding what to include in the Start menu, or by using the Shell/Restrictions options in the Default User Properties dialog box, you can control the capabilities that each user's desktop offers.

- ✔ Limiting which applications run on a workstation as well as access to the Registry.

- ✔ Preventing mapping or connection to network drives.

Group policies affect multiple users, and thus add another level of complexity to processing policies. To specify that a policy applies to a particular group, you use the Add Groups dialog box shown in Figure 13-4. To open this dialog box in the System Policy Editor, choose Edit⇨Add Group.

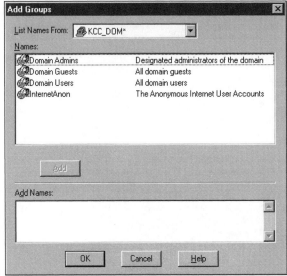

Figure 13-4:
The Add
Groups
dialog box.

Keep the following considerations in mind when you define group policies:

- ✔ The System Policy Editor uses global group memberships.
- ✔ Because a user can belong to multiple global groups, the order in which groups are processed is very important.

One group's settings may be opposite of another group's. To set the group order in the System Policy Editor, choose Options⇨Group Priority.

Configuring computer system policies

You can configure computer policies to lock down common machine settings that affect all users of that computer. You can change these settings by starting the System Policy Editor and double-clicking the Default Computer icon. Figure 13-5 shows the resulting Default Computer Properties dialog box.

Here are some common settings:

- ✔ Specifying which programs automatically run at startup.
- ✔ Setting the Administrative share on all computers at startup.
- ✔ Implementing a custom shared folder, which can be desktop folders, Start menu folders, the Start Up folder, and the Programs folder.
- ✔ Presenting a custom dialog box called the Logon Banner. You can use this dialog box to inform users of upcoming maintenance or other events.

✔ Removing the last logged on user from the Logon dialog box. This capability is a security feature because many users have predictable passwords. Knowing the last user's user name can help in guessing a user's password.

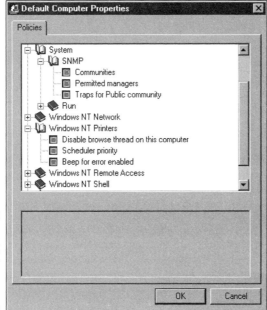

Figure 13-5:
The Default Computer Properties dialog box.

After you implement a policy for a particular computer, the Default Computer Properties dialog box adds an icon with that computer's name to the appropriate policy.

You need to know the processing order of policies:

1. The user successfully logs on to the network.

2. Windows NT reads the user profile from the NETLOGON share of the authenticating domain controller.

3. If a predefined policy exists for that user, Windows NT merges the policy into the HKEY_CURRENT_USER Registry subtree, and processing moves to Step 6.

4. If no predefined policy exists, the Windows NT uses the default policy.

5. Windows NT examines the group priority list. If the user is a member of any of the global groups for which a policy exists, Windows NT processes the account according to the group priority order. The priority is ordered from bottom to top of the list. Windows NT applies each group policy to the HKEY_CURRENT_USER Registry subtree.

6. Windows NT determines the machine policies. If a predefined machine policy exists, NT applies that policy to the HKEY_LOCAL_MACHINE Registry subtree. If no defined policy exists for this machine, NT applies the default policy to the HKEY_LOCAL_MACHINE Registry subtree.

Configuring Hardware Profiles

A hardware profile is a method for configuring which devices and services to launch at startup time depending on the location of the hardware or the tasks to be completed. A hardware profile enables a user to configure which devices are to be available for use when starting up the computer.

When making a major change to the system hardware, create a copy of the hardware profile, boot into it, and make the necessary changes. If something doesn't work, you can return to the previous configuration. Figure 13-6 shows the Hardware Profiles tab in the System Properties dialog box.

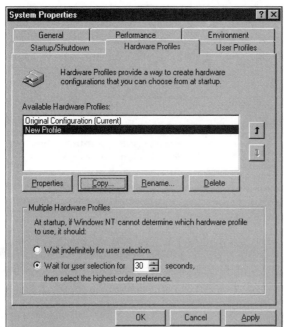

Figure 13-6:
The
Hardware
Profiles tab.

To create a copy of your current hardware profile and make it the preferred boot option:

1. Right-click the My Computer icon.

2. Choose Properties to bring up the System Properties dialog box.

3. Click the Hardware Profiles tab.

4. Select the current hardware profile, click Copy, and then enter the name for the copy in the To text box.

5. If you want to make this copy the preferred boot option, select it, and click the up-arrow button to move it to the top of the list.

6. Decide whether you want Windows NT Server to choose the new hardware profile automatically when you boot up or you want the system to wait indefinitely until you choose the hardware profile.

7. Click OK to save the new configuration and set the startup option.

1 Which registry hives are affected by using system policies? (Choose two.)

A ❑ HKEY_LOCAL_MACHINE

B ❑ HKEY_CLASSES_ROOT

C ❑ HKEY_CURRENT_USER

D ❑ HKEY_LOCAL_USER

2 User profiles are effective on which operating systems?

A ○ Windows NT Workstation

B ○ Windows for Workgroups

C ○ MacOS System 7

D ○ MS-DOS 5.0 or greater

3 Which two items assist in the centralized management of a Windows NT enterprise network? (Choose all that apply.)

A ❑ Local groups

B ❑ System policies

C ❑ User profiles

D ❑ Global groups

4 Which user profile type enables users to have their desktop settings follow them to wherever they log on the Windows NT network?

A ○ Local

B ○ Group

C ○ Roaming

D ○ Global

5 A user has a roaming profile set up on your Windows NT network. When logging on to a Windows NT Workstation that the user hasn't used before, the user sees the default desktop settings. What is a possible cause?

A ○ The PDC is down.

B ○ The server holding the user's profile is down.

C ○ The workstation is not on the network.

D ○ Nothing — this is what happens the first time a user logs on to a workstation.

6 What is the default name of the system policy file?

A ○ Config.pol

B ○ Ntconfig.pol

C ○ System.dat

D ○ System.pol

7 Using the System Policy Editor, you can create policies for which of the following? (Choose all that apply.)

A ❑ Domain

B ❑ Computer

C ❑ Group

D ❑ User

8 All property changes within the Default Computer section affect which Registry subtree?

A ○ HKEY_CLASSES_ROOT

B ○ HKEY_CURRENT_USER

C ○ HKEY_LOCAL_MACHINE

D ○ HKEY_LOCAL_USER

9 Which type of policy do you use to set a default color scheme for an individual user?

A ○ System policy

B ○ User policy

C ○ Computer policy

D ○ Domain policy

10 You use a hardware profile to _____. (Choose all that apply.)

A ❑ Configure specific devices to start at system bootup.

B ❑ Set security for network access to resources at bootup.

C ❑ Select services to start at bootup.

D ❑ Restrict users to specific areas of the network.

Answers

1 *A* and *C.* Policies affect the local machine and current user Registry hives. *The section "Setting System Policies" has more details.*

2 *A. Windows NT Workstation.* User profiles are only effective on Windows NT operating systems. *Review "Managing the User Environment."*

3 *B* and *C.* System policies and user profiles are the two key elements of centralized management in Windows NT. *See "Managing the User Environment."*

4 *C. Roaming. Review "Understanding User Profiles."*

5 *B. The server holding the user's profile is down.* If the server holding a user's profile is unreachable, Windows NT uses the default profile if this is the first time the user has used this workstation. If the user has successfully logged on before, Windows NT uses a cached copy of the user's profile. *Review "Setting up roaming user profiles."*

6 *B. Ntconfig.pol.* Ntconfig.pol is the default system policy file. *See "Setting System Policies."*

7 *B, C,* and *D.* Policies can apply to users, groups, and computers. *Review "Setting System Policies."*

8 *C. HKEY_LOCAL_MACHINE.* HKEY_LOCAL_MACHINE contains all configuration information for the computer. *See "Configuring computer system policies."*

9 *B. User policy.* A user policy is best because it affects only a single user. *Review "Specifying user and group system policies."*

10 *A* and *C.* Hardware profiles control which devices and services are started at system bootup. *See "Configuring Hardware Profiles."*

Chapter 14

Client Administration: Who's the Boss?

Exam Objectives

▶ Reviewing Network Client Administrator

▶ Creating a network installation startup disk

▶ Creating installation disk sets

▶ Copying client-based network administration tools

*W*ith server-based installations, you can automate the process of setting up operating systems and applications. You store the installation files on a Windows NT Server computer, where clients booting off of floppy disks automatically connect and run the necessary setup files.

In this chapter, we discuss the Network Client Administrator, a Windows NT administrative tool that you use for server-based installations. The Network Client Administrator may be the focus of a question or two on your exam.

Quick Assessment

Reviewing
Network
Client
Adminis-
trator

1 _____ software installations are easier and faster than installing from floppy disks or CDs.

2 _____ is a utility that enables you to make network installation startup disks, create installation disk sets, and copy client-based network administration tools.

3 The two operating systems that can administer the NT domain with the client-based administration tools are _____ and _____.

Creating a
network
installation
startup disk

4 The _____ option in the Network Client Administrator starts the installation of Windows NT Server, Windows NT Workstation, Windows 95, Windows for Workgroups 3.11, or Network Client 3.0 for MS-DOS over the network.

5 You have to create a(n) _____ with the necessary source files in order for the client to install the operating system from the server.

Creating
installation
disk sets

6 The _____ option in the Network Client Administrator installs network clients on non-Windows 95 and non-Windows NT computers.

7 The installation files for the various network clients are stored in the _____ folder on the Windows NT Server CD.

Copying
client-based
network
administra-
tion tools

8 You have greater control when using the client-based administration client tools on _____ than on Windows 95 because you have more tools available.

Answers

1   *Network.* Did you know that already? If not, review the section "Examining the Network Client Administrator."

2   *Network Client Administrator.* Review "Examining the Network Client Administrator."

3   *Windows NT; Windows 95.* See "Examining the Network Client Administrator."

4   *Make Installation Startup Disks.* If you are unfamiliar with this option, review the section "Creating a Network Installation Startup Disk."

5   *Share.* See "Creating a Network Installation Startup Disk."

6   *Make Installation Disk Set.* Review "Creating Installation Disk Sets."

7   *Clients.* See the section "Creating Installation Disk Sets."

8   *Windows NT.* Check out the section "Copying Client-Based Network Administration Tools."

Examining the Network Client Administrator

The Network Client Administrator, shown in Figure 14-1, is a Windows NT Server tool that you can use to perform the following tasks:

- ✔ Creating a network installation startup disk
- ✔ Creating installation disk sets
- ✔ Copying client-based network administration tools
- ✔ Viewing remote boot information

Figure 14-1:
Network
Client
Administrator.

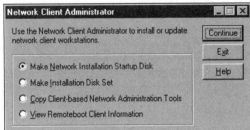

A network installation startup disk enables an operating system-less client to make a connection to a server. After the client attaches to the server, you can install the operating system shared on the server.

The Make Installation Disk Set option enables you to create a disk you can use for manually installing the network software necessary to connect a client to a Windows NT network.

The network administration tools enable a Windows NT or a Windows 95 client on a Windows NT domain to manage the domain without being on the domain controllers.

With the Copy Client-based Network Administration Tools option in the Network Client Administrator, you can create a share to the administration tools, which you can then install from the appropriate clients.

The Network Client Administrator includes a utility called View Remoteboot Client Information that you do *not* need to know for the exam. With this utility, you can view the Remoteboot service, but you can't configure it. Don't waste time studying this tool.

Creating a Network Installation Startup Disk

The first step in server-based installations is setting up the distribution files for the network installations. Copy the setup files of the operating system you want to install to a drive on the host Windows NT Server computer and create a network share. This drive must have sufficient hard disk space to store the contents for any operating systems you may want to install.

After you prepare your server for server-based installations, you can use the Network Client Administrator to create the network installation disk. For NT installation, you create an MS-DOS network client, used to access the NT share, and then you start Winnt.exe. We show you how to create this disk in Lab 14-1. After you create the network installation disk, you can use the disk to start a network installation of the following operating systems:

- ✔ Windows NT Server
- ✔ Windows NT Workstation
- ✔ Windows 95
- ✔ Windows for Workgroups 3.11
- ✔ Network Client 3.0 for MS-DOS

Lab 14-1	Creating a Network Installation Disk for a Windows 95 or MS-DOS Network Client

1. **Copy the distribution files for the operating system you want to install to the server's hard drive.**

2. **Create a network share.**

   In the Client folder on your Windows NT Server CD-ROM, find a file named Ncadmin.inf. Network Client Administrator needs this file to work. Create a network share by right-clicking the Client folder and then choosing Sharing from the resulting pop-up menu. In the dialog box that's displayed, type **OS** in the Share Name box and then click OK.

3. **Choose Start⇨Programs⇨Administrative Tools (Common)⇨Network Client Administrator.**

   The Network Client Administrator dialog box appears.

4. **Select the Make Network Installation Startup Disk option and then click Continue.**

   The Share Network Client Installation Files dialog box appears.

5. **Select the Use Existing Shared Directory option, enter the name of the Windows NT Server from which you're installing the client, enter the Share Name, and then click OK.**

   In this step, be sure to enter the same share name as the one you enter in Step 2: **OS**.

   The Target Workstation Configuration dialog box appears, as shown in Figure 14-2.

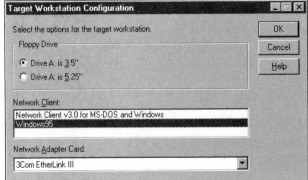

Figure 14-2: The Target Workstation Configuration dialog box.

6. **Under Network Client, highlight the client for which the network installation disk is created. Under Network Adapter Card, select the network adapter on the target computer. Click OK.**

7. **When you see the warning message about licensing, click OK.**

   You see the Network Startup Disk Configuration dialog box shown in Figure 14-3.

8. **Enter the required configuration information.**

   In the Computer Name field, enter the name used by the target computer. In the User Name field, enter the user name that you want the network installation to use to connect to the host Windows NT Server. For Domain, enter the domain to which the user account belongs. Select the network protocol that you want to use during the installation, enter any configuration settings for the chosen network protocol, and then click OK.

   The Confirm Network Disk Configuration dialog box appears, prompting you to insert an MS-DOS-formatted disk.

9. **Insert the disk and click OK to continue.**

   The network installation startup disk is created.

10. **To start the network installation, boot the target computer from the startup disk.**

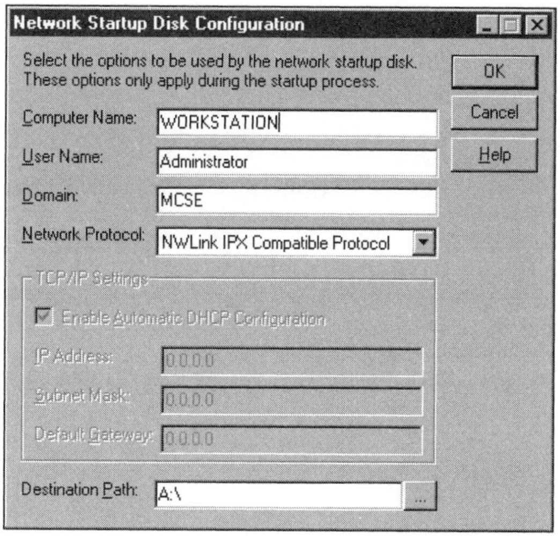

Network Startup Disk Configuration

Select the options to be used by the network startup disk.
These options only apply during the startup process.

Computer Name: `WORKSTATION`

User Name: `Administrator`

Domain: `MCSE`

Network Protocol: `NWLink IPX Compatible Protocol`

TCP/IP Settings

☑ Enable Automatic DHCP Configuration

IP Address: `0.0.0.0`

Subnet Mask: `0.0.0.0`

Default Gateway: `0.0.0.0`

Destination Path: `A:\`

OK   Cancel   Help

Figure 14-3:
The Network
Startup Disk
Configuration
dialog box.

Creating Installation Disk Sets

Microsoft Windows 95 and Windows NT come with network services and clients, such as TCP/IP and Client for Microsoft Networks. Connecting previous versions of Microsoft's operating systems to the Windows NT network requires installation disk sets. Network Client Administrator supports the creation of disk sets for the following services and clients:

✔ Microsoft Network Client 3.0 for MS-DOS

✔ Microsoft LAN Manager 2.2c for MS-DOS clients

✔ Microsoft LAN Manager 2.2c for MS-DOS OS/2 clients

✔ Microsoft Remote Access Service client 1.1 for MS-DOS

✔ Microsoft TCP/IP-32 for Windows for Workgroups 3.11

You find the files required for these network services and clients in the Client folders on the Windows NT Server CD. Lab 14-2 describes the procedure for creating installation disk sets.

Lab 14-2   Creating Installation Disk Sets

1. **Copy the Client directory from the Windows NT Server CD to the hard drive.**

2. **Create a network share named** Clients.

   See Step 2 in Lab 14-1 if you need to review the steps for creating this network share.

3. **Choose Start➪Programs➪Administrative Tools (Common)➪Network Client Administrator.**

   The Network Client Administrator dialog box appears.

4. **Select the Make Installation Disk Set option and then click Continue.**

   The Share Network Client Installation Files dialog box appears.

5. **Select the Use Existing Shared Directory option, enter the name of the Windows NT Server computer from which you're installing the installation disk sets, enter the share name** (Clients), **and then click OK.**

   You see the Make Installation Disk Set dialog box shown in Figure 14-4.

Figure 14-4:
The Make
Installation
Disk Set
dialog box.

6. **Scroll down the list and select the network client or service for which you want to create the installation disk set. Click OK.**

   Notice that we select TCP/IP for Windows for Workgroups 3.11 in Figure 14-4.

   You are prompted to insert a number of disks, depending on the network client or service you choose.

7. **Insert the disk(s) and click OK.**

   Your installation disk set is created.

You may see a question on the difference between the network installation startup disks and the installation disk set. Use the network installation startup disk to start a client computer to attach it to a share on the server, which contains the operating system installation files. An installation disk set is a set of disks with network clients and services. This set of disks is for computers that have operating systems already installed but which require network access.

Copying Client-Based Network Administration Tools

With the client-based network administration tools, managing a Windows NT domain is no longer restricted to the Windows NT Server domain controllers. Through the client-based administration tools, Windows NT Member Server, Windows NT Workstation, and Windows 95 can manage the Windows NT network. By using the Network Client Administrator, you can copy the client-based network administration tools to the hard disk and share the files or create a share to the administration tools on the NT Server CD. In Lab 14-3, we show you how to copy the client-based network administration tools.

Only clients running Windows 95 and Windows NT can administer the domain through the client-based administration tools on the Windows NT Server 4.0 CD. Users who want to administer the domain with Windows for Workgroups 3.11 or Windows 3.1 (with LAN Manager for MS-DOS) can install the client-based administration tools found on the Windows NT Server 3.51 CD.

Lab 14-3   Copying Client-Based Network Administration Tools

1. **Make sure the Windows NT Server CD is in the CD-ROM drive.**

2. **Choose Start⇨Programs⇨Administrative Tools (Common)⇨Network Client Administrator.**

   The Network Client Administrator dialog box appears.

3. **Select the Copy Client-based Network Administration Tools option and then click Continue.**

   You see the Share Client-based Administration Tools dialog box, shown in Figure 14-5. Windows NT searches for the necessary files on your CD and assigns the default path.

4. **If necessary, change the destination path and share name, and then click OK.**

   Windows NT copies the necessary files to your hard drive, shares it, and informs you when it's done.

5. **Click OK.**

   Your client-based network administration tools are now available.

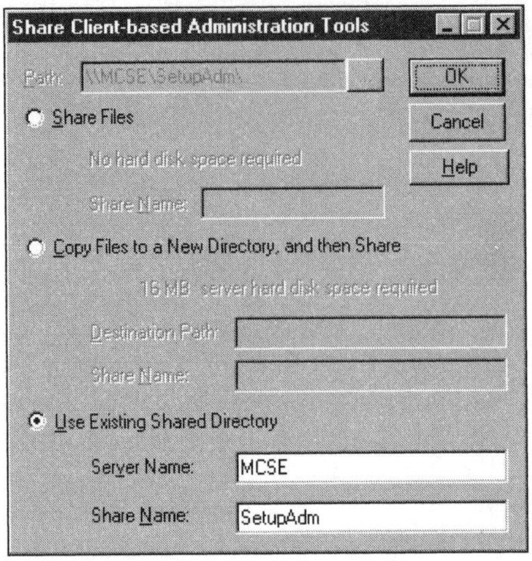

Share Client-based Administration Tools

Path: \\MCSE\SetupAdm\

☐ Share Files

   No hard disk space required

   Share Name:

☐ Copy Files to a New Directory, and then Share

   16 MB server hard disk space required

   Destination Path:

   Share Name:

☑ Use Existing Shared Directory

   Server Name: MCSE

   Share Name: SetupAdm

OK | Cancel | Help

Figure 14-5:
The Share
Client-
based
Administra-
tion Tools
dialog box.

The following client-based network administration tools are available on a Windows NT client:

- ✔ DHCP Manager
- ✔ Event Viewer
- ✔ Remote Access Administrator
- ✔ Remoteboot Manager
- ✔ Server Manager
- ✔ Services for Macintosh Manager
- ✔ User Manager for Domains
- ✔ WINS Manager
- ✔ User Profile Editor

The following client-based network administration tools are available on a Windows 95 client:

- ✔ Event Viewer
- ✔ Server Manager
- ✔ User Manager for Domains

You may see a question about the difference between the client-based network administration tools for Windows 95 and for Windows NT. Windows NT is the preferred administrative client over Windows 95 because more tools are available.

Prep Test

1 Which folder is copied from the Windows NT Server for the options of the Network Client Administrator?

A ○ i386

B ○ Client

C ○ Win95

D ○ Setup

2 Which option do you choose in the Network Client Administrator when you need to install Windows 95 on several computers?

A ○ Make Installation Startup Disk

B ○ Make Installation Disk Set

C ○ Copy Client-based Network Administration Tools

D ○ View Remoteboot Client Administration

3 Which option do you choose in the Network Client Administrator when you need to attach Windows for Workgroups 3.11 to the NT network?

A ○ Make Installation Startup Disk

B ○ Make Installation Disk Set

C ○ Copy Client-based Network Administration Tools

D ○ View Remoteboot Client Administration

4 Which option do you choose in the Network Client Administrator when you need to administer the Windows NT network but you aren't on a domain controller?

A ○ Make Installation Startup Disk

B ○ Make Installation Disk Set

C ○ Copy Client-based Network Administration Tools

D ○ View Remoteboot Client Administration

5 Which client-based administration tools are available on a Windows NT client but not on a Windows 95 client? (Choose all that apply.)

A ❑ DHCP Manager

B ❑ Server Manager

C ❑ User Manager for Domains

D ❑ WINS Manager

Answers

1 *B. Client.* The Client directory in the Windows NT Server stores the files for the Network Administrator, including the network installation startup disks and installation disk sets. *Review "Creating a Network Installation Startup Disk" and "Creating Installation Disk Sets" — in particular, Labs 14-1 and 14-2.*

2 *A. Make Installation Startup Disk.* You need to run the network startup disks. Remember that you need the disk to start up the computer because the computer probably has no operating system on it. *See "Creating a Network Installation Startup Disk."*

3 *B. Make Installation Disk Set.* You use the installation disk set to install network clients and services for a computer that has an operating system but no network clients and services installed. *See "Creating Installation Disk Sets."*

4 *C. Copy Client-based Network Administration Tools.* As its name indicates, this option copies the tools you use to manage a network on a remote computer or a client. *See "Copying Client-Based Network Administration Tools" — in particular, Lab 14-3.*

5 *A. and D. DHCP Manager and WINS Manager.* The client-based network administration tools for Windows 95 are for everyday administration. You perform network configuration and setup through a Windows NT computer. *Review "Copying Client-Based Network Administration Tools."*

Client Administration

Part V
Managing Network Resources

"Better tell the network administrator that one of our networks has gone bad."

In this part . . .

Although the Windows NT Server exam covers many aspects of managing network resources, the Enterprise exam is geared toward topics that involve managing network resources in an enterprise environment, such as internetwork routing, Dynamic Host Configuration Protocol (DHCP), and IPX. Like many other Microsoft exams, the Enterprise exam also focuses on integrating Windows NT with other network operating systems, such as NetWare. In Part V, we examine NetWare connectivity with Windows NT by discussing the NWLink protocol, Client and Gateway services, and the NetWare Migration Tool. You may see questions about Macintosh connectivity on the exam, so we also discuss connectivity and configuration with Macintosh workstations.

Chapter 15
Internetwork Routing

● ●

Exam Objectives

▶ Understanding IP routing

▶ Understanding Windows NT Server multi-protocol routing

▶ Knowing the difference between dynamic and static IP routing

▶ Integrating static and dynamic routing

▶ Using a Windows NT router

● ●

*A*s you probably know, an IP address is 32-bits, usually displayed in dotted quad notation — that is, four bytes separated by periods, such as 113.57.107.23. This address uniquely identifies a host on a network. To arrive at the intended destination, IP packets may have to be *routed,* which means that the packets are sent to their destination via a router.

Although you probably won't see many questions about IP routing on your Enterprise exam (we didn't have any questions on this topic), you should be prepared to answer one or two questions on the four routing services in Windows NT 4.0:

✔ Routing Information Protocol (RIP) for TCP/IP

✔ RIP for IPX

✔ Service Advertising Protocol (SAP) Relay Agent

✔ DHCP/BOOTP Relay Agent

Quick Assessment

Understanding IP routing

1 The _____ determines whether the destination host is local or remote.

2 The packets that aren't on the local network are sent to the _____.

Understanding Windows NT Server multi-protocol routing

3 The Service Advertising Protocol (SAP) doesn't always have to be installed; RIP for _____ can function without it.

4 If DHCP clients are located on a remote subnet, the DHCP _____ must be used.

Knowing the difference between dynamic and static IP routing

5 RIP enables your multihomed Windows NT computer to exchange information with other RIP _____.

6 If the ROUTE PRINT command shows a metric of _____, the route has been learned by sharing updates with other routers.

Integrating static and dynamic routing

7 You can point your static Windows NT router to a _____ router to take advantage of its automatic route updates.

Using a Windows NT router

8 A Windows NT computer with two network cards installed is known as a(n) _____ computer.

9 The IP _____ check box must be enabled for your Windows NT computer to act as a router.

Answers

1 *Subnet mask.* Review "Understanding IP Routing."

2 *Default gateway.* Got it wrong? Review "Understanding IP Routing."

3 *IPX.* Review "Windows NT Server Multi-Protocol Routing."

4 *Relay Agent.* Secret DHCP/BOOTP Relay Agent Man can help! See the section "Windows NT Server Multi-Protocol Routing."

5 *Routers.* Check out the section "Understanding Dynamic versus Static IP Routing."

6 *2.* Review "Isolating Routing Problems."

7 *Dynamic.* Review "Integrating static and dynamic routing."

8 *Multihomed.* Check out "Using a Windows NT Router."

9 *Forwarding.* Review "Using a Windows NT Router."

Understanding IP Routing

To answer routing questions on the exam, you must be familiar with how and why packets are routed. The IP protocol is a member of the Internet layer, which only cares about where the packet comes from and where it's going. The source and destination addresses are appended to the packet. With these addresses, the packet can be sent along its way via the router.

A *router* is a networking device that routes packets that are destined for a network other than the local network. You may remember that the subnet mask identifies the network on which a host is located. If the host isn't on the local network, the packet is sent via the default gateway. In subsequent sections of this chapter, we discuss both the subnet mask and the default gateway as they apply to IP routing.

Routers are usually expensive, but you can configure your Windows NT computer to route packets to different networks. To function as a router, a Windows NT machine requires two network interface cards: one card for the local network, and one card for the remote network. An NT computer configured in this way is known as *multihomed*. We tell you more about multihomed computers in the section "Using a Windows NT Router."

Although the Enterprise exam doesn't focus much on IP routing, you should understand the basics, just in case the exam springs a question on you. When you're cramming, focus on the following topics regarding IP routing:

- The basics of the routing process — in particular, the subnet mask and the default gateway. Don't expect anything too complicated in this area.

- The multi-protocol capabilities of Windows NT. Make sure that you understand the four routing services: RIP for TCP/IP, RIP for IPX, the SAP Relay Agent and the DHCP/BOOTP Relay Agent. We discuss these services in the section "Windows NT Server Multi-Protocol Routing," later in this chapter.

- The general concepts of static and dynamic routing. Again, don't expect anything too deep in this area.

- Microsoft loves the fact that Windows NT can function as a router, so make sure that you know what's required to configure your Windows NT computer as a router.

We remember this topic as being difficult to learn, and you may see exam questions on how to install and configure multi-protocol routing to serve as an Internet router. Yikes! The Enterprise exam doesn't go into complex IP routing issues; these issues are reserved for the TCP/IP exam.

Handling IP packets on the local network

Although the process for sending IP packets on a local network doesn't actually involve routing, you should understand how packets are sent on a local network. Not every exam question about sending IP packets involves routing to remote networks.

The subnet mask is used to determine whether the destination host is on the local network. For example, the following table lists the IP addresses and subnet masks for two hosts that are on the same network:

	Host1	*Host2*
IP address	134.36.23.118	134.36.46.22
Subnet mask	255.255.0.0	255.255.0.0

Notice that both IP addresses begin with the same two octets (134.36). Both computers also have the same subnet mask (255.255.0.0). By applying this mask to the two IP addresses, you can see that the two hosts are on the same local network. Each computer's network interface card inspects every packet that arrives on the local network to determine whether the packet is intended for that computer. Only the computer with the IP address that matches the packet's destination address will process the packet.

This method works great for small- to mid-size networks, but the traffic on the network soon grows too heavy, and performance declines. You can remedy this problem by placing some computers on another subnet, also known as *subnetting the network*. Larger networks that make use of subnetting have routers to route the packets to the other subnets.

Routing IP packets to a remote network

If the subnet mask and the IP address indicate that the destination is on a remote network, the packet must be routed appropriately. This routing makes use of the default gateway, which you configure in the TCP/IP properties for the computer, or assign via DHCP. Figure 15-1 shows an example of reaching a destination host on a remote network via a router.

You can think of the default gateway as being a router. They aren't exactly the same thing, but this idea can help you remember the purpose of the default gateway.

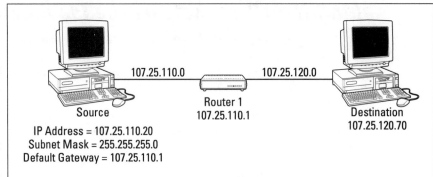

Figure 15-1:
Routing via
the local
computer's
default
gateway.

Figure 15-2 shows a more complicated routing issue: The destination host can't be found on the first network the packet was routed to, so the router must send the packet to its own default gateway.

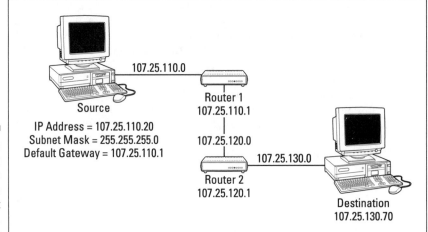

Figure 15-2:
Sending
packets via
the router's
default
gateway.

Just by looking at Figure 15-2, you can determine the default gateway for Router 1, even though it isn't specified:

✔ Router 1 has a default gateway of 107.25.120.1.

✔ You can't be certain about Router 2's default gateway.

You don't have enough information to determine the default gateway for Router 2. It will be a router on the 107.25.130 network.

Windows NT Server Multi-Protocol Routing

You can expect a question or two on the multi-protocol routing capabilities of Windows NT for the exam. As we mention in the introduction to this chapter, the four routing services in Windows NT 4.0 are

- RIP for TCP/IP
- RIP for IPX
- The SAP Relay Agent
- DHCP/BOOTP Relay Agent

RIP for TCP/IP

RIP enables a router to dynamically exchange route information with other routers. This router can broadcast routing information such as IP addresses to nearby routers, as well as route the packets accordingly. To keep all the RIP routers synchronized, each RIP router also needs to periodically send broadcast updates of all the information known to the router. You install RIP for TCP/IP on the Services tab in the Control Panel's Network applet.

RIP for IPX

RIP can dynamically route IPX packets, as well as TCP/IP packets. You accomplish this task by using RIP combined with the Service Advertising Protocol (SAP) Relay Agent. RIP for IPX also can exchange route information with other routers.

You don't always need the SAP Relay Agent for RIP routing with IPX. You only need to install the SAP Agent if you have applications that use the SAP protocol for advertising services on the network.

SAP is installed by default when you install RIP for IPX. You install RIP for IPX on the Services tab in the Control Panel's Network applet.

Secret DHCP/BOOTP relay agent man

The DHCP/BOOTP (Boot Protocol) Relay Agent is part of the Dynamic Host Configuration Protocol (DHCP), which is covered in the Internetworking with Microsoft TCP/IP exam. However, you may be asked about the purpose of this relay agent on the Enterprise exam.

The DHCP service is used to dynamically assign TCP/IP information to DHCP clients. When a client initializes on the network, it requests configuration information from the DHCP server. Because DHCP/BOOTP packets aren't designed to cross routers, the DHCP server must be on the same subnet as the DHCP client, or a DHCP/BOOTP Relay Agent must be present.

An easier alternative to installing and configuring another DHCP server on this subnet is to install the DHCP/BOOTP Relay Agent on one of the computers in the subnet. You also need to use the DHCP/BOOTP Relay Agent if your router doesn't support BOOTP forwarding. This relay agent listens for requests from the DHCP clients and forwards them to the DHCP server located on the remote subnet.

Remember that some routers do not support BOOTP forwarding. The exam may ask you why users on a remote subnet can't receive IP addressing configuration from the DHCP server on the remote subnet.

Understanding Dynamic versus Static IP Routing

As you know, routers are responsible for routing packets to different networks. This process involves one of two methods: dynamic or static IP routing. *Dynamic routing* means routers can communicate with each other and share routing information. They can query other routers for updated route information, and thus find more efficient paths to send packets, or find an alternative route if the original route fails. However, a dynamic router can't update the static route tables of a nondynamic router.

Static routing

Static routing involves creating, maintaining, and deleting static routes for the remote networks. This process involves updating route tables on each routing device, and it must be done correctly. However, maintaining route tables isn't much of a problem unless your network is extremely large and you have multiple subnets.

On a small network with only two subnets, you'll most likely be connected with one router. This configuration doesn't require an addition to the route table for the remote subnet, because the local computer's default gateway routes the packets just fine.

Static routing works fine for a network of this size. But when you begin adding more remote networks, you can no longer get by with just the default gateway. If these networks are connected by routers with static route tables, you must know exactly what you're doing to get each network to communicate with the other networks.

Dynamic routing

As we indicate earlier in this chapter, the Enterprise exam may ask you a question or two on the dynamic routing capabilities of NT Server. When you're installing the RIP protocol on your NT Server, a few subtle differences exist, depending on whether you have one or more network cards installed in the system:

- ✔ If you have only one network interface card on your system with RIP enabled, your card just listens for routing information updates. Your system doesn't advertise routes that it has learned.

- ✔ If you add more than one network interface card to a system, RIP routing is enabled, and your computer functions as a dynamic router, listening and broadcasting routing information to other RIP routers.

Make sure that you have up-to-date information when you're studying for the exam. We've seen an outdated exam preparation guide and a TechNet article, both stating that Windows NT doesn't support dynamic routing. Of course, these statements are incorrect. Yes, some similarities exist between newer versions of products, but don't let older study material lead you down the wrong path.

Integrating static and dynamic routing

If you configure your adapter on your Windows NT static router to point to a dynamic router, you can take advantage of all the benefits that these dedicated dynamic routers provide. This router can learn the most efficient routes, which can get your packets to their destinations sooner, and provide some fault tolerance, should a link in the network go down. This router can discover new paths around the congestion, to get your packets where they need to go.

By the way, the most efficient route to the destination is determined by the number of hops needed to reach the destination. Each router is considered a hop. Similar to "Name that Tune," if one router claims it can reach that network in only two hops, NT lets the router prove it.

Using a Windows NT Router

An alternative to using an expensive router is to configure Windows NT Server to act as a. Using Windows NT as a router is tested on several exams, and you may see questions about this topic on the Enterprise exam. Don't expect the questions to be too detailed, however.

To configure NT Server to act as a router, you must have more than one network adapter installed on the system. A computer with more than one network adapter installed is known as a *multihomed* computer. You usually find two network interface cards in a multihomed computer, but you can have more.

If you plan on using Windows NT as a router to route information between two networks, you must meet a few requirements. These requirements are worth noting, because they're prime candidates for a question on the exam:

✔ You must be running Windows NT version 3.5 (or higher), Windows for Workgroups 3.11, or Windows 95.

✔ You must have two network cards on the computer.

After you ensure that your system meets the hardware requirements for routing, you must attend to some configuration issues:

1. **Make sure that the network cards have valid IP addresses and subnet masks assigned to them for the network on which they participate.**

2. **Turn on the Enable IP Forwarding option, which you find on the Routing tab in the TCP/IP Properties dialog box.**

3. **Create the static routing table with entries to remote networks that the network interface cards are not attached to.**

4. **(Optional) Create a route entry to a dynamic router so that you can benefit from this router's capability to exchange routing information with other routers.**

Think of the multihomed computer as two different interfaces connecting two different networks. Each adapter in the system must have a valid configuration, such as IP address, subnet mask, and default gateway for the network on which it participates.

Isolating Routing Problems

IP routing offers plenty of chances for making errors that can leave you scratching your head. With the information we describe throughout this chapter and the troubleshooting procedures we introduce in this section, you should have no problems with IP routing troubleshooting questions on the exam. Your exam may have only one question (if any) about this topic, but you should be prepared. IP routing is a very important aspect of an enterprise network.

In the following sections, we introduce a few utilities that you use to diagnose IP routing-related problems. We don't describe every feature of these utilities — only the features that relate to IP routing and the exam.

Using the ROUTE PRINT command

The first utility you should be comfortable with is the ROUTE PRINT command, which prints the current routing table for your computer to the screen. Figure 15-3 shows the output from this command.

In this information, you should find routes to other networks. If you have trouble communicating with a particular subnet, verify the output of the ROUTE PRINT command to see if a route exists to this network.

If you see any entries with the metric of 2, you know that RIP has established this route dynamically by communicating with other routers. If you know you have dynamic RIP IP routing enabled, and you don't see any entries with the metric of 2, verify that RIP routing is, in fact, enabled.

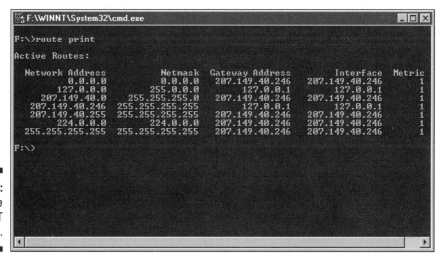

Figure 15-3:
Results of the
ROUTE PRINT
command.

The default gateway has almost the same effect as static routing, but the default gateway is used if none of the routes in the routing table can get the packet to its intended destination. If a path is first found in the routing table, the packet is sent, and the default gateway isn't used. If you don't have a route to a remote network in the routing table, and the packet still isn't arriving, check for the proper default gateway in the TCP/IP configuration. Make sure that you know this order because you can easily overlook it during the exam.

In all likelihood, you'll see troubleshooting questions on the exam, but they may not be related to IP routing. Expect questions concerning Network Monitor, Performance Monitor, and the memory dump utilities.

Checking the TCP/IP configuration with IPCONFIG

Of course, verifying the current TCP/IP configuration with IPCONFIG, or the more detailed IPCONFIG /ALL command, is crucial to troubleshooting. Here's an example of the output from the IPCONFIG /ALL command:

```
Host Name . . . . . . . . . . : cbran.direct-source.com
DNS Servers . . . . . . . . : 207.149.40.5
                                        204.157.151.3
Node Type . . . . . . . . . : Broadcast
        NetBIOS Scope ID. . . . . . :
        IP Routing Enabled. . . . . : No
        WINS Proxy Enabled. . . . . : No
        NetBIOS Resolution Uses DNS : No
        Ethernet adapter NE20005:

Description . . . . . . . . . : Novell 2000 Adapter
        Physical Address. . . . . : 00-20-18-31-7B-53
        DHCP Enabled. . . . . . . : No
        IP Address. . . . . . . . : 111.46.189.23
        Subnet Mask . . . . . . . : 255.255.255.0
        Default Gateway . . . . . : 111.46.189.1
```

You may find the routing problem has nothing to do with routing, but with the TCP/IP configuration.

Verifying connectivity with the Ping command

The Ping command verifies connectivity by trying to contact the destination host. You should learn the following procedure for the exam. This procedure uses pinging to determine which link in the chain is broken:

1. **Ping the local host (127.0.0.1) to make sure that you have TCP/IP set up correctly on your computer.**

2. **Ping another computer on the same network.**

   This connection doesn't involve routing.

3. **Ping the near side of the router — that is, the interface that's connected to the network you're on.**

   If you don't get a response, the router may not be functioning.

4. **Ping the far side of the router — that is, the opposite side of the router from your network.**

   If this connection works, the other side of the router is functioning, too.

5. **Ping another computer on the far side of the router.**

   This step determines whether the router is properly passing packets between the two networks.

6. **Ping the destination computer.**

   If the preceding steps are successful, and this last step isn't successful, the destination computer has a problem.

An easy way to remember the order in which to ping for connectivity is to think of the process starting on your machine and getting farther away. Each step of the process gets you a little closer to the destination host.

Using the TRACERT utility

You use the TRACERT (trace route) utility to trace the route the packet makes in real time as it travels to its destination. This route includes the routers (or hops) the packet passes along the way. The TRACERT utility is important for three reasons:

- ✔ It can determine whether the packet isn't reaching its destination.
- ✔ It can identify the last router the packet passed before failing.
- ✔ It can determine how long the packet travels between routers.

Prep Test

1 Two computers can't communicate with each other. Looking at the following TCP/IP information for each host, what appears to be the reason the hosts can't communicate?

	Host 1	Host 2
IP address	97.114.65.203	75.24.211.36
Subnet mask	255.255.255.0	255.255.255.0
Default gateway	97.114.65.23	145.24.27.79

A ○ The default gateway appears wrong in the first host.

B ○ The default gateway appears wrong in the second host.

C ○ The IP address appears invalid in the first host.

D ○ The problem must be a non-TCP/IP problem; this configuration looks correct.

2 (True/False). The default gateway is used before the routing table.

3 Why isn't the SAP Relay Agent always required?

A ○ Because the network may not have routers

B ○ Because you can use DHCP/BOOTP Relay Agent instead

C ○ Because your applications may not use it

D ○ Because IPX can use the Address Resolution Protocol (ARP) instead

4 What is the default gateway for the 129.31.22.106 host, with a subnet mask of 255.255.0.0?

A ○ 129.1.1.1

B ○ 129.31.0.0

C ○ 129.31.1.1

D ○ 129.1.0.0

5 (True/False). The DHCP/BOOTP Relay Agent is used for non-DHCP clients on the same subnet as the DHCP server.

6 Which option must you enable to properly route packets with your Windows NT multihomed computer?

A ○ The Enable IP Routing option on the Forwarding tab in the TCP/IP Advanced Properties dialog box

B ○ The Enable IP Forwarding option on the Routing tab in the TCP/IP Properties dialog box

C ○ The Enable IP Forwarding option on the Routing tab in the TCP/IP Advanced Properties dialog box

D ○ The Enable IP Routing option on the Forwarding tab in the TCP/IP Properties dialog box

7 (True/False). A metric of 1 from the ROUTE PRINT command means the route has been learned from dynamic RIP updates.

8 Which information is not included in the IPCONFIG /ALL command output?

A ○ Whether IP routing is enabled

B ○ DNS servers

C ○ IPX address

D ○ Physical address

9 You're trying to use your Windows NT computer to route packets between two networks. You have checked the IP Forwarding box on the Routing tab, given the network cards an IP address to share, and created a static route for each network you need to route to. What else do you need to do to configure this computer as a router?

A ○ Nothing. It will work fine.

B ○ Give each network card a unique default gateway.

C ○ Give each network card a unique subnet mask.

D ○ The configuration is invalid; you must reconfigure it.

10 You want your Windows NT router to advertise the routes that it has learned. How do you configure this to happen?

A ○ It always happens when you install the Routing Information Protocol.

B ○ You must select the IP Forwarding check box on the Routing tab.

C ○ You need to have at least two network cards installed on the system.

D ○ You must check the option for RIP broadcasting in the Network applet of the Control Panel.

Answers

1 *B. The default gateway appears wrong in the second host.* The most important fact about the default gateway is that it must be on the same network as the host. You can determine whether it's on the same network by use of the subnet mask. *See "Understanding IP Routing."*

2 *False.* The routing table is checked for the network entry before the default gateway. *See "Understanding IP Routing" for more information.*

3 *C. Because your applications may not use it.* The Service Advertising Protocol (SAP) is only needed when some applications on the IPX network advertise their services in this way. *See "Windows NT Server Multi-Protocol Routing."*

4 *C. 129.31.1.1.* Of course, you can't determine the exact IP address of the default gateway. However, you know that it must be on the same subnet as the host. 129.31.1.1 is the only address that's on the same subnet as the 129.31.22.106 host. The two addresses with zeros are examples of the network, not a host on the network. *See "Understanding IP Routing" for more information.*

5 *False.* The DHCP/BOOTP Relay Agent is used for DHCP clients on a remote subnet from the DHCP server. This relay agent forwards the DHCP messages across the router to the DHCP server. *Refer to "Windows NT Server Multi-Protocol Routing" for more information.*

6 *B.* To enable IP routing in Windows NT 4, you must activate the Enable IP Forwarding option on the Routing tab in the TCP/IP Properties dialog box. Prior versions use the IP Routing check box in the Advanced TCP/IP Properties dialog box. *Review "Using a Windows NT Router."*

7 *False.* The metric of 2 in the ROUTE PRINT command means the route was determined as a result of dynamic RIP updates. *See "Isolating Routing Problems."*

8 *C. IPX address.* The IPX protocol is a different protocol from TCP/IP, and therefore no IPX information shows up in any IPCONFIG commands. *To see sample output from the IPCONFIG command, check out "Isolating Routing Problems."*

9 *D. The configuration is invalid, and must be reconfigured.* Having IP addresses that are valid for their own particular networks is essential for configuring a Windows NT machine as a router. They can't share the same IP address. *Review "Using a Windows NT Router."*

10 *C. You need to have at least two network cards installed on the system.* With only one network card in your system, you can listen for new routes from RIP routers. With two network cards installed, you can listen for new routes, as well as broadcast the routes you've learned, to other RIP routers. *See "Using a Windows NT Router."*

Chapter 16

NetWare Connectivity

Exam Objectives

▶ Reviewing NWLink IPX/SPX Compatible Transport Protocol

▶ Understanding Client Services for NetWare

▶ Understanding Gateway Services for NetWare

▶ Using the Migration Tool for NetWare

*I*f you deal with NT in an enterprise environment, you're bound to run into other operating systems. And because more networks run Novell NetWare than all other network operating systems combined, you shouldn't be surprised to discover that the Enterprise exam asks you numerous questions involving NetWare connectivity.

Worried? Don't be. This is still an MCSE exam, and you don't need to be a NetWare expert. However, you must know how you can use NT to interact with NetWare. You also need to know how to switch an existing NetWare network over to NT.

On the Enterprise exam, what you need to know boils down to understanding the nuances of Gateway Services for NetWare, Client Services for NetWare, NWLink, and the Migration Tool. If these tools and services sound like gibberish now, don't fret. We cover each of these topics in this chapter.

Quick Assessment

Reviewing NWLink IPX/SPX Compatible Transport Protocol

1 The transport protocol _____ is based on IPX/SPX and used by NT to communicate with NetWare.

2 A common problem when one computer is unable to interact with a NetWare network, even though other computers have no problem, is _____.

3 To run GSNW, CSNW, or the Migration Tool for NetWare, _____ must be running.

Understanding Client Services for NetWare

4 _____ is a redirector used by NT Workstation when interacting with NetWare servers.

5 To successfully log on to a NetWare server, the user's _____ and _____ on NT and NetWare must match.

6 If a workstation isn't running CSNW, it needs to use _____ to interact with a NetWare server.

7 You can install CSNW only on _____.

Understanding Gateway Services for NetWare

8 You can install GSNW only on _____.

9 GSNW provides access to NetWare _____ and _____ resources.

Understanding the Migration Tool for NetWare

10 The program name of the Migration Tool for NetWare is _____.

11 The only way to preserve NetWare file and directory permissions during a migration is if the target directory is formatted as _____.

Answers

1 *NWLink.* See "Reviewing NWLink IPX/SPX Compatible Transport."

2 *Incorrect frame type.* See "Configuring NWLink and CSNW."

3 *NWLink.* See "Reviewing NWLink IPX/SPX Compatible Transport."

4 *Client Services for NetWare.* See "Understanding Client Services for NetWare."

5 *Account name; password.* See "Configuring NWLink and CSNW."

6 *Gateway Services for NetWare.* Review "Understanding Gateway Services for NetWare."

7 *NT Workstation.* See "Understanding Client Services for NetWare."

8 *NT Server.* Review "Understanding Gateway Services for NetWare."

9 *File; Print.* Review "Understanding Gateway Services for NetWare."

10 *Nwconv.exe.* See "Using the Migration Tool for NetWare: Swallows to Capistrano."

11 *NTFS.* For more information, see the section "Using the Migration Tool for NetWare: Swallows to Capistrano."

Reviewing NWLink IPX/SPX Compatible Transport

Microsoft doesn't like royalties on programs — unless, of course, another company must pay royalties to Microsoft. To avoid paying royalties on the Internetwork Packet Exchange/Sequenced Packet Exchange (IPX/SPX), Microsoft created the NWLink transport protocol. NT is well known for its interoperability with other systems, and NWLink is designed so that NT and NetWare can communicate.

Each service we mention in this chapter uses NWLink to route packets of information between NetWare and NT Server or Workstation. If any of the NetWare services offered in NT are to function, NWLink must be running.

Even though this protocol is designed so that NT and NetWare can communicate, nothing can stop you from using this protocol on a network that is solely NT. After all, this protocol is more reliable than NetBEUI, and it has less overhead than TCP/IP. Just because an exam question mentions NWLink, don't assume that NetWare is involved — unless, of course, the question tells you it is!

Understanding Client Services for NetWare

Although NWLink is designed to provide interoperability with NetWare, it's just a protocol. It routes packets on the network, but by itself, it can't access NetWare servers. It needs a redirector, and that's where Client Services for NetWare (CSNW) enters the picture.

CSNW is only available on NT Workstation 4.0. This redirector enables NT Workstations to access NetWare file and print resources. A *redirector* is a program that directs program and user requests to the appropriate target. In the case of CSNW, it also translates client requests from Microsoft network terms to statements that NetWare can understand. This capability is necessary because the two network operating systems use different commands to perform the same tasks.

The important thing to remember about CSNW is that an NT Workstation uses it to access NetWare servers directly. It doesn't need to go through a gateway, and it doesn't require anything more than a valid account and permissions on both the NT and NetWare servers. That's CSNW in a nutshell.

Installing NWLink and CSNW

Microsoft likes to give users multiple ways of doing the same thing, and installation is no exception. You can install NWLink and CSNW in several ways, at several times.

You install NWLink in pretty much the same way as you install any other protocol. During Phase 2 of NT Server or Workstation setup (the network configuration part), you select NWLink as a protocol to install. It's one of the default protocols that NT installs. The setup process loads the necessary software and binds the protocol to your network adapter card. To review the various phases in the NT Server setup process, check out Chapter 5.

If you don't install NWLink during installation of NT Server, just select the Protocols tab in the Network applet and add the protocol from there. If you choose neither of these routes, you can use still another method for installing NWLink.

Both CSNW and Gateway Services for NetWare (GSNW, which we discuss later in this chapter) require that NWLink is running on your system. If you haven't installed this protocol, it will auto-install when you add the CSNW or GSNW services to your system.

An equally easy recipe exists for installing CSNW. As with the installation of NWLink, you can install CSNW during Phase 2 of NT Workstation setup, or you can add the service after setup is complete. As we show you in Lab 16-1, you simply add the service from the Services tab of the Network applet in Control Panel.

Lab 16-1   Setting Up CSNW After You Install NT Workstation

1. **Log on with the appropriate permissions, such as with the Administrator account.**

2. **On the Services tab in the Control Panel's Network applet, click Add.**

3. **In the resulting dialog box, choose Client Services for NetWare.**

4. **When prompted, insert the Windows NT Workstation CD.**

5. **After the service is added, restart the computer.**

   After NT restarts, you just have to do a little configuration, and your work is done.

Configuring NWLink and CSNW

Configuring NWLink is relatively easy, compared to some other protocols. You have to input two configuration settings: the internal network number and frame type.

The internal network number (also known as an IPX network number) is a unique number used by NetWare file servers on the network. Unless you're connecting to a NetWare file server, you can leave its value at 00000000. If you're connecting to a NetWare file server, you can use the number shown on the NetWare Server's LAN driver information dialog box. You can find this number by wandering over to the NetWare file server and looking in NetWare Monitor. The second configuration option — frame type — is a little more involved.

One of the common issues with IPX/SPX (and Microsoft's NWLink) involves the frame type. (A *frame* is a piece of data that's transmitted on the network.) When Novell first implemented IPX/SPX, it used a frame type called 802.3. This configuration lasted until NetWare 3.12, when Novell decided to go with the 802.2 industry standard. Because older and newer versions of NetWare default to different frame types, interesting problems can arise.

If you configure a workstation or server to use a different frame type from the rest of the network, that machine can't communicate properly. Even though the other servers and workstations function on the network, the computer with the incorrect frame type can't interact. This situation makes for a simple troubleshooting rule: If one computer can't communicate on a network using IPX/SPX or NWLink, and the rest of the network can interact, always consider that an incorrect frame type is being used.

NT Server 4 has a particular problem with the issue of frame types. You configure the frame types in NWLink by choosing Auto Detection or Manual Frame Type Detection. If you choose Auto Detection, NT automatically detects the first frame type it sees on your network. Subsequently, NT can't detect other frame types. Auto Detection can cause problems in an enterprise environment where some LANs use older versions of NetWare (that is, versions previous to 3.12), while other networks use version 3.12 or later versions. Because the older versions of NetWare default to the 802.3 frame type, and the newer versions use 802.2, you must do a little tweaking in NT. This tweaking involves using manual detection and specifying all the frame types in use on your network.

If you see a question that deals with NetWare, and the question doesn't mention the transport protocol or version, assume that IPX/SPX is used. Versions of NetWare previous to 3.*x* use only IPX/SPX. NetWare 3.*x* and later versions support multiple protocols, but IPX/SPX remains the protocol of choice on many networks.

Client Services for NetWare requires very little configuration. After you install CSNW and reboot your computer, you configure CSNW as soon as you log on. If you ever need to reconfigure, just double-click the CSNW icon that the installation process places in your Control Panel.

After you log on for the first time after you install CSNW, you see a dialog box that asks you to specify the following information:

ı   ✔ Your preferred server

ı   ✔ The default tree and context

ı   ✔ Whether you want to run the NetWare logon script

The preferred server option lets you specify which NetWare server to connect with by default. If the server uses NetWare Directory Services (NDS), the default tree and context options let you specify the NDS name and context that the user will use when logging on. The context specifies where the user account resides in the NDS tree. The final option simply indicates whether the NetWare logon script should be run when the user logs on. After you enter this information, you must satisfy only one more configuration requirement.

When using CSNW, the account name and password that you use to log on to NT must also exist on the NetWare server. Remember this requirement, because it tends to crop up in Enterprise exams. These accounts must match to successfully log on to the NetWare server. If you meet this requirement, and the appropriate permissions have been set on the NetWare server, you just need to log on using the NET USE command or Network Neighborhood.

Understanding Gateway Services for NetWare

A gateway allows computers that use different protocols or services to communicate with one another. That's what Gateway Services for NetWare (GSNW) does. It gives NT Server, and computers that use NT Server, the capability to access NetWare file and print resources.

When do you use GSNW? If your NT Server needs to access a NetWare server, you can use GSNW. Also, by using an NT Server with GSNW, workstations that don't use CSNW — for example, workstations that run DOS, Windows for Workgroups, or NT Workstation without CSNW installed — can access NetWare file and print resources.

Rather than accessing a NetWare server directly (through CSNW), the workstation sends commands to the NT Server, where Gateway Services for NetWare does its stuff. GSNW translates these commands (from Microsoft network instructions into NetWare instructions), and then passes them to NetWare through a single account that belongs to GSNW. Basically, GSNW acts as the liaison between Microsoft networks and NetWare.

One of the most difficult things about Gateway Services for NetWare on the Enterprise exam is not confusing it with CSNW. People confuse the two for good reason — in part because of GSNW's full name: Gateway (and Client) Services for NetWare.

GSNW's full name includes the term *Client* because GSNW includes Client Services for NetWare, and installs it when you install GSNW. The client component allows the server to act as a NetWare client. If you use NT Server to access NetWare resources, you're using the Client services of GSNW.

Even though you install the Gateway (and Client) Services for NetWare on the server, the workstations on your network don't necessarily use CSNW. You can only install CSNW on NT Workstation, not NT Server. If a workstation requires access to NetWare resources, and doesn't have CSNW installed, it goes through the Gateway Services of GSNW on NT Server.

What CSNW is to clients, GSNW is to servers. While CSNW is used on NT Workstations, GSNW can only be installed on NT Server.

Setting up GSNW

When setting up GSNW, you notice striking similarities to CSNW. The setup of each service is almost identical (note that we say "almost"). However, after you understand how to install one, you can easily remember the procedures for installing the other. Figure 16-1 shows the Select Network Service dialog box, where you install GSNW. You access this dialog box from the Network applet in Control Panel.

To set up Gateway Services for NetWare, you must have the NWLink protocol running on your system. NWLink provides GSNW with the means for communicating with NetWare. If you don't already have it on the server, it auto-installs when you add GSNW to your system.

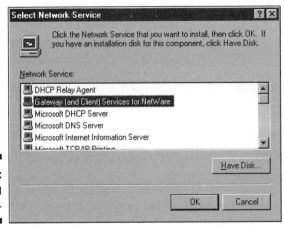

Figure 16-1:
Installing
GSNW.

Configuring the NetWare file server for GSNW

Believe it or not, the setup procedure for GSNW doesn't even start on NT Server! It starts on the NetWare server, where you need to set up a user account and a group account. On the NetWare server, you must set up a user account with the appropriate rights to NetWare's file system, and a group account named NTGATEWAY with appropriate rights to file and print resources. You must then place the NetWare user account in the NTGATEWAY group account. If you forget to set up these accounts, GSNW can't connect to NetWare.

Actually, the big difference between GSNW's installation and CSNW's installation is on the NetWare server side. Remember that a user account and password must exist for each computer that has CSNW. GSNW requires less work. Because workstations use GSNW as a gateway, you need only one user and group account for anyone using GSNW. Everyone accesses the NetWare server through the same account, and has the same rights to NetWare resources.

Installing GSNW on NT Server

A few methods exist for installing GSNW. You can add it during NT Server's setup, or after you have NT Server installed and running. During setup, add Gateway (and Client) Services for NetWare from the list of services. Although it isn't selected by default, it does come with NT Server 4.0.

If you don't select GSNW during setup, you can easily add it later. Just follow the steps we describe in Lab 16-2.

Lab 16-2   Installing Gateway (and Client) Services for NetWare

1. **Log on as an Administrator in NT Server.**

2. **Click the Services tab of the Network applet in Control Panel.**

3. **Click Add, and then select Gateway (and Client) Services for NetWare from the list of network services.**

   You're prompted for the NT Server CD, and then the software is installed.

Gee, doesn't that sound just like CSNW's installation? Yup . . . Remember one, and you remember both!

Configuring GSNW

As with setting up any software, most of the work is in configuration. If you configure GSNW properly, you'll rarely — if ever — have a problem with this service.

After you install Gateway Services for NetWare, a new icon named GSNW appears in your Control Panel. To configure GSNW:

1. **Double-click the GSNW icon in your Control Panel to open the Gateway Services for NetWare dialog box.**

   With the exception of the Gateway button, this dialog box is virtually identical to the one you use for configuring CSNW.

2. **Click Gateway to open the Configure Gateway dialog box (see Figure 16-2).**

3. **Click the Enable Gateway check box.**

   Despite all the work you've already done, the gateway isn't active until this box is checked!

4. **In the Gateway Account field, specify the account that you created on the NetWare server.**

   GSNW uses this account when logging on to NetWare on your behalf.

5. **Enter the password for this account and then confirm it.**

   The Add and Remove buttons enable you to add and remove network shares, and the Permissions button is for — you guessed it — setting the access that users have to the shared NetWare resources. You need to create a NetWare share that users of your Microsoft network can use.

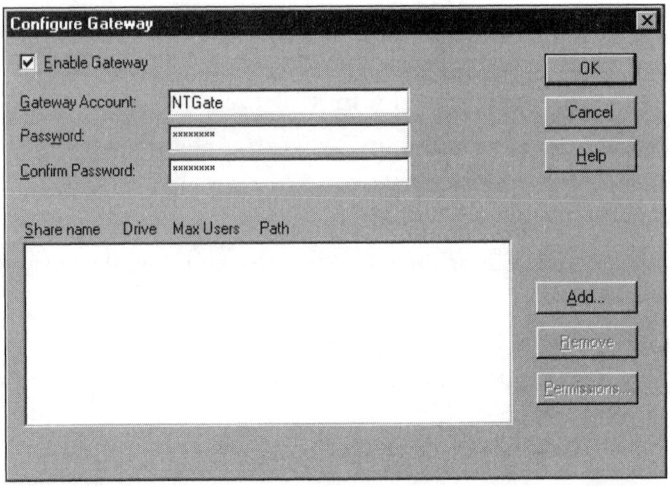

Figure 16-2:
The
Configure
Gateway
dialog box.

6. **Click Add, and the New Share dialog box opens.**

7. **Specify the Share Name that users will use to access a shared NetWare directory.**

8. **In the Network Path field, enter the UNC (Universal Naming Convention) name that specifies the location of the shared NetWare directory.**

9. **In the Use Drive field, select the drive letter to which this directory will be mapped.**

10. **If necessary, limit the number of users who can use the shared directory.**

    Remember: As the number of users increases, the performance of the gateway decreases. If the gateway bogs down, decrease the user limit.

But what's this? After all your hard work, the configuration changes haven't taken effect! Your changes don't take effect until the next time you log on to the system.

Using the Migration Tool for NetWare: Swallows to Capistrano

Microsoft provides a way to switch over from NetWare to NT — gee, that's a big surprise. In the previous sections of this chapter, we focus on making NetWare and NT work together in one network environment. But what if you want to replace your NetWare servers with NT Server? That's where the Migration Tool for NetWare comes into play.

Please allow us to point out the obvious: NetWare and NT are two different operating systems. Consequently, you can't upgrade a NetWare server to a Windows NT Server. However, NetWare administrators have spent lots of time and work on their servers, and you don't want to throw away all their work and create an NT Server from scratch. Instead, you can migrate items from one or more NetWare file servers into a single NT Server PDC.

Reviewing what you can and can't do with the Migration Tool

Although you can migrate numerous items by using the Migration Tool, you can't move everything from NetWare to an NT PDC. Some information that NetWare uses is encrypted, used differently in the two systems, or simply not used by NT.

For the items that you can migrate, the Migration Tool does an exceptional job. It allows you to select which directories and files you want to migrate, and in copying them to an NT Server, it retains the effective rights. The Migration Tool also enables you to migrate user and group accounts, and it offers features for dealing with duplicate accounts.

For good reason, numerous items exist that you can't migrate. One of the items you can't migrate is passwords. They are encrypted in NetWare, and can't be understood by NT. The only way around this limitation is by using a mapping file, which we discuss in the next section of this chapter.

Unfortunately, passwords aren't the only thing you can't migrate. Workgroup and user account managers (which you typically don't use in NetWare networks), NetWare login scripts (which aren't used by NT), and print server and print queue information cannot be migrated. Aside from these few exceptions, migration from NetWare to NT is a fairly thorough process.

Running a migration

Although few network administrators can be called good scouts, you must be prepared when running a migration. GSNW and NWLink must be running on your NT Server, and you must be a member of the Domain Admins group. And if you want to preserve the rights on the directories and files you're migrating, your NT Server's hard disks must be NTFS. If the hard disks are FAT, you lose the rights when you copy the files and directories over to NT Server.

The Migration Tool can migrate NetWare 2.x, 3.x, and 4.x to an NT Server. You must have Supervisor rights on NetWare 2.x and 3.x, or Admin rights if the NetWare server is Version 4.x. If you meet these conditions, you're ready to start.

The program that does all the work is Nwconv.exe (also known as the Migration Tool for NetWare). It ships as part of the NT Server installation CD. This program enables you to re-create a significant amount of information from a NetWare server into an NT Server. The Migration Tool for NetWare installs automatically with GSNW, and it's available from the Administrative Tools menu. In Lab 16-3, we describe the steps for performing a migration.

Lab 16-3	Performing a Migration

1. **Start the Migration Tool for NetWare (Nwconv.exe).**

   A dialog box appears with a list of NetWare server and NT Server names.

2. **Select the name of the NetWare server you want to migrate, and the NT Server to which you want to migrate.**

3. **Click the User Options and File Options buttons and select the options specific to your migration.**

4. **When you're ready, click the Trial Migration button.**

   Clicking this button takes you through the migration process (without creating files), and checks for errors.

5. **If all goes well, you then can click Start Migration to do the real thing.**

When it comes to the Enterprise exam, however, you must be prepared for certain situations in running a migration. The Enterprise exam doesn't expect you to know the specifics of each dialog box in the Migration Tool, but you must know what happens when certain events occur.

Duplicate account names are commonplace during a migration. If the Migration Tool encounters account names that are identical on both NT and NetWare, the default is to skip that account and stop migrating any additional information. However, you can get around this restriction by setting the option that permits duplicates. If you set this option, duplicate account names migrate, and the old account has a prefix added to the name. This process creates a new name, and allows the rest of the information to transfer.

By default, when the Migration Tool encounters duplicate account names, it skips the account and stops the migration.

Another method for dealing with duplicate files involves mapping files. Mapping files are particularly useful when you migrate several NetWare servers to one NT Server PDC. A mapping file renames NetWare account names to Windows NT names, and preserves NetWare passwords during the migration. This method is the only way you can transfer the encrypted passwords to NT.

If you are completely replacing NetWare servers with Windows NT, you must replace some software on client computers. After a complete migration, NetWare clients still use NetWare redirectors, which you must replace with Microsoft redirectors. If you don't replace them, NT Server can't understand the information being sent from the NetWare redirector. Of course, you can replace existing software with an operating system such as Windows NT Workstation, but this approach may not be feasible; changing the redirector is definitely the least expensive way to go.

Prep Test

1 You have numerous NT Workstations that require access to a NetWare server. Which service must you install on your NT Server if the workstations are to interact with the NetWare server?

A ○ NWLink

B ○ CSNW

C ○ GSNW

D ○ NWCONV

2 You have numerous NT Workstations that require access to a NetWare server. Which service must you install on the workstations if they are to interact with the NetWare server?

A ○ NWLink

B ○ CSNW

C ○ GSNW

D ○ NWCONV

3 You decide to migrate several NetWare servers to a Windows NT Server. Which program must you run?

A ○ NWLink

B ○ CSNW

C ○ GSNW

D ○ NWCONV

4 Which items can't be migrated with the Migration Tool unless you use a mapping file?

A ○ Workgroup and Account Managers

B ○ Login scripts

C ○ Passwords

D ○ Print queue information

5 What is the Migration Tool's default action when it encounters a duplicate account name during a migration?

A ○ It skips the duplicate and continues the migration.

B ○ It skips the duplicate and stops migrating any other information.

C ○ It adds a prefix to the duplicate name.

D ○ It logs an error to a log and continues the migration.

6 You have installed and configured CSNW on a workstation. The service is running. However, the user of this computer still can't connect with the NetWare server. What is the most likely reason?

A ○ NWLink hasn't been installed.

B ○ GSNW hasn't been installed.

C ○ The user doesn't have a valid account and password on the NT Server.

D ○ The user doesn't have a matching account and password on the NetWare server.

7 You begin installing Gateway Services for NetWare on your server, then realize that NWLink isn't one of the protocols on this server! What will happen?

A ○ An error will result, informing you to first install NWLink.

B ○ The service will use a previously installed protocol.

C ○ Nothing. GSNW will auto-install NWLink.

D ○ The server will explode.

Answers

1 *C. GSNW.* The service installed on an NT Server that enables access to NetWare servers is Gateway (and Client) Services for NetWare — GSNW. *For more information, refer to "Understanding Gateway Services for NetWare."*

2 *B. CSNW.* The service installed on NT Workstations that enables access to NetWare servers is Client Services for NetWare — CSNW. *For more information, review "Understanding Client Services for NetWare."*

3 *D. NWCONV.* NWCONV is the Migration Tool for NetWare. *See the section "Using the Migration Tool for NetWare: Swallows to Capistrano."*

4 *C. Passwords.* You can't migrate passwords from NetWare to NT unless you use a mapping file. *For more information, refer to "Using the Migration Tool for NetWare: Swallows to Capistrano."*

5 *B. It skips the duplicate and stops migrating any other information.* If duplicate account names are encountered, the Migration Tool skips the duplicate, and stops migrating any additional information. *See "Using the Migration Tool for NetWare: Swallows to Capistrano."*

6 *D. The user doesn't have a matching account and password on the NetWare server.* If the user logs on with an account name and password that doesn't match an account name and password on the NetWare server, the user can't access the NetWare server. *Review "Understanding Client Services for NetWare."*

7 *C. Nothing. GSNW will auto-install NWLink.* If NWLink isn't already installed when you add the GSNW service, it will be auto-installed. *For more information, refer to "Understanding Gateway Services for NetWare."*

Chapter 17
Macintosh Connectivity

• •

Exam Objectives

▶ Understanding NT's Services for Macintosh (SFM)

▶ Reviewing the system requirements for SFM

▶ Installing SFM

▶ Examining file sharing and SFM

▶ Configuring SFM

• •

*Y*ou want me to do what with that Mac? As strange as it may seem, the potential (and often the need) exists to connect a Macintosh to your NT domain to exchange files and print documents. Most of the major network operating systems have begun to abandon Macintosh protocols, so it's up to NT Server to provide the connection. With Services for Macintosh (SFM), Windows NT Server provides capabilities not only for routing AppleTalk, but also for sharing files and printers to those single mouse-button workstations.

You won't find too many questions about SFM on the Enterprise exam — probably only a couple of questions that cover the installation and initial configuration of SFM. In this chapter, we cover the installation steps, configuration issues, and connectivity between Macintosh clients and the NT Server. As we discuss in this chapter, you need to remember the location of the utilities installed by SFM and the differences between Macintosh and NT permissions and files.

Quick Assessment

Understanding NT's Services for Macintosh (SFM)

1 To connect to file shares and print queues on an NT Server, Mac users must select the available shared printer or Macintosh-accessible volume in the defined zone from the _____.

2 To connect a Macintosh's network to the NT Server's default network, the NT Server with Services for Macintosh installed can route the _____ protocol, thus providing a direct connection between the NT domain and the Apple network.

Reviewing the system requirements for SFM

3 To install Services for Macintosh on a Windows NT Server, you must have a(n) _____ partition with at least _____ MB of free hard disk space.

4 A Macintosh client must be running _____ and be able to use _____.

Installing SFM

5 You install the NT Services for Macintosh as a(n) _____, which you install on the Services tab in the Control Panel's _____ applet.

Examining file sharing and SFM

6 You can assign the _____, _____, and _____ permissions to Macintosh-accessible volumes.

7 To translate file extensions between NT and Mac formats, SFM provides an extensive database of _____ , and stores the information for the specific files on the _____ volume in which the files reside.

Configuring SFM

8 Macintosh users can use either an NT domain account, the _____ account, or connect to _____ volumes with a shared volume password.

Answers

1 *Chooser.* See "Understanding NT's Services for Macintosh."

2 *AppleTalk.* See "Understanding NT's Services for Macintosh."

3 *NTFS; 2.* See "Reviewing the System Requirements for SFM" and its subsections.

4 *System 6.0.7 or later; AppleShare.* See "Reviewing the System Requirements for SFM."

5 *Network Service; Network.* Review "Installing Services for Macintosh."

6 *See Files; See Folders; Make Changes.* See "File Sharing and SFM."

7 *Predefined extensions; NTFS.* See "File Sharing and SFM."

8 *Guest; Macintosh-accessible.* See "Configuring Services for Macintosh."

Understanding NT's Services for Macintosh

While you're preparing for Macintosh-related questions on the Enterprise exam, focus on how you configure the NT Server for the client, not specifically on how the end users make their connections. You need to be concerned more with the requirements and the initial configuration of the NT Services for Macintosh when studying for the exam:

- ✔ Make sure you know all the basic requirements for the services we discuss in this chapter — that is, the server, network, and client requirements.

- ✔ Make sure you understand how to create and modify a Macintosh-accessible volume. You must create all volumes on an NTFS partition.

- ✔ Finally, make sure you understand the different permission structures inherent to the Services for Macintosh. You need to know the difference between NTFS permissions and the Apple permissions.

File sharing

One of the main benefits of SFM is the capability to share files between different operating systems. With SFM, users from different computers can work on the same files on the network. For example, Mac users can open a file in Microsoft Word for the Macintosh, while PC users can work on the same file using Word for Windows. Of course, even though you can provide this common area to transfer files, you can't force your Mac users and PC users to share nicely.

The file structure doesn't change for the server clients; PC users see files and directories, and Mac users continue to see files in the Mac folder structure. SFM also stores both Mac and PC extensions on all files stored on a Mac-accessible volume, allowing both Mac and PC clients to have files associated with their respective platform's version of the application.

Print sharing

SFM allows Mac and PC users to send print jobs to any printer attached to a computer running NT Server, as well as PostScript printers that appear on the AppleTalk network. SFM also provides spooling services for Mac users, allowing Macintosh clients to use background printing.

Existing AppleTalk printers must register themselves as LaserWriters to be used by PC users.

Routing

SFM provides support for routing the primary Macintosh protocol suite —
AppleTalk — as well as support for seed routing. Seed routers can replace
the AppleTalk routers because they provide similar functions — establishing
and initializing network address information, as well as broadcasting routing
information.

The exam is more concerned with the configuration of the routing, and not
necessarily the specific details of the Apple zones to which you're connecting. In this section, we offer a brief review of the configuration screens
you use for managing the AppleTalk protocol routing configuration on the
NT Server.

After you install SFM, you need to configure the Microsoft AppleTalk Protocol properties. You must select a default network interface card and the
default Macintosh AppleShare zone. A *zone* is merely a collection of computers that show up in the Mac's Chooser — similar to a workgroup. You enter
these settings on the General tab in the Microsoft AppleTalk Protocol
Properties dialog box, shown in Figure 17-1. You access the configuration
screens from within the properties of the SFM Network Service in the
Control Panel's Network applet.

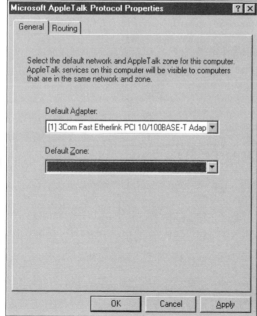

Figure 17-1:
The
General tab
of the
Microsoft
AppleTalk
Protocol
Properties
dialog box.

If necessary, you can configure the AppleTalk routing information. You enter this information on the Routing tab in the Microsoft AppleTalk Protocol Properties dialog box, shown in Figure 17-2. This information allows the NT Server to become an AppleTalk router, capable of combining two or more networks. If the NT Server is to be seen (and used) by only the default network, do not select the Enable Routing check box. You don't need to spread AppleTalk traffic across the entire network if all the Macintoshes are on the same segment on the NT Server.

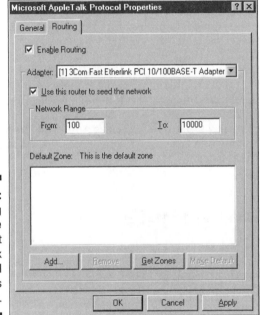

Figure 17-2:
The Routing
tab of the
Microsoft
AppleTalk
Protocol
Properties
dialog box.

Reviewing the System Requirements for SFM

The system requirements for SFM are prime candidates for the couple of Mac connectivity questions you may have on the exam. Make sure you know the requirements and the possible configurations.

NT Server requirements

In addition to the standard NT requirements, installation of SFM has the following requirements:

✔ 2MB free disk space to install the SFM services.

✔ An NTFS partition for Macintosh-accessible volumes. (If you only require printing services, you don't need the NTFS partition.)

Macintosh requirements

Three major requirements exist for connectivity between a Macintosh client and the NT Server:

✔ The Macintosh system must have the AppleShare extension installed.

✔ The Mac must be running System 6.0.7 or later.

✔ If you plan to use file transfer, the Mac must have AppleTalk Filing Protocol (AFP) Version 2.0 or later installed.

For Macs running operating systems older than System 7.5, the volume size of the Macintosh-accessible volume must not exceed 2GB. For Version 7.5 or later, the volume's readable capacity is 4GB.

Networking requirements

For purposes of the exam, the only network requirement you should remember is that the Macintosh clients and NT Server must share a common network system, connected by *one* of the following:

✔ An Ethernet card installed in your LocalTalk router and configured to pass through the LocalTalk network traffic to the NT Server

✔ Ethernet cards installed in all Macintosh clients, and configured with the same network protocol used on the server — that is, TCP/IP

✔ A LocalTalk network card installed in the NT Server running SFM, with the NT routing information configured to route AppleTalk between the Macintosh network and the server

Installing Services for Macintosh

You may be asked how to install the Services for Macintosh. As we describe in Lab 17-1, you install SFM as a Network Service.

Lab 17-1   Installing SFM

1. **Double-click the Network icon in the Control Panel.**

2. **On the Services tab in the Network applet, click Add.**

   You need the NT Server source files (CD or network source) to install the necessary files.

3. **From the list of available services, select Services for Macintosh.**

4. **Close the Network Control Panel.**

As shown in Figure 17-3, after you install SFM, you have a new MacFile icon in the Control Panel, from which you can configure many aspects of the Macintosh services. (We discuss configuration in the section "Configuring Services for Macintosh," later in this chapter.)

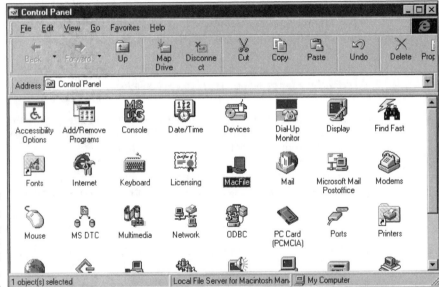

Figure 17-3: MacFile shows up as a Control Panel icon.

File Sharing and SFM

To share files, you must first create a Macintosh-accessible volume. As we mention earlier in this chapter (see "Reviewing the System Requirements for SFM"), you must create the volume on an NTFS partition.

Because the services aren't incorporated into the new Windows Explorer, you must manage all Macintosh file services from File Manager, Server Manager, or through a command-line interface. Figure 17-4 shows the MacFile services installed in File Manager.

To create a Macintosh-accessible volume:

1. Select the directory to be shared.

2. Choose MacFile⇨Create Volume.

As shown in Figure 17-5, the Create Macintosh-Accessible Volume dialog box enables you to specify a password for the volume, which all Macintosh clients must provide to make the connection. This password applies only to Macintosh clients — PC clients don't need to enter a password when connecting to the NT share.

You can set passwords for the Macintosh-accessible volumes, but they only apply to the Macintosh clients. Also, this is a shared password, similar to peer-to-peer shares on NT Workstations.

You also have the option of making the entire volume read-only, as well as opening the volume to Guests.

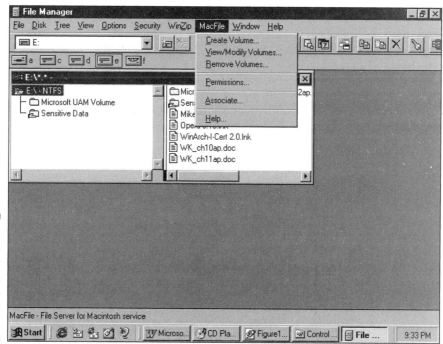

Figure 17-4:
File
Manager
with
MacFile
services
installed.

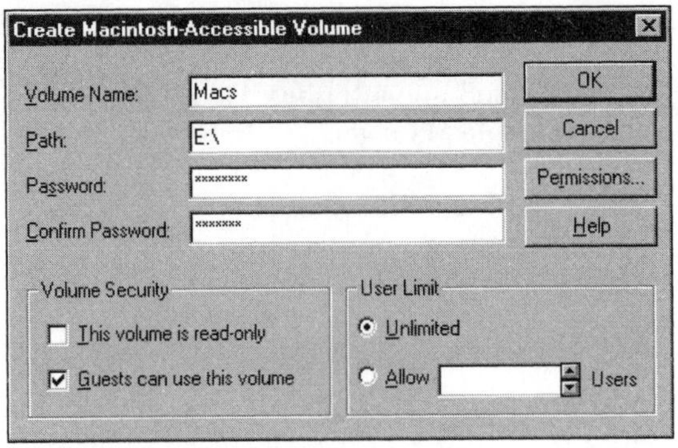

Figure 17-5:
Creating a
Macintosh-
accessible
volume.

After you create the volume, you can modify it from the View/Modify menu.
To open the View/Modify Macintosh-Accessible Volumes dialog box shown
in Figure 17-6, choose MacFile⇨View/Modify Volumes. Select the Macintosh-
accessible volume, and then click Properties to open the volume's Properties dialog box.

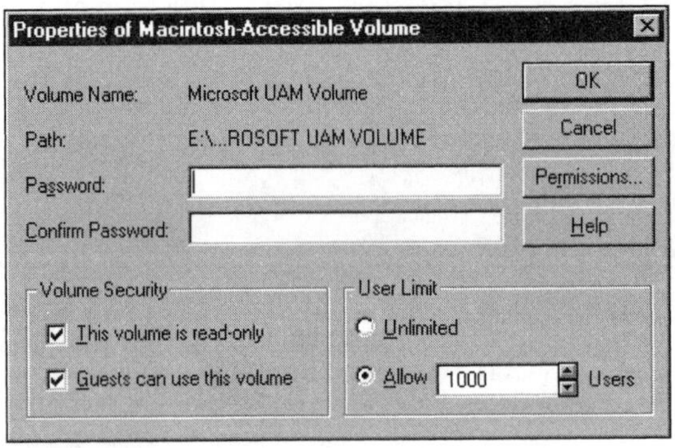

Figure 17-6:
Modifying a
Macintosh-
accessible
volume.

From the volume's Properties dialog box, you can open the Directory
Permissions dialog box by clicking Permissions. Figure 17-7 shows the
Directory Permissions dialog box.

The permissions for Macintosh-accessible volumes use a different set of
groups from those of the typical NTFS system. NT permissions are still used,
but the following permissions are used only for Macintosh platforms:

 ✔ The Macintosh See Files and See Folders permissions are similar to the
   Read permission within NT.

 ✔ The Make Changes permission gives users Write and Delete rights.

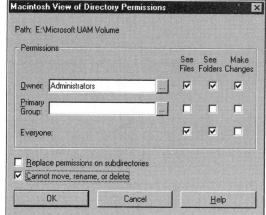

Figure 17-7:
Directory
permissions
for
Macintosh-
accessible
volumes.

The Owner of the volume is the user who created the folder or the user or group account to which you assign ownership. The Primary Group entry corresponds to an NT global group, and you can set permissions for that specific group here. The Everyone entry is equivalent to NT's Everyone — all users connecting to the volume use this set of permissions, unless you specify otherwise.

Remember these simple equations and you'll be set:

✔ See Files, See Folders = Read

✔ Make Changes = Write, Delete

Removing a Macintosh-accessible volume is similar to unsharing an NT shared directory. Simply choose MacFile⇨Remove Volumes and select one or more volumes to delete.

Unlike NT shares, you can't create a Macintosh-accessible volume from a subdirectory of an existing volume. For example, if you define the directory D:\Macfiles as a volume, you can't make the D:\Macfiles\Bananas subdirectory a separate volume.

NTFS

We can't emphasize enough that any questions on the exam related to Macintosh volumes will most likely have an answer related to NTFS. You must create all Macintosh-accessible volumes on NTFS partitions. If you don't have an NTFS partition on the system, you need to convert one to NTFS and then create your Mac volume.

Two other key features to keep in mind are the size of the volume you create, and the permissions you apply to the volume. Like the Windows 95 operating system, Macs running System 7.5 or earlier can't see volumes greater than 2GB in size. If you attempt to exceed this limit, you see the warning shown in Figure 17-8. Versions of the operating system created after System 7.5 support up to 4GB volumes.

Figure 17-8: Volume size limitations.

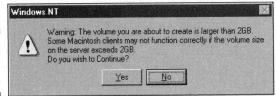

In addition to the basic Macintosh permissions you can apply, we need to address one more important feature of the security within Services for Macintosh. The Macintosh clients can use the NTFS partitions created at the root of the Macintosh-accessible volume, but permissions applied to subdirectories and files within the volume are treated differently. You can only assign more restrictive permissions within the volume. For example, a subdirectory may contain read-only permissions while the root of the drive has Change access. However, you can't apply Change permissions to a subdirectory if the volume's root has Read permissions.

SFM requires an NTFS partition to translate and support Macintosh files.

One last feature of NTFS that's worth mentioning is the native Macintosh file support that SFM provides. All Macintosh files contain both a resource fork and finder information. For exam purposes, remember that NTFS provides *multistream file access* that can support this unique file structure.

File extensions

The Macintosh operating system doesn't use file extensions in the same way as PCs. While PCs store the file type as a three-character extension to the filename, Macs embed the application information into the file itself. To ensure that files are associated with the correct applications on both platforms, Services for Macintosh provides the capability to map MS-DOS extensions to their Macintosh counterparts, as shown in Figure 17-9 and Figure 17-10.

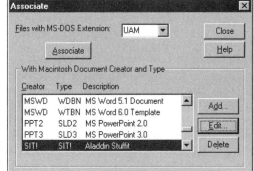

Figure 17-9:
Configuring
file
extension
conversion
information.

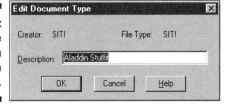

Figure 17-10:
Editing file
extension
conversion
information.

Filename translation

By now, you're accustomed to the 8.3 limitation of DOS filenames, and the 255-character limitation of NT and Windows 95. Macintosh has its own limitation of 32 characters. You must rename files with names longer than 32 characters for Macs to read them, just as with DOS. To solve this problem, the NT Server automatically generates short filenames for any filenames that don't meet the 8.3 character limitation. For files with names longer than 32 characters, Macintosh clients see the shortened 8.3 name generated by NT.

A filename created using the NTFS 256-character limit appears to Macintosh users as if it has 32 characters or less. For filenames longer than 32 characters, Macintosh clients see the name in shortened (8.3) form.

Configuring Services for Macintosh

As with many services provided for Windows NT Server, both GUI and command-line tools are available for configuring Services for Macintosh. The exam focuses more on the GUI tool, but you may be surprised with a question about the command-line utility, especially because the GUI tool and the command-line tool both have the same name: MacFile.

From the MacFile Control Panel, you can see the current number of active sessions, open file forks and locks, who's connected to the server, and which volumes and files are currently in use. Figure 17-11 shows the general properties you can access in MacFile. You can also set some of the advanced security features of SFM.

You can also get to the same GUI Control Panel from Server Manager's MacFile menu. These basic features are comparable to the properties of any NT Server as seen from the Server Manager. If you get any questions regarding MacFile on your Enterprise exam, they'll probably involve the Attributes section of MacFile.

As shown in Figure 17-12, the advanced attributes include the name of the server as it appears to Macintosh clients, the logon message received after connecting to a Macintosh-accessible volume, and some of the security measures not included within the NTFS permissions. By using this Control Panel, you can limit the number of sessions. By default, the Allow Guests to Logon option is selected. You must enable the NT domain's Guest account to use this feature.

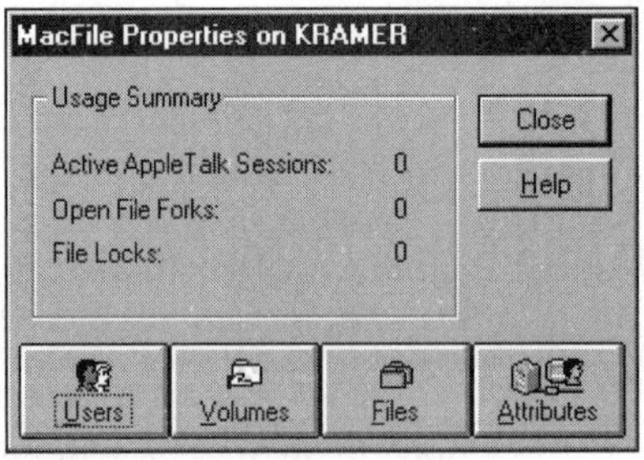

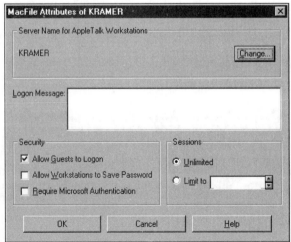

Figure 17-11: MacFile general properties.

Figure 17-12: MacFile advanced attributes.

SFM's command-line tool, also called MacFile, performs many of the services we mention in this section. Its functionality proves beneficial most often during remote administration from an NT Server that doesn't have the SFM installed.

Broken up into four commands (Volume, Directory, Server, and Forksize), the MacFile command-line application simply changes or removes Macintosh-accessible volumes. For more information on this subject, refer to the NT Resource Kit or Microsoft's technical database, TechNet. For exam purposes, however, don't spend much time worrying about these commands. Make sure you're well versed in the functions of the MacFile Control Panel properties, which we explain in the preceding paragraphs.

You may never see a question about Services for Macintosh, but if you do, it will most likely pertain to NTFS, the requirements for installation, or the permissions used for Macintosh clients. Make sure you know the tools used to configure the services — File Manager, Server Manager, and the MacFile Control Panel.

Connecting Macintoshes

1 Which of the following sets of permissions may you apply to a Macintosh-accessible volume?

A ○ See Volumes, See Files, Change Files

B ○ See Files, See Folders, Make Changes

C ○ Read, Write, Change, Full Control

D ○ Read, Write, Delete, Full Control

2 Which of the following requirements must your system meet to install Services for Macintosh to provide both printer and file sharing capabilities to NT Server? (Choose all that apply.)

A ❑ 100MB free disk space

B ❑ At least one NTFS partition

C ❑ At least one FAT partition

D ❑ 2MB of free disk space

3 Which of the following network components for Services for Macintosh are required? (Choose all that apply.)

A ❑ Apple File Server installed on all client Macintosh workstations

B ❑ A network router configured to support IPX/SPX

C ❑ A LocalTalk network interface card installed in the NT Server, with the server configured to route AppleTalk

D ❑ EtherTalk network interface cards installed in all client Macintosh workstations

4 Which utilities can you use to create a Macintosh-accessible volume? (Choose all that apply.)

A ❑ Server Manager

B ❑ File Manager

C ❑ MacFile⇨CreateVolume

D ❑ Net Share

5 Which filename formats do Macintosh clients support? (Choose all that apply.)

A ❑ Filenames up to 255 characters

B ❑ Filenames up to 64 characters

C ❑ Filenames using the 8.3 format

D ❑ Filenames up to 32 characters

6 Which of the following clients support partitions greater than 2GB? (Choose all that apply.)

A ❑ Windows 95

B ❑ Macintosh System 7.5

C ❑ Macintosh System 6.0.7

D ❑ Windows NT

7 Which of the following security measures are supported by Services for Macintosh? (Choose all that apply.)

A ❑ Allow Guests to Logon

B ❑ Volume passwords

C ❑ FAT Security

D ❑ Microsoft Authentication

Answers

1 *B. See Files, See Folders, Make Changes.* Remember, Macs use their own security structure. You configure these permissions as part of the volume properties when creating or modifying a Macintosh-accessible volume. *See "File Sharing and SFM."*

2 *B, D.* You need 2MB of free disk space to install SFM and you need an NTFS partition for Macintosh-accessible volumes. Remember, if you only require printing services, you don't need the NTFS partition. *Check the section "Reviewing the System Requirements for SFM" for a full listing of all requirements.*

3 *C, D.* You can also configure a router to support the AppleTalk protocol. *See "Reviewing the System Requirements for SFM" for more information on networking requirements.*

4 *A, B, C.* You can use both the GUI and the command-line utility to create and modify volumes. *See "Configuring Services for Macintosh."*

5 *C, D.* Remember: For all filenames longer than 32 characters, Macintosh clients only see the shortened (8.3) form of the filename. *Review "File Sharing and SFM."*

6 *A, B, D.* Mac clients running System 6.0.7 can support up to 2GB, but only those running System 7.5 or higher can see volumes greater than 2GB. They are, however, still limited to a maximum volume size of 4GB. *See "File Sharing and SFM."*

7 *A, B, D.* Remember, in order for the Guest option to work, the NT Guest account must be enabled. Volume passwords are entered for each Macintosh-accessible volume, and must be given out to each user who needs to make a connection. Microsoft Authentication is used to support NT domain accounts. *See "File Sharing and SFM."*

Part VI
Managing External Resources

The 5th Wave — By Rich Tennant

I'll tell you this—retraining for client/server isn't going to be easy. Do you know how old some of these dogs are?

In this part . . .

Our focus for Part VI is on Internet Services and Remote Access Services (RAS). We take you through installing and configuring Internet Information Server (IIS) and its various components for your intranet or Internet server. We cover the basics of RAS, including installation and configuration, connectivity options, and security configuration. We also explore the client-side issues of RAS, such as client installation and configuration, creating dial-up connections, security, and scripts.

Chapter 18

Working with Internet Services

● ●

Exam Objectives

▶ Reviewing intranets

▶ Understanding NT Internet and intranet technologies

▶ Installing and configuring Internet Information Server

● ●

*T*he Internet provides the grounds for the latest truly global communications infrastructure since the telephone. Recognizing the importance of Internet technologies, Microsoft provides a client browser — Internet Explorer — as well as fully integrated and robust server services — the Internet Information Server — with Windows NT 4.0 Server. The main focus of this chapter (and for this section of the exam) is on the Internet Information Server (IIS) services.

Quick Assessment

Reviewing intranets

1 An intranet is a(n) _____ network using the same technologies as the Internet but accessible only to users on a(n) _____.

Understanding NT Internet and intranet technologies

2 The World Wide Web (WWW) uses the _____ protocol from the TCP/IP suite.

3 (True/False). Internet Explorer is a server component for publishing Web pages.

4 At a minimum, you must have _____ physical server(s) for five virtual servers.

Installing and configuring IIS

5 Which Internet services does IIS include?

6 Which requires more overhead when creating IIS log files — logging to a plain text file or logging to a SQL database?

7 The Web server that ships with Windows NT Server 4.0 is called _____.

8 To start, stop, or pause individual IIS services, you use the _____ utility.

9 (True/False). You must have one network interface card (NIC) per IP address for a virtual server.

Answers

1   *Private; LAN.* See "Intranets: Never Talk to Strangers" for more information.

2   *HTTP.* Review "Caught in a World Wide Web of Intrigue" for definitions of terms used on the exam.

3   *False.* Internet Explorer is a client-side application for browsing pages. See "Taking a look at Internet Explorer."

4   *One.* But, you need five IP addresses. See "Creating virtual servers and directories."

5   *HTTP, FTP, and Gopher.* Review "Examining Internet Information Server" if you don't know the answer.

6   *Logging to a SQL database requires both more processor overhead and more disk space.* See "Configuring the WWW service" — in particular, the subsection titled "The Logging Tab."

7   *Internet Information Server.* See "Reviewing NT Server Internet Tools" for all the details.

8   *Internet Services Manager.* You should review "Configuring IIS" if you missed this one.

9   *False.* You can assign multiple IP addresses to the same card. Review "Creating virtual servers and directories."

Intranets: Never Talk to Strangers

We're certain that you're familiar with the Internet — the worldwide, TCP/IP-based public network of computers. If not . . . well, it's probably already too late for you. The term *intranet* refers to a local, internally contained TCP/IP network that uses technologies similar to those used on the Internet. The intranet may be connected to the Internet, but it doesn't require that connectivity. In fact, for security concerns, most companies intentionally keep their intranets as far from the Internet as possible.

Intranets can contain Web servers, FTP servers, Domain Name Servers (DNS), gopher servers — anything you commonly think of as Internet based, you can implement as an intranet component. Throughout this chapter, the technologies we explore can apply to both intranets and the Internet.

Here are some suggestions and focus points to help optimize the time you spend studying the material in this chapter:

- ✔ You'll see very little information on Internet Explorer (IE). None of the questions you may see on the Enterprise exam regarding IE require knowing configuration specifics.

- ✔ Exam questions focus on IIS.

- ✔ Be familiar with the concept of virtual servers.

- ✔ Remember that the FTP service passes logon information in clear text, and can, therefore, compromise security if you don't force anonymous logon.

Caught in a World Wide Web of Intrigue

Before we get into the details of NT's Internet tools, we want to make sure that you use the same Internet terms as we do. You need to be familiar with the following terms for this chapter, for your exam, for any Internet- or intranet-related networking, and quite possibly for the rest of your mortal life:

- ✔ **Domain name:** Also referred to as a Fully Qualified Domain Name (FQDN). The unique alphanumeric identifier (such as www.dummies.com) that refers to a specific Internet host. A Domain Name Server resolves a domain name to a standard IP address.

- ✔ **Domain Name Server (DNS):** A host machine that functions as a translator for resolving IP addresses from an FQDN. For example, www.dummies.com is an FQDN, which is mapped to the IP address 206.80.51.139 by an entry in a DNS database.

✔ **FTP:** The File Transfer Protocol. One of the more common applications in the TCP/IP protocol suite, you can use FTP to transfer files across TCP/IP networks between similar or dissimilar operating systems. NT contains a command-line version of the FTP protocol. Internet Explorer can download (but not upload) using FTP, and IIS provides an FTP server service.

✔ **Gopher:** A seldom-used service that links text-based information to other Gopher servers.

✔ **Home page:** The starting page your Internet browser uses. This term also refers to the default page of a Web server when a client connects using only the FQDN, and doesn't specify a specific directory or file to retrieve.

✔ **Host:** In the context of this chapter, any system providing active Internet or intranet server services.

✔ **HTML:** Hypertext Markup Language. HTML is the code used to create a Web page. An HTML file is a plain-text document containing formatting, layout, and content for Web documents.

✔ **HTTP:** Hypertext Transfer Protocol. This protocol provides operation for the Internet components commonly referred to as the World Wide Web (WWW).

✔ **Hyperlink:** Information tied to text or graphics on a Web page that *links* the text or graphic to a different location on the Web. Clicking a hyperlink takes you to the location of the embedded address.

✔ **Internet:** The Internet can refer to so many different components. For our purposes, however, we are talking in general terms about the worldwide, TCP/IP-based public network of computers.

✔ **Intranet:** A privately owned network, similar to the Internet in concept and operation. Intranets are often used within companies to facilitate information sharing between LAN users, without sharing that information with the outside world.

✔ **URL:** Uniform Resource Locator. The standard format for an address on the World Wide Web, a URL must contain an FQDN, and may contain a path and filename for a document.

Reviewing NT Server Internet Tools

You'd be hard pressed to find a software or hardware company that can't think of a way to utilize the technologies of the Internet. Microsoft, being one of the many corporations to recognize the importance of making the Internet easy to access, has integrated Internet-related software components with the NT operating systems.

Windows NT includes two classes of utilities to enable integrated communications with Internet-related services:

- ✔ For the client side, you have Internet Explorer (IE).
- ✔ For the server side, you use the Internet Information Server (IIS).

By default, a version of Internet Explorer automatically installs with Windows NT. And during the initial installation of networking components when you set up NT on your server, you have the option to install IIS.

You can add or upgrade either of these Internet software components after you install Windows NT, so don't worry if you didn't take the option of installing them when you set up your system. In fact, you probably need a new version of Internet Explorer, because most installations of NT Server or Workstation still include Version 2.0. At the time of this writing, IE is up to Version 4.01. The IIS component included with Microsoft Windows NT is also 2.0, but installing Service Pack 3 automatically updates IIS to Version 3.0.

Learn to perform the Sacred Dance of the Versions. To update your software to the most current releases, check out www.microsoft.com/ie for Internet Explorer, and www.microsoft.com/iis for Internet Information Server. In addition to software update downloads, you can find a wealth of information on the products, including features, troubleshooting, and third-party utilities.

Taking a look at Internet Explorer

Internet Explorer, as you know, is Microsoft's response to the consumer demand for Web-browsing software. You don't need to know how to install or configure IE for your Enterprise exam. Any questions you may see dealing with Internet Explorer are really more marketing oriented than technical.

Each passing release of IE becomes more and more integrated with its operating system. Internet Explorer truly is a full-service Web browser, capable of interacting with HTTP servers; downloading with FTP; running Java, ActiveX, and VBScript applications; and supporting other advanced formatting techniques, such as Cascading Style Sheets, frames, and Dynamic HTML.

Although the best and brightest versions of Internet Explorer are first released for Windows 95 and Windows NT, versions of IE are available for a wide range of platforms, including the following systems:

- ✔ Windows 3.1
- ✔ Windows for Workgroups
- ✔ Windows 95
- ✔ Windows NT
- ✔ Macintosh
- ✔ UNIX

Examining Internet Information Server

On the server side of consumer connectivity demand, Microsoft provides the Internet Information Server (IIS) integrated services package. IIS provides a standard interface to various Internet server services, including an HTTP (Web) server, an FTP server, and a Gopher server. IIS can provide efficient, secure publishing services for your servers on the Internet and on your intranet. On your exam, the focus for Internet Information Server is on the WWW and FTP services. You'll be required to know little, if any, information on the Gopher service.

The WWW service provides the server-side HTTP communication protocol that's needed to allow your Web server to respond to client-side Internet browsers. Microsoft's implementation of a Web server can perform any of the functions you expect from this type of software — from simple functions such as serving up standard HTML pages — to some of the more complex functions, such as providing a Secure Socket Layer or processing CGI and Perl scripts.

The FTP service is one of the more common applications in the TCP/IP protocol suite. You can use FTP to transfer files across TCP/IP networks between similar or dissimilar operating systems. The FTP service included with IIS can require user authentication or provide for anonymous connection to the FTP server. As you'd expect, authorized users can upload to or download from servers providing an FTP service. Keep in mind that authorized users can include anonymous users, if the server is set up to accept anonymous logon.

Gopher, a somewhat obsolete TCP/IP protocol, provides a menu-driven, plain-text interface to Gopher pages. As with HTML, Gopher documents can contain hyperlinks. These links appear as menus, and when followed they take a user to other Gopher servers.

Installing IIS

If you didn't install IIS when you set up your server, no problem! You can add IIS just like you would add any other network service. We go step-by-step through the setup of IIS in Lab 18-1. Before you begin, make sure you have everything you need:

- ✔ NT Server 4.0 running TCP/IP on server-class hardware.
- ✔ The NT Server Installation CD.
- ✔ A user account with Administrator rights.
- ✔ If you intend to provide services to the Internet, you need a connection to an Internet Service Provider (ISP). You must configure the network interface to the ISP with the IP address, subnet mask, and default gateway provided by the ISP.

Lab 18-1   Installing IIS

1. **Log on as Administrator.**

2. **Open the Network Properties dialog box by choosing Start⇨Settings⇨Control Panel⇨Network.**

3. **Click the Services tab.**

4. **Click Add, and select Microsoft Internet Information Server from the resulting list.**

5. **If you're prompted for a file location, insert the NT Server Installation CD, and enter *L*:\i386, where *L* represents the letter for your CD drive.**

   As shown in Figure 18-1, the IIS Setup dialog box enables you to select which components you want to install.

6. **Select all components, and click OK.**

   You're prompted to specify an installation directory.

7. **You may choose the default settings by clicking Yes, or you may enter a new installation location.**

   The installation program prompts you for the service-specific publishing directories.

8. **Again, you may choose the default settings by clicking OK, or enter a new installation location. After each dialog box, another message appears, asking if you want to create the new directory. Select Yes.**

9. **Confirm any additional dialog boxes, until you see the message notifying you of a complete installation. Click OK at this box, and your Internet server is ready to go!**

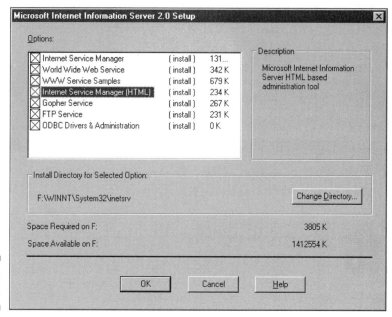

Figure 18-1:
IIS Setup.

Well . . . sort of. Your server can now respond to HTTP, FTP, or Gopher requests, but the documents for those services do not yet exist, nor have you set configuration beyond the basics.

Configuring IIS

After you install IIS, you can configure it by using the Internet Service Manager. To start the Internet Service Manager, choose Start➪ Programs➪Microsoft Internet Server➪Internet Service Manager.

Figure 18-2 shows the interface for the Internet Service Manager. From this interface, you can start, stop, pause, or configure the properties of the WWW service, the FTP service, or the Gopher service.

You'll notice many similarities in the configuration properties of these three services. We concentrate on the WWW service, then look at some of the options specific to FTP. We don't explore the Gopher service configuration, because you don't need to be familiar with this obsolete protocol for your exam.

Figure 18-2:
The Internet
Service
Manager
interface.

For any configuration changes in any of the IIS services, you must stop and restart the service before the changes take effect.

Configuring the WWW service

From the Internet Service Manager, double-click the computer name column of the WWW Service listing. Figure 18-3 shows the resulting dialog box — the WWW Service Properties interface. The WWW Service Properties dialog box has four tabs: Service, Directories, Logging, and Advanced.

The Service tab

Table 18-1 describes the properties you can set on the Service tab. We describe the other three tabs in the following sections.

The Directories tab

The Directories tab has fewer options than the Service tab. You can add directories that will be published by IIS. You can also add aliases. For example, if you have a directory named EngineeringDocuments that you want people to access as docs, you add this name as an alias in the Directory box. You can even point to directories on different physical servers.

You can also add an IP address for virtual directories. This means you can publish information located on a single server as if it were located on multiple servers. For more details on this setting, see the section "Creating virtual servers and directories," later in this chapter.

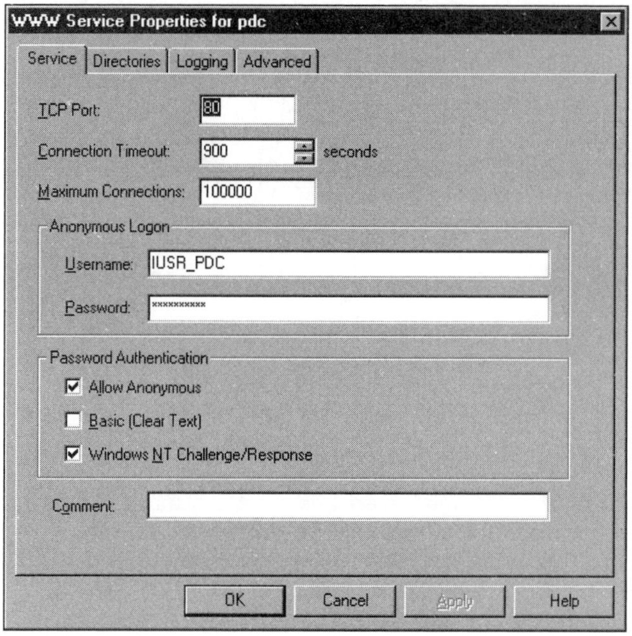

Figure 18-3:
The Service
Properties
tab.

Table 18-1	Service Properties
Property	**Description**
TCP Port	Identifies the TCP port on which the WWW service will run. Port 80 is the standard port used by the HTTP protocol.
Connection Timeout	Defines how long a connection is held open without activity before terminating. The default is 900 seconds.
Maximum Connections	Specifies how many concurrent connections are supported.
Anonymous Logon	Identifies the NT user account that's used for anonymous access.
Password Authentication	Specifies the authentication process for users of this service. Allow Anonymous uses no authentication. Basic (Clear Text) is an encoded authentication supported by most Internet browsers. Windows NT Challenge/Response encrypts user names and passwords and is supported by Internet Explorer 2.0 and later.
Comment	This option has no effect on the operation of the service.

Other options on this tab include Enable Default Document, which allows an Internet browser to request an address such as `www.microsoft.com` and have the Web server append the document to the end of the address. By default, the Default Document name is Default.htm, so IIS would respond to a user entering the previous address by displaying `www.microsoft.com/Default.htm`. Enabling the Directory Browsing Allowed button permits a user to browse to a directory without a default document and view a listing of all files in that directory.

The Logging tab

The Logging tab allows you to log system activity to a file. You can also log to a SQL database, but this method requires a bit more overhead than dropping information to a plain text file. You don't need to know how to configure a SQL database source for logging on your exam, but you should be aware of the heavier overhead requirement behind SQL logging.

The options on the Logging tab are fairly self-explanatory. All you do is select whether you want to log activity, and if so, to which directory. You also have the option to create new log files on a daily, weekly, monthly, or file-size basis.

The Advanced tab

The Advanced tab lets you grant or deny access to a specific service based on IP addresses for client systems. You can choose to grant or deny access to everyone, and then set specific IP addresses to exclude from the selected access policy. You can deny or grant access on a subnet range or on an individual address basis. When you click the Add button, you see the option for defining a group of computers or setting a single IP address for your exclusion setting.

You can also use the Advanced tab to restrict the total amount of network bandwidth (on a KB/Sec basis) that's used by a specific service, or by Internet Information Server in general.

Configuring the FTP service

The FTP service properties are quite similar to those of the WWW service. However, a few differences are worth noting before you take your exam. First, the Service tab in the FTP Service Properties dialog box provides the option of Allowing Only Anonymous connections. This option prevents user names and passwords from being sent via clear-text when users log on to the FTP server.

The other notable difference for the FTP service is the Messages tab. On this tab, you can define three messages. The Welcome message displays when someone connects to your server. The Exit message displays when a user closes the connection to your server. The third message is a Maximum Connections message. If the maximum number of users are logged on to your FTP server, this message displays to any additional users attempting a connection.

Creating virtual servers and directories

With IIS, you can create virtual directories and virtual servers, and it's important to know the difference between them for your Enterprise exam. With virtual directories, you can publish directories on multiple servers while running IIS on only one machine. Virtual directories appear to reside on the same server running the IIS service. Each Internet service can control multiple directories on multiple machines by setting up virtual directories.

To set up a virtual directory, click the Add button on the Directories tab for a selected IIS service. You see the dialog box shown in Figure 18-4. In the Directory box, you can define a local or network drive, or a UNC name for a directory. Select the Virtual Directory option, and add an alias by which clients will refer to the resource.

In contrast to virtual directories, a virtual server is a single physical server configured to appear as several separate servers. You will see a question about virtual servers on your exam. Why would you need to use virtual servers? Suppose you're providing Web hosting for multiple organizations, and each organization wants its own domain name, but none of them can afford a dedicated machine. You can create a virtual server for each company, and from a client standpoint, each system appears to be hosted on a separate machine.

Any time you see a question referring to assigning virtual servers, look for answers that involve assigning multiple IP addresses to a single network interface card (NIC) for each virtual server to be created.

You must meet a few additional requirements for virtual servers beyond what you need for a virtual directory. Before creating a virtual server, you must go into the network Control Panel and assign an additional IP address to your network card for each virtual server you host. For an intranet, you're able to determine these IP addresses, but if your server is on the Internet, you must use addresses assigned through your ISP, registered in a DNS and through the InterNIC. After determining the additional IP addresses you will use, you must assign a home directory for each IP address through the Directories tab of the Service Properties dialog box. Clicking the Add button in this dialog box opens the window shown in Figure 18-4.

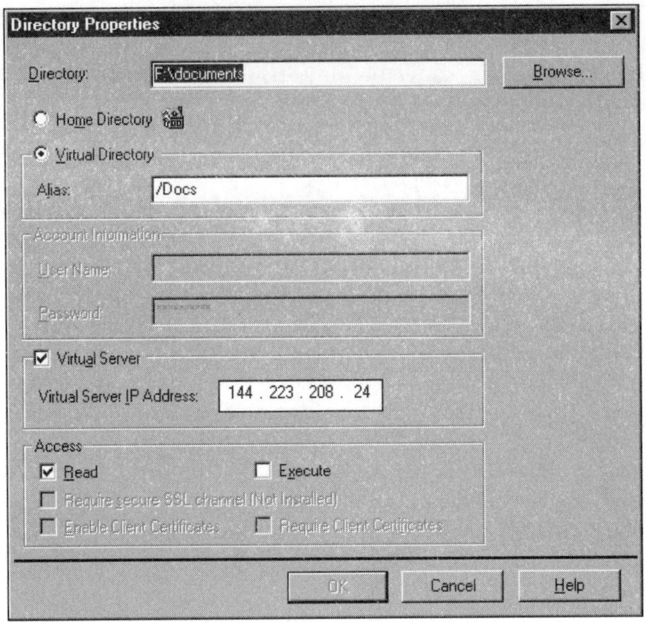

Figure 18-4:
Virtual
directories.

Prep Test

1 Your company provides Internet hosting services for organizations that don't have the resources to maintain their own Internet servers. You plan to provide three companies with virtual servers to host their Web sites from one physical server. Each organization's virtual server will have its own domain name. What are the minimum steps you must take to provide services for these three organizations?

A ○ Install IIS on your server. Install DNS and assign the server's IP address to a domain name for each organization.

B ○ Install IIS on your server. Assign three IP addresses to the single network interface card in your server. Create a WWW service folder for each organization, and assign an IP address to each folder using the Directories tab in the WWW Service Properties. Register the domain names through the InterNIC for the three organizations.

C ○ Install IIS on your server. In the Advanced properties tab, set up Virtual Directories. Assign a virtual directory to each organization.

D ○ Install IIS on your server. You must install an additional network interface card for each virtual server you want to host, and assign an original IP address to each card. Set up IIS to use all three NICs.

2 Which of the following server services are provided by IIS 3.0? (Choose all that apply.)

A ❑ WWW

B ❑ FTP

C ❑ SMTP

D ❑ Gopher

3 You want to prevent the user accounts and passwords from being transmitted over your network when users connect to your FTP service. Which options should you select on the FTP Service properties tab? (Choose all that apply.)

A ❑ Clear the Allow Anonymous connections option.

B ❑ Check the Allow Anonymous connections option.

C ❑ Check the Allow Only Anonymous connections option.

D ❑ Clear the Allow Only Anonymous connections option.

4 You want to change the default WWW document from Default.htm to Index.html. Where must you make this change?

A ○ RegEdit

B ○ The Services tab in Network Properties

C ○ The WWW Service Properties tab

D ○ The WWW Directories Properties tab

5 To conform to Internet services port setting standards, which TCP port should your HTTP service use?

A ○ 21

B ○ 23

C ○ 70

D ○ 80

6 For which of the following platforms can you install a version of Microsoft Internet Explorer? (Choose all that apply.)

A ❑ Windows 95/NT

B ❑ Windows 3.1

C ❑ Macintosh

D ❑ UNIX

7 Tim is trying to upload a file to your IIS FTP server using Internet Explorer 2.0, with no success. What is the most likely problem?

A ○ Tim is connected using an anonymous logon.

B ○ Tim doesn't have write privileges to the NTFS directory.

C ○ Internet Explorer can't be used to upload files via FTP.

D ○ The IIS FTP service doesn't allow file uploading.

8 Which of the following items is required for a virtual server?

A ○ One physical server for each virtual server

B ○ One IP address for each virtual server

C ○ One network interface card for each virtual server

D ○ One Anonymous user account for each virtual server

9 You have just disabled anonymous access to the FTP service. However, your users are still able to connect to the FTP server using an anonymous logon. What is the best way to correct this issue without interrupting the operations of any of your other services?

A ○ Stop and restart the FTP service.

B ○ Delete the anonymous account from the User Manager.

C ○ Reboot the computer.

D ○ Your FTP service is corrupt, and you must reinstall IIS.

10 How does an intranet server differ from an Internet server?

A ○ Intranet servers use NetBEUI, whereas the Internet servers use TCP/IP.

B ○ Internet servers are accessible to the public, while intranet servers are generally accessible only from the local area network.

C ○ Intranet servers must be registered with the InterNIC, while the Internet servers are maintained through DHCP.

D ○ Internet servers allow anonymous logons, while intranet servers require authentication.

Answers

1 *B.* To maintain independent Web sites for three clients on one server, you must assign three IP addresses to the single NIC. Then, create separate folders for each organization, and assign the corresponding IP address to each folder. For the servers to be accessible from the Internet by a domain name, you must register the domain names through the InterNIC. *Review "Creating virtual servers and directories."*

2 *A, B, and D.* HTTP, also known as the World Wide Web protocol, FTP, and Gopher are provided with IIS 2.0 and IIS 3.0. SMTP, the Simple Mail Transport Protocol, is not provided with Windows NT. *Review "Examining Internet Information Server."*

3 *B and C.* FTP, by nature of the protocol, only sends unencrypted user names and passwords. To prevent your user names and passwords from being sent unencrypted over the network, you must prevent FTP users from logging on with their Windows NT user accounts. To do so, you must enable *only* anonymous logon. *Review "Configuring the FTP service."*

4 *D. The WWW Directories Properties tab.* The Default Document option on the Directories tab determines the document served to a client browser when a document name isn't specified. *See the section "Configuring the WWW service" — in particular, the subsection titled "The Directories tab."*

5 *D. 80.* Port 80 is the standard TCP communications port for the HTTP protocol. Port 23 is the standard Telnet port, 21 is the standard FTP port, and 70 is the standard Gopher port. You can find a full listing of the default ports in your \WINNT\system32\drivers\etc\services file. *Review "Configuring the WWW service," paying close attention to the subsection "The Service tab."*

6 *A, B, C, and D.* Versions of Internet Explorer are available for each of the listed platforms. *Review "Taking a look at Internet Explorer."*

7 *C. Internet Explorer can't be used to upload files via FTP.* You can use Internet Explorer to browse or download from an FTP server, but you can't use it for FTP uploads. *Review "Taking a look at Internet Explorer."*

8 *B. One IP address for each virtual server.* Each virtual server needs its own IP address. You don't need to install a separate network card for each server. Each network interface card can have multiple IP addresses defined; you do this through the Control Panel⇨Network application. Select the Protocols tab, highlight TCP/IP, and click Properties. In the resulting dialog box, select the IP Address tab, and click Advanced. You can add the addresses in the IP Addresses box. *Review "Creating virtual servers and directories."*

9 A. *Stop and restart the FTP service.* Changes in configuration to any of the IIS services require stopping and restarting the affected service before those changes can take effect. *Review "Configuring IIS."*

10 B. *Internet servers are accessible to the public, while intranet servers are generally accessible only from the local area network.* The Internet is a public network, while intranets are usually not even directly connected to the Internet. Either type of server can support anonymous access, and both require TCP/IP as the network protocol. Also, the Internet server's IP address must be registered with InterNIC, whereas an intranet IP address can be maintained on a local DNS server. *Review "Intranets: Never Talk to Strangers."*

Chapter 19

Remote Access Service Basics

· ·

Exam Objectives

▶ Installing and configuring RAS

▶ Selecting RAS protocols

▶ Configuring RAS protocols

▶ Configuring RAS security

· ·

*W*indows NT 4.0 offers significantly expanded functionality in the Remote Access Service (RAS) compared to the Windows NT 3.51 implementation. As a result, Microsoft places greater emphasis on RAS on the certification exams.

One of the most powerful and versatile technologies included with Microsoft's Windows NT Server is the Remote Access Service (RAS). RAS makes network resources available to remote clients through various dial-up options, including standard phone lines, ISDN lines, and packet-switched networks such as X.25. RAS allows remote users to access network resources from anywhere in the world they can find a good telephone connection. Users can send e-mail, print, and work with data files just as if they were sitting in their offices.

RAS has many configuration options and at least two different places where it must be configured. Also, from a security perspective, RAS has the potential for serious consequences if configured improperly. To ensure that you implement this technology properly, Microsoft stresses your understanding of RAS configuration options and procedures on the Enterprise exam.

Throughout this chapter and the next one, we highlight the differences between RAS in the Windows NT 3.51 environment and the Windows NT 4.0 environment. We discuss all the new technologies that you need to know for the Enterprise exam. Even if you're already familiar with RAS in the Windows NT 3.51 implementation, you want to pay close attention to the additional functionality available in the Windows NT 4.0 implementation — for example, Multilink and Point-to-Point-Tunneling Protocol (PPTP). These new technologies receive a lot of emphasis on the Enterprise exam.

Quick Assessment

Installing and configuring RAS

1 You install RAS via the _____ tab, which you find by starting the _____ Control Panel application.

2 Windows NT Server 4.0 supports _____ simultaneous inbound RAS connection(s), while Windows NT Workstation 4.0 supports _____ inbound RAS connection(s).

3 _____ is installed on a Windows NT Workstation or a Windows 95 machine that needs to act as a client to a RAS server.

Selecting RAS protocols

4 The _____ dial-up protocol was designed as an enhancement to the original SLIP specification. This is an industry standard framing and authentication protocol that allows clients and servers to interoperate in a multivendor environment.

5 RAS supports the following LAN transport protocols: _____, _____, and _____.

Configuring RAS protocols

6 RAS includes a _____ that allows clients to gain access to NetBIOS resources, such as file and print servers, on a network regardless of which transport protocol is installed on the server.

7 Microsoft RAS provides routers for the _____ and _____ network transport protocols.

8 The _____ protocol must be installed to give remote clients the capability to use their Web browsers.

Configuring RAS security

9 _____ domain security provides for organization-wide security using a single network logon model, which eliminates the need for duplicating user accounts across a multiple-server network.

Answers

1 *Services; Network.* Review "Installing RAS Servers."

2 *256; 1.* Review "RAS Servers and Clients."

3 *Dial-Up Networking.* Review "RAS Servers and Clients."

4 *PPP.* Review "Understanding Remote Access Protocols."

5 *NetBEUI; IPX; TCP/IP.* Review "Using Local Area Network Protocols."

6 *NetBIOS Gateway.* Review "I'm a NetBEUI, you're a NetBEUI."

7 *IP; IPX.* Review "Configuring IPX."

8 *TCP/IP.* Review "Configuring TCP/IP."

9 *Integrated.* Review "Configuring RAS Security."

RAS Servers and Clients

In most cases, the RAS server and the RAS client are both Microsoft operating systems. However, this is not a requirement if you take a more liberal definition of RAS. You can use Dial-Up Networking to connect to any type of server running either the Serial Line Internet Protocol (SLIP) or the Point-to-Point Protocol (PPP) RAS protocol — including the UNIX servers that many Internet Service Providers (ISPs) use.

On the exam, a question may refer to a UNIX server. Whenever you see UNIX, at least consider the possibility of SLIP. The RAS server will always run on a Windows NT operating system, and at least for now, you can only use the PPTP RAS protocol between a Microsoft RAS server and a Microsoft RAS client. Here's a useful general rule: Unless the question specifies a different operating system, you can assume you are dealing with a Windows NT 4.0 server as the RAS server and a Windows NT 4.0 workstation as the RAS client. Another piece of helpful information that you may need for the exam is the fact that RAS on NT Server supports 256 inbound connections, while RAS on NT Workstation supports only one inbound connection.

Installing RAS Servers

Before you begin installing RAS, you should take a few moments to gather some information. By taking the time to collect the following information, you can make the installation much smoother, and greatly increase your odds for a successful installation on the first attempt:

- The model of the modem and the driver that you're using
- The type of communication port to be configured
- Whether the computer will be used for dial-out, dial-in, or both
- The client protocols and the correct options
- Modem settings such as baud rate
- Security settings

You install RAS either during or after the setup of Windows NT. If you select Remote Access to the Network as an installation option, both RAS and Dial-Up Networking are installed. You can manually install either of the services after the initial setup.

For the exam, remember that you install RAS through the Network Control Panel application. You install Dial-Up Networking by clicking the Dial-Up Networking icon in My Computer, or by clicking the Dial-Up Networking icon located on the Accessories menu. As we detail in Lab 19-1, you install RAS as a network service.

Lab 19-1   Installing a RAS Server

1. **Log on as Administrator.**

   To install a RAS server, you must use an administrator account — either the Administrator account, or a user account that has been placed in the Administrators group.

2. **Start the Network program from Control Panel.**

3. **Click the Services tab, then click Add.**

4. **In the Select Network Services dialog box, click Remote Access Service, then click OK.**

   Remember that RAS is installed as a network service. That's why you find it on the Services tab.

5. **Provide the path for your Windows NT Server distribution files.**

   This path may be a CD-ROM, a network share, or a local copy of the distribution files.

6. **When the Remote Access Setup dialog box appears, choose to run the Modem Installer.**

7. **Allow the Modem Installer to detect any modems and click Next.**

   If you know the type of modem you are using, and have the driver on a floppy disk, it may be faster to select the Don't Detect My Modem; I Will Select it from a List check box. This option enables you to configure your modem manually.

8. **Click Selected ports, select the COM port your modem is connected to, and click Next.**

9. **In the Location Information dialog box, under What Country Are You in Now, enter your area code and then click Next.**

10. **Click Finish, review the Add RAS Device dialog box, and click OK.**

Configuring analog modems

Analog modems use standard telephone lines. You may hear these phone lines referred to as POTS lines. POTS is an acronym for Plain Old Telephone Service. Don't be surprised if you also see the abbreviation PSTN. Public Switched Telephone Network is simply the fancy name for the phone company. We don't remember many exam questions dealing directly with analog modems, but you should be aware of some features of modems. Here's a list of basic modem information for you to take into the exam:

✔ Maximum modem speed right now is about 56 Kbps. Actual modem speed normally ranges between 28.8 Kbps and 38.4 Kbps.

✔ To configure a modem under NT, you may need to define a port with the Control Panel Ports applet.

✔ To configure a port, you need an available interrupt.

Modems are either synchronous or asynchronous. Synchronous modems are much more expensive than asynchronous modems, and usually provide higher throughput. On the certification exam, you should assume the word *modem* refers to an asynchronous communication device (either external or internal) that converts digital signals to analog signals and analog signals to digital signals for transmission over standard telephone lines.

Remember that modems make RAS a point-to-point connection. A one-to-one relationship exists with modem communications, which differs from the one-to-many relationship you may be familiar with from LAN communications. A modem is required at each end of the communications link to complete the connection.

Configuring ISDN adapters

Integrated Services Digital Network (ISDN) is a digital system specification that offers higher throughput than the PSTN. ISDN was designed to eventually replace all the analog telephone lines now in use by most telephone companies across the U.S. ISDN comes in two flavors: Basic and Primary — sometimes referred to as Basic Rate ISDN (BRI) and Primary Rate ISDN (PRI). For the certification exam, you only need to be concerned with BRI.

The BRI specification allows you to configure two B channels for voice or data, and one D channel for link management. Each B channel is a 64 Kbps digital transmission. If the channels are used separately, each channel has a separate telephone number and is dialed independently. With most ISDN offerings, the two B channels can be combined to form one 128 Kbps channel, most often used for data only.

For the exam, remember the following important points concerning ISDN:

✔ ISDN data transmission speed is either 64 Kbps or 128 Kbps.

✔ ISDN lines must be installed at both the server site and the remote site.

✔ An ISDN adapter must be installed in both the server and the remote client.

✔ Windows NT treats the ISDN adapter as a network adapter.

Using a Wide Area Network (WAN)

In the context of the certification exam, any connection you create with RAS is a WAN connection. However, if you run into a question that asks specifically about a WAN connection, you may want to consider the possibility that you are being asked about an X.25 connection or an ISDN connection.

Don't let the term *WAN connection* throw you. **Remember:** Aside from some configuration options specific to these technologies, a WAN connection looks and acts just like a network adapter for your LAN.

The purpose of the certification exam is not to test your knowledge of hardware, so don't expect to see any hardware-specific questions. As far as modems and ISDN adapters are concerned, if the device is on the NT Hardware Compatibility List, then it will work as a RAS communications device.

Just to be sure, you may want to brush up on your basic PC operations. Remember that a modem is a serial device, so it needs a COM port, and a COM port needs an available IRQ. If you don't remember how to tell which COM ports are available, or how to configure a COM port, take a few minutes to review the appropriate NT Server manuals. Figure 19-1 shows the RAS configuration dialog box for an analog modem showing the COM port usage configuration. If you have trouble configuring a COM port, remember that the Windows NT Diagnostic program can show you available resources such as IRQs and I/O ports.

Another connectivity option new to Windows NT 4.0 is the Point-to-Point Tunneling Protocol (PPTP). PPTP is a networking protocol that supports multi-protocol virtual private networks (VPNs). PPTP allows remote users to access private networks securely across the Internet by dialing into an Internet Service Provider (ISP) or by connecting directly to the Internet.

Figure 19-1:
The
Configure
Port Usage
dialog box.

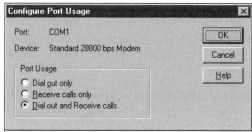

For the exam, remember the following key PPTP benefits:

✔ Being able to connect to a local ISP saves money.

✔ Other protocols can be encapsulated in IP packets for Internet routing.

✔ Data is encrypted from end-to-end.

✔ You can establish a secure connection over the Internet.

Two more connectivity options are sometimes used with RAS: X.25 networks and RS-232 null modem cables. These two options are quite a bit more exotic than PSTN, ISDN, and PPTP, so don't expect to see many questions about them on the exam. The RS-232 null modem cable is a useful option to have when you need to transfer data from one computer to another and you don't have a network available. Know that these connectivity options are available and you'll be in good shape for the exam.

Using Local Area Network Protocols

The RAS server enables multiple clients to connect by using multiple protocols. The server also allows the same client to connect using more than one protocol. The RAS server and the LAN should be running the same protocols. The RAS client can connect to network resources using any combination of the configured protocols.

When installing and configuring RAS, you should pay close attention to the LAN protocols that are already installed on the Windows NT Server. By *LAN protocols,* we mean TCP/IP, NWLink, and NetBEUI. If you do not select any additional protocols during the RAS installation, the only protocols that you have available to configure are the LAN protocols already installed on the system. If you select a LAN protocol during the installation of the RAS server that is not already installed on the system, that new protocol will be installed on the system as part of the RAS server installation.

You configure protocols by using the Network Configuration dialog box, which you access by clicking the Network button in the Remote Access Service dialog box. The Network Configuration dialog box presents you with numerous options. In the following sections, we explain three major categories of options. Table 19-1 describes the purpose of each RAS configuration option.

Table 19-1	RAS Configuration Options
Option	**Use This Option To**
Dial out Protocols	Select the dial-out protocols
Server Settings	Configure dial-in protocols
Encryption Settings	Set the authentication level required for logon
Enable Multilink	Enable PPP Multilink protocol on the server

The Multilink option allows multiple physical connections, including PSTN and ISDN connections, to be combined to form a single logical connection. The aggregate bandwidth is greater than the individual bandwidths.

Configuring TCP/IP

Of all the client protocols, TCP/IP is the most complex to configure. Consequently, it is also the protocol that the exam covers most thoroughly.

You set the TCP/IP protocol configuration for the RAS server in the RAS Server TCP/IP Configuration dialog box. You access this dialog box by selecting the TCP/IP check box in the Server Settings section of the Network Configuration dialog box. Then, click the Configure button.

For the exam, you need to be very familiar with the options in this dialog box:

✔ **Allow Remote TCP/IP Clients to Access.** This option allows you to grant clients access to resources located anywhere on the network, or to restrict clients to accessing only resources located on the RAS server. This option enables or disables the IP router function included in the RAS server. Select the Entire Network option to enable the router, or This Computer Only to disable the router.

✔ **Use DHCP to Assign Remote TCP/IP Client Addresses.** Selecting this option allows remote clients to request a DHCP-assigned address from a DHCP server located either on the RAS server or somewhere else on the network. All TCP/IP configuration information normally available through DHCP is available to remote clients.

✔ **Use Static Address Pool.** Watch out for this option! It may look like DHCP, and it may taste like DHCP, but it's not DHCP. The real trouble begins when you inadvertently overlap the range of IP addresses defined to the RAS server with the scope of addresses defined on a DHCP server. Before you know it, you have IP address conflicts spreading like wildfire! We saw questions relating to this problem on two vendor exams and on a certification exam.

✓ **Allow Remote Clients to Request a Predetermined IP Address.** If your clients require a specific IP address to function on your IP network, this option allows them to request that address. This is completely different from reserving an IP address on a DHCP server.

Configuring IPX

IPX support is required if you have Novell NetWare clients that need to gain access to NetWare servers through the RAS server. You use the RAS Server IPX Configuration dialog box to grant network access permissions and to assign network numbers to Dial-Up clients. You access the RAS Server IPX Configuration dialog box by selecting the IPX check box in the Server Settings section of Network Configuration dialog box. Then, click the Configure button.

The RAS Server IPX Configuration dialog box has the following options:

✓ **Allow Remote IPX Clients to Access:** Enables or disables the IPX gateway. By selecting the Entire Network option, you allow clients to access resources located anywhere on the network. Selecting This Computer Only allows clients to access resources located on the RAS server.

✓ **Allocate Network Numbers Automatically:** Allows the server to randomly generate and assign to the client an IPX network number. The network number is analogous to the station's address.

✓ **Allocate Network Numbers From/To:** Allows you to specify a particular range of network numbers for dial-up clients.

✓ **Assign Same Network Number to All IPX Clients:** Allows you to create a logical IPX network that contains all the RAS clients — that is, simply a logical grouping.

✓ **Allow Remote Clients to Request IPX Node Number:** Allows IPX clients to request a certain node number or IPX address.

I'm a NetBEUI, you're a NetBEUI

If NetBEUI is installed on the server, the RAS setup program automatically enables NetBEUI as a dial-in protocol. The setup program also enables the NetBIOS Gateway. NetBEUI is a very small, very fast protocol and should be enabled anytime you only need to provide support for small workgroups.

You need to configure only one option for the NetBEUI protocol. You find this option in the RAS Server NetBEUI Configuration dialog box, shown in Figure 19-2. To access this dialog box, select the NetBEUI check box in the

Server Settings section of the Network Configuration dialog box and click Configure. If you select the Entire Network option, clients can access network resources located anywhere on the network. If you select the This Computer Only option, clients can access only resources located on the RAS server.

Figure 19-2:
The
NetBEUI
Configuration
dialog box.

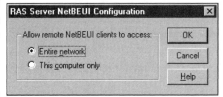

Understanding Remote Access Protocols

Alphabet soup! On top of the three LAN protocols that you need to be familiar with (TCP/IP, IPX, and NetBEUI), you must become familiar with two more RAS protocols: SLIP and PPP. Be sure you understand the differences before you go into the exam.

RAS and SLIP

The Serial Line Internet Protocol (SLIP) is an old industry standard for establishing TCP/IP connections over serial lines. SLIP is still supported under the Dial-Up Networking client, but Microsoft dropped support for SLIP at the server in Windows NT 4.0.

Remember the following key points about SLIP:

- ✔ SLIP requires a static IP address.
- ✔ It requires text-based logon sessions that often require scripting.
- ✔ It supports TCP/IP only.
- ✔ It transmits authentication passwords as clear text.

SLIP is still available on the client side, but beginning with Windows NT 4.0, RAS servers no longer support the SLIP protocol.

RAS and PPP

PPP was designed to overcome some of the limitations of the SLIP standard. The PPP specification provides a set of standard framing and authentication protocols that enable RAS clients and servers to interoperate in a multivendor environment. The PPP architecture allows clients to connect with LANs running TCP/IP, NetBEUI, and IPX. The common protocols allow client applications written to the Windows Sockets Interface (WinSock), NetBIOS, or IPX to connect to server applications using the same communication method.

PPP also allows clients that are running Client Services for NetWare (CSNW) to dial in and connect to NetWare servers. To access NetWare servers, you must have CSNW installed on the Windows NT Workstation RAS client.

One question that you may see on the test involves PPP logging. You can set this option to help troubleshoot a PPP connection. PPP logging can only be enabled through a Registry edit. You don't need to know the exact Registry key; just remember that you won't find an option in any of the RAS dialog boxes that permits you to enable PPP logging.

Configuring RAS Security

Security is a big deal to Microsoft. Industry acceptance of its operating systems and software depends, in part, on offering products that are secure and training technicians in the proper way to deploy those products. You won't pass any Microsoft certification exam without correctly answering a few security-related questions.

RAS is no exception to security scrutiny. When you configure a RAS server, you are configuring an access point to your LAN or enterprise network that anyone with a RAS client may use to gain access to your private information.

Granting permissions

To install and configure the RAS server, you must be an Administrator in the Windows NT domain that the server is a part of, or in the local Administrators group for the server.

For a user to gain access to a network through RAS, the user must have a valid Windows NT account on the RAS server or in the NT domain. That account must have been granted the Dial-In permission through one of the following utilities:

  ↙ User Manager

  ↙ User Manager for Domains

  ↙ Remote Access Administrator

The Remote Access Administrator is the tool of choice because it provides the most flexible interface. Figure 19-3 shows the Remote Access Administrator interface.

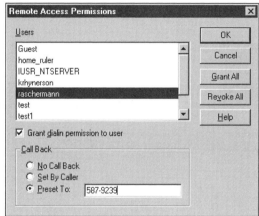

Figure 19-3:
The Remote
Access
Administrator
permissions
interface.

Using data encryption

You can use data encryption to maintain security in case of unauthorized interception of remote access transmissions. To configure data encryption, clients configure each phonebook entry to use data encryption. *Phonebook entry* refers to the collection of configuration settings that defines a dial-up server on the client. You can see your phonebook entries by opening your Dial-Up Networking folder, which you access via the My Computer icon.

Remember two things about encryption. First, information is encrypted from end-to-end. Second, you can configure data encryption from the client or the server. The server administrator can require data encryption, or the client can request it.

Prep Test

1 Which of the following network resources can a RAS client access? (Choose all that apply.)

A ❑ Printers

B ❑ File Shares

C ❑ Databases

D ❑ Mail and Scheduling

2 Which of the following is not considered a WAN protocol?

A ○ PSTN

B ○ X.25

C ○ ISDN

D ○ T1

3 Which of the following is not a protocol supported by RAS?

A ○ DLC

B ○ TCP/IP

C ○ NetBEUI

D ○ IPX

4 Which RAS protocol is needed to support TCP/IP, NetBEUI, and IPX?

A ○ SLIP

B ○ PPP

C ○ SNA

D ○ OSI

5 Which of the following is not a security feature of RAS?

A ○ Auditing

B ○ Filtering PPTP

C ○ Callback

D ○ Multilink

6 RAS on Windows NT Server supports how many connections?

A ○ 1

B ○ 10

C ○ 255

D ○ 256

7 Which of the following is not a RAS port usage setting?

A ○ Dial Out Only

B ○ Dial on Demand

C ○ Receive Calls Only

D ○ Dial Out and Receive Calls

8 You enable PPP logging through which application?

A ○ Dial-Up Networking

B ○ Network application under Control Panel

C ○ Registry Editor

D ○ RAS Monitor

Answers

1 *A, B, C, and D.* We hate to start off with a trick question, but you need to remember that any resource that isn't resident on the client or on the RAS server is a network resource. To gain access to network resources, you need to enable access to the entire network. Do you remember how to do that? *Review "Using Local Area Network Protocols."*

2 *D. T1.* A T1 line is a leased digital line. At least within the context of the exam, a T1 line isn't considered to be a WAN connection, although a T1 line may be involved as an intermediate connection. *Review "Configuring ISDN adapters."*

3 *A. DLC.* Client protocols are TCP/IP, IPX, and NetBEUI. *Review "Using Local Area Network Protocols."*

4 *B. PPP.* SLIP is the older of the two remote access protocols. It was designed primarily to extend TCP/IP networks over phone lines, so it doesn't support the NetBEUI or IPX protocols. *Review "Understanding Remote Access Protocols."*

5 *D. Multilink.* Multilink is a feature of RAS, but it isn't a security feature. Remember that Multilink and Callback don't always play well together. If this one tripped you up, you may want to check out the section "Configuring RAS Security." *Review "Using Local Area Network Protocols" — in particular, Table 19-1.*

6 *D. 256.* RAS on NT Server supports 256 inbound connections, and RAS on NT Workstation supports one inbound connection. *Review "RAS Servers and Clients."*

7 *B. Dial on Demand.* Dial on Demand is kind of a general term used to indicate that a connection is not a full-time connection. When you are configuring RAS ports, the ports are designated to Dial Out, Receive Calls Only, or Dial Out and Receive Calls. *Review "Using Local Area Network Protocols" — in particular, Table 19-1.*

8 *C. Registry Editor.* This is a trick question. Remember that turning on logging requires a Registry edit. *Review "RAS and PPP."*

Chapter 20

RAS in Action

Exam Objectives

▶ Installing RAS client software

▶ Configuring Dial-Up Networking

▶ Selecting RAS client protocols

▶ Configuring RAS security

▶ Troubleshooting RAS connections

*A*mong the most challenging topics in all the Windows NT certification exams are Remote Access Service (RAS) and Dial-Up Networking. The depth of knowledge required to successfully navigate this part of the exam ranges from analog modem signaling to network security operations.

Fortunately, you don't need to be an expert in all these areas. With a general, operational knowledge of modems and LAN/WAN protocols, you can understand RAS features and benefits, and make intelligent configuration choices. As with many other Microsoft technologies, you may find that many ways exist for accomplishing an objective, but you only get credit for knowing the Microsoft way on the certification exam.

As with any other client/server software, RAS has a server component and a client component. This chapter focuses on the RAS client, otherwise known as *Dial-Up Networking* under Windows NT and Windows 95. When configuring a Dial-Up Networking connection, you must make quite a few choices. Fortunately, the certification exam focuses on a subset of the configuration options. It's a good idea for you to familiarize yourself with all the options, but realistically, if you know where to find each option on the configuration screens, you'll be all right.

Quick Assessment

Installing RAS client software

1 The RAS client on Windows NT and Windows 95 is called _____.

Configuring Dial-Up Networking

2 You use a(n) _____ to store all the configuration information for a connection defined on a RAS client.

3 The three protocols available to a client for connecting to a server via RAS are _____, _____, and _____.

Selecting RAS client protocols

4 The _____ Gateway allows RAS clients to dial in with one protocol and access network resources with a different protocol.

5 The three LAN protocols that RAS supports are _____, _____, and _____.

Configuring RAS Security

6 You use the _____ application to grant users permission to dial into the RAS server.

7 If you configure _____ security, after the user is authenticated, the RAS server hangs up and calls the user.

8 Data _____ is a security feature in RAS that you configure at the client.

Trouble-shooting RAS connections

9 The new RAS feature called _____ allows connections to be made automatically when a user tries to access a remote resource.

10 The new RAS feature called _____ enables you to use multiple physical connections to a RAS server to increase the bandwidth of the connection.

Answers

1 *Dial-Up Networking.* Review "Installing RAS Client Software."

2 *Phonebook entry.* Review "Creating a Dial-Up Connection."

3 *SLIP, PPP, PPTP.* Review "Creating a Dial-Up Connection."

4 *NetBIOS.* Review "Configuring RAS Client Protocols."

5 *NetBEUI, IPX, TCP/IP.* Review "Configuring RAS Client Protocols."

6 *User Manager.* Review "Configuring RAS Client Security."

7 *Callback.* Review "Configuring RAS Client Security."

8 *Encryption.* Review "Configuring RAS Client Security."

9 *AutoDial.* Review "Resolving AutoDial problems."

10 *Multilink.* Review "Determining Multilink and Callback incompatibility."

Installing RAS Client Software

The RAS client on Windows NT is called *Dial-Up Networking*. Client software is also available for Windows 3.1, Windows for Workgroups, and DOS. However, you won't be tested on configurations for these older operating systems. Required knowledge about RAS client software is confined to the 32-bit Microsoft operating systems.

Dial-Up Networking is automatically installed on systems running Windows NT Workstation or Windows NT Server if you select the Remote Access to the Network option during setup.

If you're unsure whether Dial-Up Networking has been installed on a machine, open the My Computer icon on your desktop. If you have a folder called Dial-Up Networking, the software has been installed on that system.

Creating a Dial-Up Connection

You use a phonebook entry to store all the configuration information for a connection to a server. Phonebook entries can be specific to a user, or they can be available to all users on a system. On a machine running Windows NT, phonebook entries that are available systemwide are stored in the system phonebook.

You create a new phonebook entry by completing the configuration tabs in the New Phonebook Entry dialog box. You access the New Phonebook Entry dialog box by clicking the Dial-Up Networking icon under My Computer and then clicking New in the Dial-Up Networking dialog box.

For the Enterprise exam, be sure you know each tab in the New Phonebook Entry dialog box and the configuration options found on each tab:

- **Basic.** On the Basic tab, you provide a name for your new connection. You also specify the primary telephone number and any alternate telephone numbers for the connection. Alternate telephone numbers are dialed if dialing the primary number fails to establish a connection. You also specify dialing properties, such as long distance and credit card numbers, on the Basic tab. Perhaps the most important thing to remember about the Basic tab is that you enable Multilink connections on it. Remember that Multilink is used to aggregate multiple connections into a single connection to increase bandwidth.

- **Server.** On the Server tab, you must select the type of server to which you plan to connect. Your choices are PPP and SLIP. The other configuration options available on this tab differ, depending on which RAS protocol you select. If you select PPP, you can select the LAN protocol you want to use, and you have the option of selecting software data compression.

✓ **Script.** Use this tab to specify a script file that you want to run to assist log-on or log-off operations that require manual intervention. For the exam, you need to know the purpose of scripting and what you can use it for, but you don't need to worry about writing or interpreting a script.

✓ **Security.** Use this tab to set the level of authentication you want to use. Also, remember that you enable data encryption on this tab.

✓ **X.25.** The exam doesn't have any questions relating specifically to X.25. However if you needed to configure an X.25 connection or needed information about an X.25 service provider on an existing connection, the X.25 tab is the place to look.

Configuring RAS Client Protocols

The client protocols are the same for Dial-Up Networking as they are for the server configuration. The protocols are TCP/IP, IPX, and NetBEUI. You should review the TCP/IP configuration options before you take the exam. Remember that the same DHCP options that are available on a LAN are available to remote clients.

You may see a question about the NetBIOS Gateway. It's possible for a RAS client to connect to a RAS server using one protocol — for example, NetBEUI — and access NetBIOS resources on a network running a different protocol. The NetBIOS Gateway makes this possible. The client communicates with the RAS server using NetBEUI, and the RAS server communicates with the rest of the network using either TCP/IP or IPX. Remember that NetBIOS is more of an Application Programming Interface (API) than a protocol. The API is independent of the transport protocol. In this example, TCP/IP and NetBEUI are the transports.

Configuring RAS Client Security

Use the Security tab in the New Phonebook Entry dialog box to configure the level of authentication and encryption that the RAS client uses to connect to the RAS server. RAS security features include password encryption and authentication, data encryption, and callback security.

RAS negotiates the most secure form of authentication supported by both server and client. On the Security tab of the New Phonebook Entry dialog box, you can choose from three options:

✓ **Accept Any Authentication Including Clear Text.** This option uses the Password Authentication Protocol (PAP). It is not a secure method because passwords are transmitted unencrypted across open lines.

✓ **Accept Only Encrypted Authentication.** This option uses the Challenge Handshake Authentication Protocol (CHAP).

✓ **Accept Only Microsoft Encrypted Authentication.** This option uses Microsoft Challenge Authentication Protocol (MS-CHAP) and gives the user the ability to request data encryption. It also allows the user to automatically authenticate using the Windows NT account and password with which the user logged on to the workstation or server.

The Microsoft RAS server has an option that prevents clear-text passwords from being transmitted. This option enables system administrators to enforce a high level of security. For installations that require total security, the RAS administrator can set the RAS server to force encrypted communications. Users connecting to that server automatically encrypt all data sent.

RAS provides data encryption in addition to password encryption. To maintain security in case of unauthorized interception of remote access transmissions, clients configure each phonebook entry to use data encryption.

As an additional measure of security, RAS offers a Callback feature. This feature ensures that only users from specific locations can access the RAS server. It also saves toll charges for the user. When using Callback, the user initiates a call and connects with the RAS server. The RAS server then drops the call and calls back a moment later to the preassigned callback number.

Figure 20-1 shows the Remote Access Permissions dialog box. Notice the Callback settings. To access this dialog box, choose Start⇨Administrative Tools⇨Remote Access Admin. Then, in the Remote Access Admin, choose Users⇨Permissions.

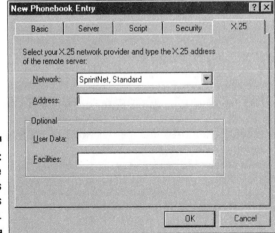

Figure 20-1:
The Remote
Access
Permissions
dialog box.

Testing a RAS Installation

Exam questions often take the form of troubleshooting scenarios. RAS troubleshooting questions fall into one of the following categories:

- ✔ Using the Event Viewer
- ✔ Enabling PPP logging
- ✔ Authentication problems
- ✔ Multilink and Callback incompatibility
- ✔ AutoDial

When you encounter a RAS troubleshooting question on the Enterprise exam, remember that you are not dealing as much with RAS as you are with Windows NT. This distinction is important to remember because Windows NT has some very helpful troubleshooting tools included with the operating system.

Using the Event Viewer

The Windows NT troubleshooting tools should be your first stop on the road to RAS problem determination and resolution. Windows NT includes a tool called the Event Viewer. Veteran system administrators can attest to the usefulness (or worthlessness) of this tool. Regardless of your personal opinion about the Event Viewer, for the exam, you should remember that the Event Viewer is the first place you look for information about a RAS-related problem.

You use the Event Viewer to monitor three separate logs: system, application, and security. For RAS, you need to be concerned with the system log.

Enabling PPP logging

If you can't solve the issue at hand with the Event Viewer, the next logical step is to make sure you are getting a good PPP connection. This is not nearly as straightforward as looking at the Event Viewer. It actually requires a Registry edit! To enable PPP logging, you need to set the value of the following Registry entry to 1:

```
\HKEY_LOCAL_MACHINE\SYSTEM\CurrentControlSet\Services\Rasman\PPP\logging
```

After you enable this option, the PPP.log file is created in the systemroot\ System32\Ras folder. The file contains detailed information about PPP connections.

You need to know how to enable PPP logging for the Enterprise exam!

Solving authentication problems

Authentication problems represent another area of RAS troubleshooting you may face on the exam. Clients who are not using the same implementation of the encryption algorithms as the server will have trouble authenticating and gaining access to network resources. To resolve this issue, select the lowest level of authentication at each end. This level is often clear-text passwords. If authentication is successful, increase the level of authentication. Continue this process until you find the highest level of authentication that is supported by both the client and the server.

Determining Multilink and Callback incompatibility

Watch out on the Enterprise exam for a question that involves both Multilink and Callback — two new RAS features included in Windows NT 4.0. You can configure only one callback number for a client. If you have four 28.8 Kbps modems connected to both your server and workstation enabled for Multilink and you are using Callback security, your throughput will be only 28.8 Kbps because the server only calls back one number for the client.

Resolving AutoDial problems

The last area of troubleshooting is the new client feature, AutoDial. When Windows NT Explorer starts up, any persistent network connectioq `or shortcuts on the desktop that point to network resources cause AutoDial to try to make the appropriate connections. This feature can be very annoying. To resolve this problem, disable AutoDial completely, or remove the shortcuts from the desktop to eliminate any persistent connections.

Prep Test

1 Which of the following is not a configuration tab of a phonebook entry?

A ○ Basic

B ○ Client

C ○ Security

D ○ X.25

2 Which RAS protocol do you select to connect to an NT Server?

A ○ SLIP

B ○ PPP

C ○ SNA

D ○ SDLC

3 (True/False). You can specify alternate phone numbers on the Server tab in the New Phonebook Entry dialog box or the Edit Phonebook Entry dialog box.

4 Which protocol is a wide area networking protocol?

A ○ TCP/IP

B ○ X.25

C ○ NetBEUI

D ○ IPX

5 Which of the following protocols is not a supported client protocol?

A ○ TCP/IP

B ○ IPX

C ○ NetBEUI

D ○ DLC

6 Which tool gives you information about failed RAS connections?

A ○ Event Viewer

B ○ User Manager

C ○ Performance Monitor

D ○ Server Administrator

7 Which log file is not viewable in Event Viewer?

A ○ System

B ○ Security

C ○ PPP

D ○ Application

8 Which log can only be enabled with a Registry edit?

A ○ System

B ○ Security

C ○ PPP

D ○ Application

9 What is the least-secure method of password encryption?

A ○ DES

B ○ CHAP

C ○ PAP

D ○ Clear text

10 Which feature allows you to aggregate connections for more bandwidth?

A ○ Multilink

B ○ Callback

C ○ CHAP

D ○ X.25

Answers

1 *B. Client.* Even though you're configuring the client, the New Phonebook Entry dialog box doesn't have a Client tab. The tabs are Basic, Server, Script, Security, and X.25. *See "Creating a Dial-Up Connection" for more information.*

2 *B. PPP.* Windows NT 4.0 no longer supports SLIP at the server. However, SLIP is available at the client to allow the client to connect to other servers such as UNIX. *See "Creating a Dial-Up Connection."*

3 *False.* You can specify alternate phone numbers for a connection, but you use the Basic tab, not the Server tab. *Review "Creating a Dial-Up Connection."*

4 *B. X.25.* X.25 is an old protocol used for wide area networking. At least in the context of the Enterprise exam, you should know the distinctions between WAN protocols such as X.25 and LAN protocols such as TCP/IP, IPX, and NetBEUI. *See "Configuring RAS Client Protocols."*

5 *D. DLC.* TCP/IP, IPX, and NetBEUI are the LAN protocols supported between a RAS server and a RAS client. *See "Configuring RAS Client Protocols."*

6 *A. Event Viewer.* Use the system log in the Event Viewer to see any failed client connections. *Review "Testing a RAS Installation" for more information on Event Viewer.*

7 *C. PPP.* The PPP.log file is a text file that must be viewed in a text editor such as Notepad. *See "Testing a RAS Installation."*

8 *C. PPP.* You enable the PPP.log file through a Registry edit. *Review "Testing a RAS Installation."*

9 *D. Clear text.* When this option is set, unencrypted passwords are transmitted over open connections. *See "Configuring RAS Client Security."*

10 *A. Multilink.* Multilink enables you to combine multiple analog phone and ISDN connections to increase the bandwidth of a connection. *See "Testing a RAS Installation" for more information.*

Part VII
Monitoring and Optimization

"OOPS - Here's the problem. Something's causing shorts in the PDC."

In this part . . .

An important subject area for your Enterprise exam involves monitoring and improving the performance of the different components in your Enterprise network. You must know how to work with Performance Monitor to analyze issues ranging from hardware utilization to network services. You also need to understand the ins and outs of using Network Monitor to gain greater insight into network-related performance issues. After you review the two chapters in this part, you'll be well-prepared for exam questions on monitoring and optimization!

Chapter 21

What a Performance!

Exam Objectives

▶ Running Performance Monitor

▶ Establishing a baseline

▶ Identifying performance bottlenecks

▶ Monitoring the processor, memory, disk, and network

▶ Using Task Manager

*H*ave you ever wanted to know just what's making your Windows NT Server run so slow? Are you interested in finding out how many of your precious system resources that new networked fax program soaks up? If you're concerned about these types of issues, Windows NT Server has just the program for you! Performance Monitor can tell you nearly everything about your server, and in many instances, about the network.

And for those times when you need a quick overview, don't forget about Task Manager. Task Manager is probably the most useful, and overlooked, utility included in Windows NT. It can certainly do more than just kill wayward programs.

You may be somewhat intimidated when you fire up the Performance Monitor. This program has literally thousands of options, and to complicate matters, some programs install additional options for Performance Monitor. And as you may expect, many of the MCSE exams — including the Enterprise exam, of course — include questions about Performance Monitor. Take heart. In this chapter, we describe the key features of both Performance Monitor and Task Manager, and we tell you just what you need to pass the exam.

Quick Assessment

Running Performance Monitor	**1** You suspect that your Windows NT Server is thrashing, but when you check Performance Monitor, you can't find any disk counters. Why?
Establishing a baseline	**2** You need to develop a baseline of information on your NT Server. The four counters should you monitor are _____, _____, _____, and _____.
	3 The two options to use for baselining are a(n) _____ and _____.
Monitoring the processor, memory, disk, and network	**4** Your NT Server has really been sluggish lately. The four counters that you can monitor to check on this situation are _____, _____, _____, and _____.
	5 The three disk counters that you can check to determine whether disk performance is a bottleneck on your system are _____, _____, and _____.
	6 You have recently added a new client/server application on your NT Server, and you want to check the processor to ensure that you have enough horsepower to handle the new application. The three processor counters that you should check are _____, _____, and _____.
	7 Your users complain that networking performance is "suffering." The three objects that you should log to properly measure network performance are _____, _____, and _____.
	8 The two counters that you should check to properly determine page file performance are _____ and _____.
	9 Your boss wants you to monitor disk performance to justify the addition of a new high performance disk array controller. The two counters that you may check to fulfill such a request are _____ and _____.
	10 You have two processors installed on your NT Server, but only one processor shows up in Performance Monitor. Why?

Answers

1 *You haven't enabled disk counters.* For details about disk counters and viewing them in Performance Monitor, review "Performance Monitor: Grading on the Curve."

2 *Disk Objects; Memory Objects; Processor Objects; Network Protocol Objects.* See "Establishing a baseline."

3 *Log; report view.* Review "Establishing a baseline."

4 *Processor Object: % Processor Time; System Object: Processor Queue Length; Memory Object: Pages / Sec; Disk Object: Ave. Disk Queue Length.* Review "Performance Monitor: Grading on the Curve."

5 *Disk Object: Average Disk Queue Length; Disk Object: % Disk Time; and Disk Object: Disk Bytes / Second.* See "Performance Monitor: Grading on the Curve."

6 *System Counter: % Total Processor Time; System Counter: Processor Queue Length; Process Counter: % Processor Time: _ Total.* See "Monitoring processor performance."

7 *Rate of bytes transferred; rate of data packages sent; rate at which files were sent and received.* Check out "Monitoring network performance."

8 *Memory Object: Page Faults Per Second; Memory Object: Pages Per Second.* See "Monitoring memory performance."

9 *% Disk Time; Ave. Disk Queue Length.* Review "Monitoring disk performance."

10 *You must select the second instance of the processor to see the second processor.* See "Monitoring disk performance."

Performance Monitor: Grading on the Curve

To track the performance of your Windows NT machine, you need to run Performance Monitor. To start Performance Monitor, choose Start⇨Programs⇨Administrative Tools⇨Performance Monitor.

When you first load Performance Monitor, it really doesn't look like much of anything. Don't be fooled by its rather plain appearance. Performance Monitor can tell you nearly everything about your server, including what it had for breakfast! So how do you use this tool? It's actually very easy, after you understand a few basic concepts.

Performance Monitor enables you to configure four views:

- ✔ Chart view
- ✔ Log view
- ✔ Alert view
- ✔ Report view

As you work with Performance Monitor, you'll want to configure a custom workspace that includes some or all of these views. By doing so, you avoid the hassles of setting up your workspace every time you start Performance Monitor. Nothing is worse than setting up everything the way you like it and then forgetting how you had it set. In addition, as you perform baseline monitoring, you can easily identify the settings for which you have baseline information.

Performance Monitor divides the things you can check into categories called objects. An *object* is a part of your server that you can measure. Table 21-1 lists the default objects available in Windows NT Server 4.0.

Each object has counters associated with it. For example, the Physical Disk object has numerous counters that you can monitor. Using Performance Monitor on the Physical Disk object, you can check average disk queue length, percentage of disk time, and other items that can assist in your troubleshooting or optimization task.

In addition to objects and counters, you can specify *instances*. For example, if you have three physical disks in your server, you have three instances of the Physical Disk object. They are numbered 0, 1, and 2.

Table 21-1	Performance Monitor Objects
Object	**Description**
Cache	Part of physical memory that holds recently used information
Logical Disk	Logical views of disk space, such as disk partitions
Memory	Random-access memory (RAM) used to store either program information or data
Objects	Various software objects used by the system
Paging File	Virtual memory — such as your Windows 95 swap file
Physical Disk	The actual hard disk or RAID device
Process	A running program
Processor	Your CPU
Redirector	The file system that diverts (redirects) requests that can't be satisfied locally to a network server
System	System hardware and software
Thread	The smallest part of a program or process that requires use of the processor

To start monitoring performance, you need to add a counter by clicking the Add button (the button with the plus sign) on the Performance Monitor toolbar. As shown in Figure 21-1, Performance Monitor opens a dialog box that enables you to select from numerous objects you may want to monitor.

Figure 21-1:
Adding a counter in Performance Monitor.

You can add counters for Processor, Disk, Memory, Page File, and many other objects. In addition to these counters, certain programs add counters to Performance Monitor. For example, installing Proxy Server activates counters that enable you to monitor the number of users connected to the Proxy Server. And if you install the TCP/IP protocol, Performance Monitor adds counters for that protocol. Indeed, Performance Monitor's extensibility is one of its greatest features.

Establishing a baseline

Finding bottlenecks takes more than occasionally firing up Performance Monitor. You must create a baseline of information that you can use for evaluating the counters you monitor. So how do you create this baseline, and which counters should you monitor?

To create a baseline, you run Performance Monitor in Log view over a period of time, and at different times of the day, to find your peak usage times, and to determine how the server is running. A useful rule is to set Performance Monitor to collect data every 60 seconds for three to four days. Of course, the longer you run Performance Monitor, the more accurate your data becomes. For example, usage may be abnormally high at certain times of the day, or even certain times of the month. If you don't sample during these times, the baseline information regarding your maximum load is skewed.

You can compare this baseline information with the counters you use for monitoring your system's performance. For example, if your baseline information indicates that your processor normally runs with a 35 percent utilization rate, and you suddenly experience a 75 percent processor utilization rate, you can start looking around and figure out what is taking all the processor time.

 Baselining will show up in scenario-based questions on the exam. If the scenario objective is to establish a baseline of information, and the Log view isn't selected, that objective is not met.

Monitoring processor performance

At the outset, we must point out that processor bottlenecks are rare. Although many items may peak processor utilization, and some bottlenecks may manifest themselves with increased processor demands, real, honest-to-goodness processor bottlenecks rarely occur on a Pentium, Pentium Pro, or Pentium II server. Of course, that wasn't the case in the olden days of 486 servers.

In most cases, what seems to be a processor bottleneck is really a memory problem. Occasionally, the bottleneck may be a network problem, but it's seldom a problem with the processor.

The symptoms of a processor bottleneck are easy to remember. In fact, they are among the few real guidelines available in working with Performance Monitor. As you prepare for the exam, memorize these guidelines for identifying a processor bottleneck:

- ✔ Processor Object: % Processor Time often exceeds 90 percent.
- ✔ System Object: Processor Queue Length is often greater than 2.
- ✔ On multiprocessor systems, the System Object: % Total Processor Time is often greater than 50 percent.
- ✔ Server Work Queues: Queue Length is greater than 4 over a sustained period.

In Tables 21-2 through 21-5, we list some of the more important counters for monitoring the processor in your NT Server. You need to look at a few counters from the system object, the processor object (of course), the process object, and the thread object. Although these tables present lots of information for you to remember, knowing these counters helps you in three ways: on this exam, on other exams, and in real life.

Table 21-2	System Object Counters
Counter	**Description**
% Total Processor Time	A measure of the activity on all processors.
In a single-processor machine:	This value is equal to the Processor Object: % Processor Time counter.
In a multiple-processor machine:	This value equals the sum of the % Processor Time counters for all processors in the machine, divided by the number of processors in the machine.
Processor Queue Length	An instantaneous count of how many threads are ready to be serviced, but must wait for the processor to become available. Because this counter isn't an average, it's best viewed in chart form.

Table 21-3	Processor Object Counters
Counter	**Description**
% Processor Time	The percentage of time the processor is busy.
% User Time	How often the processor runs threads in User mode. User mode threads use their own application code.
% Privileged Time	How often the processor runs threads in Privileged mode. Privileged mode threads use operating system services.

Table 21-4	Process Object Counters
Counter	**Description**
% Processor Time	The amount of time the processor works on threads for a particular process (program)
% Processor Time: Total	The total time all the threads run on the processor
% User Time	How often the particular process runs its own code
% Privileged Time	How often the particular process uses operating system services
Priority Base	The likelihood that the process can gain access to the processor during times of heavy utilization

Table 21-5	Thread Object Counters
Counter	**Description**
Thread State	An instantaneous counter that indicates whether the thread is ready (and waiting) or active
Priority Base	The likelihood that the thread can gain access to the processor during times of heavy utilization
Priority Current	The current priority of the thread
% Privileged Time	The amount of time the thread runs its own code, as opposed to using the operating system services

Processor bottlenecks occur when the processor is so busy responding to requests that it can no longer handle any more requests. When this happens, the processor queue length continues to climb and the server does no additional work.

To correct a processor bottleneck, you must determine which process is hogging all the resources, and then try to balance the load a little better on your servers. You also may be able to adjust the priority at which the application is running and therefore better allocate the resources. After you make changes, run the same set of counters to ensure that you've fixed the processor bottleneck.

Monitoring memory performance

Processor bottlenecks are rare, but memory bottlenecks are common. In fact, a memory problem often looks like an underpowered processor, or a sluggish disk array.

Windows NT Server uses a memory system that combines physical memory and virtual memory, which stores information on disk until needed. When the system must retrieve information from disk and move it into physical memory, a slow, resource-intensive process ensues. When the server *pages* data from the hard disk into memory, the processor is involved, the disks are involved, and the controller for the disks is involved. All these resources are being pulled away from other activities, which degrades the performance of the server. If this paging happens often enough, you have a memory bottleneck.

A sustained hard page fault rate of more than 5 per second means that you have a memory bottleneck. A *hard page fault* occurs when a program needs some data that it can't find in the physical memory on the server, which means the data must be retrieved from the disk.

To find memory problems, you need to log System, Memory, Logical Disk, and Process objects at 60-second intervals for several days. After you collect that baseline information, monitor the counters we describe in Table 21-6 and then compare the counters to your baseline information.

Table 21-6	Counters for Monitoring Memory
Counter	**Description**
Page Faults/Sec	How often data needed for a process isn't available in physical memory.
Pages Input/Sec	How many pages are coming from the physical disk to satisfy memory requirements of a process.
Pages Output/Sec	How many pages are being written to the physical disk to free up space in memory for the faulted pages. If the process changes a page, the page must be written to disk.
Pages/Sec	The sum of the Pages Input / Sec and the Pages Output/Sec.
Page Reads/Sec	How often the system reads from disk because of page faults.
Page Writes/Sec	How often the system writes to disk because of page faults.
Available bytes	How much memory the system has left to allocate. This counter is an instantaneous number, not an average.

If you're looking for a memory bottleneck, you want to look closely at three counters:

- ✔ Page Faults/Sec
- ✔ Pages Input/Sec
- ✔ Page Reads/Sec

By examining these three counters, you can determine whether you have a memory bottleneck.

Monitoring disk performance

The old saying, "Storage requirements always expand to meet the available disk space," certainly is true. However, disk performance involves how long the system takes for writing to and reading from those storage bins.

Unfortunately, disk counters are not enabled by default. You must turn them on separately because they require a little bit of processor time, and on earlier models of 486 servers they can adversely affect performance of the server. However, on modern servers, the effect is negligible.

To enable disk counters, complete the following steps:

1. **Go to a command prompt.**

2. **Enter the following command:**

```
diskperf -y
```

   Note: You must be a member of the Administrators group to issue this command.

3. **Restart the computer.**

Disk counters remain in effect until you turn them off. Even if you reboot the system, they remain in effect. To determine whether they are in effect, enter the following command:

```
diskperf
```

To turn off disk counters, complete the following steps:

1. **Go to a command prompt.**

2. **Enter the following command:**

```
diskperf -n
```

3. **Restart the computer.**

If you need to activate disk counters on a stripe set, complete the following steps:

1. **Go to a command prompt.**

2. **Enter the following command:**

```
diskperf -ye
```

3. Restart the computer.

After you install the disk counters, which ones should you look at, and how do you interpret them? Table 21-7 describes the more important disk counters.

Table 21-7	Disk Monitoring Counters
Counter	**Description**
% Disk Time	The percentage of time the disk is busy.
Ave. Disk Queue Length	The average number of operations waiting for the disk to become available.
Current Disk Queue Length	The current number of operations waiting for the disk to become available.
Ave. Disk/Sec Transfer	The average duration of each data transfer in seconds. The size of each transaction doesn't matter.
Disk Bytes/Sec	How fast the data is being moved in bytes. The primary measure of disk throughput.
Ave. Disk Bytes/Transfer	The average number of bytes moved with each transfer. This counter is a measure of efficiency.
Disk Transfers/Sec	How quickly transfers are serviced. This counter doesn't consider the size of the transfers.

Remember the following guidelines for identifying a disk bottleneck:

✔ Disk activity is regularly greater than 85 percent.

✔ Disk queues are greater than 2, while paging occurs at a rate of less than 5 per second.

You can obtain the paging value from the following memory counters:

✔ Pages read/second

✔ Pages write/second

You need to keep in mind that high disk use, in and of itself, is not a cause for alarm. Disk activity remaining at 40 I/O operations per second is not unusual. But if you see constant use, and long disk queue lengths, you may have cause for concern.

Remember that high disk use and long queue lengths are typically signs of a memory shortage. You must first rule out memory as a problem, before concluding that you have a disk bottleneck. Keep the preceding guidelines in mind when taking the exam (they'll show up in multiple rating questions) as well as in real life.

Monitoring network performance

Network performance is largely a function of network bandwidth and network capacity. *Bandwidth* is how fast data is transmitted and received over a communication link between the computer and the network. *Network capacity* is a broader term that takes into account the capability of the server and the network link to support the traffic and the resources using the network.

In examining bandwidth issues, you typically look at the following items:

✔ The rate at which bytes are transferred to and from the server

✔ The rate at which data packages (including frames, packets, segments, and datagrams) are sent by the server

✔ The rate at which files are sent and received by the server

To measure network capacity, you examine the following types of counters:

✔ Number of connections established by the server

✔ Number of connections maintained by the server

To measure transmission rates with Performance Monitor, you need to install the SNMP protocol through the Protocol tab in the Network Properties dialog box. By installing this protocol, you gain access to the TCP counters, the IP counters (if TCP/IP is installed), and the network interface performance counters. Each of the installed protocols has performance counters to enable you to monitor network performance.

Viewing collected data

To work with the data collected over time, you need to create a log. After you create the log, you can examine the information in Performance Monitor and use the tools there to perform your analysis. In Lab 21-1, we guide you through the steps for creating a log file from Performance Monitor.

Lab 21-1   Creating a Performance Monitor Log

1. Open Performance Monitor by choosing Start⇨Programs⇨ Administative Tools⇨Performance Monitor.

2. Choose View⇨Log.

3. Click the Add button (the button with the plus sign) to bring up the Add Counter dialog box.

4. Select Processor from the list and then click Add.

5. Select Memory from the list and then click Add.

6. Select Process from the list and then click Add.

7. Click Done.

   After selecting the counters for the log, you need to save the log and then begin collecting the data.

8. Choose Options⇨Log.

9. Give the log a name, such as base.log, and click Save.

10. Choose Options⇨Log.

11. Select the log file you created in Step 9.

12. Accept the default for Update Time, and click Start Log.

13. After a few minutes of collecting data, choose Options⇨Log.

14. Click Stop Log.

   You have created a Performance Monitor Log file.

At times, however, you may want to create a report from your data — perhaps to justify the expenditure for a system upgrade, or to provide a detailed evaluation of the performance of your system. In Lab 21-2, we walk you through this process using the data you collected in Lab 21-1.

Lab 21-2   Creating a Report in Performance Monitor

1. In Performance Monitor, choose View⇨Report.

2. Choose Options⇨Data From.

3. In the resulting dialog box, select the Log File radio button.

4. Click the ... button, select the log file you created in Lab 21-1, and then click OK.

5. Click the Add button (the button with the plus sign) to add data to the report.

(continued)

Lab 21-2 (continued)

6. Select the Processor: % Processor Time object and then click Add.

7. Select the Memory: Pages/sec object and then click Add.

8. Select the Process: %Processor Time, Total counter and then click Add.

9. Click Done.

You have created your first report in Performance Monitor.

In addition to the two views we mention in Lab 21-1 and Lab 21-2, you can choose to export the previously collected data into an Excel spreadsheet or into an Access database. After you export the data, you can manipulate the data and create the appropriate presentation method for the data.

Using Task Manager

Task Manager provides a quick and easy way to get a look at what's going on under the hood of your server. By simply pressing Ctrl+Alt+Del, and then selecting Task Manager, you bring up a very useful little utility. In the following sections, we look at each of the tabs available through Task Manager, and explore a few ways to use it in your day-to-day server management duties.

Applications

The Applications tab gives a quick view of the applications that are running on your server. It also gives you the status — whether they're running, not responding, or whatever. If you need to kill an application, you can do so by selecting the task, and then clicking the End Task button at the bottom of the screen.

Processes

The Processes tab lists the processes running on the server that run in their own memory space, or use operating system services. It also indicates the amount of memory usage, CPU usage, and processor time each process consumes.

If you want to look at 16-bit tasks, choose Options⇨Show 16 bit Tasks. Keep in mind that Task Manager shows the memory values in Kilobytes. Performance Monitor shows the values in bytes. Therefore, if you want to compare values between the two utilities, you need to multiply the values in Task Manager by 1,024.

Performance

The Performance tab provides real-time graphs of CPU utilization and memory utilization. Under the two graphs, this tab displays information about handles, threads, and memory on the server. If you want to graph the percentage of time spent in privileged or kernel mode, choose View⇨Show Kernel Times.

Prep Test

1 Your boss doesn't want you to add another processor to the server. However, you think the server needs another processor. To prove the situation one way or the other, you decide to use Performance Monitor. Which counters should you examine? (Choose all that apply.)

A ❑ Processor Object: % Processor Time

B ❑ System Object: Processor Queue Length

C ❑ Disk Object: Disk Queue Length

D ❑ Memory: Pages per Second

2 You want to monitor Disk Object counters, but you can't find them in Performance Monitor. Why?

A ○ By default, Disk object counters are not installed.

B ○ By default, Disk object counters are installed, but someone turned them off.

C ○ Which Disk object counters you have available depends on which types of drives you have on the server.

D ○ You have a disk array installed, and Disk object counters only work on single drives.

3 Which views are available in Performance Monitor? (Choose all that apply.)

A ❑ Log view

B ❑ Detail view

C ❑ Trend view

D ❑ Alert view

E ❑ Pay per view

4 You want to quickly find a process using all the CPU resources. What do you do?

A ○ Select the CPU object and choose Processes in Performance Monitor.

B ○ Select the Process object in Performance Monitor, and choose All.

C ○ Start Task Manager, select the Processes tab, and look for a resource-hogging process.

D ○ Select the Processor object, and choose the Max process object.

5 You suspect you have a memory bottleneck on your NT Server machine. To confirm your suspicion, you select which of the following counters? (Choose all that apply.)

A ❑ Page Faults per Second

B ❑ Pages Input per Second

C ❑ Page Reads per Second

D ❑ Percentage of Processor Utilization

E ❑ Average Disk Queue Length

6 You want to check a number of TCP counters and a few IP counters to monitor Network protocol performance. When you start looking for the objects, you can't find them. Why? (Choose all that apply.)

A ❑ The counters aren't available if TCP/IP isn't installed on the server.

B ❑ The counters aren't available if SNMP isn't installed on the server.

C ❑ The counters aren't available if SMTP isn't installed on the server.

D ❑ The counters aren't available unless you have the DLC protocol installed.

Answers

1   *A, B, C, and D.* In addition to monitoring the processor object, you need to look at memory and disk objects, to ensure that they're not putting an additional load on the processor. *Review "Performance Monitor: Grading on the Curve."*

2   *A. By default, Disk object counters are not installed.* You must install them from the command line. They're left out due to the load they can create on some older servers. *Review "Performance Monitor: Grading on the Curve."*

3   *A, D.* Log view and Alert view are available in Performance Monitor. *Refer to "Establishing a baseline."*

4   *C. Start Task Manager, select the Processes tab, and look for a resource-hogging process.* To see a list of running processes, start Task Manager, select the Processes tab, and look for the process consuming the most CPU time. *Refer to "Using Task Manager."*

5   *A, B, C.* To get a good overview of memory performance, you check Page Faults per Second. This counter is a total number of page faults and a good indicator of lack of memory. Additionally, you should check Pages Input, and Page Reads per Second to see where the paging is going. The other two choices don't provide direct input on memory performance. *Refer to "Monitoring memory performance."*

6   *A, B.* To access certain Network counters, the protocol must be installed, and SNMP must be installed. *Refer to "Monitoring network performance."*

Chapter 22

Network Monitor: NT's Traffic Reporter

Exam Objectives

▶ Monitoring network traffic

▶ Optimizing performance

▶ Collecting, presenting, and filtering data

*N*etwork Monitor is the tool you need when you want to find out what's really going on with your network. This powerful tool, which is included with Windows NT 4.0, enables you to look at the data stream on your network and thus troubleshoot protocol and connectivity issues at a very low level.

By using Network Monitor, you can capture and display frames of information (also called *packets*) sent from computers on your network to the server. Armed with this information, you can then use Network Monitor to analyze the data to search for a wide variety of problems that may be causing bottlenecks or network congestion and slowing the performance of your finely tuned network. In addition to all these benefits, a good understanding of Network Monitor can add a couple of points to your score when you take the Enterprise exam.

Quick Assessment

Monitoring network traffic

1 To run Network Monitor you must first _____, and then _____ this tool.

2 The default maximum buffer allowed by Network Monitor is _____.

3 The two passwords that you can set for Network Monitor are _____ and _____.

Optimizing performance

4 (True/False). You're having connectivity problems, and you suspect that they're related to the IP protocol. You can examine only this protocol in Network Monitor.

5 The area of Network Monitor that displays the percentage of network utilization on your network is _____.

Collecting, presenting, and filtering data

6 You can easily provide maximum CPU resources to Network Monitor by _____.

7 You're having network problems, and a consultant asks you for a network capture. The easiest way to get the data to the consultant is by saving the capture as a _____ file.

8 The two steps that you can take to avoid dropped frames from your captured files are configuring the _____ size and using the _____ mode.

9 You suspect someone else may be running Network Monitor on your network. Can you find the person?

10 The most efficient method for checking out a suspected problem with a particular computer on the network is creating a _____ and specifying only that computer.

Answers

1 *Install; configure.* Refer to the section "Taking a Look at Network Monitor" for more information.

2 *8MB less than the memory installed on the machine.* Review "Manually executing a capture."

3 *Display password; capture password.* Review "Password protection."

4 *True.* Refer to "Filtering Captured Data" for more information.

5 *The Network Monitor Capture window.* Review "MCSE Games: Capture the Data."

6 *Running Network Monitor in dedicated capture mode.* See "Manually executing a capture."

7 *.cap.* Refer to "Saving captured data."

8 *Capture buffer; dedicated capture.* See "Manually executing a capture."

9 *Yes.* See "Detecting other Network Monitor installations."

10 *Capture filter.* Refer to "Filtering Captured Data" for more information.

Taking a Look at Network Monitor

Before Network Monitor, if you needed to perform packet sniffing (collecting network traffic at the packet level), you had to buy an expensive device made just for that purpose. You could also run specialized programs for that purpose, but you needed an Ethernet card that supported *promiscuous mode* — that is, the card was set to accept all packet traffic on the network, regardless of whether it was directed to that computer.

With Network Monitor, your network card doesn't have to support promiscuous mode. Network Monitor uses the new NDIS 4.0 specification to copy all the frames it detects into a *capture buffer* — a resizable area of memory.

Network Monitor can capture only as much information as fits in available memory. But this limitation doesn't cause any problems because you can select which part of the frame you need to see by designing a capture filter. By designing a filter (which works sort of like doing a query on a database), you can capture only certain addresses, protocols, or protocol properties. (For more information about capture filters, see the section "Filtering Captured Data," later in this chapter.)

Because Network Monitor provides capabilities for capturing data from your network, you need to address security for this tool. You can take several steps to help protect your network from unauthorized use of this tool. We discuss these steps in the section "Maintaining Network Monitor Security," later in this chapter.

Before you can use Network Monitor, you have to install the program, because by default it isn't installed. To install Network Monitor:

1. **Open the Control Panel's Network applet.**

2. **Click the Services tab.**

3. **Select Network Monitor Tools and Agent.**

4. **Click Add.**

After you install Network Monitor, you can launch it from the Administrative Tools (Common) menu, which you open by clicking the Start button.

MCSE Games: Capture the Data

With Network Monitor installed, you can capture some data. Your Ethernet card passes on a portion of the frames it sees on the network to the capture buffer. If the capture buffer overflows, it uses FIFO (first in, first out) to determine what it retains in memory.

To prevent the capture buffer from overflowing, you can design a capture filter to refine what the card passes on to the capture buffer. For more information about capture filters, see "Filtering Captured Data," later in this chapter.

You begin your capture session by choosing Capture⇨Start. As shown in Figure 22-1, Network Monitor displays statistics about the capture session while it runs. These statistics provide lots of valuable information.

You can resize any of the panes in this window to get a better representation of the data in which you're interested. In the Graph pane (the upper-left pane in Figure 22-1), you can see a quick representation of your network's status. This feature is particularly useful when you're monitoring the progress of a capture. This high-level overview can assist in troubleshooting by providing the following information:

   ✔ % Network Utilization

   ✔ Frames Per Second

   ✔ Bytes Per Second

   ✔ Broadcasts Per Second

   ✔ Multicasts Per Second

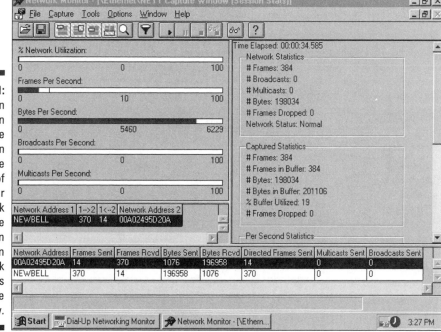

Figure 22-1: You can glean valuable information about the health of your network from the session statistics in Network Monitor's Capture window.

The upper-right pane of the screen is called the Total Statistics pane (refer to Figure 22-1). Here, you have a numerical summary of the information contained in the graphs on the left side of the screen, such as Network Statistics. In addition, you have statistics regarding the captured data. These statistics tell you how many frames you have in the buffer, how much of your buffer is in use, and whether you've dropped any frames because of a full buffer. As shown in Figure 22-2, by clicking the scroll bar in the Total Statistics pane, you can see additional statistics that provide information about the network card, and whether frames are being dropped.

The Session Statistics pane (under the Graph pane) lists network addresses of the computers talking in the current capture session. This pane details how many frames are being passed about, and the directions in which they're going. Pay close attention to the arrows that Network Monitor uses to indicate the direction of data flow (also used in designing capture filters). The arrow always points toward the computer that will receive the information. For example, in Figure 22-2, NEWBELL sends 370 frames of information to the computer at network address 2. NEWBELL receives 14 frames from the other computer.

The Station Statistics pane (under Session Statistics) breaks down the information from the Session Statistics even further by listing the number of bytes sent and received from each station represented in the capture buffer.

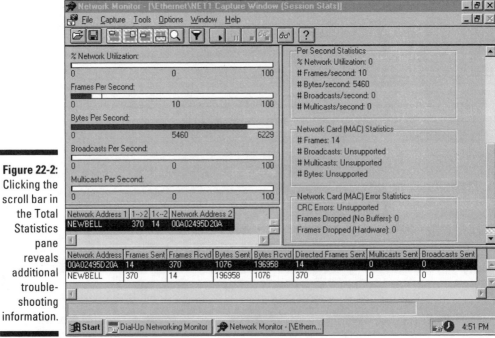

Figure 22-2: Clicking the scroll bar in the Total Statistics pane reveals additional troubleshooting information.

The information on broadcasts sent and multicasts is particularly helpful for pointing out potential problems on your network. In addition, you may want to investigate the direction of data flow and the sizes of the various exchanges taking place. All this information can help to identify possible bottlenecks on the network.

Manually executing a capture

To control a manual capture, you use the Capture menu shown in Figure 22-3. However, before you choose Start, you probably want to set the buffer size. To configure the buffer, choose Capture⇨Buffer Settings. In the resulting dialog box, you can select the size (in MB) of the buffer you need to use, as well as how much of the frame (in bytes) you want to capture. The default maximum capture buffer size that Windows NT allows is 8MB less than the amount of RAM installed on the machine. Although you can use virtual memory for your capture buffer, it's better not to do this in order to ensure that critical frame information is reliably captured.

In addition to selecting the buffer size, you can select the frame size to capture. For example, if you're only interested in header information for a particular protocol, you can set that information in the Capture Buffer Settings dialog box, and not waste space by capturing extraneous frame

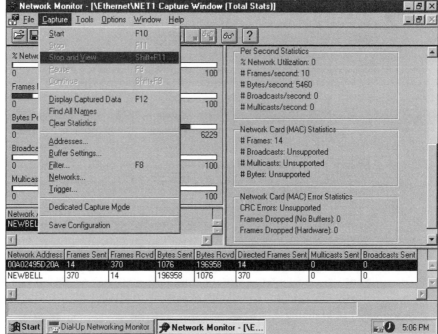

Figure 22-3:
Use the Capture menu to start, stop, or pause a capture session, and configure the buffer size.

data. This information is dependent upon the protocol being investigated, and is beyond the scope of both this book and the NT Enterprise exam. The Network Monitor Help file includes resource information about the various protocols.

The Capture Statistics window (refer to Figure 22-2) actually puts a load on the CPU that may not be needed. By choosing Capture⇨Dedicated Capture Mode, you can avoid the load associated with updating the display and thereby provide additional resources for capturing frames. As shown in Figure 22-4, when in Dedicated Capture Mode, you have the option of switching to Normal Mode to view real-time data and from there you can switch back to Dedicated Mode if you desire.

Figure 22-4:
Dedicated
Capture
Mode
reduces the
CPU load,
thereby
helping to
avoid frame
loss during
a capture
session.

Reviewing captured information

After you run a capture session, what do you have? Network Monitor simplifies the task of analyzing the data by organizing the captured data into several different views, and performing much of the protocol analysis for you. Figure 22-5 shows the Summary view. This view is helpful for gaining an overview of the information contained in the captured data. In Figure 22-5, the large number of UDP frames are due to someone listening to streaming audio from the Internet.

By adding the Detail and the Hex views from the Window menu, you can find information such as the source address and the destination address of the frame (see Figure 22-6). Armed with this information, you can go to the machine and do a little investigative work to find out why the machine is flooding your network with useless information. These views also give you the detail you need about the protocols to change your buffer settings if you're focusing on one particular item.

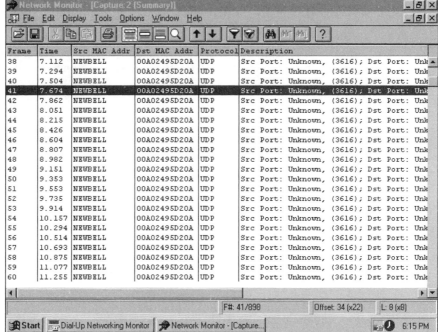

Figure 22-5:
Network Monitor's Summary view provides an overview of the captured data, enabling you to quickly spot anomalies.

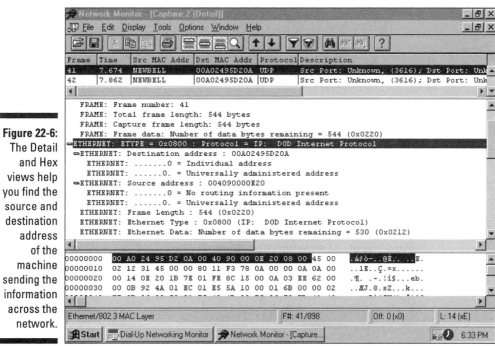

Figure 22-6:
The Detail and Hex views help you find the source and destination address of the machine sending the information across the network.

Saving captured data

After you capture the data from the network, you may want to save the information so that you can either forward it for expert analysis, or use it as baseline information while you do some network tuning. In either case, you save the captured data as a .cap file that you can open in Network Monitor later. Remember to save the data to a .cap file before you start another capture session, or you can lose the data.

To save your captured data, simply choose File⇨Save. Network Monitor gives you the opportunity to choose the location, as well as the range of frames you want to save. The default is to save all the frames in the capture.

Filtering Captured Data

Like a database query, a filter enables you to select a portion, or a subset, of the available data. For example, if you narrow down a problem to a specific computer, you can filter out all the other traffic and focus only on that computer. You can use two kinds of filters with Network Monitor:

- ✔ A capture filter selects only the information you tell it to during the capture session.
- ✔ A display filter enables you to see only the information you configure after the capture session.

Network Monitor can't export data to another program. On a couple of questions during the Enterprise exam, we were able to eliminate Network Monitor from the list of possible answers due to this requirement.

You can save your filters and reuse them. This feature is helpful when you're trying to correct a particular problem. You save a data set, and after you make changes, you run the filter again, thereby enabling you to track your progress.

Both filter types work in a similar fashion. Lab 22-1 details the steps for designing a capture filter.

Lab 22-1   Designing a Capture Filter

1. **Choose Capture⇨Filter.**

    Network Monitor opens the Capture Filter dialog box shown in Figure 22-7.

2. **Change the Protocol filter by selecting the first line (SAP/TYPE = . . .) and click the Edit Line button on the right.**

3. **Click Disable All to quickly remove all protocols from the filter.**

4. **Select TCP, IP, and ARP (or whatever protocols you are running on your network) and click Enable.**

5. **Select the Address Pair line to filter traffic direction.**

6. **Select a computer from the Station 1 list and select the arrow that points toward Station 2.**

7. **Select the *Any option in the Station 2 column.**

   This option means traffic to any computer on the network.

8. **Click OK to close the Edit Line dialog box.**

9. **Click OK to close the Capture Filter dialog box.**

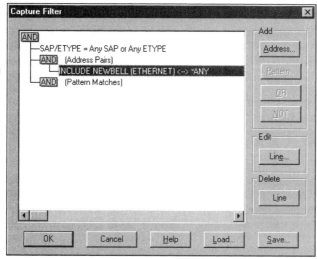

Figure 22-7:
Like a database query, a capture filter allows you to specify a subset of data for analysis.

By using the Capture Filter dialog box, you can design a capture filter to filter data by Protocol, by Address, or by Data Pattern (or by a combination of all three). For example, if you want to filter by Protocol, you select the SAP/ETYPE line and then click the Edit Line button. Clicking this button opens a menu from which you can select the type of protocol you want to filter. To select one particular protocol, simply disable all protocols, and then enable the one protocol you want to examine.

If you're interested in just one machine, you select the address pairs, and then click the Edit Line button. As shown in Figure 22-8, Network Monitor opens a menu from which you can select the address you want to examine. You have options for including or excluding an address. You also can pick the direction of information flow. You select the name for Station 1 in the left column, select the direction arrow (remember, the arrowhead points in the direction of data flow), and then select the recipient under the Station 2 column. For example, in Figure 22-8, the filter includes data traffic from NEWBELL to any station on the network, as well as traffic from any station on the network to NEWBELL.

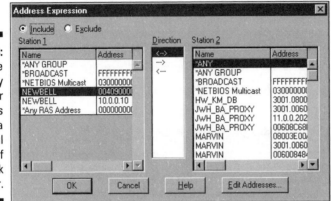

Figure 22-8: The capability to filter addresses is a powerful feature of Network Monitor.

A display filter works much like a capture filter. Because it works only on data already captured, however, it doesn't affect the contents of the capture buffer.

With the display filter, you can choose a particular protocol, address, or data property to help you sort through the data. You make the selections in the same manner as you do when designing a capture filter. However, you can also apply the logic expressions of AND, OR, and NOT. This capability gives you a greater range of selectivity when creating your filter than is available in the capture filter mode.

Maintaining Network Monitor Security

With the power available in Network Monitor, you must take appropriate security measures to safeguard your network from misuse of this tool. One security feature has already been implemented for you by Microsoft: Network Monitor only monitors traffic between the server that it's running on and the rest of the network. This feature safeguards you from a certain amount of misuse. However, the version that ships with Systems Management Server (SMS) can capture frames sent to or from any computer on the network, as well as capture frames over a remote network.

Password protection

By using the Monitoring Agent icon in the Control Panel, you can set two passwords for Network Monitor:

- ✔ The Display Password
- ✔ The Capture Password

The Display Password enables access to a saved capture (a .cap file). If you have this password, you can open only a previously saved capture file. You can't capture new data.

The Capture Password enables unlimited access to Network Monitor. If you have this password, you can open saved capture files, and create new captures.

If you've installed Network Monitor Agent on your computer and the service is running without password protection, anyone with the SMS version of Network Monitor can connect to your server and use it to capture data from your network.

Detecting other Network Monitor installations

To protect your network from unauthorized snooping, Network Monitor can easily detect other instances of the program on your network, even if the program isn't running. For example, if the driver is installed on a machine, Network Monitor can tell you the name of the machine, the name of the user logged on to the computer, the Ethernet address of the machine, the version number of the program, and whether the program is capturing data, or merely installed. To obtain this information, choose Tools⇨Identify Network Monitor Users.

If you have network segments separated by a router that doesn't forward multicasts, you can't detect Network Monitor installations on the other segment without being connected to that segment.

Prep Test

1 Your boss asks you to use Network Monitor to find any problems on the network. He also asks you whether the server Ethernet card supports promiscuous mode. Why would your boss ask such a question?

A ○ Because promiscuous mode is required to support Network Monitor

B ○ Because older sniffers require promiscuous mode and your boss is unaware of the new NDIS 4.0 specification

C ○ Because your boss made up a phrase to test whether you know what you're doing

D ○ Because your card must support promiscuous mode if you want to monitor all traffic on the network

2 You're looking over session statistics while you monitor a data capture session, and your boss walks in. Pointing to the arrows under the network address section, your boss asks you what they mean. What do you tell your boss?

A ○ The arrows indicate the computer that I'm currently monitoring.

B ○ The arrows indicate the direction of data flow. The arrowhead points away from the direction of flow.

C ○ The arrows indicate the direction of data flow. The arrowhead points in the direction of flow.

D ○ The arrows are just placeholders. They hold a space where you can put data at a later date.

3 Name two ways you can save space in your capture buffer.

A ❑ Edit the Registry. Set the MaxMem key to a multiple of 512.

B ❑ Create a display filter to show only desired information.

C ❑ Set the frame size in the Buffer Settings menu.

D ❑ Create a capture filter to grab only the information you want.

4 List the two types of passwords that you can set on Network Monitor installations.

A ❑ Administrator

B ❑ Supervisor

C ❑ Display

D ❑ Capture

5 You suspect someone else is running Network Monitor on the network. What can you do to detect the other user?

A ○ You can't.

B ○ You can find the other user by using Performance Monitor.

C ○ You can find the other user by choosing Tools⇨Identify Network Monitor Users.

D ○ You can find them by choosing Security⇨Find Other Installations.

6 How can you reduce the CPU load on the server that's running Network Monitor?

A ○ Add more RAM.

B ○ Increase the paging file.

C ○ Run Network Monitor minimized.

D ○ Run Network Monitor in Dedicated Capture Mode.

7 You ran a 40MB Network Monitor data capture session, but it wasn't filtered. Now you have a rather large collection of data, and are having trouble sorting it out to make heads or tails of it. What can you do?

A ○ Save the data as a capture (.cap) file, import it into an Excel spreadsheet, and then sort the data.

B ○ Save the data as a capture (.cap) file, export it as a .csv (comma-separated value) file, import it into an Excel spreadsheet, and then sort the data.

C ○ Save the data as a capture (.cap) file, import it into an Access database, and then create your report.

D ○ Save the data as a capture (.cap) file and then create a display filter to select the data you are interested in examining.

Answers

1 *B. Because older sniffers require promiscuous mode and your boss is unaware of the new NDIS 4.0 specification.* Older sniffers require the Ethernet card to support promiscuous mode. However, with the advent of NDIS 4.0 (which Network Monitor supports), you don't need support for promiscuous mode. *Refer to "Taking a Look at Network Monitor."*

2 *C. The arrows indicate the direction of data flow. The arrowhead points in the direction of flow.* The arrowheads displayed in the Session Statistics screen while you monitor a data capture session point in the direction of data flow. You also use this principle when you create a capture filter. *Review "MCSE Games: Capture the Data."*

3 *C and D.* If you want to save space in your capture buffer, you can limit the size of the Frame Size (in bytes) by choosing Capture⇨Buffer Settings. This setting effectively determines what is captured, and is dependent upon the protocol you're monitoring. You can also design a capture filter to select only specified items, such as a certain protocol, or a certain computer on the network. *For more information, see "Manually executing a capture," and "Filtering Captured Data."*

4 *C and D.* The two types of passwords you can set on Network Monitor are Display and Capture. The Display password only enables you to examine previously captured data. The Capture password enables you to examine previously captured data, as well as create new captures. To protect your network from unauthorized use of these tools, you must set these passwords. *For more information, refer to "Maintaining Network Monitor Security."*

5 *C. You can find the other user by choosing Tools⇨Identify Network Monitor Users.* By choosing Tools⇨Identify Network Monitor Users, you can detect other people running Network Monitor, and you can detect whether they have the driver installed on their computers. *For more information on this subject, see "Detecting other Network Monitor installations."*

6 *D. Run Network Monitor in Dedicated Capture Mode.* If you need to view session statistics, you can click the Normal Mode button. After you look at the statistics, you can again choose Capture⇨Dedicated Capture Mode. *For more information, refer to "Manually executing a capture."*

7 *D. Save the data as a capture (.cap) file and then create a display filter to select the data you are interested in examining.* A display filter gives you a great deal of control over the way the data is displayed in Network Monitor. You can select only certain protocols, certain computers, or any combination of these criteria. *For more information on creating display filters, review "Filtering Captured Data."*

Part VIII
Troubleshooting

"I DON'T THINK OUR NEWEST NETWORK CONFIGURATION IS GOING TO WORK. ALL OF OUR TRANSMISSIONS FROM OHIO SEEM TO BE COMING IN OVER MY ELECTRIC PENCIL SHARPENER."

In this part . . .

Every network environment has its share of troubleshooting issues. In Part VIII, we examine troubleshooting of numerous common problems you may see in questions on your exam. We cover some basic techniques for resource troubleshooting and repair strategies, as well as advanced problem resolution.

This part also includes chapters on conflict resolution and fault tolerance. In addition, you can find information on troubleshooting hardware issues from installing new hardware to failure in the boot process and working with your Boot.ini file.

Chapter 23

Conflict Resolution

• •

Exam Objectives

▶ Resolving printing problems

▶ Resolving RAS problems

▶ Troubleshooting connectivity problems

▶ Solving resource access and permissions problems

▶ Using the Event Log Services

▶ Resolving configuration errors

▶ Performing advanced problem resolution

• •

*W*ouldn't it be great if you could install a network operating system and never have to worry that it might not work correctly? No matter which operating system you use, it will probably need coaxing at some point in time. You face many challenges as you attempt to implement Windows NT in an enterprise environment, and you must find out how to troubleshoot the various problems that can occur.

In this chapter, we provide you with tools to help troubleshoot Windows NT configuration errors that you may encounter. We focus on those tools you need to know to answer exam questions on troubleshooting.

Quick Assessment

Resolving printing problems

1 To repair a print spooler that has stalled, go to Control Panel, open Services, then _____ and _____ the spooler service.

Resolving RAS problems

2 When troubleshooting connection problems in RAS, use the least-secure option for authentication, which is Allow Any Authentication, Including _____.

Trouble-shooting connectivity problems

3 When installing the IPX/SPX protocol, you must make sure that you use the correct _____.

4 If a server running only TCP/IP can communicate on its own subnet, but not on any other subnet, it's not correctly configured for a _____.

Solving resource access and permissions problems

5 Whenever a conflict exists between share permissions and NTFS permissions, both permissions are evaluated, and the _____ restrictive permissions are enforced.

Performing advanced problem resolution

6 (True/False). You can use the Emergency Repair Disk (ERD) alone to boot an NT Server in the event of a fatal system error.

7 Use the _____ command-line utility to determine the integrity of a memory dump file.

Using the Event Log Services

8 When Windows NT encounters a data loss or failure of major functions, it produces kernal STOP errors that you can view using _____.

Answers

1 *Stop; start.* See "Resolving Printing Problems" — in particular, Table 23-1.

2 *Clear Text.* Review "Troubleshooting RAS."

3 *Frame type.* See "Troubleshooting Connectivity Problems."

4 *Default gateway.* Review "Troubleshooting Connectivity Problems."

5 *Most.* Review "Solving File and Resource Access Problems."

6 *False.* Review "Using the ERD to Restore the System" — in particular, the steps in Lab 23-1.

7 *Dumpchk.* Review "Advanced Problem Resolution."

8 *Event Viewer.* Review "Using the Event Log Services."

Resolving Printing Problems

Troubleshooting Windows NT Server printing problems can be very difficult. The process can become complicated because of the many variables involved in printing and the numerous clients and print devices that Windows NT Server supports. However, we can offer some general guidelines that can help isolate printer problems:

- **Verify that you're using the correct print driver.** To ensure that you have the correct driver and it isn't corrupted, you may want to reinstall the print driver.

- **Try printing from another client system using the same server.** If you can print from a different client system, the print problem is located on the troubled client. If you can't print from a different client, the problem is on the server.

- **Verify that you have enough space on the hard drive where the spooler is located.** If necessary, move the spooler or increase available hard disk space.

- **Try to print using another application.** If the problem occurs only with certain applications, check the appropriate subsystem.

- **Print the document to a file and copy the output to a printer port.** If this method works, your spooler is the problem. If this method doesn't work, the problem is related to the driver or application driver.

Table 23-1 lists solutions for common printing problems you may encounter.

Table 23-1   Common Printing Problems and Resolutions

Problem	Resolution
Disk drive starts thrashing and print job never completes.	You're out of hard disk space for spooling. Either create more room or move the spooler to another partition.
No one can print to the server; a job at the server won't print and you can't delete it.	The print spooler is stalled. From Control Panel, go to Services, stop the Spooler Service, and then restart it.
Print job doesn't print completely or comes out garbled.	You're using an incorrect printer driver. Replace it with the correct printer driver.
A printer has stopped printing even though it is still online, and people are still submitting print jobs to the Print Server.	Add the Universal Naming Convention name of the replacement printer to the port on the printer that stopped functioning.

Problem	Resolution
Applications running on the system seem to be slowing down the printing process	The spooler priority isn't set high enough. Adjust the PriorityClass Registry entry contained in HKEY_LOCAL_MACHINE\ System\CurrentControlSet\Control\Print.

Troubleshooting RAS

If you have a Dial-Up Networking (DUN) client that has difficulties being authenticated over Remote Access Service (RAS), try changing the Security option on both the server and the client to Allow Any Authentication, Including Clear Text. Because of the wide variety of DUN clients available, the clients may not support the same encryption methods as those that Windows NT Server supports. By switching to the Allow Any Authentication, Including Clear Text option, you can try the lowest authentication method on each side. If you have success with that setting, you can start increasing the authentication options until you determine the highest level of authentication that you can use between the client and the server.

If a DUN client has problems with authentication over Point-to-Point Protocol (PPP), a Ppp.log file offers a handy means for troubleshooting the problem. The Ppp.log file is not enabled by default. To enable the Ppp.log file, change the following Registry entry to a 1:

```
\HKEY_LOCAL_MACHINE\System\CurrentControlSet\Services\Rasman\PPP\Logging
```

The Ppp.log file is stored in the %systemroot%SYSTEM32\RAS folder.

The Device.log file is another log file that you may find very useful in troubleshooting RAS, especially if you have a modem problem. Device.log captures the initialization information between the system and the modem. Device.log contains entries that show RAS issuing the initialization string, the modem echoing the command, and the modem responding with OK. This information can be very helpful if RAS can't dial or if it returns hardware-related errors.

Like Ppp.log, Device.log isn't enabled by default. You must turn it on by changing the following Registry entry to a value of 1:

```
\HKEY_LOCAL_MACHINE\System\CurrentControlSet\Services\Rasman\
   Parameters\Logging
```

This change doesn't take effect until you stop RAS and then restart it. After you restart RAS, it creates Device.log in the %systemroot%SYSTEM32\RAS folder. Here's an example of a Device.log file:

```
Remote Access Service Device Log 12/14/98 19:24:06
-----------------------------------------------------------
Port Handle: 108 Command to Device:
Port Handle: 108 Command to Device:ATS0=1
Port Handle: 108 Echo from Device:ATS0=1
Port Handle: 108 Response from Device:
OK
```

After the `Response from Device` line, you should see a positive response from the device. If Device.log doesn't show the modem responding, you probably have RAS configured for the wrong modem or the modem has a hardware configuration problem.

Troubleshooting Connectivity Problems

We could easily fill an entire book with information on troubleshooting network problems! They can be the toughest types of problems to trouble-shoot because you have so many components where something can go wrong. Worse yet, the path causing the problem may not be active when you arrive to troubleshoot the problem. The following list offers solutions to common connectivity problems:

- ✔ **Loose adapter cable:** Check to make sure the network cable is plugged in to the network adapter card. This may seem obvious, but it happens more than you might expect.

- ✔ **Network interface card failure:** Check the Event Viewer System log for errors related to the network adapter, the workstation, and the server components. If you're using TCP/IP, use PING to determine whether the system is getting out on the wire.

- ✔ **Protocol mismatch:** If two machines are active on the same network but still can't communicate, they may be using different protocols. Use the Control Panel's Network applet to determine which protocols are in use on each machine. Keep in mind that NetBEUI is not a routable protocol, so it won't traverse any routers on your network.

- ✔ **System on an IPX/SPX network can't communicate:** Make sure the system is using the correct frame type.

- ✔ **External network problem:** If the hardware on the local system is functioning correctly and you're using TCP/IP, use PING to attempt to isolate the problem. Try to PING in increasing distances until you see a problem. You may want to use Network Monitor to help locate conges-tion and broadcast storms.

✔ **System on a TCP/IP network can't communicate outside the local subnet:** The system has the wrong default gateway settings. Check the default gateway settings under TCP/IP properties and verify that the values match the actual address of the network's default gateway (router).

Network Monitor has some built-in limitations when it comes to solving network problems. The Network Monitor that ships with Windows NT Server doesn't support promiscuous mode, which allows the capture of any packet that goes over the wire, regardless of whether the packet is intended for your machine. The version of Network Monitor that comes with Windows NT Server can only capture packets sent from or to one of your server's network cards. If you need to monitor traffic on your entire network, you need to use a different tool. The Network Monitor that comes with Systems Management Server (SMS) does support promiscuous mode.

Solving File and Resource Access Problems

File and resource access problems typically involve conflicts between shared permissions and local NTFS permissions. When you share resources on an NTFS partition, you limit remote access by combining two sets of permissions — the network share permissions and the local NTFS permissions. All shared permissions except for No Access are evaluated by accumulation, and all NTFS permissions except for No Access are evaluated by accumulation. Then the system looks at both the shared result and the NTFS result and uses the most restrictive permissions as the effective permissions.

For example, assume that Joe's assigned share permission for C:\Stuff is Change (RXWD) and his assigned NTFS permission for this resource is Read (RX). The system uses the most restrictive permission — Read (RX) — as Joe's effective permission for this resource.

If you encounter a permission problem with a network share, be sure to verify the effective permissions for the user.

Inevitably, someone will lose access to a resource. Of course, this problem can only happen if you're using NTFS. Assuming you have Administrator privileges, you can easily solve the dilemma by taking ownership of the resource and then sharing it (with Full Control) to the person who needs access so that person can gain ownership of the resource. The new owner must initiate the Take Ownership step after you assign Full Control of the resource to that person. You cannot give that person ownership directly.

Using the ERD to Restore the System

You can use the Emergency Repair Disk (ERD) to restore a Windows NT system to the configuration it had the last time you updated your Emergency Repair Disk. This disk can repair missing Windows NT system files and restore the Registry to include disk configuration and security information. To create an ERD, you use the Repair Disk utility (Rdisk.exe) from a command prompt.

If you select the Update Repair Info option, the Repair Disk utility overwrites some of the files located in the %*systemroot*%\Repair directory. After the Repair Disk utility updates the %*systemroot*%\Repair directory, the program prompts you to create an Emergency Repair Disk. The disk it creates is the same as if you had chosen the Create Repair Disk option.

If you click the Create Repair Disk button, the Repair Disk utility formats the disk, then creates the ERD. This procedure overwrites any repair information that may exist on a previous ERD.

The Repair Disk utility doesn't automatically update the Security Accounts Manager (SAM) and security files. To update those files, you need to use the /S switch in conjunction with rdisk.

After you create an up-to-date ERD, you can use it in the emergency repair process. You use the emergency repair process when your system doesn't function correctly and using the Last Known Good configuration doesn't solve your problem. This process requires booting the system from the original installation disks used when you first installed Windows NT Server. You also need the up-to-date ERD. Lab 23-1 shows you how to complete the emergency repair process.

ERDs are computer-specific, so don't get them mixed up if you have several systems.

Lab 23-1   Using the ERD with the NT Setup Disks

1. **Start your system using the Windows NT Setup boot disk.**

2. **Insert Disk 2 when the system prompts you for it.**

3. **When the first screen appears, press R to start the emergency repair process.**

   Four options are displayed on your screen:

   • Inspect Registry Files

   • Inspect Startup Environment

- Verify Windows NT System Files

- Inspect Boot Sector

4. **Select only the options that you require for this repair.**

5. **Select the Continue (perform selected tasks) line and press Enter.**

6. **Windows NT asks whether you want to perform mass storage detection; go ahead and let it do that.**

7. **When the system prompts you, insert Disk 3 and press Enter.**

8. **Press Enter to skip the Specify Additional Mass Storage Devices step.**

9. **When the system prompts you, insert the ERD you created.**

   Several choices are displayed on your screen.

10. **Select the appropriate options based on your situation.**

11. **Select Continue (perform selected tasks) and press Enter.**

   The system copies the correct data back to your Windows NT Server partition.

12. **After the data is copied, remove the ERD and press Enter to restart your system.**

You must regularly update the system repair information in the %systemroot%\Repair directory on your hard drive and remember to create and maintain an up-to-date ERD. Your system repair information must include new configuration information such as drive letter assignments, stripe sets, volume sets, and mirrors. Otherwise, you may not be able to access your drive in the event of a system failure.

Troubleshooting Registry Problems

The Registry is structured as a set of four subtrees. Keys within each subtree contain per-computer and per-user databases. Values within each key contain entries and additional subkeys. Table 23-2 identifies the four subtrees.

Table 23-2	Registry Keys
Root Key Name	*Description*
HKEY_LOCAL_MACHINE	Static hardware and software configuration settings, such as system memory and device drivers
HKEY_CLASSES_ROOT	Data relating to Object Linking and Embedding (OLE) and file associations

(continued)

Table 23-2 *(continued)*

Root Key Name	Description
HKEY_CURRENT_USER	Information about the user who is currently logged on, such as personal program groups, desktop settings, network connections, and printers
HKEY_USERS	Preferences for every user who has ever logged on to this computer

Many tools are available to work with the Registry. Windows NT Diagnostics provides a graphical display of Registry hardware information. You can change drivers, protocols, and display settings through Control Panel applications.

Some settings in the Registry (for example, some TCP/IP settings) are not accessible through any means other than using a Registry editor. The Registry Editor is Regedt32.exe. If you use the Registry Editor to change entries, remember that the Editor doesn't recognize syntax errors. You don't get any error warning if you inadvertently mistype a name or value.

Use the Registry Editor's Read-Only mode when you're reviewing the Registry's contents and you don't plan to make any changes. This built-in safety precaution ensures that you don't accidentally change or delete any part of the Registry. You can find the Read-Only option on the Registry Editor's Options menu.

Before you make any changes, back up the Registry. We describe the methods you can use for backing up the Registry in the following section.

Backing up the Registry

In this section, we introduce you to the basics of backing up the Registry. For a more in-depth look at Registry backups, check out Chapter 25.

You have four ways to back up Registry entries:

- **Windows NT Backup.** After starting the Windows NT Backup application, choose Save Registry. This method is useful for making a tape backup. One of the benefits of using the Windows NT Backup and Restore applications is that they can access Registry hives while Windows NT is running. Many backup programs see these as open files and won't back them up.

- **Regback.exe and Regrest.exe.** You use these utilities to back up and restore individual Registry hives while Windows NT is running. You can find these utilities in the Windows NT Resource Kit.

✔ **Registry Editor.** Within the Registry Editor, choose Registry⇨Save Key. This command saves a single key and everything beneath it in a designated file. Unfortunately, online restores are not guaranteed. Windows NT Backup and RegBack provide more reliable backups.

✔ **Emergency Repair Disk.** Although you can use Rdisk.exe as a Registry backup method, it doesn't back up the entire Registry. RDISK was not designed to restore the system to its original state. You can view RDISK as a last option.

Gaining access to a remote computer's Registry

The Registry Editor contains a troubleshooting option to edit information contained in the Registry of another computer. The two keys that you can access remotely are HKEY_LOCAL_MACHINE and HKEY_USERS. You can use the capability to edit a remote Registry as a troubleshooting tool if you are familiar enough with the format of the Registry to know which keys you need to change to fix a given problem.

You can access a remote computer's Registry by choosing Registry⇨ Select Computer from the Registry Editor's menus. The Registry Editor responds by displaying a list of the domains and computers you can choose. Figure 23-1 shows the Registry Editor and the Registry keys.

Figure 23-1:
The
Windows
NT Registry
Editor.

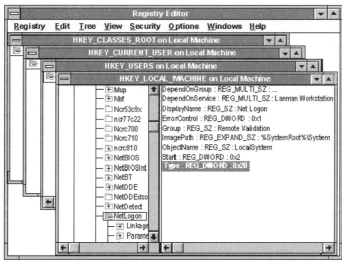

To close a remote Registry, make sure that one of the key windows for the remote Registry is the active window within the Registry Editor. Then choose Registry⇨Exit. You follow this same procedure if you need to close the local Registry. If you forget to close the remote Registry when you exit the Registry Editor, or inadvertently close the local one, the next time you start the Registry Editor, the remote Registry will appear.

Be very careful with the Registry Editor. Remember to make backups of the Registry, and to use read-only mode whenever possible.

Using the Last Known Good configuration

What happens if you load a new device driver that doesn't function correctly and it stops the system from booting correctly? Do you have to reload Windows NT? We hope you answered with a resounding NO! You can get around this problem by reverting to the Last Known Good configuration.

Last Known Good is the configuration that was saved to a special control set in the Registry after the last successful logon to Windows NT. Instead of reloading the entire operating system, you can restart the computer without logging on, then select Last Known Good during the boot sequence. NT loads the previously known good control set and bypasses the bad device driver. You can also initiate Last Known Good if Windows NT has a fatal error at boot time. Lab 23-2 leads you through the process of booting using the Last Known Good configuration.

Lab 23-2	Booting Using the Last Known Good Configuration

1. **When Boot.ini displays the OS menu, select Windows NT Server.**

   A message displays, telling you to press the spacebar for the Last Known Good configuration.

2. **Press the spacebar immediately, because you have only a few seconds to make this choice before it disappears.**

3. **Select L to choose the Last Known Good configuration from the Hardware Profile/Configuration Recovery menu.**

4. **Press Enter to confirm your choice.**

   After the system boots, it displays a message confirming it loaded from a previous configuration.

The Last Known Good configuration can't help you in all situations. For example, it can't solve problems such as user profiles and file permissions, which aren't related to changes in control set information. Nor can it solve startup failures caused by hardware failures or corrupted files. So, although the Last Known Good configuration may save the day in some situations, like the Windows NT boot floppy, it doesn't work in all cases.

Advanced Problem Resolution

In some cases, you can't easily diagnose or repair problems with a Windows NT Server. When basic troubleshooting techniques don't reveal the source of your problems, more advanced techniques may be required. These advanced techniques are generally implemented by on-site networking personnel. Analyzing the results generated by these tools may require the help of Microsoft support engineers.

Understanding NT Server's STOP messages

Have you ever heard someone talking about the NT "blue screen of death"? The blue screen is actually a text-mode STOP message. The message identifies hardware and software problems that happen while you are running Windows NT Server.

The STOP message information can be very valuable for troubleshooting a problem. The information on the screen includes the text translation of the contents of memory, the addresses of the violating call, and the drivers loaded at the time of the STOP error. If you have configured your system to write debugging information, NT Server also generates that file.

Although the "blue screen of death" can be somewhat cryptic, if you concentrate on the following items, you can find the information you need for determining the source of the error:

- Error code and parameters (first line of the screen)
- Modules that were successfully loaded and initialized (middle of the screen)
- Modules that were on the stack (bottom of the screen)

This information tells an experienced engineer the extent of the problem, as well as the cause of the problem. A normal STOP message begins with information similar to the screen in Figure 23-2.

Some errors are immediately indicative of the problem. Other errors require Microsoft Product Support Services (PSS) assistance. Solving some errors may even require that you set up NT in kernel debugger mode.

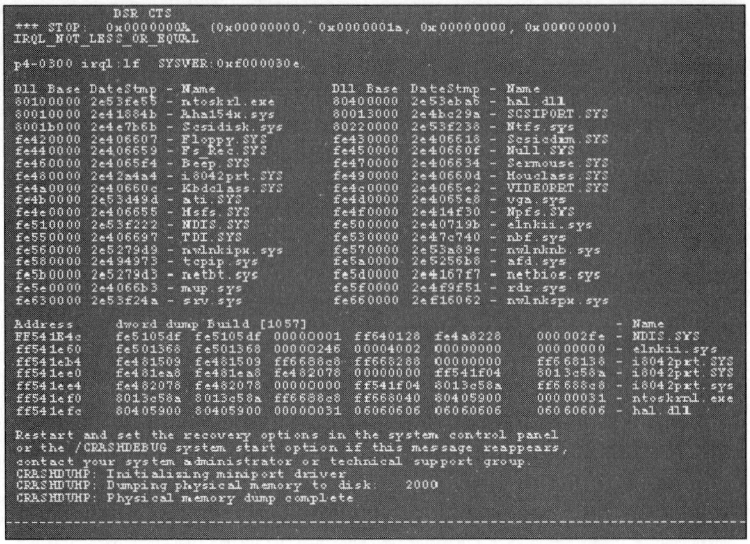

Figure 23-2:
The blue
screen of
death.

Configuring a memory dump: High-tech landfill

Occasionally, you find a problem that requires some in-depth analysis on Microsoft's part. A Microsoft engineer may ask you to collect a Crashdump file, put it on a magnetic tape, and send it in for analysis.

The Crashdump file is the preferred method of debugging in many cases because it lets you get the server up and running again very quickly while maintaining all the information you need for analyzing the issue. This Crashdump facility writes the contents of memory to a file on a disk when a STOP error occurs.

The file created by the Crashdump utility can be viewed remotely by Microsoft PSS via a RAS connection, or you can send the file to Microsoft via e-mail, an FTP utility, or by mailing in a magnetic tape. To generate a Crashdump file

  ✔ Recovery must be enabled. On the Recovery tab in the System Control Panel, select the Write Debugging Information To option, and enter a filename for saving the crash information. This filename defaults to Memory.dmp.

  ✔ The paging file must be resident on the system drive and must be at least 1MB larger than physical RAM.

  ✔ The system drive must contain free disk space that is at least the size of the paging file.

In addition, you may select the following options on the Recovery tab in the System Control Panel:

- ✔ Overwrite Any Existing File
- ✔ Write an Event to the System Log and/or Send an Administrative Alert
- ✔ Automatically Reboot

With Recovery properly configured, a STOP message generates the following events:

- ✔ The system automatically dumps the RAM contents to the pagefile.
- ✔ The computer is automatically restarted (if designated in Control Panel).
- ✔ The pagefile contents are written to %*SystemRoot*%\Memory.dmp.

To ensure that your memory dump was successful, and the Memory.dmp file is not corrupted, use the Dumpchk utility. Dumpchk is located on the Windows NT CD in the following location:

Support\Debug*platform*\Dumpchk.exe.

When you're sure you have a good Memory.dmp file, you typically send it to Microsoft for analysis. Remember that the size of the file will be at least the size of the physical RAM in the computer. On a server with lots of RAM, the file that Crashdump generates can take a long time to transmit. However, you can reduce the size of the file.

Although Microsoft prefers to receive the whole memory dump file, you may be able to use a command line utility called Dumpexam.exe to examine the Crashdump file and extract pertinent information from it. The result is usually a text file containing the information that you selected. The file created by Dumpexam.exe — Memory.txt — will be significantly smaller than Memory.dmp. In many cases, Memory.txt provides enough information for Microsoft to adequately analyze the situation. If the needed information isn't in the text file after running Dumpexam.exe, you have to send in the entire Memory.dmp file.

Three files are required to run Dumpexam.exe, and they all must be in the same directory. They are located in the \SUPPORT\DEBUG*platform* directory (where *platform* is I386, ALPHA, MIPS, or PPC) of the Windows NT Server CD. The first file depends on the platform of the computer on which the dump file was generated. The last two files are

- ✔ Dumpexam.exe
- ✔ Imagehlp.dll

The Dumpexam.exe utility has the following syntax:

```
dumpexam [options] [CrashDumpFile]
```

Table 23-3 describes the options for Dumpexam.exe.

Table 23-3	Dumpexam.exe Optional Switches
Option	*Description*
-?	Displays the command syntax.
-v	Specifies verbose mode.
-p	Prints the header only.
-f *filename*	Specifies the output filename. Required only if the dump file is not located in %*systemroot*%, or the name is not Memory.dmp.
-y *path*	Sets the symbol search path.

You should run Dumpexam.exe with no parameters if

✔ No hot fixes or service packs have been applied to Windows NT Server 4.0.

✔ The memory dump file is in the location specified in the Recovery dialog box in the System option in Control Panel.

Using the Event Log Services

Using Event Viewer, you can monitor events and STOP errors within your system. You can use Event Viewer to view and manage System, Security, and Application event logs. You can also archive event logs. Through User Manager for Domains, you can enable Auditing, which allows designated user and system events to be logged to appropriate log files within Event Viewer.

The event-logging service starts automatically when you run Windows NT. You can stop event logging with the Services tool in the Control Panel.

You may find the Event Viewer to be an immense help in troubleshooting your system — especially when server services don't start. Figure 23-3 shows an example from the System log. The red flag deals with Remote Access Service. By displaying the event details for that log entry, as shown in Figure 23-4, you can see that the RAS Connection Manager failed to start because it couldn't load a specified DLL. Based on the error you receive, you can quickly isolate the malfunction.

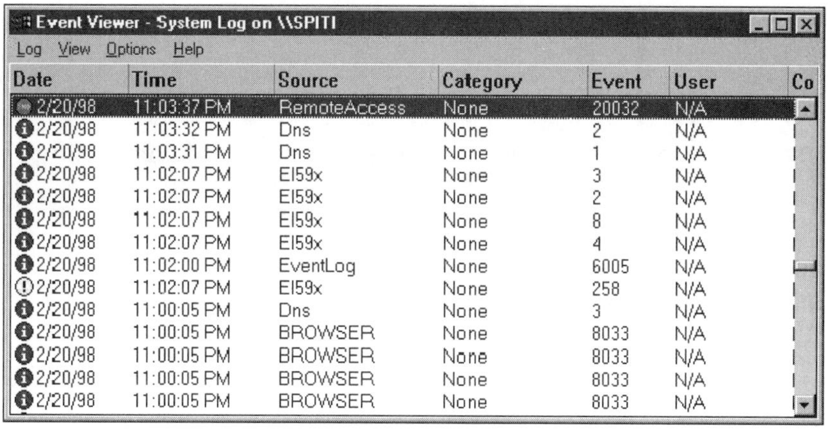

Figure 23-3:
System log
from the
Event
Viewer.

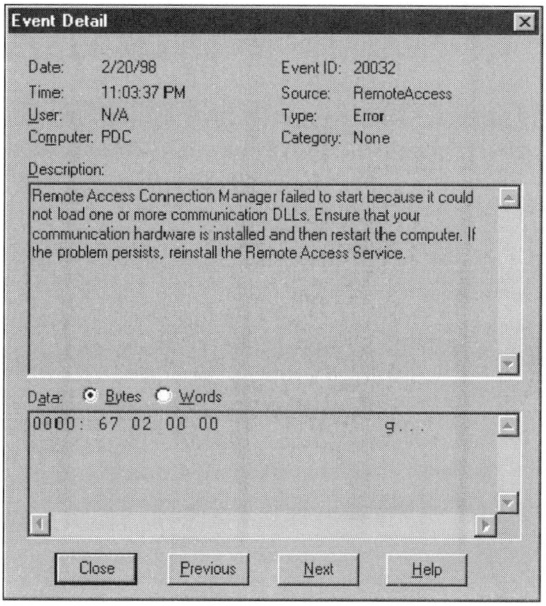

Event Viewer - System Log on \\SPITI

Log View Options Help

Date	Time	Source	Category	Event	User	Co
2/20/98	11:03:37 PM	RemoteAccess	None	20032	N/A	
2/20/98	11:03:32 PM	Dns	None	2	N/A	
2/20/98	11:03:31 PM	Dns	None	1	N/A	
2/20/98	11:02:07 PM	EI59x	None	3	N/A	
2/20/98	11:02:07 PM	EI59x	None	2	N/A	
2/20/98	11:02:07 PM	EI59x	None	8	N/A	
2/20/98	11:02:07 PM	EI59x	None	4	N/A	
2/20/98	11:02:00 PM	EventLog	None	6005	N/A	
2/20/98	11:02:07 PM	EI59x	None	258	N/A	
2/20/98	11:00:05 PM	Dns	None	3	N/A	
2/20/98	11:00:05 PM	BROWSER	None	8033	N/A	
2/20/98	11:00:05 PM	BROWSER	None	8033	N/A	
2/20/98	11:00:05 PM	BROWSER	None	8033	N/A	
2/20/98	11:00:05 PM	BROWSER	None	8033	N/A	

Figure 23-4:
Event detail
for the RAS
Connection
Manager
error.

Event Detail

Date: 2/20/98   Event ID: 20032
Time: 11:03:37 PM   Source: RemoteAccess
User: N/A   Type: Error
Computer: PDC   Category: None

Description:

Remote Access Connection Manager failed to start because it could
not load one or more communication DLLs. Ensure that your
communication hardware is installed and then restart the computer. If
the problem persists, reinstall the Remote Access Service.

Data: ⦿ Bytes ◯ Words

0000: 67 02 00 00   g...

[Close] [Previous] [Next] [Help]

1 Which command line-utility can verify the integrity of the Memory.dmp file?

A ○ Rdisk.exe

B ○ Verify.exe

C ○ Dumpexam.exe

D ○ Dumpchk.exe

2 When a domain user loses access to an NT object, the administrator must reestablish access by _____ and then assigning Full Control permissions to the user.

A ○ Taking ownership

B ○ Deleting permissions

C ○ Backing up

D ○ Enabling logon

3 When network communication is working on the LAN, but not across the WAN, which items should you check within NT Server? (Choose all that apply.)

A ❑ A properly configured default gateway

B ❑ A routable protocol such as TCP/IP or IPX/SPX

C ❑ The DHCP Server Service

D ❑ The Replicator Service

4 What's the default location for the Memory.dmp file?

A ○ \%systemroot%

B ○ \%WinDir%

C ○ C:\Windows

D ○ C:\

5 You want to restore the SYSTEM key in the Registry. You don't have an ERD, but you do have a disk that contains configuration information stored in the SYSTEM key. You created this disk using the Save Key command in the Registry Editor. Which program can you use if you want to restore the SYSTEM key using this disk?

A ○ Registry Editor

B ○ User Manager for Domains

C ○ Disk Administrator

D ○ NT Backup

6 All computers on your WAN use NWLink IPX/SPX as the only network protocol. A member server in your domain can't connect to the network. What is the most likely cause of the problem?

A ○ Incorrect frame type

B ○ Protocol mismatch

C ○ Upper-memory area conflicts

D ○ Faulty network devices

7 Your Windows NT Server encounters a series of critical STOP errors. How do you configure Windows NT to save STOP error information to a memory dump file?

A ○ Specify the Recovery option in Dr. Watson.

B ○ Specify the Recovery option in Performance Monitor.

C ○ Specify the proper Recovery option on the Startup/Shutdown tab in System Properties.

D ○ Specify the Recovery option in Server Manager.

8 You have given share-level access to the E:\DATA directory to the Everyone group with Change permissions (RXWD). Users are complaining that they can read, but can't write or delete within the directory. What is the likely cause of this problem?

A ○ The users are not members of the Everyone group.

B ○ The users are not members of the Administrators group.

C ○ The users don't have change permissions within NTFS to E:\DATA.

D ○ The share for E:\DATA doesn't currently exist.

9 Several users dialing in to the corporate NT Server can't authenticate their correct user name and password. Other users can establish a dial-up connection without errors. You have determined that RAS is configured to allow only Microsoft encryption. What is the likely cause of this problem?

A ○ Users are dialing in to the network using Microsoft Windows 95.

B ○ Users are accessing the network using various dial-up networking clients.

C ○ Users are forgetting their passwords.

D ○ Users have locked out their Windows NT user accounts.

10 You can correct certain startup problems by running the Emergency Repair Disk (ERD). Which tasks can the ERD process perform? (Choose all that apply.)

A ❑ Verifying Windows NT system files

B ❑ Inspecting the startup environment

C ❑ Inspecting the boot sector

D ❑ Replacing the master boot record

Answers

1 *D.* The Dumpchk.exe utility enables you to verify the integrity of the Memory.dmp file before you attempt to use it for system diagnosis. *See "Configuring a memory dump: High-tech landfill."*

2 *A.* The administrator can't give ownership directly to the desired user; he or she must first initiate Take Ownership, and then assign Full Control to the designated user. The user must then initiate a Take Ownership action to become the new owner of the object. *Review "Solving File and Resource Access Problems."*

3 *A, B.* Both items are possible causes for local LAN communication not being able to work in a WAN environment. The default gateway tells TCP/IP packets how to find networks not defined as local. Only routable protocols can pass over a router-based network or WAN. *See "Troubleshooting Connectivity Problems."*

4 *A.* This location is normally the \WINNT directory, but may have been changed by the administrator during system setup. *See "Configuring a memory dump: High-tech landfill."*

5 *A.* Use this tool to restore the key in question because you have no tape record for use with NT Backup. (NT Backup is the preferred method for restoring the Registry.) *See "Gaining access to a remote computer's Registry."*

6 *A.* IPX/SPX requires a compatible frame type from all communicating devices on the network. The 802.3 and 802.2 frame types are both valid frame types, but they don't communicate with each other, so selecting the frame type currently in use on your network is important. Auto-frame type selection is a good option to choose in most cases. *See "Troubleshooting Connectivity Problems."*

7 *C.* During a critical STOP error (which results in the "blue screen of death), this option allows the system to save important information to a designated location for troubleshooting purposes. *Review "Configuring a memory dump: High-tech landfill."*

8 *C.* If NTFS permissions are more restrictive than the assigned share level permissions, the most restrictive permissions apply to the users. Add Change permissions (RXWD) to the E:\DATA directory using Explorer. *See "Solving File and Resource Access Problems."*

9 *B.* By selecting Allow Only Microsoft Encryption, you prevent DUN clients from other vendors from accessing your network. Remove this restriction to allow all clients to authenticate using RAS. *See "Troubleshooting RAS."*

10 *A, B, C.* During the repair process, you are given the opportunity to select each of these areas for possible recovery by the ERD. *See "Using the ERD to Restore the System."*

Chapter 24

Implementing Fault Tolerance: Earning Your Disaster Recovery Stripes

• •

Exam Objectives

▶ Understanding Windows NT RAID support

▶ Implementing fault tolerance

▶ Recovering from disk failure

• •

*A*n important part of planning your enterprise environment is planning for hardware failure. You don't want a production server going down with no way to recover the data. Regular backups help protect your data, and fault tolerance can get your system up and running faster in the event of hard disk failure.

NT provides fault tolerance through a method known as a Redundant Array of Inexpensive Disks (RAID). NT supports three levels of RAID, and two of those levels provide fault tolerance. In this chapter, we describe the levels of RAID that NT supports, and we explain the process for implementing RAID and recovering from disk failure using the Windows NT RAID implementation.

Quick Assessment

1 RAID level 0 is also referred to as _____.

2 RAID level 1 is also referred to as _____.

3 RAID level 5 is also referred to as _____.

4 Which of NT's software-supported RAID levels is not fault tolerant?

5 At a minimum, you need _____ drives to implement RAID 5 fault tolerance.

6 (True/False). RAID in Windows NT doesn't require special RAID-compliant hardware.

7 (True/False). Fault tolerance eliminates the need for regular backups.

8 To implement fault tolerance, you use the NT utility known as _____.

9 (True/False). Windows NT Workstation can use the same RAID levels as Windows NT Server.

Answers

1   *Disk striping.* See "Reviewing RAID Support in NT."

2   *Disk mirroring.* See "Reviewing RAID Support in NT."

3   *Disk striping with parity.* Again, check out "Reviewing RAID Support in NT."

4   *RAID 0, disk striping (without parity).* See "Reviewing RAID Support in NT" (be sure to review Table 24-1).

5   *Three.* And the maximum is 32. See "Reviewing RAID Support in NT" — in particular, the subsection on RAID 5.

6   *True.* Although hardware solutions are available, Windows NT Server can implement RAID strictly through software. That's the focus of this entire chapter!

7   *False.* For more information, see the section "Recovering from Disk Failure."

8   *Disk Administrator.* You can find more information in the section "Reviewing RAID Support in NT."

9   *False.* See "Reviewing RAID Support in NT."

Reviewing RAID Support in NT

Redundant Array of Inexpensive Disks (RAID) is a method of joining groups of smaller inexpensive drives together to form larger storage devices. Several levels of RAID exist, and Windows NT supports three of them.

You implement NT's software RAID through Disk Administrator. To start Disk Administrator, choose Start⇨Programs⇨Administrative Tools⇨ Disk Administrator.

Your exam asks a number of questions concerning the three different types of RAID supported by NT. You need to be familiar with all three types and know how to calculate the aggregate capacity of each type. While you prepare for the exam, focus on the following points:

- ✔ RAID levels provided with NT, and which of those levels provide fault tolerance

- ✔ Disk space utilization for the various RAID levels

- ✔ Benefits and drawbacks of the available RAID levels

- ✔ How to recover from hardware failure when fault tolerance has been implemented

In addition to the software implementation of RAID available with Windows NT, many vendors produce hardware-based solutions. Hardware solutions are generally fairly expensive, but you typically see better performance and more features, such as instant recovery via hot-swappable drives.

Six levels of RAID exist, defined by different levels of price, performance, and reliability. On your exam, you don't need to know all six levels. The exam only focuses on the three levels of RAID supported by Windows NT Server: RAIDs 0, 1, and 5. We offer in-depth explanations of these three levels in the following sections of this chapter. Table 24-1 outlines all six RAID levels.

Table 24-1	Levels of RAID
Level	*Description*
RAID 0	Disk striping without parity. Doesn't provide fault tolerance, but provides enhanced performance.
RAID 1	Disk mirroring. Provides fault tolerance, but a degraded level of performance.
RAID 2	Disk striping with error-correction code. Not included with NT.

Level	Description
RAID 3	Disk striping with error-correction code stored as parity. Not included with NT.
RAID 4	Disk striping with parity information stored on one drive. Not included with NT.
RAID 5	Disk striping with parity distributed across all drives in the stripe set.

NT Server supports these three RAID levels:

- ✔ RAID 0
- ✔ RAID 1
- ✔ RAID 5

Only RAID 1 and RAID 5 are fault tolerant. RAID 0, while not fault tolerant, provides a higher level of performance. RAID 1 and RAID 5 are only supported on NT Server; they are not available on NT Workstation. Be familiar with all three supported RAID levels for your exam.

RAID 0

RAID 0 is striping without parity. Striping spreads information evenly across all disks in an array, but without parity, no way exists to recover data in the event of a single disk failure except from a backup.

This level provides no fault tolerance, but is very fast and requires a minimum of only two disk drives. RAID 0 can use a maximum of 32 disks. Read and write times are faster because the operations are performed across multiple disks.

On your exam, you will see questions asking about recovery from stripe sets. The key phrase you should look for is "with parity." You can only rebuild data from single disk failures on a stripe set with parity. You can't recover from a stripe set without parity without restoring from tape backup.

RAID 0 provides the greatest amount of disk space. You calculate logical drive size by multiplying partition size by the number of drives in your stripe set:

logical drive size = partition size × number of drives

All partitions must be of the same size. The system and boot partition can't be contained in a stripe set.

To create a stripe set without parity:

1. Start Disk Administrator.

2. Select blank, same-sized partitions on two or more separate drives.

3. Choose Partition⇨Create Stripe Set.

For example, Figure 24-1 shows two selected partitions with 200MB of free space. By choosing the Create Stripe Set option, you create a drive with total usable capacity of 400MB, but it won't be a fault-tolerant system.

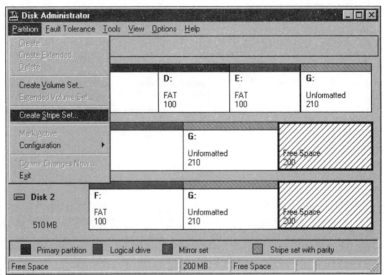

Figure 24-1:
Creating a
stripe set.

RAID 1

RAID 1 is disk mirroring. The mirrored drive contains an exact image of the data stored on the primary disk. This level provides a reasonable level of protection but carries with it degraded performance levels.

Mirroring requires two drives. You get the least efficient utilization of drive space with RAID 1, making it one of the more expensive software solutions. Although mirroring doesn't affect read times, it causes degradation in write times, because each time the system writes data to the drive, it must copy that data to the mirror.

You can mirror any partition, including the system and boot partitions. Size of the logical drive is determined by the size of one of the partitions, and the partition sizes must be identical. The mirror doesn't increase the available storage of the logical drive:

logical drive size = partition size of original drive

If the two drives being used with RAID 1 are controlled by separate controller boards, this method is known as *disk duplexing* rather than disk mirroring. The controller overhead required for duplexing is minimized because the read and write operations are on separate controllers. The redundancy that duplexing provides protects your data in the event of both drive failure and controller failure.

To create a drive mirror:

1. **Start Disk Administrator.**
2. **Select an existing partition on one disk, and a partition at least as large as the first one on a separate disk.**
3. **Choose Fault Tolerance⇨Establish Mirror.**

RAID 5

RAID 5 is striping with parity. Striping, as previously mentioned, spreads information evenly across all disks in an array. With parity, one of the stripes always contains parity information, allowing for data recalculation in the event of a single disk failure.

This level provides the highest level of protection. RAID 5 involves only a minimal performance loss compared to RAID 0, but increased write performance compared to RAID 1, and increased read and write performance compared to no RAID. RAID 5 has an additional overhead cost, as well as a loss in overall storage capacity.

RAID 5 can use between 3 and 32 drives. The size of a RAID 5 disk set is calculated as the size of the partition multiplied by the number of drives minus one:

logical drive size = partition size × (number of drives − 1)

All partitions must be of the same size. For example, if you have three blank, unpartitioned areas on three disks, and the smallest partition is 210MB, the stripe set with parity can occupy 210MB on each of the three disks. In other words, the stripe set with parity will occupy 630MB of disk space, with 420MB of usable space, and 210MB used for storing parity information.

A RAID 5 is a fault-tolerant system, spreading parity information across all drives in a disk set. The parity information is a mathematical combination of the data contained on a disk. If a single drive in the stripe set fails, you can use the parity information to recalculate the missing data and regenerate a failed partition after the disk has been replaced. In addition, when a single drive fails, you can still access information through parity recalculation. Of course, using a system with a failed drive requires quite a bit more overhead, runs slower, and uses roughly three times as much memory for parity recalculation as a system with a fully functional array. The system and boot partitions can't be contained on a striped partition.

To create a stripe set with parity:

1. **Open Disk Administrator.**

2. **Select empty, same-sized partitions on three or more physical disks.**

3. **Choose Fault Tolerance⇨Create Stripe Set with Parity.**

   NT creates your fault-tolerant stripe set.

The system and boot partition can never be contained in a software-based stripe set, such as the RAID 0 or RAID 5 implementation available with NT. If you have a requirement for fault tolerance on a system with only two drives, or fault tolerance for the system and boot partitions, your answer must be either disk mirroring or disk duplexing (RAID 1). For fault tolerance across three or more drives containing the system or boot partitions, you may also use a hardware implementation of RAID 5.

Recovering from Disk Failure

Fault tolerance does you no good if you don't know how to successfully recover from failure. Your disaster recovery plan should include keeping a spare hard disk available to replace members of your disk sets if they unexpectedly fail. In the following sections, we look at recovery from failure in RAID 1 and RAID 5 fault-tolerant environments.

Recovering from disk mirroring failure: Seven years of bad luck

If the original disk in your mirrored set fails, you don't lose data because everything is written to the mirror. The system automatically switches over to the mirror upon failure.

If your failed mirror set is simply a data partition, you can easily repair your disk:

1. **Start Disk Administrator.**

2. **Break the mirrored set by choosing Fault Tolerance⇨Break Mirror.**

3. **Delete the failed partition by right-clicking and choosing Delete from the pop-up menu.**

4. **Replace the failed disk.**

5. **Use Disk Administrator to establish a new mirror set.**

Repairing a failed mirror set on a system or boot partition is slightly more complicated. Before you reboot the system, you must edit the Boot.ini file to change the ARC name to point to the mirrored partition. Lab 24-1 steps you through the recovery of a failed mirror set on a system or boot partition.

Lab 24-1   Recovering a Mirrored System or Boot Partition

1. **Edit the Boot.ini file to point to the mirrored drive.**

2. **Use Disk Administrator to break the mirror.**

   As shown in Figure 24-2, you complete this step by choosing Fault Tolerance⇨Break Mirror.

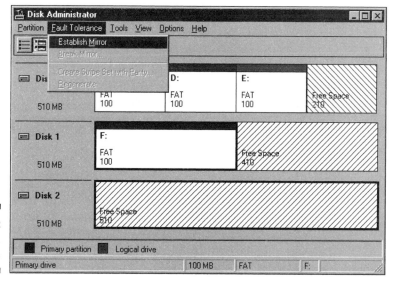

Figure 24-2:
Breaking a
mirror set.

3. Replace the failed drive.

4. Boot the system from the mirrored drive.

5. In Disk Administrator, re-create the mirror set by choosing Fault Tolerance⇨Establish Mirror.

Recovering from disk failure on a stripe set with parity (a fashion mistake?)

To recover from a single disk failure in a stripe set with parity:

1. Replace the faulty disk with a drive of the same or greater physical size.

2. In Disk Administrator, choose Fault Tolerance⇨Regenerate.

   The system re-creates the data that was stored on the failed drive through parity calculations.

You can only recover from a single disk failure in a stripe set with parity, regardless of how many disks your array contains. If your array includes 12 disks, and a single unit fails, you can recover using the process we describe in this section. If two drives fail, however, the only recovery solution is to replace the failed hardware and restore your data from backup. If you see a question on the exam that asks you how to recover from two failed disks, look for the answer containing this solution.

Prep Test

1 Which of the following RAID types provide fault tolerance in Windows NT Server? (Choose all that apply.)

A ❑ RAID 0

B ❑ RAID 1

C ❑ RAID 3

D ❑ RAID 5

2 Christi has decided to create a stripe set with parity across three disks with 250MB of free space on each disk. How much disk space will be utilized by the stripe set with parity, and how much of that space will be usable for storing data?

A ○ 500MB utilized, 500MB for data storage

B ○ 750MB utilized, 500MB for data storage

C ○ 500MB utilized, 250MB for data storage

D ○ 750MB utilized, 750MB for data storage

3 You want to utilize fault tolerance for your system and boot partition. Which of the following fault-tolerant systems can you implement? (Choose all that apply.)

A ❑ Disk mirroring

B ❑ Disk duplexing

C ❑ Disk striping

D ❑ Disk striping with parity

4 Two of the disks in your RAID 5 array of 30 disks have failed. What is the easiest way for you to restore your system?

A ○ Replace the two disks, and choose Partition⇨Regenerate from the Disk Administrator menus.

B ○ Replace the two disks, and choose Fault Tolerance⇨Regenerate from the Disk Administrator menus.

C ○ Replace the two disks, and restore your system from backup.

D ○ Replace the two disks, and choose Fault Tolerance⇨Establish Mirror from the Disk Administrator menus.

5 You want to create a stripe set with parity with exactly 500MB of usable storage space. You have three disks in your system. How much free, unpartitioned space do you need on each disk to create a 500MB logical drive?

A ○ 500MB

B ○ 250MB

C ○ 167MB

D ○ 750MB

6 Tim is using a mirror set to store important computer-aided design (CAD) drawings on a partition separate from his NT Server system and boot partition. One of the disks in his mirror set fails. What must you do to repair Tim's system?

A ○ Replace the failed disk. Using Disk Administrator, establish a new mirror set between the disk that didn't fail and the new disk.

B ○ Replace the failed disk. Choose Fault Tolerance⇨Regenerate in Disk Administrator.

C ○ Break the mirror set from the Fault Tolerance menu in Disk Administrator. Replace the failed disk. Using Disk Administrator, establish a new mirror set between the disk that didn't fail and the new disk.

D ○ Simply replace the failed disk. NT automatically re-creates the mirror set when you reboot.

7 One of the three physical disks used in your stripe set has failed. After replacing the failed hardware, how can you repair your stripe set?

A ○ Run Disk Administrator. Choose Partition⇨Regenerate.

B ○ Run Disk Administrator. Choose Fault Tolerance⇨Regenerate.

C ○ Run Disk Administrator. Choose Fault Tolerance⇨Reestablish.

D ○ Run Disk Administrator. Re-create your stripe set, and restore from tape backup.

8 Which of the following fault-tolerant systems has the fastest read time?

A ○ Disk mirroring

B ○ Disk duplexing

C ○ Disk striping

D ○ Disk striping with parity

9 Which of the following fault-tolerant solutions provides the highest level of usable disk space?

A ○ RAID 0

B ○ RAID 5

C ○ Disk mirroring

D ○ Disk duplexing

10 Barbara, a manager in your accounting department, wants to implement fault tolerance for her data storage partitions on her NT Workstation computer. Which of the following solutions would work?

A ○ Implementing disk duplexing

B ○ Implementing disk mirroring

C ○ Implementing software-based RAID 5

D ○ Implementing hardware-based RAID 5

Answers

1 *B and D.* RAID 0 is not fault tolerant, although it's supported by Windows NT Server. NT doesn't support RAID 3. RAID 1 may also be referred to as disk mirroring. *See "Reviewing RAID Support in NT."*

2 *B. 750MB utilized, 500MB for data storage.* 250MB will be needed from each disk. To determine the storage capacity for a RAID 5 array, subtract one from the total number of partitions in your array, and multiply the result by the smallest partition size. *See "Reviewing RAID Support in NT" — in particular, the subsection "RAID 5."*

3 *A and B.* You can use only disk duplexing or disk mirroring for fault tolerance on system and boot partitions. *See "Reviewing RAID Support in NT."*

4 *C. Replace the two disks, and restore your system from backup.* If more than one disk in a stripe set with parity fails, your only option is to restore from backup. *See "Recovering from disk failure on a stripe set with parity (a fashion mistake?)."*

5 *B. 250MB.* To create 500MB of usable space in a stripe set with parity across three disks, you must create a stripe set across three 250MB partitions. Total space required for this solution is 750MB. Only 500MB of that space can be used to store data; the remaining 250MB is for storing parity information. *See "Reviewing RAID Support in NT" — in particular, the subsection "RAID 5."*

6 *C.* You must break the mirror set before replacing the disk. Reestablish the mirror set in the same way as you originally created it. The Regenerate command is only for stripe sets with parity. *See the section "Recovering from disk mirroring failure: Seven years of bad luck."*

7 *D. Run Disk Administrator. Re-create your stripe set, and restore from tape backup.* Notice that the question refers to a stripe set, not a stripe set with parity. A stripe set isn't fault tolerant; therefore, the only way to repair your data is from tape backup. *See "Recovering from disk failure on a stripe set with parity (a fashion mistake?)."*

8 *D. Disk striping with parity.* Disk striping with parity has the fastest read time because the read operations are performed across multiple disks. Disk mirroring and disk duplexing both read from a single disk, and disk striping is not a fault-tolerant system. *For more information, see "Reviewing RAID Support in NT."*

9 *B. RAID 5.* Software-based RAID 5 provides the greatest amount of usable storage space. Mirroring and duplexing each provide only 50 percent usable data storage across the disk set. RAID 5 provides a minimum of 66 percent usable disk space when implemented on the minimum number of disks, three. RAID 0 is not fault tolerant. *See "Reviewing RAID Support in NT."*

10 *D. Implementing hardware-based RAID 5.* Windows NT Workstation doesn't support fault-tolerant disk schemes. The only solution for the options listed is to implement a hardware-based RAID array. Hardware RAID can generally operate independently of an operating system. Other solutions, of course, include upgrading Barbara's computer to Windows NT Server and implementing one of the available fault-tolerant schemes. *See "Reviewing RAID Support in NT" — in particular, the subsection "RAID 5."*

Chapter 25

Hardware Woes

Exam Objectives

▶ Resolving installation failures

▶ Resolving boot failures

▶ Resolving configuration errors

*Y*ou don't need to be a hardware technician to pass the Enterprise exam, but you must answer a few basic hardware troubleshooting questions. These questions focus on resolving installation, boot, and configuration failures. The Enterprise exam doesn't cover repairing broken hardware devices.

In this chapter, we cover installation failures and how to get around them. We discuss boot failures and the Boot.ini file, and we cover configuration errors and troubleshooting the Registry.

Keep the following tips in mind as you prepare for the hardware trouble-shooting questions on the exam:

✔ Concentrate on the boot-up process. Understand what happens when NT Server boots up, what can go wrong, and how you can fix it.

✔ Don't get bogged down memorizing the details of the Boot.ini file. Understand the purpose of each of its sections and focus on the switches used for troubleshooting.

✔ Don't memorize all the system Registry subkeys and values. For the exam, you need to know the purpose of each system key.

✔ Be aware of the types of errors that you may encounter during the NT Server installation. You don't need to know the contents of the Hardware Compatibility List, but you need to know its purpose.

Quick Assessment

Resolving installation failures

1 You can create new NT boot and setup floppy disks by using the _____ switch in conjunction with the NT Server setup program.

2 The _____ helps you determine whether you can expect your hardware to work with NT Server.

Resolving boot failures

3 _____ is the name of the configuration file that holds the settings for the boot loader menu.

4 The _____ naming convention is used to specify the location of operating systems in the Boot.ini file.

5 The Boot.ini file contains the _____ and _____ sections.

6 You can add the _____ switch to an Operating Systems entry in the Boot.ini file to have the names of the device drivers displayed when NT Server boots.

Resolving configuration errors

7 A copy of the Registry is contained on the _____, which when combined with the NT setup disks, you can use to restore a nonbootable NT Server.

8 The _____ and _____ utilities on the NT Server Resource Kit allow you to back up and restore all or part of the Registry to a file(s).

9 The _____ option provides an automatic backup of system Registry keys.

10 The _____ holds essential system configuration information and is composed of hives, keys, and values.

Answers

1 */ox.* See "Troubleshooting Installation Errors."

2 *Hardware Compatibility List.* See "Troubleshooting Installation Errors."

3 *Boot.ini.* See "Resolving Boot Failures."

4 *ARC.* See "Resolving Boot Failures" for more information.

5 *Boot Loader; Operating Systems.* Review "Resolving Boot Failures."

6 */sos.* See "Resolving Boot Failures."

7 *Emergency repair disk.* See "Resolving Configuration Errors with the Registry."

8 *RegBack; RegRest.* Review "Resolving Configuration Errors with the Registry."

9 *Last Known Good.* Review "Resolving Configuration Errors with the Registry."

10 *Registry.* See "Resolving Configuration Errors with the Registry."

Troubleshooting Installation Errors

The NT Server installation process is robust and relatively straightforward. In most cases, the installation process detects a system's hardware devices, and little need exists for user involvement beyond choosing setup options. In some cases, however, the installation process doesn't go as smoothly as you would hope. You may encounter the following installation errors:

- ✔ Hardware incompatibility
- ✔ Device detection failure
- ✔ Lack of NT-specific drivers
- ✔ Installation media failure
- ✔ Inability to connect to the domain controller

To pass the Enterprise exam, you need to know the basic steps for overcoming all these installation obstacles.

Hardware troubleshooting isn't easily taught. Good troubleshooters usually learn most from their experiences. All the MCSE exams contain a healthy dose of situational questions, and this is especially true of the hardware troubleshooting area. The best way to prepare for these questions is to gain hands-on experience with the technology. You don't have to intentionally break your NT Server, but taking a firsthand look at the Boot.ini file and the system key of your server's Registry can go a long way toward helping you gain the understanding necessary to answer these questions on the exam.

Hardware incompatibility

Before you purchase new hardware or attempt to install NT Server on an existing machine, Microsoft recommends that you check its Hardware Compatibility List (HCL) to determine whether the device is NT certified. The HCL identifies all the devices that Microsoft has tested for compatibility with Windows NT Server 4.0. This list tells you whether Microsoft finds your device to be compatible. If your device isn't listed on the HCL, Microsoft hasn't tested it and you're on your own.

Although an uncertified device may seem to work fine with NT Server, using such a device is like buying a used car without a warranty — you have no guarantee that it will continue to work properly, and Microsoft (like the used car dealer) won't provide support for it. If you have Internet access, use the copy of the HCL that's maintained on Microsoft's Web site, as it is more current than the copy on the NT Server CD.

Device detection failure

Another common installation problem occurs when the NT setup program doesn't automatically detect a mass storage device (such as a hard drive or a CD-ROM drive) on your machine. In such cases, you need to know how to install a device driver manually. Lab 25-1 outlines the procedure for installing device drivers manually. You should be familiar with this portion of the installation process for the exam.

Lab 25-1	Installing a Mass Storage Device Manually

1. **At the setup screen that asks whether you want to specify additional mass storage devices, press S.**

   The setup program displays a list of the device drivers that ship with NT Server.

2. **If your device is on the list, highlight it using the arrow keys and then press Enter.**

   The setup program performs a more thorough search of your machine for the device and installs the device driver from the NT installation media.

3. **If the manufacturer of your device has provided you with a disk that contains an NT driver, highlight Other and then press Enter.**

4. **Insert the disk that contains the driver and press Enter.**

   The device driver is read from the disk and installed.

Lack of NT-specific drivers

You won't find any questions about this topic on the MCSE exam, but driver availability is another cause of installation failure. Despite the popularity of NT Server, you occasionally run across a device that doesn't have NT Server drivers. This is especially true of older hardware. In such cases, you must ask the manufacturer of the device to create an NT driver for it.

Installation media failure

Installation failure often results from floppy disk failure. This problem occurs when one of the three setup disks becomes corrupted. Exposing these disks to dust, magnetic fields, heat, and moisture can easily turn them into high-tech coasters. If you experience a media failure, you should toss out that floppy disk and re-create it using the NT setup program and its /ox switch (see Chapter 7). You need to be familiar with the /ox setup switch for the exam.

Inability to connect to the domain controller

If the system you're installing will serve as a backup domain controller, it must connect to the primary domain controller to obtain the contents of the domain's Security Accounts Manager (SAM) database. If you receive the error message `Unable to connect to the domain controller,` make sure that the primary domain controller is up and running, the network is operable, your NIC driver is installed, and you are using the same network protocol(s) on both machines. If you're using TCP/IP, both systems should have the same subnet mask.

Resolving Boot Failures

To understand boot failures, you need to study the boot process. If you understand what happens during boot-up, you can recognize what can go wrong, and you can begin to formulate a repair strategy. You can answer many of the boot failure troubleshooting questions on the exam by utilizing a basic understanding of the boot process.

Understanding the boot process

The boot process encompasses everything that happens from the time you turn on your NT Server until you successfully log on. We divide the boot process into four sequences:

- ✔ The preboot sequence
- ✔ The load sequence
- ✔ The initialization sequence
- ✔ The Win32 subsystem sequence

The boot process merits careful study because the exam includes various questions about this process. If you understand the purpose of each file involved in the boot process, and the sequence in which these files are executed, you should be able to answer all the related questions. Figure 25-1 offers a graphical depiction of the NT boot process.

Don't be intimidated by the technical jargon. Just concentrate on the main purpose of each file and its place in the boot sequence.

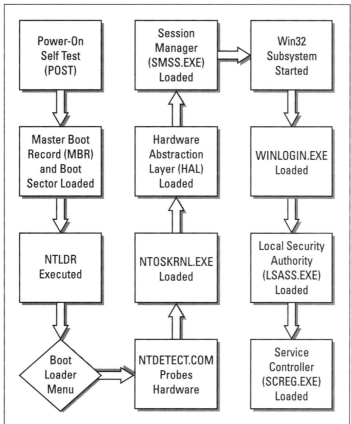

Figure 25-1:
The NT boot
process.

The preboot sequence involves the following steps:

1. When you turn on your machine, it immediately performs some low-level hardware diagnostic tests. This step is called the Power-On Self Test (POST).

2. The POST is followed by the loading and execution of the Master Boot Record (MBR) and the boot sector.

3. Ntldr executes. Ntldr is a program that starts operating systems. It can execute a variety of Microsoft operating systems, including various versions of DOS, Windows, and NT.

The load sequence comprises the following steps:

1. Ntldr switches to a 32-bit memory model and then starts a miniature file system. The miniature file system allows Ntldr to access other configuration files.

2. Ntldr then uses the information in the Boot.ini file to build the boot loader menu.

3. If Windows NT is chosen as the operating system, the Ntdetect.com file executes. Ntdetect.com probes the computer for its hardware configuration and returns its findings to Ntldr.

4. Ntldr then kicks off Ntoskrnl.exe and passes the hardware configuration information it received from Ntdetect.com to Ntoskrnl.exe.

5. Ntoskrnl.exe loads the Hardware Abstraction Layer (HAL) and reads in the HKEY_LOCAL_MACHINE\SYSTEM keys. The device drivers specified in the SYSTEM key load (but don't execute).

The initialization sequence has only two steps:

1. Ntoskrnl.exe executes all the loaded device drivers and starts the Session Manager (Smss.exe).

2. The Session Manager loads and executes all the subsystems listed in the HKEY_LOCAL_MACHINE\SYSTEM\CurrentControlSet\ Control\Session Manager\SubSystems Registry key, including the Win32 subsystem.

The Win32 subsystem sequence involves the following steps:

1. The Win32 subsystem loads the video subsystem and executes Winlogon.exe. Winlogon.exe executes the Local Security Authority subsystem (Lsass.exe), which displays the logon dialog box.

2. The Win32 subsystem executes the Service Controller (Screg.exe), which loads and executes the services marked for automatic execution in the HKEY_LOCAL_MACHINE\SYSTEM\CurrentControlSet\Services Registry key.

3. If a user successfully logs on to the machine, the system configuration information contained in the HKEY_LOCAL_MACHINE\SYSTEM\Clone key is copied into the Last Known Good control set.

The average human being can only remember three or four items in an ordered list at a time. So unless you're an elephant, you may want to tackle the boot process in pieces. Study the contents of each sequence separately. Then study the order of the sequences.

Troubleshooting the boot process

If you understand the boot process, you possess the knowledge needed to troubleshoot it. The Enterprise exam covers three main types of boot failures: hardware failures, device driver failures, and missing or corrupt system files.

Hardware failures

Even the best hardware eventually fails. Boot failures may result from bad memory chips or worn-out hard drives. When the operating system tries to access a failed memory chip, the infamous "blue screen of death" often results. (For all the gory details about NT's so-called "blue screen of death," refer to Chapter 23.) For help with memory failure troubleshooting, see the discussion of the maxmem switch in the section "Reviewing the Boot.ini switches," later in this chapter. File system corruption as well as odd grinding or squeaking noises often signal an impending hard drive failure. If the Check Disk program begins to run every time the system boots, trouble is surely ahead.

Device driver failures

Poorly written or conflicting hardware device drivers often result in a boot failure. If you install a new device driver and your system no longer boots, you can be reasonably sure that the new driver is at the root of your problems.

To restore your previous configuration settings, use the Last Known Good option or the Emergency Repair Disk (ERD). For more information about these procedures, see Chapter 23. If you aren't sure which drivers are being loaded or which driver is causing your system to fail, use the /sos switch in your Boot.ini file section. For more information about this switch, see "Reviewing the Boot.ini switches," later in this chapter.

Missing or corrupt system files

A common cause of boot failure is missing or corrupt system files. Here's a quick rundown on the most frequently encountered file-related errors, their causes, and potential remedies:

- ✔ **BOOT: Couldn't find Ntldr. Please insert another disk.** You have a nonbootable disk in the drive, or the Ntldr file is missing. Remove the disk from the drive or restore the system using the ERD.

- ✔ **Windows NT could not start because the following file is missing or corrupt: \winnt root\system32\ntoskrnl.exe Please reinstall a copy of the above file.** The Boot.ini file is missing or points to the wrong location, or the Ntoskrnl.exe file is missing. Check for the existence of the Boot.ini file. If it exists, check the Operating Systems entries in the Boot.ini file to make sure they're correct. If all else fails, restore the system using the ERD.

- ✔ **I/O error accessing boot sector file: multi(0)disk(0)rdisk(0)partition(1)\ bootsect.dos.** The Bootsect.dos file is missing from a DOS/Windows partition. Restore the system using the ERD.

- ✔ **NTDETECT V1.0 Checking Hardware . . . NTDETECT failed.** The Ntdetect.com file is missing. Restore the system using the ERD.

Understanding the Boot.ini configuration file

The Boot.ini file is located at the root of the boot partition. The information in this file is used to build the boot loader menu that's displayed at startup. You should be familiar with the structure of the Boot.ini file for the Enterprise exam.

The Boot.ini file contains two sections: Boot Loader and Operating Systems. Brackets enclose the names of the two sections. The Boot Loader section contains boot menu options. The Operating Systems section contains information about the operating systems to be listed on the boot loader menu. Figure 25-2 shows a typical Boot.ini file.

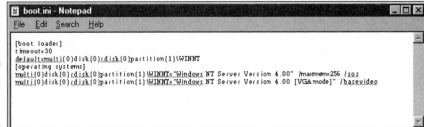

Figure 25-2:
A typical
Boot.ini file.

Examining the Boot Loader section

The Boot Loader section usually contains two entries. The timeout entry specifies the number of seconds that the boot loader menu displays before the default operating system entry loads. The default entry specifies the location of the default operating system using ARC notation (see "What is ARC notation?" a bit later in this chapter).

Understanding the Operating Systems section

The Operating Systems section contains one or more entries for each installed operating system. At the very least, each entry contains the location of the operating system using ARC notation, and the description that's used to refer to it in the boot loader menu. You can add additional switches after the description.

If you're asked whether an entry would appear in a Boot.ini file, look for answers that begin with one of the following keywords:

```
timeout=
default=
multi(x)
scsi(x)
```

If an answer doesn't begin with one of these keywords, you can safely assume that it's incorrect.

What is ARC notation?

ARC stands for Advanced RISC Computer and is a standard naming convention that's used to reference the location of information on a mass storage device such as a hard drive. An ARC location contains five distinct parts. Table 25-1 describes each part.

Table 25-1	ARC Notation
Part	*Description*
multi(x) or scsi(x)	This part tells you which drive controller interface manages the drive holding the operating system. Use scsi(x) for SCSI drives and multi(x) for IDE, EIDE, MFM, and RLL drives (0 = first controller).
disk(x)	You can daisy-chain as many as seven SCSI devices on each SCSI controller interface. This part represents the SCSI device number. Use 0 if your drive is not a SCSI device.
rdisk(x)	Non-SCSI controller interfaces (such as IDE) can also support multiple devices. Use this setting to specify a non-SCSI drive number. If your drive is SCSI, set this part to 0 (1 = first drive).
partition(x)	All drive types can be divided into multiple partitions. This setting specifies which drive partition the operating system is located on (1 = first partition).
\xxx	This part is the path (from the root of the partition) where the operating system files are located.

If you come across a question on the Enterprise exam that asks you to identify the ARC notation that would represent a particular installation, you can eliminate a couple of the answers simply by identifying the type of drive that is involved. For a SCSI drive, you can immediately eliminate all answers that begin with multi(x). For an IDE drive, you can eliminate all answers that begin with scsi(x).

Reviewing the Boot.ini switches

You can use several switches in conjunction with the entries in the Operating Systems section of the Boot.ini file. You should be familiar with the /sos, /basevideo, and maxmem switches for the Enterprise exam, because these switches are regularly used for hardware troubleshooting purposes. Table 25-2 describes the purpose of each switch. Lab 25-2 guides you through the process of adding a troubleshooting switch to your Boot.ini file.

Table 25-2	Boot.ini Switches
Switch	**Purpose**
/basevideo	Boots the computer in standard VGA mode. If you install the wrong video driver or use a video setting that your video card or monitor doesn't support, you can use this switch to recover.
/sos	Displays the name of each driver as it loads. You can use this switch to identify which driver causes a machine to fail.
/noserialmice= [COMx,y,z]	Specifies that no check is made for the specified serial pointing device(s). You can use this switch to determine whether a serial device conflict is causing the machine to fail.
/debug	Enables the kernel debugger. You can use the kernel debugger to send kernel operations information to a remote system for analysis.
/crashdebug	Enables the creation of a Memory.dmp file when a fatal error occurs. You can analyze the Memory.dmp file to determine the reason for the crash.
/nodebug	Disables the collection of debugging information, and thus speeds server performance.
Maxmem:x	Sets an upper limit on the amount of RAM NT Server can utilize. If you suspect that you have a bad memory chip, you can place it in the uppermost memory bank and see whether your problems disappear.

The Boot.ini file has file attributes of read-only and system. To edit it directly, perform the steps we describe in Lab 25-2.

Lab 25-2   Adding a Troubleshooting Switch to the Boot.ini File

1. **Remove the read-only and system attributes from the Boot.ini file.**

2. **Open the Boot.ini file with a text editor such as the Windows Notepad and add the /sos switch to the default operating system entry (see Figure 25-2).**

3. **Save your changes and close the text editor.**

4. **Reinstate the read-only and system attributes to the Boot.ini file.**

   When you reboot the system, you should see all the drivers that are being loaded during bootup.

All unanswered questions on the exam are marked as incorrect, so answer as many questions as possible in the allotted time. Some of the situational hardware troubleshooting questions are very time-consuming to read and answer. Fortunately, the MCSE exam software allows you to skip questions and come back to them later. Rather than getting hung up on a tough question, move on to the next question. You can always return to that question again if time permits.

Resolving Configuration Errors with the Registry

The list of ways in which you can misconfigure NT Server is endless. Installing the wrong device drivers and entering important system configuration settings incorrectly are just two actions that can leave your system in a sorry state. Fortunately, NT Server stores all important system configuration settings in a single place: the NT Registry. Consequently, you can fix most configuration errors by restoring the copy of the Registry that existed before the misconfiguration took place. The configuration error troubleshooting section of the Enterprise exam focuses on this premise.

You must be familiar with the NT Registry to pass the Enterprise exam. The Registry is a database that acts as a central repository for configuration information. It's organized in a hierarchical manner like an inverted tree and is composed of hives, keys, and values:

✔ Hives (also called subtrees) are collections of keys. Table 25-3 describes the contents of the five root hives in the NT Server Registry.

✔ Keys can contain other keys or values.

✔ A value represents a single configuration setting.

Table 25-3	Root Hives in the NT Registry
Root Hive	*Contents*
HKEY_LOCAL_MACHINE	Static hardware and software configuration settings.
HKEY_USERS	The preferences for every user that ever logged on to this computer.
HKEY_CURRENT_USER	The currently logged-on user's preferences.
HKEY_CLASSES_ROOT	Data relating to Object Linking and Embedding and file associations.
HKEY_CURRENT_CONFIG	The current hardware and software configuration settings. This subtree is dynamic and is copied into HKEY_LOCAL_MACHINE during shutdown.

Backing up the Registry automatically

As we discuss in Chapter 23, the Last Known Good boot-up option allows you to restore an NT Server to the same state as when it last successfully booted up. What does the Last Known Good option have to do with backing up the Registry? The Last Known Good option's operation depends on the creation of a backup copy of the portion of the Registry that holds system configuration information.

When you make changes to the configuration of an NT system, these changes are written to the current control set (HKEY_LOCAL_MACHINE\ SYSTEM\CurrentControlSet) in the Registry. If you allow NT to boot up using the default configuration, the values in the current control set are copied into a temporary repository called the clone control set (HKEY_LOCAL_MACHINE\SYSTEM\Clone). On the other hand, if you boot up using the Last Known Good configuration, the values in the Last Known Good control set (HKEY_LOCAL_MACHINE\SYSTEM\ControlSet00X) are copied into the clone control set. Either way, the settings contained in the clone control set are the ones used during boot-up.

When someone successfully logs on to the system, the values stored in the clone control set are copied into the LastKnownGood control set and the clone control set is cleared. So at any given time, an NT Server contains at least two sets of hardware configuration keys — one contained in the CurrentControlSet, and another contained in a control set to be used by the Last Known Good option. In this way, NT Server backs up important hardware configuration information without any human intervention.

All the Registry keys and values that are involved in troubleshooting configuration errors are located in the HKEY_LOCAL_MACHINE hive. If you come across a question that involves using the Registry to repair a configuration error, you can safely assume that any answer that includes another hive is incorrect.

Restoring the Registry using the Last Known Good option

You may make a hardware configuration change that renders your server unbootable. Perhaps you have installed the wrong device driver. Or maybe a rogue application or a disk failure has corrupted the Registry. In these cases, you may need to restore the Registry.

Before you try any other methods for restoring the Registry, you should choose the Last Known Good option from the boot loader menu. When you choose this option, NT Server copies the information stored in the control set of the last good boot into the CurrentControlSet hive. For more information about this procedure, see Chapter 23.

Backing up and restoring the Registry using the ERD

Given the importance of the Registry as a repository of vital system configuration information, you must back it up manually on a regular basis. You can perform this task in several ways. Many commercial backup programs do the trick. However, you can also use Windows NT itself to do the job.

If your attempt to repair a nonbooting server using the Last Known Good boot menu option ends in failure, your next course of action is to recover the server using the Emergency Repair Disk (ERD). The ERD holds copies of some of the key Registry files. You should create the ERD shortly after installation, and you should update it whenever you successfully upgrade the system. The restoration process works by overwriting defective Registry settings with those found on the ERD. You must understand how to create and use ERDs for the Enterprise exam. To learn more, see Chapter 23.

Backing up and restoring the Registry using the RegBack and RegRest utilities

The Windows NT Resource Kit includes a command-line utility called Regback.exe. RegBack allows you to back up all or parts of the NT Registry to a set of files. The Resource Kit also contains a complement to the RegBack utility called Regrest.exe. RegRest enables you to recover the Registry from the backup files that RegBack creates. You won't be tested on the syntax of the RegBack and RegRest utilities, but you should be aware of their existence.

Backing up and restoring Registry keys with the Registry Editor

You can back up individual Registry keys to a file and restore them to the Registry by using the Registry Editor itself. You must have proper rights, and the key can't be in use for the restoration to take place. Lab 25-3 guides you through this operation.

Lab 25-3	Backing Up and Restoring Registry Keys with RegEdt32

1. **Open the Registry Editor (Regedt32.exe).**

2. **Highlight the key you want to back up.**

   For this lab, choose the HKEY_CURRENT_USER\AppEvents key.

3. **Choose Registry⇨Save Key from the main menu.**

4. **Enter a filename for saving the backup, and then click Save.**

   For example, you can save the HKEY_CURRENT_USER\AppEvents key in a file named C:\Appevent.key.

5. **Highlight the key you want to restore.**

   For the example, highlight the HKEY_CURRENT_USER\AppEvents key again.

6. **Choose Registry⇨Restore from the main menu.**

7. **Enter the filename you used for backing up the selected key, and then click Open.**

   A warning dialog box appears.

8. **Click Yes to restore the key.**

Editing the Registry

In some cases, you may need to edit the contents of the Registry directly. For example, you may need to take the direct approach if you can't set a configuration setting through the Control Panel or through an application's user interface.

To edit Registry keys, you use the Registry Editor (Regedt32.exe). Figure 25-3 shows this graphical utility. You should be very familiar with the functionality of the Registry Editor for the Enterprise exam. Refer to Chapter 23 for more detailed information about the NT Registry and the Registry Editor.

Professionals only — don't try this at home! Editing the Registry directly is recommended only if no other alternative exists. Mistakes you make in the Registry can easily leave your machine in an unrepairable state. Use extreme caution!

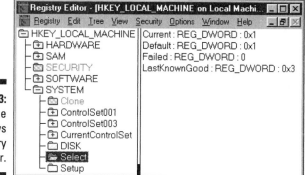

Figure 25-3:
The
Windows
NT Registry
Editor.

Prep Test

1 Which entry may be found in the Operating Systems section of the Boot.ini file?

A ○ default=multi(0)disk(0)rdisk(0)partition(1)

B ○ timeout=30

C ○ multi(0)disk(0)rdisk(1)partition(1)\WINNT="Windows NT Server 4.0"

D ○ path=c:\winnt\;c:\winnt\system32;c:\winnt\system

2 Which ARC name represents the WINNT directory on the first partition of the second SCSI hard drive with device address of 2?

A ○ scsi(1)disk(2)rdisk(0)partition(1)\WINNT

B ○ scsi(2)disk(2)rdisk(0)partition(1)\WINNT

C ○ multi(2)disk(2)rdisk(0)partition(1)\WINNT

D ○ scsi(2)disk(2)rdisk(1)partition(1)\WINNT

3 You receive the following error message when you attempt to boot up your NT Server: Which of the following statements are potential causes of this problem? (Choose all that apply.)

```
BOOT: Couldn't find NTLDR. Please insert another disk.
```

A ❏ You have a nonbootable disk in the floppy disk drive.

B ❏ The Ntldr file is missing.

C ❏ Ntdetect has failed to detect your hard drive.

D ❏ The Operating Systems entry in the Boot.ini file points to the wrong ARC location.

4 Which key serves as a temporary repository for Registry values that are collected while the operating system is loading?

A ○ HKEY_LOCAL_MACHINE\SYSTEM\Clone

B ○ HKEY_LOCAL_MACHINE\SYSTEM\CurrentControlSet

C ○ HKEY_LOCAL_MACHINE\SYSTEM\Select

D ○ HKEY_LOCAL_MACHINE\SYSTEM\ControlSet001

5 You just purchased a built-to-order system from a small value-added reseller. The NT Server Hardware Compatibility List (HCL) doesn't list your new system. Which of the following statements cannot be correct?

A ○ Microsoft has found your system to be incompatible with NT.

B ○ Microsoft Hardware Quality Labs haven't tested your system.

C ○ Your system may be compatible with NT Server.

D ○ Your reseller has tested the server for compatibility with NT Server.

6 Which boot sequence is correct?

A ○ Win32 subsystem loaded, kernel initialized, POST, hardware detected
B ○ Kernel initialized, POST, hardware detected, Win32 subsystem loaded
C ○ POST, hardware detected, kernel initialized, Win32 subsystem loaded
D ○ Hardware detected, Win32 subsystem loaded, POST, kernel initialized

7 You receive the following error when you turn on your system:

```
Windows NT could not start because the following file is missing
          or corrupt: \winnt root\system32\ntoskrnl.exe Please
          reinstall a copy of the above file.
```

Which statement doesn't provide a reasonable explanation for this error?

A ○ The Boot.ini file is missing.
B ○ The Ntoskrnl.exe file is missing.
C ○ An Operating Systems entry in the Boot.ini points to the wrong ARC location.
D ○ The Bootsect.dos file is missing or corrupt.

8 Why must the backup domain controller have the capability to connect to the primary domain controller during installation?

A ○ It needs to replicate the SAM database.
B ○ It needs to have the same SID as the PDC.
C ○ To test its network configuration.
D ○ To access installation files quicker.

9 The NT setup program doesn't detect your CD-ROM drive but the drive comes with an NT driver disk. Which of the following statements is true?

A ○ You can't use this device with NT.
B ○ The driver for your device is probably on the NT Resource Kit CD.
C ○ You can install the device driver from the vendor-provided disk.
D ○ The Advanced Device Probe option probably can detect your drive.

10 Which operating system can you not start with the NT boot loader?

A ○ DOS 6.22
B ○ Windows 95
C ○ NT Workstation 3.51
D ○ Linux

Answers

1 *C. multi(0)disk(0)rdisk(1)partition(1)\WINNT="Windows NT Server 4.0".* You find the entries listed in choices A and B in the Boot Loader section. Choice D isn't a valid Boot.ini entry. *Review "Resolving Boot Failures."*

2 *A. scsi(1)disk(2)rdisk(0)partition(1)\WINNT.* B is incorrect because the scsi() value is an ordinal number (first drive = 0, second drive = 1). C is incorrect because the multi entry is for use with non-SCSI disks, and D is incorrect because rdisk has a value of zero for SCSI disks. *Review "Resolving Boot Failures."*

3 *A and B.* C and D are incorrect because Ntldr initiates Ntdetect and reads the Boot.ini file. Neither of these actions could take place if the Ntldr file could not be found and executed first. *Review "Resolving Boot Failures."*

4 *A. HKEY_LOCAL_MACHINE\SYSTEM\Clone.* The hive in choice B holds the currently active control set. The hive in choice C holds keys that specify the functions of all the control sets, and the hive in choice D is one of two to four control sets that are stored in the Registry. *Review "Resolving Configuration Errors with the Registry."*

5 *A. Microsoft has found your system to be incompatible with NT.* Such a finding would appear in the HCL. *Review "Troubleshooting Installation Errors."*

6 *C. POST, hardware detected, kernel initialized, Win32 subsystem loaded.* The Power-On Self Test occurs first, hardware detection occurs second, kernel initialization occurs third, and Win32 subsystem loading occurs fourth. *Review "Resolving Boot Failures."*

7 *D. The Bootsect.dos file is missing or corrupt.* Bootsect.dos is only used for non-NT boots. *Review "Resolving Boot Failures."*

8 *A. It needs to replicate the SAM database.* Choice B is incorrect because all NT Servers must have unique Server IDs. Choice C is incorrect because network connectivity is tested earlier in the installation. Choice D is incorrect because the NT installation files are all contained on the installation media. *Review "Troubleshooting Installation Errors."*

9 *C. You can install the device driver from the vender-provided disk.* The vendor-supplied device driver, if written specifically for NT, should work. *Review "Troubleshooting Installation Errors."*

10 *D. Linux.* The Windows NT boot loader can only start Microsoft operating systems. *Review "Resolving Boot Failures."*

Part IX
The Part of Tens

The 5th Wave · By Rich Tennant

ON A BET, HOWIE LENDELMAN, THE OFFICE TINKERER, TRIES LINKING HIS CALCULATOR INTO THE WORKGROUP'S NETWORK FILE SERVER.

HE'S GETTING FILES! HE'S GETTING FILES!

In this part . . .

In Part IX, we provide top-ten lists with information that can help you pass the Enterprise exam. We list the top ten resources that are certain to help you pass the exam and become an MCSE. We also offer ten nuggets of advice gathered from veteran exam takers to make your Enterprise exam experience more enjoyable, and of course, to help you pass the exam. Turn to Part IX for our favorite exam day tips, a great list of online resources for getting extra information, up-to-date exam specifics, and moral support.

Chapter 26

Ten Terrific Exam Day Tips

In This Chapter

▶ Practicing with NT before the exam

▶ Staying focused

▶ Pacing yourself

▶ Dumping your brain

▶ Keeping your cool

*A*s with any new challenge, having some insight and advice from those who have already taken the Enterprise exam is helpful. In this chapter, we offer ten suggestions for increasing the likelihood that your exam experience is a successful one.

Don't Memorize the Practice Exams

Many MCSE certification candidates make the mistake of memorizing the answers to the practice exams. Because the chances of the practice questions being on the actual exam are pretty slim, this technique won't help you at all. If you miss a question on the practice exam, don't just look up the answer and commit it to your memory. Try to figure out which concept the question tests and then study that concept thoroughly.

Work with the Software

Passing an MCSE exam without having any hands-on experience with Windows NT is extremely difficult. Take the time to sit down and work with the software. Having access to a network is extremely helpful when you're preparing for the Enterprise exam. If the resources are available, you may want to set up your own NT-based LAN. Many people who have passed the Enterprise exam say that they found the process of setting up such a LAN extremely helpful.

Beware of "Meaning-Changing" Words

Many questions on the MCSE certification exams have one or more "meaning-changing" words. These words are so important to your understanding of the question that if you miss one, you will surely answer incorrectly. Look out for "meaning changing" words such as *always, never,* and *not,* as in the following question: "Which of the following network protocols is *not* supported by NT Server?" The best way to avoid falling victim to this mistake is to read the questions very carefully.

Eliminate Potential Distractions

You need to focus all your attention on the exam. Distractions during the exam can eat up the most valuable asset you have — your time. Sources of distractions include pagers, cell phones, and watch alarms. These distractions can increase your chance of failure, so make an effort to eliminate them. For example, leave your pager at home. You don't want to waste valuable time digging it out and turning it off if someone pages you during the Enterprise exam.

Watch the Clock

Pace yourself. You have 90 minutes to answer 51 questions. So, you have an average of approximately one minute and 45 seconds per question. If you find that you're spending several minutes on a question, mark it and come back to it later if you have the time. If you allow yourself to get hung up on more than a few questions, you will almost certainly run out of time.

Prioritize Questions

Your time is limited and unanswered questions are marked as incorrect, so you should answer as many questions as you possibly can. Because you can answer short questions relatively quickly, you should give them top priority. Longer questions (such as those involving multiple scenarios) take the most time to answer; therefore, you should leave them for last. Use the marking feature of the MCSE exam software to aid you in your prioritization efforts. Mark the long questions and return to them only after you answer all the shorter questions.

Don't Click the Start Button until You're Ready

The timer in the MCSE exam software doesn't begin until you click the Start button. Before you click that button, take a few moments to compose yourself. Get comfortable and relax. Perform a "brain dump" by writing some of the key concepts that you want to remember on your pieces of scratch paper. You have absolutely no reason to begin the exam before you're ready.

Stay Calm

You can easily become frustrated when you run into a series of tough questions during the MCSE exams. The more frustrated and worked up you get, the worse you will do. In your anger, you may begin to make silly mistakes that you wouldn't make if you had only kept your wits. If you find yourself in such a flustered state, don't allow yourself to panic. Stop for a moment. Take a deep breath, relax, and compose yourself before continuing.

Use the Process of Elimination

You can use the multiple-choice process of elimination that you learned in grade school to help you with some of the MCSE exam questions. In case you've forgotten how the process of elimination works, it's based on the premise that half the answers to a multiple choice question are obviously wrong and you can immediately eliminate them, leaving a couple of likely candidates. You then choose which of the likely candidates you believe to be the better answer. By eliminating the answers that are obviously wrong, you reduce the complexity of the problem and double the likelihood of answering the question correctly.

Get Back on the Horse

The advantage (or disadvantage, depending on your point of view) of having computerized exams is that you know immediately after the exam ends whether you have passed. If you fail the exam, don't despair. You aren't alone. The majority of MCSE exams end in failure.

You will receive a score report that lists your areas of strength and weakness. Use this report to develop a new study plan that emphasizes the concepts in which you performed poorly. After studying these concepts, take the exam again. Remember that you won't be taking the same exam again. You receive different questions each time that you take the exam.

Chapter 27

Ten MCSE Certification Resources

In This Chapter

▶ Utilizing Internet-based MCSE resources

▶ Employing other MCSE resources

*N*umerous resources are available to assist you in your pursuit of MCSE certification. In this chapter, we describe resources of all types. Some of these resources are strictly Internet-based, while others can be utilized when you're disconnected.

Internet-Based Resources

Some of the best MCSE resources are located on the Internet. The advantages of this medium include its widespread availability, its capability to link professionals from around the world, and its timeliness. In the following sections, we describe a few of our favorite Internet-based MCSE resources.

Mailing lists

When you subscribe to a mailing list, you receive messages from other members of the list pertaining to its subject. You also can send messages to the list server, which distributes your message to the rest of the mailing list's members. If you join an active mailing list, you may receive several dozen messages daily.

Two popular MCSE mailing lists are administered by CompuNotes and Sunbelt Software Distribution. To subscribe to the CompuNotes mailing list, send a message to ListServer@compunotes.com with the following phrase in the body:

```
subscribe MCSE your first name your last name
```

To subscribe to the Sunbelt mailing list, fill out the form found on Sunbelt's Web site (www.ntsoftdist.com).

Online training

MCSE training courses are available online from the Free Academy of Career Training (www.freeacademy.london.on.ca) and Scholars.com (www.scholars.com). The Free Academy of Career Training (FACT) is a Canadian-based site that offers free technical courses. To enroll, fill out the form at the FACT Web site. Scholars.com is a Microsoft Authorized Technical Education Center and requires the payment of tuition.

Forums and message boards

Forums or message boards are analogous to online bulletin boards and are similar in nature to newsgroups. You can read others' posts as well as create your own. Two popular MCSE-focused forums are hosted by *Microsoft Certified Professional Magazine* (www.mpcmag.com) and Saluki.com, Inc. (www.saluki.com). These forums are great places for asking questions, answering others' questions, or simply exchanging information with other MCSE candidates.

Online exams and exam notes

Numerous Web sites offer notes, tips, and tricks from folks who have already taken the NT Server in the Enterprise exam. The following sites offer a great way to get the inside scoop on the contents and structure of the actual exam from people who have already been there:

- www.masontech.clara.net/7068.htm
- www.asb.com/usr/hollwrth/mcse/enterprise.htm
- www.saluki.com/mcp/nts40ent.htm
- home.att.net/~tpgugliotta/enterprise.htm
- www.hal-pc.org/~pchou/enterprise.html
- www.shine1.com/pdeboer.mcse/Test_enterprise.htm

You can also test your knowledge by checking out Kevin W. Hammond's "How Prepared Are You?" NT in the Enterprise exam (www.mcs.net/~hammond/exam/70_68/default.htm) and the Test Free Web site (www.testfree.com). Both of these sites offer free online MCSE exams.

Usenet newsgroups

Several Usenet newsgroups are dedicated to various NT Server topics, and one newsgroup focuses on issues related to MCSE certification (`comp.professional.mcse`). Usenet newsgroups enable you to read old posts, reply to posts, and post new topics. Like forums, they are great places for getting answers to your questions as well as sharing your expertise with other people.

Here are some NT Server newsgroups that contain information helpful to anyone taking the NT Server in the Enterprise exam:

- ✔ `comp.os.ms-windows.nt.networking`
- ✔ `comp.os.ms-windows.nt.admin.misc`
- ✔ `comp.os.ms-windows.nt.admin.security`
- ✔ `comp.os.ms-windows.nt.setup.hardware`
- ✔ `comp.os.ms-windows.nt.setup.misc`
- ✔ `comp.os.ms-windows.nt.misc`

Web sites

Literally dozens of Web sites are available on the Internet that focus on MCSE certification. Many of these sites contain certification information, exam tips and tricks, and links to other MCSE resources. For example, check out the Hard Core MCSE Web site (`www.hardcoremcse.com`), which contains MCSE sample questions, exam tips, and links to other MCSE-related Web sites. Also, take a look at The MCSE Wizard (`people.a2000.nl/denneman/index.html`), which contains links to MCSE exam-related tools, newsgroups, information, and magazines. You can find other Web sites concentrating on MCSE certification by entering such keywords as *MCSE, certification,* and *exam* into a search engine such as Yahoo! (`www.yahoo.com`), Lycos (`www.lycos.com`), or Alta Vista (`www.altavista.digital.com`).

Online magazines

A few online magazines serve the NT community. The following e-zines, as they are sometimes called, contain technical articles about NT Server that can provide valuable insight to anyone who is about to take the NT Server in the Enterprise exam:

- ✔ ENT Online (`www.entmag.com`)
- ✔ NT! NT! (`www.sdwntug.org/ntnt`)

ENT Online is the Internet-based version of *ENT Magazine,* which focuses its content on the use of NT as an enterprise platform and is available free to qualified professionals. NT! NT! is published by the San Diego County Windows NT User Group and contains informative articles about the Microsoft BackOffice product suite.

Other MCSE Resources

Not all MCSE resources are Internet-based. In the following sections, we describe resources that you can use in your pursuit of MCSE certification when you're disconnected.

Practice exam software

Various companies sell software programs that simulate the MCSE exams. These practice exams are probably the best way for you to familiarize yourself with the content, style, and structure of the MCSE exams. They come highly recommended by people who have successfully passed using these programs as a guide. Three prominent vendors of MCSE practice exam software are

- ✔ VFX Technologies (www.vfxtech.com)
- ✔ Cyber Pass, Inc. (www.certify.com)
- ✔ PC Age, Inc. (www.pcage.com)

Flashcards

Flashcards is a software program developed by StarText Computing Services Ltd. As the name implies, Flashcards is a study aid that helps students prepare for the MCSE exams by subjecting them to memory drills of MCSE exam material. Flashcards is a great way to memorize the large amount of information that you need to know in order to pass the exams. For more information on Flashcards, browse to www.flashcards.com or call 403-244-9636.

User groups

Joining a user group dedicated to Windows NT is a great way to learn more about the operating system as well as to meet other professionals who are pursuing MCSE certification. To find the Windows NT user group nearest to you, visit the Windows User Group Network Web site (www.wugnet.com), attend a local computer fair, or ask your colleagues. We find our local NT user groups to be great sources of NT and MCSE certification information.

Part X
Appendixes

The 5th Wave — By Rich Tennant

"WE SORT OF HAVE OUR OWN WAY OF PREDICTING NETWORK PROBLEMS."

In this part . . .

The name of this part may be "Appendixes," but we wouldn't be surprised if you turned here first for some real juicy (and useful) stuff. Included is a sample exam such as you'll see come test time — around 50 questions to test your Windows NT in the Enterprise knowledge. You'll also find an appendix telling you about the contents of the companion CD — which includes demo tests, a collection of test tips from the book, and an incredibly cool game.

Appendix A

Practice Exam

• •

Practice Exam Rules

▶ 90 minutes

▶ 52 questions

▶ No peeking anywhere else in the book while you take the practice exam

• •

*W*e designed the following practice exam to show you what you can expect on the NT Server 4.0 in the Enterprise exam. Passing scores for Microsoft certification exams typically fall somewhere in the range from 55 percent to 80 percent. For this practice exam, shoot for at least 40 correct answers.

Read each question carefully. Although some questions may seem similar, they have slightly different wording, variations on themes, or different answers.

To a great extent, your success on a Microsoft exam depends on carefully considering what each question asks as well as the possible solutions. Also remember that a question may have more than one correct answer, so get used to choosing all that apply. Good luck!

Practice Exam

1 What is the maximum recommended number of accounts that a directory services database can contain?

A ○ 10,000

B ○ 20,000

C ○ 30,000

D ○ 40,000

2 How many trust relationships must exist in a complete trust model with seven domains?

A ○ 42

B ○ 49

C ○ 70

D ○ 90

3 Your company has a moderate-sized network that requires centralized administration of accounts. You want to use a model that allows user and group administration to be performed by one domain, while resources are controlled by the domains that host them. Which domain model should you use?

A ○ Single domain

B ○ Master domain

C ○ Multiple master domain

D ○ Complete trust domain

4 The insurance company you work for has several branch offices that are located in the same city. Each branch wants to control its own local resources, and security isn't an issue. You must implement a domain model for this company.

Required results:

- You must be able to administer the network from any location.

- Users from each location must be able to access the servers and resources at each of the other locations.

Desired (optional) results:

- Users and resources should be grouped by branch location.

- The model should be scalable to meet the expansion of the company.

The proposed solution involves the use of a complete trust model. Which results does the proposed solution produce?

A ○ The solution produces the required results and both of the optional desired results.

B ○ The solution produces the required results, but only one of the optional desired results.

C ○ The solution produces the required result, but none of the optional desired results.

D ○ The solution doesn't produce the required results.

5 Which option does the Change log control?

A ○ Full synchronization

B ○ Partial synchronization

C ○ Whether full or partial synchronization occurs

D ○ Whether full or partial backup occurs

6 What is the default size of the change log?

A ○ 32KB

B ○ 64KB

C ○ 128KB

D ○ 4MB

7 Which application do you use to create trust relationships?

A ○ Server Manager

B ○ Network Administrator

C ○ Trust Manager

D ○ User Manager for Domains

8 In a multiple master domain, with three master domains and 15 resource domains, how many trusts do you need to establish?

A ○ 18

B ○ 25

C ○ 51

D ○ 62

9 You set up a one-way trust with Domain A as the trusting domain and Domain B as the trusted domain. A user from Domain A knows this trust relationship exists, and tries to access resources on Domain B. The user fails to access anything on Domain B. Why?

A ○ The user doesn't have an account on Domain B.

B ○ The user logged directly on to Domain B, and therefore can't enjoy the trust between the two domains. Have the user log on to Domain A first.

C ○ Domain A isn't trusted.

D ○ Domain B isn't trusted.

10 Your network uses NWLink as its transport protocol. You want to view its configuration information. Which command do you type at the command prompt to view this information?

A ○ IPCONFIG

B ○ IPXROUTE CONFIG

C ○ NWLINK CONFIG

D ○ NWLINK /c

11 You decide to use the Registry Editor to troubleshoot software problems in Windows NT Server 4.0. After you start RegEdit, which Registry subtree do you use?

A ○ HKEY_CURRENT_CONFIG

B ○ HKEY_USERS

C ○ HKEY_CURRENT_DATA

D ○ HKEY_LOCAL_MACHINE

12 What are the four main phases in the Windows NT boot process?

A ○ Initial, Boot, Kernel, Logon
B ○ Initial, Boot, User, Logon
C ○ Initial, Boot, Load, Logon
D ○ Boot, Real, Kernel, Logon

13 You are having problems with Windows NT. You decide to check which files are being loaded during the boot and load sequences. Which program can you use to help identify missing drivers and services?

A ○ Crashdump
B ○ WinDmp
C ○ Kernel Debugger
D ○ DumpExam

14 Account information is stored in a file that contains information on all users, groups, and permissions in a domain. What's the name of this file?

A ○ SAM
B ○ LMHOSTS
C ○ User.dat
D ○ System.dat

15 You have installed TCP/IP, and you decide to have IP addresses assigned to computers on your network. Which tool do you use for this task?

A ○ DNS
B ○ DHCP
C ○ DLC
D ○ DCHP

16 You have 255 users connected to your RAS server, and a Macintosh computer attempts to make the 256th simultaneous connection by using AppleTalk. Why can't this computer connect?

A ○ RAS only supports 255 simultaneous connections.
B ○ The RAS server doesn't have AppleTalk installed.
C ○ RAS doesn't support AppleTalk.
D ○ The user doesn't have an account on the system.

17 What resolves host names to IP addresses?

A ○ DHCP
B ○ DNS
C ○ WINS
D ○ DMB

18 Your company has just merged with a company that uses NetWare. Your 50 Windows NT Workstations now need to access the new NetWare server. What do you need to install on your NT server?

A ○ Gateway Services for NetWare

B ○ Client Services for NetWare

C ○ Server Service for NetWare

D ○ Proxy Service for NetWare

19 What information do you need for printing to a TCP/IP print device?

A ○ Printer name

B ○ IP address

C ○ Both the printer name and the IP address

D ○ None of the above

20 A computer on a network can have different roles. Which role allows a computer to contain a list of all resources in a domain? Choose the most appropriate answer.

A ○ PDC

B ○ BDC

C ○ Master browser

D ○ Master domain browser

21 Synchronization between servers is causing considerable traffic on your network. Which settings should you change in the PDC's Registry to increase performance?

A ○ Decrease the value of the Pulse setting, and increase the value of PulseConcurrency.

B ○ Increase the value of the Pulse setting, and decrease the value of PulseConcurrency.

C ○ Increase the value of the Pulse setting, and increase the value of PulseConcurrency.

D ○ Decrease the value of the Pulse setting, and decrease the value of PulseConcurrency.

22 Your system dual boots between Windows NT and DOS. When you try booting to DOS, you find it doesn't load. Which boot file should you check first to solve this problem?

A ○ Boot.ini

B ○ Bootsect.dos

C ○ Ntoskml.dos

D ○ Ntldr

23 During installation, on which partition does Windows NT store its system files? Choose the best answer.

A ○ Primary partition

B ○ Extended partition

C ○ Boot partition

D ○ System partition

24 In which of the following choices must the process voluntarily give up the processor to the scheduler?

A ○ Cooperative multitasking

B ○ Preemptive multitasking

C ○ Symmetric multiprocessing

D ○ Asymmetric multiprocessing

25 Your company is implementing a new WAN with domains in New York, Boston, Chicago, Toronto, and London, Ontario. Accounts are to be maintained by the chief offices in each country (New York and Toronto), and resources are regularly accessed from the Boston, Chicago, and London domains. Trusts have yet to be established among any of these domains.

Required results:

- Allow the domains with user accounts access to each other, so that account information can be shared between domains.

- Allow the user domains of New York and Toronto access to resources in all other domains.

Desired (optional) results:

- The solution should be scalable to meet with growth of the company.

- The complexity of trust relationships should be minimal.

The proposed solution involves the use of a multiple master domain model. You must set up two one-way trusts between New York and Toronto. You also must set up one-way trusts between resource domains to each of the user domains.

Which results does the proposed solution produce?

A ○ The solution produces the required results and both of the optional desired results.

B ○ The solution produces the required results, but only one of the optional desired results.

C ○ The solution produces the required results, but none of the optional desired results.

D ○ The solution doesn't produce the required results.

26 Marni needs access to a folder called Test on a server named Tester. You grant her permissions to this share, but she complains that she still can't access it. What is the most likely reason?

A ○ The user's access token has been corrupted.

B ○ The new permissions don't take effect until the next time you start the server.

C ○ The new permissions don't take effect until the next time the user logs on.

D ○ None of the above.

27 Darren is a member of the Sales and Marketing groups, and requires access to a shared folder. The folder's ACL allows Full Access. Darren's user account allows Read and Write, the Sales group has No Access, and the Marketing group has Change permissions. Which access does Darren have to the share?

A ○ Read and Write

B ○ Full Access

C ○ Change

D ○ No Access

28 The Administrator account is a known account on Windows NT. Every NT Server is installed with this account present. You want to safeguard your server from would-be hackers who may try to use this account to get into your system. How can you do this?

A ○ In User Manager for Domains, delete the Administrator account.

B ○ In User Manager for Domains, rename the Administrator account.

C ○ In User Manager for Domains, disable the Administrator account.

D ○ Nothing. Windows NT doesn't allow deletion, disabling, or renaming of the Administrator account.

29 You have a network consisting of 30,000 users, 30,000 computers, and 400 groups. What is the minimum number of user domains that you must implement in a multiple master domain?

A ○ 1

B ○ 2

C ○ 3

D ○ 4

30 The PDC in Domain A serves a large number of users, but is slower than the computer in Domain B, which serves a smaller number of users. You decide to switch the PDC in Domain A to Domain B, and the PDC in Domain B to Domain A. Now users in both domains complain that they can't access the network. What is the most likely reason for this problem?

A ○ You forgot to change the domain names in each of the servers when you switched them.

B ○ You forgot to change the workgroup names in each of the servers when you switched them.

C ○ You forgot to change the SIDs in each of the servers when you switched them.

D ○ You can't move a PDC from one domain to another without reinstalling Windows NT.

31 Which statement is true?

A ○ The HOST file maps host names to IP addresses, whereas LMHOSTS maps IP addresses to NetBIOS names.

B ○ The HOST file maps IP addresses to NetBIOS names, whereas LMHOSTS maps host names to IP addresses.

C ○ The HOST file maps host names to NetBIOS names, whereas LMHOSTS maps NetBIOS names to host names.

D ○ The HOST file maps host names to WINS, whereas LMHOSTS maps host names to IP addresses.

32 Two domains are connected by a Windows NT Server that acts as a router. Both domains use TCP/IP, and you want the DHCP server in the one domain to issue IP addresses to clients in both domains. What must you install on the router for clients in both domains to acquire IP addresses from the DHCP server?

A ○ RIP for IP

B ○ DLC

C ○ DHCP Relay Agent

D ○ Proxy server

33 Which application do you use to create an emergency repair disk?

A ○ ERD

B ○ RDISK

C ○ Dr. Watson

D ○ EMU

34 Which protocol is supported by both the dial-in and dial-out capabilities of RAS?

A ○ PGP

B ○ PPP

C ○ SLIP

D ○ DLC

35 Which file stores user profiles?

A ○ Ntuser.dat

B ○ User.dat

C ○ System.dat

D ○ Ntconfig.pol

36 You have added numerous Macintosh clients to your network. Which file system must you have on your NT Server's hard disk if these clients are to have access to it?

A ○ FAT

B ○ NTFS

C ○ HPFS

D ○ CDFS

37 You have installed IIS on your server, and you want to implement the password authentication that has the highest level of security. Which password authentication option should you choose?

A ○ Basic

B ○ Clear Text

C ○ Allow Anonymous

D ○ Challenge/Response

38 Of the following choices, which is not a quality of DNS?

A ○ Maps IP addresses to fully qualified domain names (FQDNs).

B ○ Flat database namespace.

C ○ Requires manual configuration.

D ○ Hosts can have multiple aliases.

39 Which application do you use to promote a BDC to a PDC on your network?

A ○ Network Administrator

B ○ Server Manager

C ○ Windows NT Explorer

D ○ Disk Administrator

40 You set up directory replication between a PDC and a BDC. Both servers use FAT partitions, and directory replication fails. Why?

A ○ The export directory must be on an NTFS partition for replication to work.

B ○ The import directory must be on an NTFS partition for replication to work.

C ○ The export and import directories must be on NTFS partitions for replication to work.

D ○ Replication can only occur between two PDCs or two BDCs.

41 You notice that the network's performance is slowing considerably. You discover that performance degrades during times when users log on. Which course of action offers the most effective means for improving performance?

A ○ Install more RAM on the server.

B ○ Install a faster processor on the server.

C ○ Add a BDC to the domain.

D ○ Add another PDC to the domain.

42 Darren is a member of the Sales and Marketing groups, and requires access to a shared folder. The folder's ACL allows Read and Execute. Darren's user account allows Read and Write, the Sales group has Delete, and the Marketing group has Read and Write permissions. What access does Darren have to the share?

A ○ Read and Write

B ○ Read and Execute

C ○ Change

D ○ Delete

43 You work for a large company with domains in New York, Boston, and Chicago. The New York domain contains the master account database. The Boston domain needs to work with electronic documents from the New York office. New York already trusts users, and has set up a folder for them to work from called \Bostwork on a server named Master.

Required result: Users from the Boston domain must have full access to the \Master\Bostwork share.

Desired (optional) results:

- Users of the \Master\Bostwork share should be grouped by location.

- Administration over these users should be as simple as possible.

Proposed solution:

- Create a global group in the Boston domain called BMaster, and add users needing access to the share to this group.

- Create a global group named NMaster in the New York domain, and add the global group Boston\BMaster to it.

- Give NMaster Full Control over the \Master\Bostwork share.

Which results does the proposed solution produce?

A ○ The solution produces the required result and both of the optional desired results.

B ○ The solution produces the required result, but only one of the optional desired results.

C ○ The solution produces the required result, but none of the optional desired results.

D ○ The solution doesn't produce the required result.

44 You want to use RAID to get the best possible disk reads and writes to increase performance. Which RAID level should you use?

A ○ RAID Level 0
B ○ RAID Level 1
C ○ RAID Level 4
D ○ RAID Level 5

45 In which of the following choices are all processes, including those of the operating system, shared equally among all processors?

A ○ Cooperative multitasking
B ○ Preemptive multitasking
C ○ Symmetric multiprocessing
D ○ Asymmetric multiprocessing

46 You attempt to check your server's hard drive with Performance Monitor, but you can't. What must you run to enable these counters?

A ○ PERFMON
B ○ DISKPERF
C ○ DISKMON
D ○ RDISK

47 You create a network share in Windows NT. What permissions does the Everyone group have to this share by default?

A ○ No Access
B ○ Read
C ○ Change
D ○ Full Control

48 You want to create a baseline with Performance Monitor. Which view mode should you use for this task?

A ○ Report
B ○ Chart
C ○ Log
D ○ Numeric

49 You want to decrease network traffic while synchronizing over a slow WAN link between your New York and Chicago offices. Which setting must you modify?

A ○ NetLogon idle value
B ○ Replication Governor Reg_Dword value
C ○ Sync Pulse Reg.Class value
D ○ Current Control Set Replication value

50 In an election, which device will always be the domain master browser by default?

A ○ PDC
B ○ BDC
C ○ Member server
D ○ Stand-alone server

51 On which operating system can global groups reside?

A ○ Windows 95
B ○ Windows NT Workstation
C ○ Windows NT stand-alone servers
D ○ Windows NT domain controllers

52 Which statement is true?

A ○ BDCs synchronize simultaneously.
B ○ BDCs synchronize by order of their SIDs.
C ○ BDCs synchronize by alphabetical order of their NetBIOS names.
D ○ BDCs synchronize by order of their IP addresses.

Answers

1 *D. 40,000.* The maximum recommended number of accounts that a directory services database can contain is 40,000 accounts. *Objective: Plan the implementation of a directory services architecture (Chapter 3).*

2 *A. 42.* A complete trust model with seven domains requires 42 trust relationships. You calculate this value by using the following formula:

$$T = N \times (N - 1)$$

where T is the number of trusts, and N is the number of domains. In the case of seven domains, this equation is $7 \times (7 - 1)$, which equals 42. *Objective: Plan the implementation of a directory services architecture (Chapter 4).*

3 *B. Master Domain.* The master domain model has centralized account administration performed at the master domain, while the resource domain controls resources. *Objective: Plan the implementation of a directory services architecture (Chapter 3).*

4 *A. Solution produces the required results and both of the optional results.* The complete trust model is suitable for any size organization that doesn't require centralized administration. It allows for administration to take place from any server on the network. You can group users and resources by location or department, and users can access any server or resource. This model meets the requirements for this situation. *Objective: Plan the implementation of a directory services architecture (Chapter 3).*

5 *C. Whether full or partial synchronization occurs.* The change log controls whether full or partial synchronization occurs. *Objective: Configure Windows NT core services (Chapter 6).*

6 *C. 128KB.* The default size of the change log is 128KB. *Objective: Configure Windows NT core services (Chapter 6).*

7 *D. User Manager for Domains.* You use User Manager for Domains for creating trusts. *Objective: Plan the implementation of a directory services architecture (Chapter 4).*

8 *C. 51.* You must establish 51 trusts. You calculate this value by using the following formula:

$$T = M \times (M - 1) + (R \times M)$$

Where M is the number of master domains, R is the number of resource domains, and T is the number of trust relationships. If you have three master domains and 15 resource domains, this equation is $3 \times (3 - 1) + (3 \times 15)$, which equals 51. *Objective: Plan the implementation of a directory services architecture (Chapter 4).*

9 *C. Domain A isn't trusted by Domain B.* You set up a one-way trust, and Domain B is the only domain trusted to access resources from the other domain. *Objective: Manage user and group accounts (Chapter 4).*

10 *B. IPXROUTE CONFIG.* To view configuration information on NWLink, type IPXROUTE CONFIG from the command prompt. *Objective: Configure protocols and protocol bindings (Chapter 16).*

11 *D. HKEY_LOCAL_MACHINE.* You can solve software problems by using the HKEY_LOCAL_MACHINE Registry subtree. *Objective: Choose the appropriate course of action to resolve configuration errors (Chapter 23).*

12 *A. Initial, Boot, Kernel, and Logon.* The four main phases of the boot process are Initial, Boot, Kernel, and Logon. *Objective: Choose the appropriate course of action to resolve boot failures (Chapter 23).*

13 *C. Kernel Debugger.* You use Kernel Debugger to help identify drivers and services that are missing from the boot and load sequences. *Objective: Choose the appropriate course of action to resolve boot failures (Chapter 23).*

14 *A. SAM.* Account information is stored in the SAM (Security Accounts Manager) file. *Objective: Manage user and group accounts (Chapter 10).*

15 *B. DHCP.* You use DHCP (Dynamic Host Configuration Protocol) to assign IP addresses to computers. *Objective: Configure protocols and protocol bindings (Chapter 8).*

16 *C. RAS doesn't support the AppleTalk protocol.* AppleTalk, the protocol used by Macintosh computers, isn't supported by RAS. *Objective: Install and configure Remote Access Services (Chapters 19 and 20).*

17 *B. DNS.* DNS (Domain Name Services) resolves host names to IP addresses. *Objective: Install and configure Internet services (Chapter 18).*

18 *A. Gateway Services for NetWare.* Gateway Services for NetWare (GSNW) enables Windows NT Workstations to access NetWare server resources. *Objective: Choose the appropriate course of action to resolve connectivity problems (Chapter 16).*

19 *C. IP address and printer's name.* You must have both the IP address and the printer's name when printing to a TCP/IP printer. *Objective: Configure printers (Chapter 7).*

20 *C. Master browser.* The master browser contains a list of all resources in a domain. A computer can have many roles on a network. Although a computer acting as a PDC will always be master browser, it isn't the fact that it's a PDC that allows it to hold the list. It is the computer's role as a master browser that allows it to contain a list of all resources in a domain. *Objective: Configure NT Server core services (Chapter 6).*

21 *B. Increase the value of the Pulse setting, and decrease the value of PulseConcurrency.* To improve performance and decrease traffic caused by synchronization, increase the value of the Pulse setting, and decrease the value of PulseConcurrency. *Objective: Configure Windows NT Server core services (Chapter 6).*

22 *B. Bootsect.dos.* If you're having problems dual booting to DOS, the first boot file to check is Bootsect.dos. *Objective: Choose the appropriate course of action to take to resolve boot failures (Chapter 23).*

23 *C. Boot partition.* During installation, Windows NT stores its system files on the boot partition. *Objective: Install Windows NT Server to perform various server roles (Chapter 5).*

24 *A. Cooperative multitasking.* In cooperative multitasking, the process must voluntarily give up the processor to the scheduler. If the process doesn't give up the processor, the computer locks up. *Objective: Choose the appropriate course of action to take to resolve configuration errors (Chapter 25).*

25 *A. The solution produces the required results and both of the optional desired results.* The fact that accounts are to be maintained in the chief offices of each country indicates that you need to use a multiple master domain model. Each master domain requires two one-way trusts, while each resource domain requires a one-way trust to the master domains. As such, the proposed solution produces all the required and desired results. *Objective: Plan the implementation of a directory services architecture (Chapters 3, 4).*

26 *C. The new permissions don't take effect until the next time the user logs on.* Changes to a user or group account don't appear to users who are currently logged on. Users must log off and then log back on for changes to the account to take effect. *Objective: Manage user and group accounts (Chapter 12).*

27 *D. No Access.* The No Access setting overrides any other permissions that a user may have. *Objective: Manage user and group accounts (Chapter 12).*

28 *B. In User Manager for Domains, rename the Administrator account.* Windows NT doesn't allow you to delete or disable the Administrator account, but you can rename it. *Objective: Manage user and group accounts (Chapter 10).*

29 *B. 2.* One user domain can consist of 26,000 user accounts, 26,000 computer accounts, and 250 groups. For the amount specified in this question, you need to implement at least two user domains. *Objective: Plan the implementation of a directory services architecture (Chapter 3).*

30 *D. You can't move a PDC from one domain to another unless you reinstall NT.* The Security Identifier is created on the server when you install NT. The SID defines the domain, and you can't change this SID. Consequently, you can't move a PDC from one domain to another without reinstalling NT. *Objective: Configure Windows NT Server core services (Chapter 6).*

31 *A. The HOST file maps host names to IP addresses, while LMHOSTS maps IP addresses to NetBIOS names.* The HOST file is used to map host names to IP addresses, while LMHOSTS maps IP addresses to NetBIOS names. *Objective: Choose a protocol for various situations (Chapter 9).*

32 *C. DHCP Relay Agent.* DHCP Relay Agent is used to obtain IP addresses for clients that are separated (on different segments or domains) from the DHCP server. *Objective: Choose a protocol for various situations (Chapter 8).*

33 *B. RDISK.* You use RDISK to create an emergency repair disk. *Objective: Choose the appropriate course of action to take to resolve boot failures (Chapter 23).*

34 *B. PPP.* PPP is supported by both the dial-in and dial-out capabilities of RAS. *Objective: Choose the appropriate course of action to take to resolve RAS problems (Chapter 19).*

35 *A. Ntuser.dat.* Ntuser.dat stores user profiles. *Objective: Create and manage policies and profiles for various situations (Chapter 13).*

36 *B. NTFS.* If Macintosh clients are to access a hard disk on an NT Server, the disk must be formatted in NTFS. *Objective: Configure a Windows NT Server computer for various types of client computers (Chapter 17).*

37 *D. Challenge/Response.* Of the password authentication schemes, Challenge/Response offers the greatest level of security. *Objective: Manage user and group accounts (Chapter 12).*

38 *B. Flat database namespace.* A flat database namespace is not a quality of DNS but of WINS. *Objective: Choose a protocol for various situations (Chapter 9).*

39 *B. Server Manager.* You use Server Manager to promote BDCs to PDCs. *Objective: Install Windows NT Server to perform various server roles (Chapter 6).*

40 *A. The export directory must be on an NTFS partition for replication to work.* For replication to work, the export directory must be on an NTFS partition. *Objective: Configure Windows NT Server core services (Chapter 6).*

41 *C. Add a BDC to the domain.* Because performance degrades during logon times, installing a BDC can balance the load of users logging on to the network. You can't install another PDC, because you can have only one per domain. *Objective: Install Windows NT Server to perform various server roles (Chapter 6).*

42 *C. Change.* Permissions to a share are cumulative. To determine which access the user has, you add the permissions from each group the user is a member of, the user's account, and the object's ACL. Because Change consists of Read, Write, Execute, and Delete, the user's permission set is Change. *Objective: Manage disk resources (Chapter 12).*

43 D. *The solution doesn't produce the required result.* The solution doesn't meet the required result because it places one global group inside of another global group. Global groups can only contain users; they can't contain other groups (global or local). *Objective: Manage user and group accounts (Chapter 11).*

44 A. *RAID Level 0.* RAID Level 0, disk striping without parity, provides performance but no fault tolerance. *Objective: Plan the disk drive configuration for various requirements (Chapter 24).*

45 C. *Symmetric multiprocessing.* In symmetric multiprocessing, all processors are shared equally among all processes, including those of the operating system. *Objective: Choose the appropriate course of action to take to resolve configuration errors (Chapter 25).*

46 B. *DISKPERF.* To enable the disk counters for Performance Monitor, you need to run DISKPERF. To start the counters, run DISKPERF –y. To deactivate the counters, run DISKPERF –n. *Objective: Monitor performance of various functions by using Performance Monitor (Chapter 21).*

47 D. *Full Control.* By default, the Everyone group has full access to a newly created network share in Windows NT. This default is unlike most operating systems, where network users get No Access. *Objective: Manage user and group accounts (Chapter 11).*

48 C. *Log.* Log view records counters that you can subsequently reference, and is the proper choice for creating a baseline. *Objective: Establish a baseline for measuring system performance (Chapter 21).*

49 B. *Replication Governor Reg_Dword value.* To reduce network traffic while synchronizing, change the value of the Replication Governor Reg_Dword. *Objective: Configure Windows NT Server core services (Chapter 6).*

50 A. *PDC.* The PDC will always be the master browser, unless it has been configured not to or is unavailable. *Objective: Configure NT Server core services (Chapter 6).*

51 D. *Windows NT domain controllers.* Global groups reside on PDCs and BDCs. *Objective: Manage user and group accounts (Chapter 11).*

52 A. *BDCs synchronize simultaneously.* BDCs synchronize simultaneously. *Objective: Configure NT Server core services (Chapter 6).*

Appendix B

About the CD

• •

*Y*ou'll find the following on the *MCSE NT Server 4 in the Enterprise For Dummies* CD-ROM:

- ✔ The QuickLearn game, a fun way to study for the test
- ✔ Practice and Self-Assessment tests, to make sure you're ready for the real thing
- ✔ Practice test demos from Specialized Solutions, Super Software, and Transcender
- ✔ A bonus chapter about Computerized Adaptive Testing
- ✔ A Links file to help you find resources on the Web

System Requirements

Make sure that your computer meets the minimum system requirements listed next. If your computer doesn't match up to most of these requirements, you may have problems using the contents of the CD.

- ✔ A PC with a 486 or faster processor.
- ✔ Microsoft Windows 95 or later.
- ✔ At least 16MB of total RAM installed on your computer.
- ✔ A CD-ROM drive — double-speed (2x) or faster.
- ✔ A sound card.
- ✔ A monitor capable of displaying at least 256 colors or grayscale.
- ✔ A modem with a speed of at least 14,400 bps.

Important Note: To play the QuickLearn game, you must have a 166 or faster computer running Windows 95 or 98 with SVGA graphics. You must also have Microsoft DirectX 5.0 or later installed. If you do not have DirectX, you can install it from the CD. Just run D:\Directx\dxinstall.exe. Unfortunately, DirectX 5.0 does not run on Windows NT 4.0, so you cannot play the QuickLearn Game on a Windows NT 4.0 or earlier machine.

Using the CD

To install the items from the CD to your hard drive, follow these steps:

1. **Insert the CD into your computer's CD-ROM drive.**

2. **Click Start⇨Run.**

3. **In the dialog box that appears, type** D:\SETUP.EXE.

   Replace *D* with the proper drive letter if your CD-ROM drive uses a different letter.

4. **Click OK.**

   A license agreement window appears.

5. **Read the license agreement, nod your head, and then click the Accept button if you want to use the CD. After you click Accept, you'll never be bothered by the License Agreement window again.**

   The CD interface Welcome screen appears. The interface is a little program that shows you what's on the CD and coordinates installing the programs and running the demos.

6. **Click anywhere on the Welcome screen to enter the interface.**

   The next screen lists categories for the software on the CD.

7. **To view the items within a category, just click the category's name.**

   A list of programs in the category appears.

8. **For more information about a program, click the program's name.**

   Sometimes a program has its own system requirements or requires you to do a few tricks on your computer before you can install or run the program. This screen tells you what you need to do, if necessary.

9. **If you don't want to install the program, click the Go Back button to return to the preceding screen.**

10. **To install a program, click the appropriate Install button.**

    The CD interface hides while the CD installs the program.

11. **To install other items, repeat Steps 7 through 10.**

12. **When you finish installing programs, click the Quit button.**

    You can eject the CD now. Carefully place it back in the plastic jacket of the book for safekeeping.

To run some of the programs on the *MCSE Windows NT Server 4 in the Enterprise For Dummies* CD, you need the CD in your CD-ROM drive.

What You'll Find

This section offers a summary of the software on the *MCSE Windows NT Server 4 in the Enterprise For Dummies* CD.

Dummies test prep tools

This CD contains questions related to Windows NT Server 4 in the Enterprise. Most of the questions are topics that you can expect to be on the test. We've also included some questions on other topics that may not be on the current test, but that you will need to perform your job.

QuickLearn Game

The QuickLearn Game is the *...For Dummies* way of making studying for the Certification exam less painful. OutPost is a fast-paced arcade game.

Answer questions to defuse dimensional disrupters and save the universe from a rift in space-time. (The questions come from the same set of questions that the Self-Assessment and Practice Test use, but isn't this way more fun?) Missing a question on the real exam almost never results in a rip in the fabric of the universe, so just think how easy it'll be when you get there!

QUIKLERN.EXE on the CD is just a self-extractor, to simplify the process of copying the game files to your computer. It will not create any shortcuts on your computer's desktop or Start menu.

Don't forget, you need to have DirectX 5.0 or later installed to play the QuickLearn game; and it does not run on Windows NT 4.0.

Practice Test

The Practice test is designed to help you get comfortable with the MCSE testing situation and pinpoint your strengths and weaknesses on the topic. You can accept the default setting of 60 questions in 60 minutes, or you can customize the settings. You can choose the number of questions, the amount of time, and even decide which objectives you want to focus on.

After you answer the questions, the Practice test gives you plenty of feedback. You can find out which questions you answered correctly and incorrectly and get statistics on how you did, broken down by objective. Then you can review the questions — all of them, all you missed, all you marked, or a combination of the ones you marked and the ones you missed.

Self-Assessment Test

The Self-Assessment test is designed to simulate the actual MCSE testing situation. You must answer 60 questions in 60 minutes. After you answer all the questions, you find out your score and whether you pass or fail — but that's all the feedback you get. If you can pass the Self-Assessment test regularly, you're ready to tackle the real thing.

Links Page

I've also created a Links Page, a handy starting place for accessing the huge amounts of information on the Internet about the MCSE tests. You can find the page at D:\Links.htm.

Bonus Chapter: Computerized Adaptive Testing For Dummies

This special CD chapter describes computerized adaptive testing (CAT) — how it works and how it differs from both computerized testing in general and other types of tests. The chapter also includes a FAQ about certification CATs specifically. There is even a section where test takers discuss their reactions to the CATs they have survived. A final section discusses the use of simulations in performance-based testing and shows how such tests are superior to multiple-choice and other types of questioning for certification exams. This chapter is in PDF format, and you will need Adobe Acrobat Reader to view it. If you don't have Acrobat Reader, install it from the CD.

Screen Saver

A spiffy little screen saver that the Dummies team created. Screen shots of test questions will fill your screen, so when your computer is not doing anything else, it can still be quizzing you!

Commercial demos

MCSEprep Exam Simulator, from Super Software, Inc.

This demo, designed to help you prepare for the Windows NT Server 4 in the Enterprise exam, gives you 5 practice questions — just enough to get a taste. Learn more by visiting the Web site, www.mcseprep.com.

QuickCert, from Specialized Solutions

This package from Specialized Solutions offers QuickCert practice tests for several Certification exams. Run the QuickCert IDG Demo to choose the practice test you want to work on. For more information about QuickCert, visit the Specialized Solutions Web site at www.specializedsolutions.com.

MCSE Windows NT Server 4 in the Enterprise, from Specialized Solutions

This is a demo of some of the training aids you get from Specialized Solutions self-study courses. A practice quiz, video training, simulations, and an electronic dictionary give you a taste of the training module.

Transcender EnterpriseCert demo, from Transcender Corporation

Here is a demo of Transcender's Windows NT Server 4 in the Enterprise exam simulation. You can get a taste of Transcender's other products through the Certification Sampler, also on the CD. To learn more about what Transcender has to offer, check out their Web site at `www.transcender.com`.

Transcender NT ServerFlash, from Transcender Corporation

This demo from the good folks at Transcender is designed to help you learn fundamental concepts and terminology. You provide short answer-type explanations to questions presented in a flash card format, and grade yourself as you go.

Transcender Certification Sampler, from Transcender Corporation

The Certification Sampler offers demos of many exams.

SimDemo, from Sylvan Prometric

This demo shows you two simulation questions and lets you work them through, to help you get comfortable with this question format.

Computer Adaptive Testing Demonstration, from Galton Technologies

This little program is designed to demonstrate how computer adaptive testing works. When you start the Math CAT test, you are presented with a series of math problems. If you remember high school algebra, you'll be done with this test pretty quickly. Otherwise it might take you a little longer.

If You Have Problems (Of the CD Kind)

I tried my best to compile programs that work on most computers with the minimum system requirements. Alas, your computer may differ, and some programs may not work properly for some reason.

The two most likely problems are that your computer doesn't have enough RAM for the programs you want to use, or that other running programs are affecting the installation or running of a program. If you get error messages such as `Not enough memory` or `Setup cannot continue`, try one or more of the following actions and then try using the software again:

- ✔ **Turn off any antivirus software you have on your computer.** Installers sometimes mimic virus activity and may make your computer incorrectly believe that it is being infected by a virus.

- ✔ **Close running programs.** The more programs you're running, the less memory is available to other programs. Installers usually update files and programs; if other programs run, installation may not work.

- ✔ **In Windows, close the CD interface and run demos or installations directly from Windows Explorer.** The interface can tie up system memory or conflict with interactive demos. Use Windows Explorer to browse the files on the CD and launch installers or demos.

- ✔ **Have your local computer store add more RAM to your computer.** This is a somewhat expensive step. If you have a Windows 95 PC with a PowerPC chip, however, more memory can help the speed of your computer and enable more programs to run at the same time.

If you still have trouble installing from the CD, please call IDG Books Worldwide Customer Service: 800-762-2974 (outside the U.S.: 317-596-5430).

Index

• **P** •

• X •

• Y •

IDG Books Worldwide, Inc., End-User License Agreement

READ THIS. You should carefully read these terms and conditions before opening the software packet(s) included with this book ("Book"). This is a license agreement ("Agreement") between you and IDG Books Worldwide, Inc. ("IDGB"). By opening the accompanying software packet(s), you acknowledge that you have read and accept the following terms and conditions. If you do not agree and do not want to be bound by such terms and conditions, promptly return the Book and the unopened software packet(s) to the place you obtained them for a full refund.

1. **License Grant.** IDGB grants to you (either an individual or entity) a nonexclusive license to use one copy of the enclosed software program(s) (collectively, the "Software") solely for your own personal or business purposes on a single computer (whether a standard computer or a workstation component of a multiuser network). The Software is in use on a computer when it is loaded into temporary memory (RAM) or installed into permanent memory (hard disk, CD-ROM, or other storage device). IDGB reserves all rights not expressly granted herein.

2. **Ownership.** IDGB is the owner of all right, title, and interest, including copyright, in and to the compilation of the Software recorded on the disk(s) or CD-ROM ("Software Media"). Copyright to the individual programs recorded on the Software Media is owned by the author or other authorized copyright owner of each program. Ownership of the Software and all proprietary rights relating thereto remain with IDGB and its licensers.

3. **Restrictions on Use and Transfer.**

   (a) You may only (i) make one copy of the Software for backup or archival purposes, or (ii) transfer the Software to a single hard disk, provided that you keep the original for backup or archival purposes. You may not (i) rent or lease the Software, (ii) copy or reproduce the Software through a LAN or other network system or through any computer subscriber system or bulletin-board system, or (iii) modify, adapt, or create derivative works based on the Software.

   (b) You may not reverse engineer, decompile, or disassemble the Software. You may transfer the Software and user documentation on a permanent basis, provided that the transferee agrees to accept the terms and conditions of this Agreement and you retain no copies. If the Software is an update or has been updated, any transfer must include the most recent update and all prior versions.

4. **Restrictions on Use of Individual Programs.** You must follow the individual requirements and restrictions detailed for each individual program in Appendix B ("About the CD") of this Book. These limitations are also contained in the individual license agreements recorded on the Software Media. These limitations may include a requirement that after using the program for a specified period of time, the user must pay a registration fee or discontinue use. By opening the Software packet(s), you will be agreeing to abide by the licenses and restrictions for these individual programs that are detailed in Appendix B ("About the CD") of this Book and on the Software Media. None of the material on this Software Media or listed in this Book may ever be redistributed, in original or modified form, for commercial purposes.

5. Limited Warranty.

(a) IDGB warrants that the Software and Software Media are free from defects in materials and workmanship under normal use for a period of sixty (60) days from the date of purchase of this Book. If IDGB receives notification within the warranty period of defects in materials or workmanship, IDGB will replace the defective Software Media.

(b) **IDGB AND THE AUTHOR OF THE BOOK DISCLAIM ALL OTHER WARRANTIES, EXPRESS OR IMPLIED, INCLUDING WITHOUT LIMITATION IMPLIED WARRANTIES OF MER-CHANTABILITY AND FITNESS FOR A PARTICULAR PURPOSE, WITH RESPECT TO THE SOFTWARE, THE PROGRAMS, THE SOURCE CODE CONTAINED THEREIN, AND/OR THE TECHNIQUES DESCRIBED IN THIS BOOK. IDGB DOES NOT WARRANT THAT THE FUNCTIONS CONTAINED IN THE SOFTWARE WILL MEET YOUR REQUIREMENTS OR THAT THE OPERATION OF THE SOFTWARE WILL BE ERROR FREE.**

(c) This limited warranty gives you specific legal rights, and you may have other rights that vary from jurisdiction to jurisdiction.

6. Remedies.

(a) IDGB's entire liability and your exclusive remedy for defects in materials and workmanship shall be limited to replacement of the Software Media, which may be returned to IDGB with a copy of your receipt at the following address: Software Media Fulfillment Department, Attn.: *MCSE Windows NT Server 4 in the Enterprise For Dummies,* 2nd Edition, IDG Books Worldwide, Inc., 7260 Shadeland Station, Ste. 100, Indianapolis, IN 46256, or call 800-762-2974. Please allow three to four weeks for delivery. This Limited Warranty is void if failure of the Software Media has resulted from accident, abuse, or misapplication. Any replacement Software Media will be warranted for the remainder of the original warranty period or thirty (30) days, whichever is longer.

(b) In no event shall IDGB or the author be liable for any damages whatsoever (including without limitation damages for loss of business profits, business interruption, loss of business information, or any other pecuniary loss) arising from the use of or inability to use the Book or the Software, even if IDGB has been advised of the possibility of such damages.

(c) Because some jurisdictions do not allow the exclusion or limitation of liability for consequential or incidental damages, the above limitation or exclusion may not apply to you.

7. U.S. Government Restricted Rights. Use, duplication, or disclosure of the Software by the U.S. Government is subject to restrictions stated in paragraph (c)(1)(ii) of the Rights in Technical Data and Computer Software clause of DFARS 252.227-7013, and in subparagraphs (a) through (d) of the Commercial Computer–Restricted Rights clause at FAR 52.227-19, and in similar clauses in the NASA FAR supplement, when applicable.

8. General. This Agreement constitutes the entire understanding of the parties and revokes and supersedes all prior agreements, oral or written, between them and may not be modified or amended except in a writing signed by both parties hereto that specifically refers to this Agreement. This Agreement shall take precedence over any other documents that may be in conflict herewith. If any one or more provisions contained in this Agreement are held by any court or tribunal to be invalid, illegal, or otherwise unenforceable, each and every other provision shall remain in full force and effect.

Installation Instructions

To install the items from the CD to your hard drive with Microsoft Windows, follow these steps:

1. **Insert the CD into your computer's CD-ROM drive.**

2. **Click Start⇨Run.**

3. **In the dialog box that appears, type** D:\SETUP.EXE.

   Replace *D* with the proper drive letter if your CD-ROM drive uses a different letter.

4. **Click OK.**

   A license agreement window appears.

5. **Read through the license agreement, and then click Accept. You'll never see the License Agreement window again.**

6. **Click anywhere on the Welcome screen to enter the interface.**

7. **To view the items within a category, click the category's name.**

   A list of programs in the category appears.

8. **For more information about a program, click the program's name.**

9. **To install a program, click the appropriate Install button.**

   The CD interface drops to the background while the CD installs the program you chose.

10. **When you finish installing programs, click Quit.**

    The CD interface closes, and you can eject the CD. Carefully place it back in the plastic jacket of the book for safekeeping.

To run some of the programs on the *MCSE Windows NT Server 4 in the Enterprise For Dummies,* 2nd Edition CD, you may need to keep the CD inside your CD-ROM drive.

For details about the contents of the CD-ROM and instructions for installing the software from the CD-ROM, see Appendix B "About the CD" in this book.

IDG BOOKS WORLDWIDE
BOOK REGISTRATION

We want to hear from you!

Visit **http://my2cents.dummies.com** to register this book and tell us how you liked it!

- ✔ Get entered in our monthly prize giveaway.

- ✔ Give us feedback about this book — tell us what you like best, what you like least, or maybe what you'd like to ask the author and us to change!

- ✔ Let us know any other ...*For Dummies*® topics that interest you.

Your feedback helps us determine what books to publish, tells us what coverage to add as we revise our books, and lets us know whether we're meeting your needs as a ...*For Dummies* reader. You're our most valuable resource, and what you have to say is important to us!

Not on the Web yet? It's easy to get started with *Dummies 101*®: *The Internet For Windows*® *98* or *The Internet For Dummies*®, 5th Edition, at local retailers everywhere.

Or let us know what you think by sending us a letter at the following address:

...*For Dummies* Book Registration
Dummies Press
7260 Shadeland Station, Suite 100
Indianapolis, IN 46256-3945
Fax 317-596-5498

**BESTSELLING
BOOK SERIES
FROM IDG**